Metalcasting
Principles & Techniques

Yury S. Lerner, PhD
Professor Emeritus Of Technology
University Of Northern Iowa

P. N. Rao, PhD
Professor Of Technology
University Of Northern Iowa

Technical Editor:
Ian Kay

Editor:
Karen Frink

American Foundry Society, Schaumburg, IL 60173

Technical Editor, Ian M. Kay

Copy Editor, Karen A. Frink

Cover and layout design by H. Parrilli (AFS).

Published by the American Foundry Society, Schaumburg, IL USA
© 2013 American Foundry Society

All rights reserved. Published 2013
Printed in the United States of America

Printed 2014 softcover

ISBN 978-0-87433-428-9

Printed in the United States of America.
Printed on acid free Sustainable Forestry Initiative (SFI) paper.

DEDICATION

This book is dedicated to our students from all over the world, whose motivation has inspired us to develop this educational material, and to our fellow metalcasters, who choose this profession, which is not always an easy and pleasant one, nevertheless continuing their hard work, improving existing and developing new metalcasting techniques and technology, thus becoming leaders of the foundry industry.

The Authors have also dedicated this book to their families, who have always encouraged the Authors' research and technical writing, and their love of teaching.

TABLE OF CONTENTS

PREFACE

Metalcasting is one of the oldest manufacturing methods that is still used extensively in the modern world. Lately, it has been going through a lot of fundamental changes and innovations.

There are a number of books in the market dedicated to metalcasting technology. Most of them were excellent when they were originally published, but have become out-of-date in view of the technological and scientific advances in the metalcasting industry. Other books that have been published in recent years are either not comprehensive enough to provide all the material needed for the curriculum or too detailed, making them unsuitable as textbooks. Thus, it was felt that there was the need to develop a comprehensive textbook that provides all the material required in a course on metalcasting.

The material contained in this textbook summarizes known basics and compliments them with the latest developments in all areas of metalcasting technique, technology and quality testing.

The book is divided into four parts: Casting Alloys (Foundry Metallurgy), Tooling Practice (Tooling, Gating and Risering), Molding Practice and Melting Practice. Additional chapter discusses Rapid Prototyping in various metalcasting processes. Each part consists of one or more chapters. All chapters are structured into brief summary of topic/objectives followed by chapter content and concluded by review questions. Some chapters are supplied with practical examples/exercises with solutions or case studies designed to enhance the learning process.

The textbook is the main book. There is also a Lab & Safety Manual, which contains detailed instructions on major foundry laboratory testing methods, and has exercises aimed at obtaining practical "hands-on" experience in all aspects of metalcasting. The Lab Manual also contains general safety information and specific safety precautions applied to each testing procedures.

The Solutions Manual contains answers on review questions and problems that are assigned to each Chapter of the textbook.

The textbook is comprised of teaching and lecture material developed during many decades at different Universities and, lately the University of Northern Iowa, as part of the manufacturing/metallurgical curriculum. Its objective is to serve as a primary textbook for the beginners-undergraduate students at Universities, which are accredited by the Foundry Educational Foundation (FEF), the educational program of the metalcasting industry at the college level, for vocational schools, community colleges, four-year technology schools and traditional engineering school students.

Metalcasting Principles and Techniques is also recommended as instructional tool for metalcasting facilities to train new employees, for suppliers to learn more about metalcasting and for libraries as reference material.

ACKNOWLEDGEMENTS

The authors wish to thank the following foundry professionals for their reviews, valuable comments and suggestions rendered during preparation of this manuscript:

- Mike Riabov, Director, Metallurgy and Technical Services, Neenah Foundry Co., Neenah, WI
- Mike Kuebler, Manager, Quality, and Service, John Deere Foundry, Waterloo, IA
- Karl Dance, Manager, Technical Services, Foundry, Viking Pump Incorporated, A Unit of IDEX Corporation

The authors also gratefully acknowledge the following organizations and companies for their help and permissions in using their materials:

American Foundry Society (AFS)

ASM International

North America Die Casting Association (NADCA)

Ductile Iron Society (DIS)

Foundry Management and Technology Journal

Modern Casting

Simpson- Gerosa Corporation

Gradient Lens Corporation

Stahl Specialty Co.

Foseco Metallurgical, Inc.

Laempe+Reich Co.

Loramendi S. Coop.

Roberts Sinto Corporation

Rimrock Corporation

ISA Industries, Inc.

Finite Solutions, Inc.

Inductoterm Corporation

CMH Manufacturing

Iron Casting Research Institute

POM Group

Heraeus Electro-Nite

Eirich Machines, Inc.

Very special thanks to Ian Kay of the Cast Metals Institute (retired) for his part as Technical Editor. His painstaking review, many thoughtful suggestions and contributions to the manuscript are deeply appreciated.

The authors would also like to thank Jennifer Head, Director of Education at AFS and the Institute, and Fred Kohloff, Director of Environmental, Health and Safety, AFS, for their help and useful suggestions. It was very much appreciated.

The authors also wish to thank the American Foundry Society and Special Publications Director Laura Moreno, Graphic Designer Henry Parrilli and Editor Karen Frink (retired), for their help with the preparation and publication of this book.

BIOGRAPHIES

Yury S. Lerner

Yury S. Lerner, PhD., is an AFS/FEF Distinguished Professor and Professor Emeritus of the University of Northern Iowa. He obtained his BS and MS degrees in Metallurgical/Metalcasting Engineering from the State Polytechnic University of Odessa, Ukraine, and earned his PhD. in Foundry Engineering from the Ukrainian Academy of Sciences. He began his career in as a plant metallurgist and during those years progressed to various management positions in the foundry industry.

While working, Dr. Lerner began his academic career, first, as an adjunct Professor, then, as a full Professor, in the areas of metallurgy and foundry technology.

Dr. Lerner has authored and co-authored more than 200 publications in national and international professional journals and conference proceedings, including two books, in the areas of metallurgy, materials science and metalcasting processes. He holds also several dozen patents in these fields. Dr. Lerner is also a member of the Foundry Educational Foundation (FEF) and a member of the American Foundry Society (AFS).

P.N. Rao (Nageswara Rao Posinasetti)

P.N. Rao received his B.E. from Sri Venkateswara University, Tirupati and M.E. from Birla Institute of Technology and Science, Pilani, India in Mechanical Engineering and PhD, from Indian Institute of Technology, New Delhi, India. He has conducted post-doctoral research at the University of Manchester Institute of Science & Technology, Manchester, UK, and Loughborough University of Technology, Loughborough, UK. Earlier he worked in the Indian Institute of Technology, New Delhi from 1976 until 1995, and at MARA University of Technology, Malaysia (1995 until 2001) before arriving in the United States. He has authored and co-authored more than 190 papers in national and international journals, and conferences.

Dr. Rao has also authored several books about manufacturing technology, which were published by McGraw Hill, India.

Dr. Rao teaches at the University of Northern Iowa, Cedar Falls, Iowa, in the Department of Technology, where he has been since 2001. Dr. Rao is also a member of the American Foundry Society (AFS).

INTRODUCTION TO METALCASTING

Objectives

Metalcasting is one of the key processes and one of the largest in the manufacturing industry. After studying this chapter, the reader should be able to:

- Define metalcasting
- Discuss a brief history of metalcasting over the years
- Compare the advantages and limitations of the casting process
- Describe the terminologies that are relevant to metalcasting
- Classify the foundries based on various criteria
- Discuss the present as well as the future of the foundry industry

Keywords

Casting, Metalcasting, Casting Process, Foundry, Jobbing Foundry, Captive Foundry, Flask, Ladle, Parting Line, Mold, Mold Cavity, Cope, Drag, Pattern, Core, Core Print, Runner, Gate (Ingate), Bottom Board, Riser, Chill, Vent, Chaplet, Pouring Cup, Molding Sand, Refractory Material, Foundry Sand, Investment Casting Process, Sand Mold, Molten Metal, Molten Metal Flow, Scrap, Binder, Iron, Steel, Aluminum, Magnesium, Nondestructive Techniques, Casting Yield, Solidification Modeling.

Brief History of Metalcasting

Casting is one of the earliest metal shaping methods known in the history of civilization. It generally means pouring a molten metal into a refractory mold (sand or metal) with a cavity of the shape to be made, and allowing it to solidify in the mold. When solidified, the desired metal object is taken out of the mold either by breaking the disposable sand mold or taking the mold apart when a reusable metal mold is used. The solidified object is called a casting. This process is also called casting, metalcasting or founding.

The archaeological data indicates that the casting process originated probably around 5,000 years ago in the Black Sea area and then spread into Mesopotamia and the Middle East. Copper was the first metal used to make castings. In many parts of the world during that period, copper axes and other flat objects were cast in open sand molds or molds cut in stone or baked clay. These molds were essentially in a single piece. But in later periods, when more complicated objects were cast, the mold was split into two or more parts to facilitate the withdrawal of the pattern.

The Bronze Age (2000 BC) brought far more refinement into the casting process. For the first time perhaps, cores, for making hollow sockets in the cast objects, were invented. These cores were made of baked clay. At this time, the lost wax or investment casting process was also extensively used for making ornaments and fine craftwork.

Casting technology has been greatly improved by the Chinese from around 1500 BC. Archaeological excavations revealed usage of multipiece molds for making highly intricate castings. They spent a lot of time in perfecting the mold to the last detail so that hardly any finishing work was required on the casting made from the molds.

Indus valley civilization (1000 BC) is known for their extensive use of copper and bronze for casting of weapons, ornaments, agricultural tools and cookware. From the various objects and figurines that were excavated from the Indus valley sites, those people appear to have been familiar with all the known casting methods, including the wax pattern process.

The discovery of iron is believed to have happened around 2000 BC. China made its first iron castings about 600 BC. There are evidences that iron casting had also started in Syria and Persia around 1000 BC. India could be credited with the invention of crucible steel, but iron casting technology in India was not used until the times of the invasion of Alexander the Great, around 300 BC. The famous iron pillar, cast around 400 AD, is an example of the metallurgical skills of ancient Indians. The pillar is made of a solid shaft of iron, 7.3 m (23 ft 8 in) tall with 93 cm (37.2 in) buried below the present floor level. Its diameter varies from 0.5 m (20 in) to 0.29 m (16.4 in) (Fig. 1-1). The rate of rusting of this pillar, which stands outside, is practically zero and even the buried portion is rusting at an extremely slow rate. It is believed that it was first cast of high phosphorus malleable iron and then hammered to the final shape. It is a wonder that the iron has not rusted, despite the seventeen centuries that have passed since then, and it is an excellent example of advanced metallurgy of those times.

In Europe, iron casting was not widespread until the 14th Century. Earlier, in the 13th Century, foundries, particularly in England and Italy, made a lot of improvements in the casting processes of making bronze church bells and cannons, where their production achieved the greatest results. A significant role in the progress of metalcasting art was played by the first foundry textbook, developed in the 16th Century by Italian foundryman Vannocio Biringuccio, who was head of the papal foundry in Rome. The book summarized all practical foundry knowledge known at that time, and covered topics from moldmaking procedures to foundry metallurgy.

From the late 16th Century, Russia began to cast the world's largest bronze bells weighing from 36 up to 220 metric tons (79,200 to 484,000 lb). The monument of casting art of the 18th Century, the largest in the world, known as Tsar Bell (Fig. 1-2), is 6.2 m (20 ft) tall and is 6.6 m (22 ft) in diameter, was poured in a pit mold made with the aid of sweep molding in Moscow (Russia) in 1735, and was left in the pit to cool off. Approximately

two years later, while in the pit, during a fire, water was accidentally poured on the red-hot bell. It cracked because of uneven cooling, and an 11.5 ton piece broke off. The bell remained in the pit for over 100 years and only after that was it raised and placed on a granite pedestal.

At that time, foundries, making cast bells and cannons, became the first industrial scale metalcasting facilities. Figure 1-3 shows the world-famous 5.5 m (18 ft) long

Fig. 1-2. The largest in the world Tsar Bell weighing 220 metric tons (485,020 lb) cast of bronze in Russia in 18th Century with an 11.5 metric ton (25,353 lb) piece that broke off.

Fig. 1-3. The giant, world famous Tsar Cannon, weighing more than 40 metric tons (88,000 lb) along with the cannon balls designed to be shot from it, with weight of nearly one ton (2200 lb) each. Cast in Russia of bronze in 16th Century.

Fig. 1-1. Cast iron pillar made in India around 400 A.D. is 7.3 m (23 ft 8 in) tall; it weighs approximately 6.5 metric tons (143,300 lb), and during almost 1700 years showed no rust.

Introduction to Metalcasting

Tsar Cannon with a 5.34 m (17.5 ft) long barrel, weighing more than 40 metric tons (88,000 lb) along with the cannon balls, designed to be shot from it with a weight of nearly one ton (2200 lb) each. The cannon was cast of bronze in the 16th Century in Russia and later, in the 19th Century, it was placed on the decorative cast iron gun carriage.

The Big Ben, officially known as the Great Bell, housed in the Great Clock of Westminster in London (England), was cast on April 10, 1858. This iconic bell measuring 2.74 m (9 ft) in diameter and 2.286 m (7.5 ft) tall, and weighing approximately 14 metric tons (30,272 lb), was the largest bell cast in Britain.

In the U.S. the first foundry, known as Saugus Iron Works, was established in 1642 near Lynn, Massachusetts. Figure 1-4 shows the first American casting, an iron pot, made at this facility.

Nonferrous metals such as copper, lead and tin were used for thousands of years, but aluminum has been produced commercially only for about 150 years. Although aluminum is the most abundant metallic element in the Earth's crust, it is very rare in its free form and was once considered a precious metal, more valuable even than gold. Napoleon III of France is said to have had a set of aluminum plates reserved for his finest guests, while other guests had to make do with gold ones.

The statue, known as Eros, in Piccadilly Circus London (England), made in 1893, is one of the first statues to be cast in aluminum. In 1884, aluminum was selected as a cast material for the apex of the Washington Monument (Washington D.C., USA), the world's tallest stone structure and the world's tallest obelisk, standing 169.294 m (555 ft 5⅛ in) (Fig.1-5). Today, more aluminum is produced than all other nonferrous materials combined.

During all times, from ancient days up to today, metalcasting played an important role in the evolution of every society allowing manufacturing of a large variety of agricultural equipment, such as tractors and combines, construction of gigantic bridges, building cars, trains, and airplanes. Castings are also used in all stages of food preparation, from cutting and processing to the actual cooking such as making pots, pans and grills. Art castings such as jewelry, silverware, sculpture and bells are made using the latest technological innovations in metalcasting.

In general, metalcasting remains, and will continue in the future, being the key manufacturing process.

Fig. 1-4. The first American casting; an iron pot made at the first American foundry, known as Saugus Iron Works, which was established in 1642 near Lynn, Massachusetts. (From B.L. Simpson. Courtesy: American Foundry Society.)

Fig. 1-5. The Washington Monument (Washington, D.C., USA) is the world's tallest stone structure and the world's tallest obelisk standing 169.294 m (555 ft 5 1/4 in).

1.2. Casting Advantages and Applications

The casting process is extensively used in manufacturing because of its many advantages, and may be summarized as follows:

- There are no limitations on size, geometry or weight of castings to be made. Today, components of the most intricate shape, varying in weight from a few grams to several hundred tons, are made by the casting process.

- Practically, the casting process may use any cast alloy, while not every metal-shaping method may be used to make metal components. For example, cast iron cannot be forged due to brittleness, but can be easily cast by any casting process.

- The casting process offers to designers and consumers near-net-shape, thin-wall cast components made with minimum operational cost in comparison with other metal-shaping processes.

- Further, the necessary tools required for the production of casting molds is very simple and relatively inexpensive.

- Castings are generally cooled uniformly from all sides and, therefore, they are expected to have no directional properties.

A great variety of every possible shape and size casting is successfully used in each part of industrial manufacturing. Brief examples of some typical applications of castings are given below.

- **Automotive industry:** gray iron, compacted graphite iron and aluminum alloy engine cylinder blocks and engine heads; alloyed iron liners and camshafts; ductile iron crankshafts; aluminum alloy wheels and space frames; ductile iron steering knuckles, yokes, pistons, piston rings, gears, exhaust manifolds, differential parts, parts for suspension and break systems.

- **Machine tool:** gray iron beds and tables for precision machinery; ductile iron connecting rods and heavy section structural components for hydraulic presses.

- **High-pressure hydraulic equipment:** ductile iron cylinders, pump and hydraulic motor housings, distribution, valves, housing for monitoring and regulating apparatus.

- **Railroad industry:** cast steel wheels, parts for couplers, frames for freight cars.

- **Construction machinery:** cast steel shoes, pads and wheels for earth-moving equipment, cable bend saddles for suspension bridges.

- **Mining and crushing machinery:** alloyed iron, alloyed steel and austempered ductile iron mill rolls, crushers, grinding mills and impellers.

- **Construction:** gray, malleable and ductile iron municipal castings, pipe fittings, hydraulic water supply pipes and special pressure pipes.

- **Military:** ductile iron artillery projectiles, aluminum and magnesium alloy parts for aircraft and marine engines, housing for electronics, etc.

- **Medical devices:** alloyed steel and super alloy surgical instruments, surgical implants, bone implants.

Lately, with the introduction of new cast alloys and new casting methods, in addition to existing areas of castings applications, a practically new and rapidly growing market has been opened for a wide range of cast components, particularly for heavy cast components used in the manufacturing of wind turbines. For instance, depending on the size, only one land windmill generator requires between 10 and 25 metric tons (22,000-550,000 lb) of ductile iron castings. On the other hand, offshore wind farms are much larger and its market demands are broader.

Currently, sand molding accounts for approximately 70% of castings made. However, the dimensional accuracy and surface finish achieved by the conventional sand casting process, in many cases, is not satisfactory and would not be adequate for final parts applications. Also, the traditional sand casting process is labor intensive to some extent and, despite the many improvements aimed at increasing accuracy of molding and coremaking machines and mechanization and automatization of foundry operations, improving overall casting quality still has certain limitations. As an alternative, for this purpose, special precision casting processes, such as diecasting, lost foam, vacuum molding or permanent mold casting and others have been developed, allowing production of thin-walled, near-net-shape cast components with low or no subsequent finishing or machining operations. The details of these processes are given in later chapters.

1.3. Foundry Process and Terminology

Before going into the details of casting technology, defining major foundry terminology would be appropriate. It will be done with the reference to Fig. 1-6, which illustrates a typical sand casting process that utilizes a disposable mold, formed out of foundry sand, containing a binder, which is a material that holds foundry sand in molds and cores together.

In this process, the mold cavity is formed by the molding sand, using a pattern that has the same shape as an actual casting. The metallic or wooden frame, called a flask, holds the sand mold cavity along with cavities of the gating system and riser. The upper part of the flask is called the cope, and the lower part is called the drag. The gating system, consisting of a pouring basin, runner and gates or ingates, delivers molten metal from the pouring ladle into the mold cavity. The riser feeds the casting during solidification and serves as a reservoir of molten metal, compensating for reduction in volume and eliminating shrinkage in the casting. The sand core is installed to cast a central hole in the casting. It may be supported by metal inserts called chaplets. If it is necessary to locally increase cooling rate and promote solidification, chills made of metal or graphite would be used. To allow the escape of gases, formed as a result of sand mold and core components reaction with the molten metal, vents in the shape of different passages are made in the mold and core.

For better understanding of subsequent material, some essential foundry terminology and their definitions are summarized below.

Bottom board is a flat base, usually made of wood, used at the start of the moldmaking to support the flask. The pattern is first kept on the bottom board; sand is sprinkled on it and then it is rammed.

Chaplet is used to support a core inside the mold cavity to take care of core weight and overcome the metallostatic forces. If a chaplet is made of metal, it becomes an integral part of the casting.

Chill (external or internal) is a metallic or graphite object, which is placed in the mold cavity or core to locally increase the cooling rate of castings, provide desired solidification mode and eliminate shrinkage. Metal internal chills become part of the casting.

Core is inserted into the mold to make openings or hollow cavities in castings. Special binders are used to make the sand mix for cores.

Core setting is an operation of placing the core into the mold. The core prints hold the core in the predetermined fixed position.

Facing material is a thin layer of carbonaceous or any other material sprinkled, sprayed or applied by other methods on the inner surface of the mold cavity or core to give better surface finish to the castings; also called mold wash or coating.

Flask is a frame or container without bottom and top, used for making and holding the sand mold. Depending upon the position of the flask, it is referred as drag (lower molding flask) or cope (upper molding flask). A snap flask is removed after completion of molding, while a tight flask stays with the mold during pouring until mold shakeout. Flasks may be made up of wood, for temporary applications, or, more generally, of metal, for long term use.

Gate(s) or ingate(s) are the actual entry points, through which molten metal enters the mold cavity. In some cases, they may control mold filling rate.

Ladle is a metal receptacle, lined inside with a refractory material, used for transporting and pouring of molten metal.

Molding sand is a freshly prepared refractory material, mixed with the binder. Molding sand surrounds the pattern while making the mold.

Parting line or parting plane is the line on the pattern or on the mold or on the casting showing the line of separation of the pattern between its halves or a dividing line between the molding flasks that make up the sand mold. In permanent mold or diecasting, the parting line also shows how the sections of a metal mold are separated.

Pattern is a replica or prototype of the final casting to be made with some dimensional modifications. The mold cavity is made with the help of the pattern.

Pouring cup or pouring basin is a small funnel-shaped cavity at the top of the mold into which the molten metal is poured. It is typically connected to the sprue.

Riser is a reservoir of molten metal provided in the casting so that hot metal can flow back into the mold cavity when there is a reduction in volume of metal due to solidification.

Runner(s) are passageways in the parting plane through which molten metal flow is regulated before it reaches the mold cavity. The runner connects the sprue with the ingates.

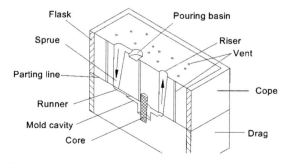

Fig. 1-6. Cross-section of a sand mold, showing major components of sand casting involved in the process.

Sprue is a vertical channel, connecting the pouring basin (pouring cup) with the runner. Through the sprue the molten metal reaches the mold cavity. In many cases, it controls the flow of the molten metal into the mold.

Vents are small opening in the mold or in the core allowing gases to escape during pouring.

1.4. Classification of Foundries

There are different classification criteria by which foundries may be divided. For example, depending on the casting alloy poured, the foundry may be identified as an iron foundry or a malleable iron foundry or a ductile iron foundry or an aluminum foundry. Depending upon the prevailing molding method, foundries are also specified as sand mold foundry or permanent mold foundry or investment casting foundry.

There are also other features that classify all foundries into two categories:

- Jobbing foundry that makes castings for customer's needs;
- Captive foundry that produces casting for the company's internal consumption. Sometimes, when capacity allowed, a portion of the castings may be made for outside customers. In this case, the term captive does not reflect actual foundry standing and the term partially captive foundry may be more appropriate.

1.5. Present and Future of the Foundry Industry

Today, the American foundry industry consists of more than 2000 foundries with a total annual production of about 12 million tons of castings made of various ferrous and nonferrous alloys.

Lately, the domestic foundry industry has undergone fundamental technological changes due to the development of new machines and tooling for producing dimensionally accurate molds, cores, and castings that required only minimal cleaning or finishing. Installing automatic molding and core setting equipment significantly increases process repeatability. Automatic pouring systems have almost entirely eliminated human involvement in all stages of the pouring process, ensuring better and consistent casting quality, which along with improved melting with automatic preheating and charging of melting furnaces, resulted in significant reduction of scrap, metal losses and increased casting yield. Technological advances were also directed at making foundry processes and core binders more environmentally clean and user friendly.

Developments in computer-aided design (CAD) software allowed importing 3-D model files directly from customer's computer to the foundry and building the pattern and delivering prototype castings to the customer in the shortest time. Implementation of new and improved solidification modeling systems allowed more precise modeling of the casting process, to predict and verify the castings' quality before production starts, which resulted in quicker job start-ups, least cost and increased yield.

Fluid flow analysis and solidification modeling are now done not only at large casting operations, but also at small castings producers' facilities using a variety of affordable software. It is assumed that design of more than 60% of currently made castings is optimized with the aid of the contemporary computerized stress analysis and CAD systems. Significant progress was achieved in production of clean, slag-free, thin-wall castings due to the wide use of filtration systems in all areas of molten metal processing: from melting to pouring into the molds.

The requirements for lighter weight, near-net-shape, high-volume automotive castings have driven car makers to convert many castings from iron to aluminum, which resulted in overall weight reduction and less fuel consumption. For example, the aluminum cylinder head production is now more than 90%, while the aluminum share of engine blocks is expected to grow up to 70%. Today, passenger vehicles contain an average of 145 kg (319 lb) of aluminum castings, which places aluminum second only to steel in automotive applications.

Development and implementation of the aluminum lost foam process for high-volume automotive powertrain and marine engine castings significantly increased cast components quality and engine performance.

Marked growth of magnesium castings applications is seen in automotive, aircraft and aerospace industries due to their high strength-to-weight ratio and excellent mechanical and service properties.

New developments in nondestructive techniques and diagnostic processes such as real-time x-ray and neutron radiography have allowed using these methods not only for quality testing, but also to study the actual mold pouring process. This has provided fundamental knowledge and understanding of processes taking place inside the mold, enabling the development of accurate mathematical models and the realization of improved control systems.

Due to continuous improvements, concepts of lean manufacturing were introduced to the foundry industry, which completely changed the way foundries do business, from ordering castings to their processing. Significant changes in people and management techniques enhanced the entire foundry workforce throughout participation in the team-based organization system.

It is forecasted that global casting production will reach more than 100 million tons in year 2015 with aluminum alloy and ductile iron castings leading the production. Long-term growth is also expected for magnesium and copper-based alloys.

Growing casting production trends are also forecasted for the domestic foundry industry. It is also expected that, besides quantitative changes, major strategic changes will occur in foundry techniques and technologies in the near future.

Chief improvements are expected in foundry metallurgy, such as developments of new inoculants and inoculation methods that would eliminate iron carbide in thin-wall iron castings, development of new aluminum and magnesium alloys having significantly shorter heat treatment time or even with no requirements for heat treatment. These, along with better structure control in cast alloy components, will allow better energy conservation and overall cost reduction.

The development of environmentally friendly binder systems, which produce low volatile organic compounds and are easy to remove from the castings, will continue. Further implementation of robotic systems with improved vision capability will enable the use of them to make cores and molds, pour molds, clean and grind castings. It will reduce process variations, improve quality requirements, reduce cost and improve casting yield. More improvements of existing precision casting methods for mass production, as well as development of new molding methods and casting processes will allow foundries to produce superior quality and consistency in thin-wall castings with reduced molding media, material handling and the least environmental impact.

Developments of low-energy consumption sand reclamation systems and new molding media will significantly improve working conditions in the foundry industry. Finally, advances in metalcasting technology will enable U.S. foundries to enhance their ability to produce the highest quality castings at a competitive price.

References

1. Hodges, H., "Technology in the Ancient World," Allen Lane, The Penguin Press, London, 1970.

2. Jaggi, O.P., "Dawn of Indian Technology," Atma Ram, New Delhi, 1969.

3. Simpson, B. L., "History of the Metalcasting Industry" (Second Edition), American Foundrymen's Society, Des Plaines, IL, 1997.

4. Lessiter, M.J., Kotzin, E.L., "Timeline of Casting Technology," *Modern Casting*, No.11, November 2003.

5. Kirgin, K., "Demand Expansion Forecast for Iron, Diecast Aluminum," *Modern Casting*, No. 3, March 2006.

6. Schleg, F.P., "Technology of Metalcasting," American Foundry Society, Des Plaines, IL, 2003.

7. Modern Casting Staff Report, "46th Census of World Casting Production," *Modern Casting*, No.12, December 2012.

Review Questions

1.1 Explain briefly the metalcasting process.

1.2 List the main advantages of the casting process.

1.3 State the typical applications of castings in the automotive industry.

1.4 Discuss the latest developments in the foundry industry.

1.5 Describe criteria by which the foundries are classified.

1.6 Summarize the major limitations of the sand casting process, and how they are overcome.

1.7 Give the points a designer should consider in deciding which casting process to use.

1.8 Define the following terms as related to sand casting: cope, drag, and bottom board.

1.9 Give a brief write-up on the following casting terms: sprue, gate and runner.

1.10 Sketch the cross section of a sand mold, which is ready for pouring, and label its major parts.

1.11 Briefly explain the role of the riser.

1.12 Give the definition of parting line.

1.13 Discuss the role of a core.

1.14 Describe the function of vents in a casting.

1.15 Define the function of chaplet.

1.16 Give a definition of a pattern.

1.17 Describe a foundry ladle.

CASTING ALLOYS

Objectives

Each metalcasting process aims toward production of quality castings with desirable structure, mechanical and service properties. That is why properties of foundry alloys play a major role in the development and use of the castings. After studying this chapter, the reader should be able to:

- Recognize basic types of metallurgical structure found in cast metals, which will help in understanding their solidification behavior and strengthening mechanisms

- Discuss cooling curves and equilibrium diagrams

- Describe important properties of cast alloys and their testing methods

- Define different types of ferrous alloys, such as steels and cast irons, that are commonly cast in foundries, and discuss their characteristics

- Compare properties and applications of nonferrous alloys such as aluminum, copper and magnesium alloys

- Explain heat treatment procedures used for ferrous and nonferrous alloys to control their structure and properties.

Keywords

Solid State, Molten State, Solidification, Solidification Structure, Microstructure, Transformation Temperature, Phase Transformation, Cooling Curve, Grain, Solid Solution, Ferrite, Cementite, Austenite, Pearlite, Martensite, Equilibrium Diagram, Eutectoid Transformation, Eutectic Transformation Strength, Strain, Cast Alloys, Ferrous Alloys, Nonferrous Alloys, Mechanical Properties , Tensile Strength, Elongation, Ductility, Hardness, Toughness, Modulus of Elasticity, Residual Stress, Wear Resistance, Steel, Alloyed Steel, Graphite Shape, Graphite Flakes, Graphite Nodules, Metallic Matrix, Cast Iron, Gray Iron, Ductile Iron, Malleable Iron, Temper Graphite, White Iron, Austempered Ductile Iron, Compacted Graphite Iron, Alloyed Iron, Aluminum Alloys, Copper Alloys, Brass, Bronze, Magnesium Alloys, Heat Treatment, TTT Diagram, Annealing, Normalizing, Quenching, Case

Hardening, Carburizing, Nitriding, Carbonitriding, Tempering, Dimension Stability, Distortion, Knoop Hardness, Brinell Hardness, Rockwell Hardness, Micro Hardness, Vickers Hardness, Hardenability, Machining, Corrosion Resistance, Stress Relieving, Precipitation Hardening, Abrasion Wear, Age Hardening.

Cast alloys used in industrial metalcastings are typically divided into two major classes:

- Ferrous Alloys
- Nonferrous Alloys

The ferrous alloys are iron-based alloys. This class of alloys consists of two groups: steels and irons. In general, steels contain up to 2% carbon, and cast irons contain above 2% carbon. In addition to C (carbon), steels and irons contain Si (silicon), Mn (manganese), S (sulfur), P (phosphorus) and other elements, called alloying elements, such as Cr (chromium), Ni (nickel), Cu (copper), Mo (molybdenum), etc. The principal difference between these two classes of ferrous alloys, besides chemical composition, is that the microstructure of irons (except white irons) contains free carbon in the form of graphite particles.

There are two groups within nonferrous alloys: light alloys and heavy alloys. Typical representatives of light alloys are aluminum, magnesium and titanium alloys. Heavy alloys are copper, nickel and cobalt alloys.

The successful application of cast components greatly depends on the ability of the foundry to develop and deliver to the consumer a product with required mechanical and service properties that ensure predictable and reliable part performance.

2.1. Structure of Cast Alloys

Before proceeding to study the properties of alloys, a brief survey of the solidification structure formation of cast alloys would be beneficial, to better understand the subject.

Alloys are metallic solids, complex in composition and are formed as a result of the solidification of molten liquid of two or more elements. When an alloy solidifies, it changes from liquid to solid state and crystals are formed. A definite geometrical order is observed in all the crystalline solids in the internal arrangement of atoms, which form the space or crystal lattice. The space lattice of any solid is made up of a number of conjugate unit cells, inside which the atoms are arranged in a definite order. The unit repeating volume in three dimensions is called a unit cell. This is the simplest volume, which completely fills space, and has all the characteristics of the whole crystal.

The three most common lattice systems in metals are: cubic, hexagonal and tetragonal (Fig. 2-1a-e). Figure 2-1(b) shows a unit cell of the type called body-centered cubic (BCC) cell, wherein atoms are present at all eight corners of the cube and at the body center. This unit cell is not in isolation but surrounded on all sides by similar unit cells. As a result, the corner atoms are shared by all of the adjacent eight unit cells. Iron (α, ferrite) at room temperature has the structure of BCC with an edge radius (lattice constant) of 0.24824 nm. Metals such as chromium, molybdenum and vanadium have BCC space lattice.

In a face-centered cubic (FCC) lattice (Fig. 2-1c) atoms are present not only at all eight corners of the cube, but also in the middle of each six faces. Metals such as aluminum, copper and nickel have FCC space lattice. Austenite or γ-iron has the structure of FCC.

Similarly, there are other atom arrangements such as body-centered tetragonal (BCT) lattice (Fig. 2-1d), which is present in the metallic matrix of quenched ferrous alloys and called martensite, and hexagonal close-packed (HCP) lattice (Fig. 2-1e), typical for such metals as magnesium and titanium.

Other metals, besides iron, may also exist in more than one crystalline (allotropic) form, depending upon the temperature.

Cobalt:	HCP	below 420°C (788°F)
	FCC	420°C to 1495°C (788 to 2723°F)
Chromium:	HCP	below 20°C (68°F)
	BCC	20°C to 1799°C (68 to 3270°F)

2.1.1. Nucleation and Grain Growth

When the free energy of a parent phase is reduced by means of temperature or pressure, it is a driving force leading to solidification. For example, at the melting point, the thermal fluctuations result in the formation of tiny particles (containing only a few atoms) of the product phase within the parent volume. Such a tiny particle has an interface that separates it from the parent matrix. It grows by transfer of atoms across its interface. The process of formation of the first stable tiny particles is called nucleation. The process of increase in the sizes of these particles is called grain growth. The grain size in the alloy phase depends on the relative rates of nucleation and growth.

Each nucleating particle becomes a grain in the solid. High nucleation rate means a larger number of grains. Also, when this is combined with a low growth rate, more time is available for further nucleation to take place in the parent phase that lies between slowly growing particles. A combination of a high nucleation rate and a low growth rate yields a fine grain size. On the other hand, a low nucleation rate combined with a high growth rate yields a coarse grain size.

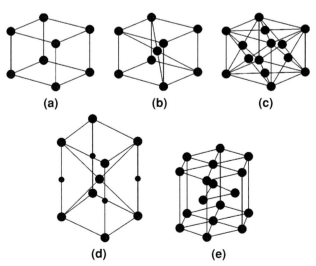

(a)   (b)   (c)

(d)   (e)

Fig. 2-1. The most common types of space lattice structure in cast alloys: (a) cubic; (b) body-centered cubic; (c) face-centered cubic; (d)tetragonal; (e)hexagonal.

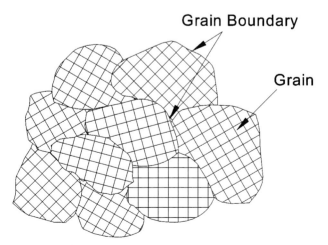

Fig. 2-2. Grain formation in solidifying cast alloys.

An increase in cooling rate lowers the effective transformation temperature and results in the combination of a high nucleation rate and a relatively slow growth rate and, ultimately, yields a fine grain size. Figure 2-2 schematically presents grains, formation in cast alloys, where each square inside the grain represents a unit cell.

Grain size has a significant effect on the properties of cast alloys. For example, coarse-grained cast steels possess less strength and have a higher tendency toward distortion than those having fine grain, although they offer better machinability and hardenability. Fine-grained steel alloys are tougher and more ductile and do not distort or crack during heat treatment.

2.1.1.1. Solid Solutions in Cast Alloys

Metallic alloys are a combination of a number of metals mixed in many different ways. One predominant form is solid solution. A solution is formed when solute atoms are dissolved in solvent atoms. If a solution were allowed to freeze without separating the constituents, a solid solution would result. In a solid solution, the elements are present only as a mixture, but not as chemical compounds. The solid solutions are the essential parts of cast alloys.

There are generally two types of solid solutions: one called the *interstitial* and the other the *substitutional*.

In an interstitial solid solution, the solute atom would be positioned in the interstitial sites (empty space between the adjacent atoms) formed by the solvent atoms. It is possible only when the solvent atom is much larger compared to the solute atom. Also the extent of solubility depends on the difference in the atomic sizes.

For example, carbon would form an interstitial solid solution with iron:

Carbon atomic radius = 0.0750 nm

Iron atomic radius = 0.1241 nm

The addition of alloying elements (solute) to pure metals (solvent) may cause lattice distortion or, in other words, may change lattice parameter or its configuration. The change in lattice configuration results in improving the mechanical properties.

In the substitutional solid solutions, the solute atoms would replace the solvent atoms. This is only possible if both the atoms are similar in size and also in nature.

All processes in liquid and solid alloys, including heat treatment, are linked to a phenomenon called diffusion. Diffusion is the physical process of movement of atoms from one location of higher concentration to another of lower concentration or to a vacant place. Diffusion of atoms would be faster at high temperatures and in liquid phase. It is also a time-dependent process, as the atoms have to physically travel from one site to the other.

In an alloy system, elements are completely soluble in the liquid state, and the component metals may combine within a certain temperature range to form two homogeneous coexisting portions. Each of these portions may have different compositions and, consequently, different properties. These homogeneous physically different portions of the alloy systems are termed a phase. A phase may be defined as any part of a chemical system that possesses distinctive physical characteristics. An alloy may consist of one phase or a combination of different phases.

When the alloy, which is completely soluble in the liquid state, solidifies or is transformed from liquid to solid state, several solid phases may be formed. Sometimes, when the amount of alloy metal that can be dissolved in a solid solution is exceeded, the 'parent' metal and the alloy metal will together form an intermetallic compound. Though the intermetallic compounds are shown with a chemical symbol such as Fe_3C, which is called cementite or iron carbide, they are not like the chemical compounds such as CO_2, which are actually formed by a chemical reaction. In the present case, it is only an atomic arrangement. Intermetallic compounds are usually very hard. Even if only a small amount of intermetallic compound is present, the alloy will combine the toughness of a solid solution with the hardness of the intermetallic compound.

2.1.2. Equilibrium Diagrams

These diagrams are based on a series of cooling curves of given alloy compositions. The cooling curve represents the temperature changes against time for a given metal or alloy, showing the phases present within. But for an alloy system, containing various compositions of the constituent elements, a phase diagram or equilibrium diagram, wherein the phases found at various temperatures and compositions are plotted in a single chart, are more informative. These diagrams show the solidification process and the structural and phase transformation of the given alloy system. They are developed using thermal analysis combined with precise microstructure evaluation.

Note: Details of solidification and thermal analysis of cast alloys on the example of lead-tin alloy are given in the Lab Manual, which accompanies this textbook.

These diagrams enable us to determine the temperature levels at the beginning and end of the solidification of various alloy compositions, the structure of alloys for various temperatures under equilibrium conditions and, also, the phase transformation during cooling and heating. Equilibrium conditions mean that sufficient time would be available for the changes of phases to take place.

An equilibrium diagram is plotted by laying off the percentage concentrations of the two components along the horizontal axis X (abscissa) and the temperature along the vertical axis Y (ordinate). Any point on the diagram refers to a definite composition of the alloy at a particular temperature, as shown in Fig. 2-3 for the tin (Sn)–lead (Pb) system.

Eutectic Composition

In certain alloy systems, alloying causes a lowering of the melting points and at a certain composition, called the eutectic composition, the melting point is the lowest. For example, the alloy of 62% tin and 38% lead has a melting point of 183°C (361.4°F), whereas lead melts at 327°C (620.6°F) and tin melts at 232°C (449.6°F) as shown previously in Fig. 2-3. The low melting point of this alloy, called solder, enables delicate parts of metal to be soldered without damage by heat.

2.1.2.1. Iron-Carbon Equilibrium Diagram

The iron-carbon equilibrium diagram is shown in Fig. 2-4. As it was stated before, iron, depending upon temperature, exists in different allotropic forms.

The structural form of pure iron at room temperature is called ferrite or α-iron, which is a solid solution of carbon in α-iron. Ferrite is soft and ductile. Since ferrite has a body centered cubic structure, the inter-atomic spaces are small and pronouncedly oblate, and cannot readily accommodate even a small carbon atom. Therefore, solubility of carbon in ferrite at room temperature is very low at about of 0.006%. The maximum carbon content in ferrite is 0.05% at 723°C (1333°F). In addition to carbon, a certain amount of silicon, manganese and phosphorus or some alloying elements may be found in ferrite.

The face-centered modification of iron is called austenite or γ-iron. It is the stable form of pure iron at temperatures between 910°C (1670°F) and 1400°C (2552°F). At this temperature, austenite is nonmagnetic, soft and ductile. The face-centered cubic structure of iron has larger interatomic spacing than in ferrite. Even so, in the FCC structure the interstices are barely large enough to accommodate carbon atoms, and lattice strains are produced. As a result, not all the interstitial sites can be filled at any one time. The maximum solubility is only 2% of carbon at 1130°C (2066°F).

The solidification of the liquid iron and carbon melt begins along the liquidus denoted in Fig. 2-4 as ABCD.

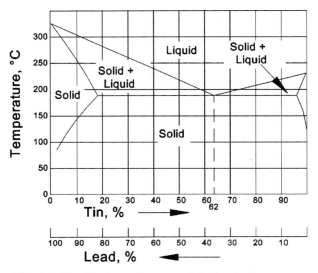

Fig. 2-3. Equilibrium diagram of tin-lead alloy.

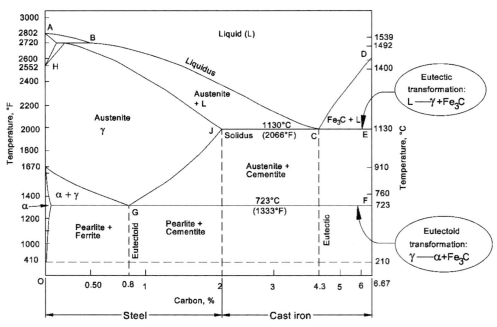

Fig. 2-4. Iron-carbon equilibrium diagram.

Above the liquidus, the alloy is in a liquid state and is a homogeneous system. Along the liquidus, AB, the crystals of the solid solution of carbon in δ-iron, which has a body centered cubic structure and is similar to α-iron, are separated from the liquid. Crystals of austenite or γ-iron are also separated from the liquid along the line BC, with the compositions of carbon ranging from 0.18 to 2.0%. The complete solidification of these alloys proceeds along the solidus line HJ. Those with 2.0 to 4.3% carbon are completely solidified on line JCE. The solidification of the last portion of the liquid phase, enriched in carbon to 4.3%, takes place along this line. The liquid is completely solidified at 1130°C (2066°F); at the same time crystals of austenite, containing 2% carbon and cementite (iron carbide) containing 6.67% carbon, get separated from it. The solidification of alloys containing from 4.3 to 6.67% carbon begins along line CD, with the separation of primary cementite from the melt.

At a temperature of 723°C (1333°F), the eutectoid reaction, i.e., formation of two solids (ferrite and cementite) from a single solid (austenite) takes place. This temperature, called the eutectoid temperature, and the composition at which this reaction occurs (0.80% C), represents the eutectoid composition.

Cementite or iron carbide is the hardest microstructural constituent in ferrous alloys, and is brittle. The new microstructural constituent, called pearlite, is a mechanical mix of ferrite and cementite. This mixture is lamellar, i.e., it is composed of alternate layers of ferrite and cementite and has high tensile strength. It is much harder than ferrite, but softer than cementite.

The alloy containing 0.80% carbon is called eutectoid steel and its microstructure contains 100% pearlite at room temperature. Alloys with less than 0.80% C are called hypoeutectoid steels, and those with higher carbon composition are called hypereutectoid steels.

In the iron portion of the diagram, which is located between 2 and 6.67% carbon, an alloy with 4.3% carbon content is called eutectic and it has the lowest melting point. Iron containing from 2% to 4.3% carbon is called hypoeutectic and from 4.3% to 6.67% is called hypereutectic.

2.2. Properties and Testing of Cast Alloys

2.2.1. Mechanical Properties

2.2.1.1. Strength

Cast components, depending on their applications, may be subjected to one of the following loads or stresses: tension, compression, torsion, impact, fatigue or shear.

$$\text{Stress} = \frac{\text{applied load}}{\text{area of cross section opposing the load}}$$
$$\text{lb/in}^2 \text{ (psi) (MPa)}$$

The resistance of a material to the external force is called strength.

Subsequently, depending on the type of load applied, the strength could be tensile or compressive or one of the above mentioned.

When a load is applied, the material is elastically deformed; the ratio of deformation to the original dimension is called strain. It can be calculated as:

$$\text{Strain} = \frac{\text{change in dimension}}{\text{original dimension}} \text{ unitless}$$

Elastic deformation occurs when the material returns back to its normal shape after the applied load is removed. Plastic deformation is, on the other hand, permanently set in a material and cannot be regained after removal of load.

The traditional method of mechanical properties testing is a destructive method that involves quasi-statically tension testing of the standard test specimens and measuring of the stresses and corresponding strains. As a result of this testing, the stress-strain diagram is established and tensile and elastic properties of the material are determined. A tensile test is carried out on a universal testing machine. This involves the preparation of a test specimen, as shown in Fig. 2-5. The typical ASTM (American Society of Testing and Materials) standard specimen is cylindrical in cross section with a diameter of 0.5 in. (12.5 mm) and the gage length of 2 in. (50 mm).

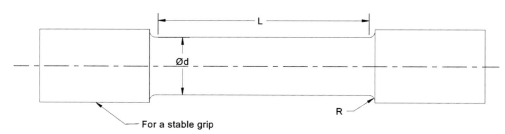

Fig. 2-5. ASTM standard test specimen for tensile test.

The specimen is placed into the tensile test machine and a uniformly increasing tensile load is applied on the specimen. As the load increases, the specimen initially gets elastically deformed, and then begins to yield or undergo plastic deformation when the material goes beyond the elastic limit and starts necking at some point, and finally breaks. Typically, a load cell system is used to measure load, while a strain gauge called an extensometer records strain. The stresses and strains are calculated from the above data and plotted in a diagram as shown in Fig. 2-6 for low-carbon steel.

As seen, in the linear portion of the diagram, the applied stress is directly proportional to the induced strain. It is called the proportional limit. If the load within the proportional area is removed, the specimen will return to its original length without any residual deformation. The end of the linear portion of the diagram is called the yield point (A), above which the material starts plastically deforming. The value of stress at this point gives yield strength. In the plastic region, there is a nonlinear relationship between the stress and strain, as evidenced by the bow-shaped portion of the curve (C to E). Finally, when the force of the applied load goes beyond the limit that the material can withstand, the specimen breaks.

Because for most nonferrous alloys and high-strength steels, yield point is hard to determine with desirable accuracy, the practical method, called the offset method, is used to calculate yield stress as a point on the stress-strain diagram that is offset by 0.2% strain, as is shown in Fig. 2-6. In this method, a straight line is drawn from the point representing 0.2% strain parallel to linear portion of the diagram. The intersection of this line with the diagram at point B gives the value of the stress and is used to calculate yield strength.

It needs to be noted that stress-strain diagrams have different shapes for different alloys. For example, for gray iron, which is a brittle material, it consists only of the straight-line portion of the stress-strain diagram, where a yield point doesn't exist. The latter explains why gray irons are specified only by tensile strength. The maximum stress reached in a material before the fracture is called the ultimate strength or tensile strength.

As a result of this testing, besides major tensile properties, other properties such as ductility and modulus of elasticity of the material are determined.

Ductility indicates the amount of plastic deformation that a material can undergo, under tensile forces without fracture.

Quantitatively it may be expressed in two ways as:

- The ratio of elongation of the material at fracture during the tensile test to the original length, expressed as a percentage. Since the elongation is dependent upon the gauge length chosen for the tensile test, the length needs to be specified along with the elongation values.

- The ratio of reduction in cross-sectional area in the fractured specimen to the original cross-sectional area, expressed as a percentage. This is independent of the gauge length and, hence, is a more convenient measure for ductility.

Brittleness is the property opposite of ductility and typically manifests itself as loss of impact toughness.

Modulus of Elasticity or ***Young's Modulus*** indicates the stiffness of a material and is defined from the straight-line portion of stress-strain diagram as the ratio of stress to strain. Modulus of elasticity is very important to designers in many engineering calculations such as in load-deflection, thermoelastic stress and fracture mechanics.

Compression Strength is the ability of material to resist pressing or crushing deformation. The test is opposite to tensile test, but utilizes the same testing machine. In this test, compression load is applied to a standard cylindrical specimen and maximum stress is related to the height changes.

2.2.1.2. Impact Toughness

This property signifies the amount of energy absorbed by a material at the time of fracture under impact loading at fixed temperatures. In short, it is the capacity of a material to take an impact load. Toughness of a material

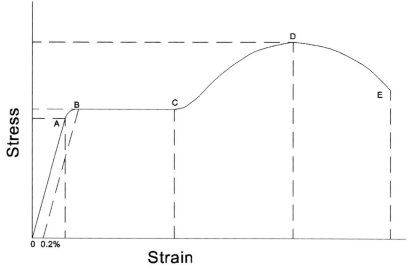

Fig. 2-6. Typical stress-strain diagram for low-carbon steel.

is measured by means of ASTM standard impact tests. In this test (Fig. 2-7), a notched bar made of the test material is held in a vice, and a pendulum of fixed weight is allowed to swing from a known height in such a way that it hits the notched bar in its path and breaks it.

In the Charpy impact test, the specimen is held between two grips and is hit behind the notch (Fig. 2-7(a)), whereas in the Izod impact test the specimen is held at one end like a cantilever and is hit above the notch as shown in Fig. 2-7(b).

Since the material has absorbed some amount of energy during its fracture, a pendulum loses part of its energy and, therefore, will not be able to reach the same height from where it started. The loss in height multiplied by the weight represents the energy absorbed by the specimen during fracture, which can be directly measured from the indicator on the tester. In another ASTM impact test, called the drop weight test, the specimen is fractured by a falling weight (Fig. 2-7c). The standard test specimens used in the impact tests are bars with a square cross section of 10-mm, 55-mm long and different standardized shaped notches.

The impact resistance is dependent upon the cast alloy composition as well as its heat treatment. As-cast structures would tend to have lower ductility compared to annealed or normalized. The annealed ductile irons normally would have better toughness than the corresponding normalized or quenched alloys. Normalized and tempered, and quenched and tempered steels have higher toughness than annealed steel. (Heat treating will be discussed later in this chapter.)

2.2.1.3. Hardness

Hardness is a measure of a material's resistance to indentation or penetration of a harder material. Although hardness testing does not give direct measurements of any performance properties, hardness correlates fairly well with other properties such as tensile strength, for example for irons and steels, wear resistance and machinability of cast alloys.

The indentation made depends upon the applied load, the indenter's material and the time for which the applied load is maintained. There are a number of indentation tests to measure the hardness of cast alloys, and involve a ball, a cone or a pyramid of a harder material that is indented into the material with a specified load. The indentation made is measured to give an indication of the hardness on the given scale for the test. The most commonly used are Brinell and Rockwell hardness test methods.

Brinell Hardness (HB) test utilizes a ball (usually 5 or 10 mm in diameter), made of hardened steel, which is indented at a right angle, with a gradually applied load to the specimen surface. The indentation (impression) diameter made on the specimen is then measured. The use of hardened steel (as a ball material) limits the application of Brinell hardness tests to relatively low-hardness materials, because the hardness of a tested material must be significantly less than the hardness of the indenter. The applied load depends on the hardness of the material being tested: the 500-kg load is used for copper alloys, the 1500-kg load is used for aluminum alloys and the 3000-kg load applies when tests are done on cast irons or steels. The load is usually applied for 10 to 15 seconds.

After the impression is made, the diameter of the indentation is measured using a low magnification portable microscope with an accuracy of ±0.05 mm. Then the Brinell hardness number, HB is calculated as:

$$HB = \frac{2P}{\pi D[D - \sqrt{D^2 - d^2}]}$$

Where:

P is the applied load in kg,

D is the diameter of the ball, mm

d is the diameter of the indentation, mm

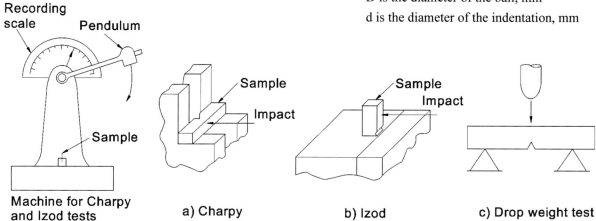

Fig. 2-7. Impact testing machine and ASTM standard impact toughness testing methods.

To simplify the calculations, calibrated charts are provided with testing machines that give HB values for each diameter of the indentation made by applying available test loads.

The contemporary Brinell testing machine may be furnished with a portable optical scanning system that eliminates the operator influence on the Brinell measurements by automatically scanning the Brinell impression and providing a Brinell reading and measurement. In general, the Brinell hardness tests may be done on specimens or lightweight castings having enough material underneath the indentation and on all sides to give a proper value for hardness readings.

Rockwell Hardness (HR) tests measure the depth of penetration of the indenter (ball or diamond pyramid) into the test material surface. The hardness is indicated directly on the scale attached to the testing machine. Thus, the Rockwell hardness measurement is more universal and faster compared to the Brinell method. Depending on the hardness of the material, Rockwell tests may use nine combinations of three types of indenters (steel balls or diamond-point) and three loads (60, 100 and 150 kg) utilizing one of its scales.

For relatively soft materials such as copper and aluminum alloys, a steel ball, 1.6 mm (1/16 or 0.0625 in) diameter, is used with a load of 100 kg and the hardness is read on the B scale. In testing harder materials such as quenched steel or white irons, a 120°-diamond cone is used with a 150-kg load and hardness value is read on the C scale. Rockwell hardness (HR) test result is expressed as a hardness number followed by a letter, indicating specific scale. For example, 75 HRB indicates that material has a hardness reading of 75 on the B scale.

Other Hardness Tests. Besides the above mentioned, there are other hardness (micro hardness) tests available such as Vickers and Knoop, to measure hardness over a small area or hardness of a microstructure. These methods utilize a range of loads using a diamond indenter to make an indentation, which is measured and converted to a hardness value. In the Vickers (HV) hardness test, a square base pyramid diamond indenter, having 136° between the opposite faces, is used. The Vickers hardness number (Vhn) is calculated as:

$$\mathrm{Vhn} = \mathrm{Vhn} = \frac{1.854P}{D^2}$$

Where:

P is the applied load,

D is the measured average of two diagonals of the indentation, mm.

The Vickers method is more commonly used for hardness measurements of surface (case) hardened parts, making a series of indentations to describe a profile of the change in hardness along the cross section of the part, or for micro hardness evaluation of microstructural constituencies in cast alloys.

In Knoop hardness tests, a narrow rhombus-shaped diamond indenter is used along with a very light load. This method is used only for micro hardness tests, mostly on small parts and thin sections when indentations are closely spaced or very close to the edge. All contemporary micro hardness testers allow for both Vickers and Knoop testing.

The Shore Scleroscope hardness testing method is based on a different principle to measure the hardness, which depends on the rebound height of a ball from the test specimen surface. The harder the material, the higher is the height to which the ball rebounds. The testers, built on this principle, are portable and even lately, hand-held, which makes it suitable for foundry applications, as shown in Fig. 2-8.

As can be seen from previously discussed materials, hardness can be measured by various methods and expressed in many different units. The widely available ASTM conversion charts allow converting hardness data obtained from different hardness measurements. It is necessary to keep in mind that these are approximate relationships, which may be used merely as a guideline.

Fig. 2-8. Portable hand-held hardness tester suitable for foundry applications.

Note: More details of mechanical properties and hardness tests are given in the Lab Manual, which accompanies this textbook.

2.2.2. Specific Properties Affecting Service Performance

Residual stresses are stresses that remain in the part after the original cause of the stress is removed. Residual stresses, present in cast metal components, are generated in nearly every step of the metalcasting process.

The most widespread causes of castings' residual stresses are mold and core restraint contraction, different thermal gradients from variations in the casting sections' cooling rates, and microstructure transformation during solidification of the casting. The amount of retained stresses affect the casting dimensional stability and life cycle.

Dimensional stability characterizes the ability of material to maintain its shape and dimensions by resisting elastic distortion during the service. This is particularly important when cast parts are machined and used in precision machinery or for hydraulic parts. When some of the metal is removed by machining, the rebalance of residual stresses occurs causing distortion or warping of cast parts.

Identifying and managing these stresses, and using this knowledge to implement tighter quality process controls, significantly improves the cast component's performance, increases fatigue life, prevents premature failures, and minimizes scrap rates and castings returns. Of all the residual stress measuring techniques, the X-ray diffraction (XRD) method is widely accepted as the most general and reliable nondestructive method of quantifying the residual stress levels in castings. This technique uses the atomic planes of the crystalline grains within the material as very sensitive strain sensors. A diffraction analysis technique measures the strain and converts it to stress. A low-energy X-ray beam diffracts off of the sample. Changes in strain in the sample translate into changes in the diffraction angle that are measured by two X-ray detectors and then processed by special software into a stress value.

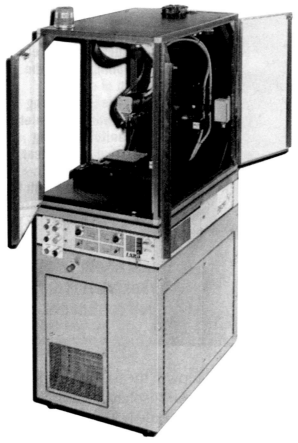

Fig. 2-9. The lab-based X-ray diffraction residual stress measurement system, recommended for small castings.

Fig. 2-10. Portable version of the X-ray diffraction residual stress measurement system. It has fiber optic-based solid-state detectors that allow the detector electronics to be remote from the sensing head. To be used for large castings such as engine blocks.

The method employs the use of fiber optic-based solid-state detectors. The fiber optics allow the detector electronics to be remote from the sensing head, thus enabling configurations of the measurement head that are small enough to allow access to tight locations. A stress measurement can be performed in a few minutes. Small castings can be loaded for inspection into the lab-based test machine (Fig. 2-9). For larger castings, a portable system can be brought to the cast component (Fig. 2-10).

The XRD residual stress measurement method can be used to measure stress at the stage of the casting design or after pouring, heat treatment, machining and surface treatments.

Wear Resistance characterizes the ability of a material to resist its removal from the surface as a result of physical or mechanical contact with other material or medium.

Wear commonly is classified according to its three major modes:

- *Adhesive* (frictional) wear (sliding and rolling) is caused by contact with another metallic surface. Frictional wear is typical for automotive and tractor crankshafts, camshafts, various axis and shafts for machine tools, etc.

- *Abrasive* wear is caused by contact with metallic (shots, turnings) or nonmetallic abrasives (sand, coal, cement, slag, etc.) materials. Abrasive wear takes place in agriculture machines, coal pulverizing equipment, slurry pumps, etc.

- *Erosion* wear is caused by impact of dispersed particles in flowing fluids or gases. Erosion wear may be combined with localized abrasive, for example, at bends and valves in pneumatic conveying systems in coal pulverizing equipment, and pump impellers.

The following tests are carried out to evaluate cast alloy's wear behavior and rank their performance under different wear modes. Three duplicate tests are typically conducted with the same test materials.

- *Rotating sliding test* (Fig. 2-11) simulates dry or lubricated sliding wear mode that is typical for bushing/bearing applications. In this test, a stationary block made from test material is held under a specific pressure against a shaft (counter face) rotating at a desired surface speed. The steel shaft is made of quenched medium carbon steel 1045 (48-52 HRC); testing period takes from 2 to 48 hours; running-in period varies until consistent friction coefficient values are obtained. In this testing mode, wear behavior of both the test material (stationary block) and counter surface wears (steel shaft) are

measured. The latter is very important, because in real bearing/bushing applications the counter surface material significantly affects net system operation performance.

Wear resistance is determined from the loss in weight and expressed as wear rates of the test material and the steel shaft (counter surface).

- *Reciprocating wear tests* with abrasive-contaminated lubricant are conducted in a special device simulating working conditions typical for guideways and other similar parts (Fig. 2-12). Tests are performed at a specific load and a sliding speed over a testing period that varies from 30 to 60 minutes. The lubricant is prepared by adding cast iron turnings crushed to 0.05 to 0.1 mm size to industrial SAE-20 oil in a ratio of 1:10. All specimens are tested against gray iron grade 30, and the rate of wear is recorded as ratio of linear wear to the testing period. Because the wear rate is proportional to the actual wear, the lower value implies greater wear resistance.

- *Abrasion wear test* is developed to simulate the conditions of erosion wear combined with localized abrasive wear, typical, for example, for bends and valves in pneumatic conveying systems in coal pulverizing equipment, slurry pumps, and pump impellers, using a device shown on Fig. 2-13. The test cycle consists of rotating the specimens fixed on the rotating head at a speed of 1000 rpm inside the container filled with an abrasive medium (alumina sand with particles size approximately 2 mm) for a period of 15 hours. After each test, a fresh portion of slurry is used.

Specimens made from the test materials are prepared in the shape of rectangular 25 x 75 mm and 10 mm thick (1 x 3 x 0.4 in.) bars. A holding fixture is designed to hold

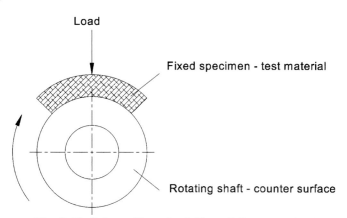

Fig. 2-11. Schematics of rotating sliding wear test.

simultaneously six specimens. Three similar specimens made from the reference material are alternated with the three test specimens, and averages of wear rate for each material is calculated. The rate of wear is determined as the ratio of weight loss of test material to the weight loss of reference material (quenched and tempered medium carbon steel 1050). In order to accelerate the wear and create more local stress by the impeller effect, the test specimens are held in the holding fixture at a 30- degree angle.

Thermal Shock Resistance characterizes the ability of a material to withstand thermal stress as a result of a sudden exposure to elevated temperature; testing typically involves repeated cycling simulating thermal shock conditions. This property is greatly influenced by thermal conductivity of a material, its modulus of elasticity and tensile and impact toughness at elevated temperature.

Corrosion Resistance characterizes the ability of a material to withstand chemical attack by the environment.

Machinability specifies the capacity of a material to be machined easily. Typically it is measured by a machinability factor–a relative measure of the machinability of an engineering material under specified standard conditions.

2.3. Ferrous Alloys

The basic source of all iron and steel is iron ore, which is an oxide of iron mixed with alumina, silica, phosphorus, manganese, sulfur and other materials. Major iron ores are hematite and magnetite, which contain about 55% iron.

Pig iron, the principal base material for almost all steel and iron melting processes, is the product of the blast furnace. Pig iron contains about 4% carbon, 1% silicon, 1% manganese and small percentages of phosphorus and sulfur. Pig iron is hard and brittle. It lacks the great strength, ductility and resistance to shock that steel possesses.

Absolutely pure iron is very difficult to obtain. In this state, it is a soft and highly ductile metal of a light gray color having a specific weight of 7.86 g/cm^3. The mechanical properties of commercial grade iron, containing from 0.1 to 0.2% impurities, are:

Hardness	60 to 80 HB
Tensile strength	180 to 310 MPa (26,100 to 44,960 psi)
Yield point	200 MPa (29,000 psi)
Reduction in area	75%

The only application that can be found for pure iron is in the making of magnets, in view of its high permeability. Otherwise, the extensive use of iron is in the form of its large number of alloys. Iron can be alloyed with many elements.

Alloys of iron and carbon in amounts more than 2% are called cast irons and are most widely used in metalcasting. They contain certain amounts of silicon, manganese, chromium, nickel and other elements.

2.3.1. Cast Irons

As stated before, the ferrous alloys that have carbon contents of more than 2% are called cast irons. Though cast irons can have any carbon percentage between 2 and 6.67, the practical limit is normally between 2 and 4%.

From the iron-carbon equilibrium diagram (Fig. 2-4), it can be observed that high hardness and brittleness cementite or iron carbide may be present in the microstructure of cast irons. When cast iron is slowly cooled, the cementite decomposes into iron and carbon in the form of graphite; this process is called graphitization.

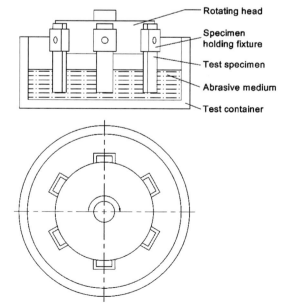

Fig. 2-13. Schematics of an abrasion wear test device.

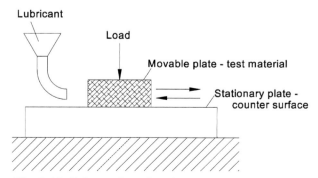

Fig. 2-12. Schematics of reciprocating wear test.

In the presence of graphitizing elements such as silicon, nickel or copper, iron carbide decomposes as follows:

$$Fe_3C \rightarrow 3\,Fe + C$$

The decomposition of cementite is also controlled by the cooling rate, which is affected by casting section thickness. The dissociated carbon, present in the microstructure in the form of graphite, is very soft, and has very low strength. Thus, it reduces the hardness and increases the machinability of cast iron.

The shape of graphite, present in cast irons, would greatly affect its strength. In gray iron, graphite particles are in the form of flake, whereas ductile iron features nodular or spheroidal graphite. In malleable iron, graphite particles are in the shape of irregular or temper graphite nodules. Due to graphite precipitation, cast irons expand during solidification. In high carbon and silicon content iron, this expansion may even compensate for shrinkage.

2.3.1.1. Gray Iron

In gray iron, graphite is present in the form of flakes and the mechanical properties are mainly dependent upon graphite size, shape and distribution. This characteristic is called graphite morphology. The graphite breaks up continuity of the iron structure and greatly weakens it. But it also helps in absorbing vibration energy, as a result of which gray cast iron is commonly used for the beds and tables of machine tools.

Figure 2-14 illustrates typical graphite structure in gray iron containing graphite flakes. Metallic matrix in unalloyed gray iron may contain a different ferrite/pearlite ratio. For the best combination of properties, a metallic matrix of predominantly pearlite is recommended.

ASTM A48 specification (Table 2-1) specifies gray iron castings intended for general engineering applications where tensile strength is a major consideration. Castings produced to this specification are classified by the minimum tensile strength measured by testing specimens cut from separately cast test bars.

Classes are designated by tensile strength, which is increased from 20 to 60 in increments of 5 ksi, and by the letter A, B, C or S, depending on the test bar diameter that represents the overall thickness of the casting:

- Test bar diameter A = 0.80 in. (20 mm) represents the casting controlling wall thickness from 0.25 to 0.5 in. (5 - 14 mm);
- Test bar diameter B = 1.2 in. (30 mm) represents the casting controlling wall thickness from 0.51 to 1.0 in. (15 - 25 mm);
- Test bar diameter C = 2.0 in. (50 mm) represents the controlling wall thickness from 1.01 to 2.0 in. (26 - 50 mm);

- Test bar S represents the controlling wall thickness over 2 in. (50 mm) and its dimensions are determined by agreement between the foundry and consumer.

For example, Gray Iron Class 30B indicates that minimum tensile strength of 30 ksi (207 MPa) is obtained on 1.2 in. (30 mm) diameter test bar B. A typical gray iron Class 30 for general use contains (%): 3.2–3.5 C; 1.6–2.2 Si; 0.5–1.0 Mn; 0.05–0.15 S and 0.02–0.15 P. This chemistry in regards to iron-carbon diagram is considered as hypoeutectic.

Alloying elements such as Cu, Ni, Cr and/or Mo are commonly used to increase mechanical properties of gray iron or promote some specific service properties. The carbon and silicon contents are the most important chemical elements influencing microstructure and properties of cast irons. Their combined effect is commonly expressed as the carbon equivalent (CE) and calculated as:

$$CE = \%C + 0.33\,(\%\,Si + \%P)$$

Table 2-1. ASTM A48 Standard Specifies Gray Iron Castings Intended for General Engineering Applications where Tensile Strength is a Major Consideration.

Gray Iron Grade or Class	Minimum Tensile Strength, psi (MPa)
20	20,000 (138)
25	25,000 (172)
30	30,000 (207)
35	35,000 (241)
40	40,000 (276)
45	45,000 (310)
50	50,000 (345)
55	55,000 (379)
60	60,000 (414)

Fig. 2-14. Typical flake graphite structure in gray iron. 100X; unetched.

In gray iron, decreasing CE results in increasing tensile strength and hardness. The cooling rate, which represents the combined effect of section thickness and mold material (foundry sand, or ceramic or metal) has considerable effect on graphite morphology. A rapid cooling produces fine graphite structure, a very slow cooling results in coarse graphite particles. Subsequently, bigger flakes lessen tensile strength and hardness. Inoculation of iron with Si-based alloys produces finely dispersed graphite flakes in a pearlitic matrix. The presence of graphite flakes, serving as a lubricant during machining, ensures excellent machinability of gray iron.

ASTM A159 (SAE J431) specifies different grades of gray iron recommended for automotive and tractor applications such as brake drums and clutch plates, cylinder blocks and cylinder heads, flywheels, liners, cylinders, pistons, as well as alloy gray iron for automotive camshafts. Castings produced to this specification are graded by Brinell hardness range, minimum tensile strength, carbon content and microstructure.

Due to exceptional damping capacity and good wear resistance, gray iron is widely used in the machine tool industry to cast high precision bases and tables weighting up to 100 metric tons (220,000 lb). High thermal conductivity and the ability to withstand high stresses at elevated temperatures, make gray iron very effective for casting various capacity ingot molds used in iron and steel foundries. Its excellent corrosion resistance is the primary cause of wide use of gray iron as material for pipes and sanitary castings. Gray cast iron is easily machinable and is the cheapest form of cast iron. Because of its low melting temperature in comparison to cast steel, higher fluidity and, in most cases, negligible shrinkage during solidification, it is extensively used in casting processes.

2.3.1.2. White Cast Iron

Cast iron in which graphitization has not taken place, i.e., all the carbon is in solution or in the form of cementite or iron carbide (Fe_3C), is called white cast iron. The graphitization process requires time; therefore, when liquid cast iron is cooled rapidly, white cast iron would result. The other method of white iron casting production is by adding chemical elements such as Cr (up to 30%) or Mo (up to 3%), called carbide stabilizers, to the base iron.

White cast iron is a highly brittle material. Its tensile strength varies between 170 and 345 MPa (24,650 and 50,030 psi) and is usually about 240 MPa (34,810 psi), and the hardness ranges from 450 to 600 HB. In view of the very high hardness, the machinability is poor and

grinding commonly finishes cast parts. White cast iron is typically used for low and high stress abrasive wear applications in mining, coal crushing and milling, and for cast parts of earth handling equipment.

2.3.1.3. Malleable Iron

Malleable cast iron is a heat-treated iron-carbon cast alloy, which solidifies in the as-cast condition as a white iron with a graphite-free structure, i.e., the total carbon content is present as cementite or iron carbide form (Fe_3C). A following, controlled graphitizing heat treatment transforms the cementite to temper graphite nodules uniformly distributed either in ferritic or pearlitic metallic matrix or in its combination.

Figure 2-15 represents typical graphite structure in malleable iron obtained as a result of graphitizing heat treatment. It needs to be noted that because of the diffusion in the solid state in which graphite is formed in malleable iron, the nodules are not actually spherical as they are in ductile iron, but are irregularly shaped aggregates.

Due to the combination of temper graphite and low-carbon metallic matrix, malleable iron possesses considerable ductility and toughness. The base chemistry of malleable iron has low carbon and silicon content ensuring formation of an as-cast metallic matrix of mostly iron carbide.

The typical chemical composition of malleable iron is as follows (%): 2.2–2.8 C, 1.2–1.8 Si, 0.2–0.8 Mn, 0.02–0.20 S and 0.02–0.15 P. Small amounts of elements such as bismuth or tellurium may be added to promote an as-cast iron carbide structure; micro additions of boron and/or aluminum may be used to shorten the annealing cycle. The addition of alloying elements such

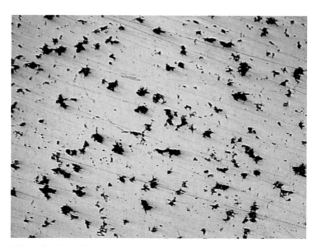

Fig. 2-15. Typical temper graphite structure in malleable iron. 150X; unetched.

as copper, from 0.5 to 1.0%, or nickel, from 0.5 to 0.8%, and molybdenum from 0.35 to 0.5% stabilizes pearlite formation and improves tensile properties.

Depending upon the type of heat treatment applied, different grades of malleable cast iron are specified, differentiated by resulting microstructure and mechanical properties. ASTM A47 standard specification designates two grades of ferritic malleable castings for general applications, based on their mechanical properties.

For example, in Grade 32510, the first three digits of the grade indicate the minimum yield strength (x 100 psi)–32,500 psi (224 MPa), and the last two digits indicate the minimum elongation, % in 2 inches = 10%. To obtain a desirable ferritic microstructure, castings made of this grade are subjected to two-stage annealing.

ASTM A220 standard specification of pearlitic malleable castings is also based on the same designation system as ASTM 47, in which each grade is specified by five digits indicating minimum yield strength and minimum elongation. For example, Grade 45008 means that minimum yield strength is 45,000 psi (310 MPa) and elongation is 8%.

The microstructure of pearlitic malleable cast iron has a matrix, according to the grade specified, of predominantly pearlite or of transformation products of austenite obtained after normalizing and tempering. Graphite is present in the form of temper carbon nodules.

Disadvantages of malleable iron include lengthy and costly heat treatment and limited application by section thickness. This is because section thickness greater than 2 inch cannot be cast as white iron structure without using special methods. It explains why, lately, significant amounts of malleable castings have been converted to ductile iron. Today, malleable iron is used mostly as a material for thin-section castings such as pipe fittings, flanges, caps for electric insulators and valve parts.

2.3.1.4. Ductile Iron

Ductile iron, sometimes referred to as nodular or spheroidal graphite iron, is a relatively new casting material. Since its invention in the 1940s, ductile iron production has been growing rapidly, successfully replacing malleable iron, steel castings, forgings and steel weldments in a wide variety of industrial applications.

In ductile iron (Fig. 2-16), graphite is present as small, round, and well-distributed particles called nodules, and their weakening effect on the metallic matrix is less than in gray or malleable iron. As a result, the mechanical properties of ductile iron are similar to cast and even forged steel (high strength, ductility and shock

resistance), while maintaining all the advantages of cast iron (high damping capacity, corrosion and wear resistance).

Addition of small amounts of magnesium or cerium, or a combination of these two elements to molten cast iron, can achieve the nodular form of graphite. Typical residual magnesium content in ductile iron is within the range of 0.025–0.06%. The base chemical composition of unalloyed ductile iron is as follows (%): 3.2–3.6 C, 2.2–2.8 Si, 0.3–0.6 Mn, max 0.03 S, max 0.06 P. As can be seen, due to high carbon and silicon contents, ductile iron's CE is considerably high, and in regard to the iron-carbon diagram, its chemistry is referred to as hypereutectic.

Tables 2-2 and 2-3 detail the major mechanical properties of standard ASTM A536 grades of ductile iron. The grades listed in Table 2-2 are recommended for general use and grades listed in Table 2-3 are recommended for special castings such as pressure pipes, fittings, etc. Three double-digit numbers that specify minimal tensile strength, tensile yield and elongation designate each grade of ductile iron. For example, annealed ferritic ductile iron Grade 60-40-18 has minimum tensile strength of 60,000 psi (414 MPa), minimum tensile yield of 40,000 psi (276 MPa) and minimum elongation of 18%.

The tensile strength of ductile iron ranges from 60,000 to 120,000 psi (415 to 827MPa). Ductility is gradually reduced and hardness is increased with increasing tensile strength. The yield strength of ductile iron is a minimum of 40,000 psi (276 MPa). This is higher than some grades of cast steels or any gray iron, which has no true yield strength. The impact resistance depends upon ferrite content in the microstructure. Annealed ductile iron grade

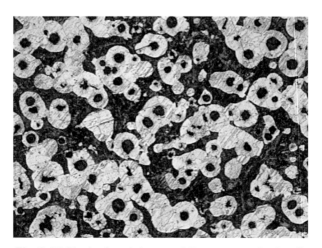

Fig. 2-16. Typical nodular graphite structure in ductile iron. Graphite nodules are surrounded by ferrite, the rest of the metallic matrix is pearlitic.100X; etched.

60-40-18 is fully ferritic and has higher impact resistance than other grades. Its impact strength measured on Charpy unnotched specimens has value of up to 100 ft-lb (135 joules). Samples made of this grade of ductile iron can be bent or deformed without fracturing.

The modulus of elasticity of ductile iron is comparable to cast steel and has its value between 24 and 26 million psi. The greatest value applies to pearlitic grades that possess high tensile strength, considerably higher than the modulus of elasticity of gray iron, which has a value of only 15 million psi.

Due to its excellent fatigue properties, ductile iron has replaced steel forgings in many applications such as automotive crankshafts, camshafts and connecting rods. Ductile iron wear resistance is comparable to some grades of carbon and alloy steel and is superior to gray irons in heavy load or impact load applications. This has been confirmed by service performance of diesel engine cylinder liners, crankshafts, gears, different machine tool and press components exposed to wear with high local loadings.

The corrosion resistance of ductile iron is similar to gray cast iron and is superior to cast steel in many corrosives. It is extensively used as a material for pressure-cast pipes and for equipment handling of a wide variety of corrosive materials.

Ductile iron exhibits excellent pressure tightness because the nodular graphite reduces discontinuities in the structure and prevents the capillary leakage often encountered in gray cast irons. This makes ductile iron ideal for high-pressure hydraulic parts. Table 2-4 illustrates typical applications of ductile iron for this purpose.

Because ductile iron can be cast with almost the same low-cost operational procedures as gray iron, ductile iron castings are only fairly more expensive than gray iron, but are less expensive than cast steel. The substantial advantages of ductile iron's high strength and ductility combined with exceptional wear and shock resistance make it a good economical choice for many industrial applications such as automotive steering knuckles, brake calipers, piston rings, exhaust manifolds, gears, molds for glass industry, steel mill rolls, etc.

Table 2-2. Mechanical Properties of ASTM A536 Grades of Ductile Iron.

Mechanical Properties	Grade 60-40-18	Grade 65-45-12	Grade 80-55-06	Grade 100-70-03	Grade 120-90-02
Tensile strength, min, psi	60000	65000	80000	100000	120000
Tensile strength, min, MPa	414	448	552	689	827
Yield strength, min, psi	40000	45000	55000	70000	90000
Yield strength, min, MPa	276	310	379	483	621
Elongation in 2 in. or 50 mm, min, %	18	12	6.0	3.0	2.0

Table 2-3. Mechanical Properties of
ASTM A536 Grades of Ductile Iron for Special Applications.

Mechanical Properties	Grade 60-42-10	Grade 70-50-05	Grade 80-60-03
Tensile strength, min, psi	60000	70000	80000
Tensile strength, min, MPa	415	485	555
Yield strength, min, psi	42000	50000	60000
Yield strength, min, MPa	290	345	415
Elongation in 2 in or 50 mm, min, %	10	5.0	3.0

Table 2-4. ASTM Grades of Ductile Iron Recommended for Hydraulic Parts Applications.

Castings group	Working conditions of components	Typical representative castings	Recommended ASTM grade of ductile iron
A	Exposed to wear and pressure > 30 MPa (4350 psi)	Distributor bodies; rotors, liners and bushes for piston, axial-, and radial-piston pumps and hydraulic motors.	80-55-06 100-70-03
B	Not exposed to wear, pressure > 30 MPa (4350 psi)	Pump and hydraulic motor housing; end-covers; distribution, monitoring and regulating apparatus.	60-40-18 65-45-12

The weight of complex ductile iron castings ranges from a fraction of kilograms (ounces) to tons. The heaviest ductile iron casting ever poured (283 metric tons /622,600 lb) was done recently at a German foundry for a new forging press. This component, measuring 10.9 x 3.95 x 2.74 m (36 x 13 x 9 ft.), is the upper crossbeam for a closed-die forging press, and was poured at about 1,350 °C (2462 °F) from five ladles in approximately 120 seconds. After cooling in the mold for about four weeks, the casting was lifted out of the casting pit and machined on high-capacity machines capable of handling parts with a clamping length of up to 22 meters (72.18ft). The previous record for heaviest ductile iron casting was a 270 metric ton (594,000 lb) component cast last year by the same foundry.

2.3.1.5. Austempered Ductile Iron

Austempered ductile iron (ADI) is a heat-treated nodular cast iron with a microstructure that consists of stabilized high-carbon austenite and acicular ferrite with dispersed graphite nodules. According to ASTM A644, the standard name of this specific microstructure is ausferrite. In order to get its unique properties, the as-cast ductile iron is subjected to the special austempering heat treatment cycle consisting of two subsequently performed operations:

- Austenitizing is heating to 840–900°C (1550–1700°F) and holding at this temperature for a period of time necessary to produce austenite;
- Rapid Cooling to 220–400°C (430–750°F), typically in the molten salt bath, and isothermal holding at this temperature, produces ausferrite with a desirable austenite/ferrite ratio, depending upon the desirable ADI grade.

ASTM designates five grades of ADI that, depending on the heat treatment parameters, have the mechanical characteristics shown in Table 2-5. As can be seen, ADI exhibits more than twice the strength for a given level of ductility, compared to conventional ductile iron. Although the level of its mechanical properties is almost the same as in high-alloy steels, the production cost of ADI is significantly lower. ADI is successfully used in many industrial applications requiring high strength, combined with relatively high-impact toughness and ductility.

ADI also offers great potential for cast parts in applications involving impact loads combined with wear (automotive transmission and suspension, earth moving equipment, tractors, etc.) as an alternative material to:

- Alloyed and unalloyed steel castings and forgings that are used under abrasive wear conditions. In this case, ADI may permit an 8–10% reduction in part weight and cost with equivalent or better service performance;
- White iron castings in applications requiring both wear resistance and high impact toughness. ADI may enable significant cost reduction with better service performance;
- Bronzes and pearlitic DI in rotating dry sliding wear applications, typical for bushings/ bearings used at relatively high PV factors (where P is applied pressure and V is sliding velocity) and in a dirty environment, where reliable fluid lubrication is not assured. ADI may lower cost with better service performance.

2.3.1.6. Alloyed Irons

Alloying of cast irons has the purpose to improve mechanical or specific properties influencing the life cycle of cast components. The following are some typical groups representing alloyed irons used in foundries:

- Austenitic gray (ASTM A436) or (ASTM A439) ductile irons or Ni-resists, intended for heat, corrosion or wear-resistant applications may contain subsequently up to 22% and 37% nickel. These irons contain carbon from 2.4 to 3% and up to 6% silicon in both gray and ductile irons. Minimum tensile strength of austenitic gray irons vary from 138 to 207 MPa (20,000 to 30,000 psi), and hardness values 124–212 HB. Austenitic ductile irons possess minimum tensile strength from 380 to 450 MPa (55,000 to 65,000 psi), elongation from 6 to 20 % and 140–202 HB.

Table 2-5. ASTM A897 Grades and Properties of Austempered Ductile Iron.

ADI Grade	Minimum Yield Strength, MPa (ksi)	Minimum Tensile Strength, MPa (ksi)	Minimum Elongation, %	Minimum Unnotched Charpy, J (ft-lb.)	Typical Brinell Hardness, HB
850/550/10	550 (80)	850 (125)	10	100 (75)	269-321
1050/700/7	700 (100)	1050 (150)	7	80 (60)	302-363
1200/850/4	850 (125)	1200 (175)	4	60 (45)	341-444
1400/1100/1	1100 (155)	1400 (200)	1	35 (25)	388-477
1600/1300/–	1300 (185)	1600 (230)	–	–	444-555

- High nickel and chromium irons (ASTM A532) or Ni-Hards, developed for abrasion resistant applications such as crushing and grinding balls used in coal pulverizing, contain 3.3–5.0% nickel and 1.4–3.5% chromium.

- High silicon iron for corrosion resistant service (ASTM A518) contains 14–15% of silicon, while carbon content varies from 0.7 to 1.1%.

2.3.1.7. Compacted Graphite Iron

The compacted graphite iron (CGI) is cast iron, whose microstructure contains a combination of compacted graphite, sometimes called vermicular graphite, in the form of interconnected flakes (80% min) and up to 20% of nodular or spheroidal graphite, uniformly distributed in ferrite/pearlite metallic matrix (Fig. 2-17).

As a result of this intermediate graphite structure, mechanical and other properties affecting service life of cast components are between those properties of gray and ductile iron. Originally, CGI was developed as under-treated ductile iron with a reduced addition of magnesium-bearing nodulizer and, subsequently, with a low-residual magnesium content (up to 0.01%). The problem is that it is very difficult to regulate residual magnesium content in molten iron in such a low range.

One of the practical methods used to develop controlled CGI production technology is to treat the molten iron with a decreased amount of magnesium-bearing nodulizer. This is done to obtain nodular graphite. After that, small amounts of denodulizer elements, such as 0.15 to 0.20% titanium, are added to the molten iron. This is done to suppress the more-than-desired percentage of nodular graphite in the solidification structure. The base chemistry (CE) of CGI is almost similar to ductile iron and is considered hypereutectic with 3.5–3.8% C and 2.5–3.0% Si; manganese content varies in the range of 0.30 to 0.60% depending upon desirable ferrite/pearlite metallic matrix. The disadvantages of this method include reduced machinability of iron due to the presence in the microstructure of hard titanium-bearing inclusions in the case of high-uncontrolled residual titanium content.

ASTM A842 covers microstructure and mechanical property specification of compacted graphite castings. Table 2-6 shows typical ASTM A842 standard tensile and hardness requirements for five grades of CGI castings. Castings produced to this specification are classified by the minimum tensile strength measured by testing of specimens cut from separately cast test bars. For example, CGI Grade 350 indicates that minimum tensile strength of 350 MPa (50,760 psi). CGI Grade 250 is ferritic grade, Grade 450 is a pearlitic grade and grades between these

Table 2-6. Typical Range of Properties for ASTM A842 Grades of Compacted Graphite Iron.

Mechanical Properties	Grade 250	Grade 300	Grade 350	Grade 400	Grade 450
Tensile strength, min, MPa (psi)	250 (36,250)	300 (43,510)	350 (50,760)	400 (58,010)	450 (65,260)
Yield strength, min, MPa (psi)	175 (25,380)	210 (30,450)	245 (35,530)	280 (40,610)	315 (45,690)
Elongation in 2 in. or 50 mm, min, %	3.0	1.5	1.0	1.0	1.0
Brinell Hardness, HB	179 max	143–207	163–229	197–255	207–269

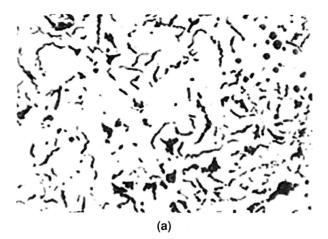

(a)

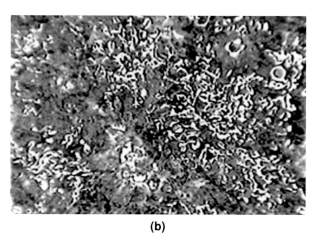

(b)

Fig. 2-17. Typical graphite structure in compacted graphite iron: (a) 100X; unetched; (b) etched.

grades represent CGI with different ferrite/pearlite ratio. CGI is suitable for cast components such as diesel engine blocks, heavy-duty automotive brake drums, wheel hubs, gears and ingot molds.

2.3.2. Cast Steels

As stated before, steels are iron-carbon alloys containing up to 2% carbon. There are three classes of plain carbon steels determined by carbon content:

Low   up to 0.25% C

Medium from 0.25 to 0.60% C

High   > 0.60%C

The properties of steel are influenced significantly by carbon content (Fig. 2-18): with increasing carbon content, tensile strength and hardness are increased, but ductility is decreased.

Low-carbon steels are used where ductility and softness are important and high tensile strength is not required. These steels are tough, but not resistant to wear. Since these are soft, they are very easily formed and machined and later can be carburized to increase the hardness and wear resistance. Low-carbon steels are not responsive to normal heat treatment but are responsive to case hardening. They form the largest percentage of steel produced and, because of being the cheapest engineering material, are used for auto bodies, large pipes and various components in bridges, ships and other structural applications

Medium-carbon steels are less ductile but harder and have greater tensile strength than low-carbon steels. They also have better machinability and are more responsive to heat treatment. Medium-carbon steels are used for making shafts, connecting rods, spindles, rail axles, gears, turbine bucket wheels, steering arms and other machine parts requiring medium strength and wear resisting surfaces.

High-carbon steels have higher tensile strength and are harder than other plain carbon steels. They also readily respond to heat treatment. These are used for making different types of tools, railroad wheels, etc.

The following is a general designation system adopted for plain carbon steels in which a two-digit number identifies the composition range of alloying elements followed by a two-or three-digit number indicating an average carbon content in hundredths of a percent. Some of the most generally used steels are as follows:

10XX - Plain carbon

13XX - Manganese 1.75

25XX - Nickel 5.0

31XX - Nickel 1.25; chromium 0.65

40XX - Molybdenum 0.25

41XX - Chromium 0.50 or 0.95; molybdenum 0.12 or 0.20

43XX - Nickel 1.80; chromium 0.50 or 0.80; molybdenum 0.25

44XX - Manganese 0.80; molybdenum 0.40

46XX - Nickel 1.85; molybdenum 0.25

51XX - Chromium 1.00

61XX - Chromium 0.60, 0.80 or 0.95; vanadium 0.12 or 0.10 min or 0.15 min

81XX - Nickel 0.30; chromium 0.40; molybdenum 0.12

92XX - Manganese 0.85; silicon 2.00

93XX - Nickel 3.25; chromium 1.20; molybdenum 0.12

For example, in steel 5120, the first two digits (51) signify that chromium is the major alloying element in the amount of 1% and the last two digits (20) indicate that the approximate carbon content is 0.2%. If carbon content is 1% or more, it will be indicated by the last three digits; for example, steel 51100.

ASTM standard A27 covers carbon steel castings for general applications that require up to 70 ksi (485 MPa) minimum tensile strength. Except for two grades, the two-digit number, reflecting minimum tensile yield and tensile strength in ksi (MPa), specify all other grades. For example, Grade 70-36 specifies minimum tensile strength of 70 ksi (485 MPa) and minimum tensile yield of 36 ksi (250 MPa). Ductility (elongation from 22 to 24 % and reduction in area from 30 to 35 %) is also specified for these grades.

Recommended by the standard, typical chemical composition of cast steel contains carbon in the amount of 0.25–0.35%, 0.2–0.8% silicon, 0.6–1.2% manganese, and max 0.06% sulfur and max 0.05% phosphorus.

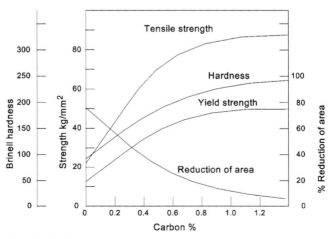

Fig. 2-18. Mechanical properties as a function of carbon content in steels.

Small quantities of elements such as sulfur and phosphorus are considered as impurities and, therefore, must be controlled. Sulfur forms with iron to become iron sulfide, FeS, which solidifies along the grain boundaries making the steel brittle at elevated temperature, caused by the excessive sulfur content. If an equal amount of manganese is present in the steel, then manganese sulfide, MnS, forms and the harmful effect of sulfur is reduced. It is generally recommended that manganese should at least be three times that of sulfur. However, the very small quantities of sulfur that are generally present contribute to better machinability.

Phosphorus in small amounts increases the strength and hardness of steels. Most of the steels contain about 0.02% or 0.025% typical phosphorus. Increased amounts of phosphorus caused room- and low-temperatures brittleness.

Steel castings may be heat-treated by full annealing, normalizing, normalizing and tempering or quenching and tempering. Steel castings are widely used in automotive, tractor and agricultural industries, construction machinery, mining and crushing equipment, electrical machinery and power generating equipment, railroad, military and marine applications.

The weight of these castings varies from less than 0.45 kg (1 lb), used to make small gears and axles, up to 145 metric ton (325,000 lb) parts, for forging presses. Just recently, an English foundry poured the upper and lower rams for a hydraulic forging press, requiring 360 and 380 metric tons (792,000 and 836,000 lb) of liquid steel respectively.

2.3.2.1. Effect of Alloying Elements

Alloying elements are added to improve special properties of cast steels such as mechanical properties at low or elevated temperatures; improve corrosion and oxidation resistance or abrasion wear resistance; increase machinability or electrical and magnetic properties; and improve hardenability.

Since the microstructure of steels essentially consists of ferrite or pearlite and cementite, the mechanical properties can be controlled by changing either the ferrite/pearlite ratio or the property of iron carbide and ferrite phases, by the alloying elements or by controlled dispersion of iron carbide in the ferrite matrix.

Some of the alloying elements act as austenite stabilizers. The austenite stabilizers lower the eutectoid temperature, thereby expanding the temperature range in which austenite is stable. Alloying elements such as nickel, silicon and aluminum do not form any carbides, whereas manganese, chromium, tungsten, molybdenum,

vanadium, titanium and niobium increase carbide stability. When nitrogen is present, many of these carbide stabilizers form carbonitrides or nitrides, which are highly abrasion resistant. The following is a detailed description of the effect of individual alloying elements on the mechanical properties of carbon steels.

- *Manganese* is the most common alloying element in all steels. It decreases the critical temperatures appreciably, thus increasing the hardenability of steels. It forms carbide Mn_3C but its carbide-forming tendency is the lowest of all the alloying elements. It counteracts the brittleness caused by sulfur in steels. Equal amounts of manganese and sulfur in steel readily form manganese disulfide, which is evenly distributed in it. This greatly improves the hot working characteristics and also the lubrication in machining, ensuring good surface finish. Manganese in amounts from 2 to 10% imparts brittleness to steel.

- *Chromium* is a strong carbide former and forms a complex series of carbide compounds of chromium and iron. Chromium raises the critical temperature and increases hardenability, wear resistance, corrosion and oxidation resistance.

- *Nickel* is not a carbide former, but strengthens and toughens the ferrite phase. It increases the tensile strength without appreciable decrease in ductility. In many ways, its effect on properties is similar to manganese. In combination with chromium, it provides greater hardenability, higher impact and fatigue resistance.

- *Tungsten* is a very strong carbide former and forms abrasive-resistant particles in tool steels. At larger percentages, it improves hardness and strength at elevated temperatures and, as such, are useful in cutting and hot-working tools. Tempering does not soften it. In tungsten steels, much higher tempering temperatures may be employed with less loss in hardness and with reduction in internal strains, compared to plain carbon steels.

- *Molybdenum* greatly increases the hardenability. It is also a strong carbide former. It increases the hot hardness and hot strength when used in combination with chromium and vanadium. The typical amounts present are 0.15 to 0.50% molybdenum.

- *Vanadium* is a strong carbide former. It increases the hardenability and also the secondary hardening effect upon tempering. Grain growth tendency at heat-treating temperatures is minimized. Vanadium steels have a much finer structure than steels without vanadium. It increases hardness at elevated temperatures.

- *Silicon* slightly increases the hardenability. One of the important uses of silicon is as a deoxidizer in molten steel, and for its ability to resist oxidation in steel. In large quantities above 2.5%, it raises tensile strength without great reduction of ductility, but it develops poor machinability and steel's susceptibility to decarburization. Silicon increases the electrical resistivity of iron, thus reducing eddy current effects with alternating current. Thus, silicon steels are used extensively for electrical applications. Silicon steels can be easily magnetized, and they are also used for magnetic applications.

- *Aluminum* is primarily used as a steel deoxidizer. It is most effective in inhibiting grain growth. In those steels, which are to be nitrided, aluminum provides an extremely high hardness of the nitrided case due to the formation of hard and stable aluminum nitride compounds.

- *Titanium* has the highest carbide-forming tendency of all the alloying elements, but has no effect on hardenability. Titanium is a good deoxidizer; it inhibits grain growth and is used to tie up nitrogen.

- *Niobium,* also called columbium, reduces the hardenability and increases the ductility slightly, which results in an increase in impact strength. It imparts a fine grain structure, retards softening during tempering and also is used to tie up nitrogen.

- *Cobalt* decreases the hardenability. It strengthens ferrite, when dissolved in it, and resists softening under elevated temperatures, but promotes surface decarburization.

Cast steels, containing, in addition to carbon, up to 8% of alloying elements, are considered low-alloy steels. Steels containing more than 8% alloying elements are referred to as high-alloy steels. Stainless steels are a class of chromium-containing steels, with chromium content from 10 to 12%; they are widely used for their excellent corrosion resistance and for long service life at elevated temperatures. Cast corrosion-resistant steels are generally low in carbon, usually lower than 0.20%, and also contain from 1 to 30% nickel. The addition of nickel to iron-chromium alloys improves ductility and imparts strength.

Austenitic manganese steel or Hatfield steel, named by its inventor, contains about 1.2% carbon and 12% manganese. Its microstructure, after solution annealing and quenching, is austenitic with the hardness of about 200 HB. When impacted (work-hardening), austenite transforms to martensite, and surface hardness increases up to 500 HB. This steel has a unique combination of high toughness, ductility and abrasion wear resistance achieved as a result of work-hardening. It is used extensively in impact abrasion-resistant applications for earthmoving, mining, and excavation equipment, in rock crushers, grinding mills and pumps for handling gravel and rocks. Other applications include caterpillar tractor and tank track pads.

Austenitic steels with higher manganese contents (>15%) have recently been developed for applications requiring low-magnetic permeability, low-temperature (cryogenic) strength and low-temperature toughness. These cast parts are used in transportation systems and nuclear fusion equipment to store and transport liquid.

Another class of austenitic steels with high manganese content have been developed for cryogenic and for marine applications with resistance to cavitation corrosion. These alloys have been considered as economical substitutes for conventional austenitic stainless steels because they contain aluminum and manganese instead of chromium and nickel. As a result, these alloys are generally of higher strength but lower ductility than conventional stainless steels.

2.4. Nonferrous Alloys

2.4.1. Aluminum Alloys

Aluminum and its alloys are the most widely used nonferrous cast materials because of their low density (2.7 g/cm^3/0.09755 lb/in.^{3}), low melting temperature interval (580–650°C/1080–1200°F) and excellent thermal and electrical conductivity.

Another feature of aluminum alloys is its high corrosion resistance. Aluminum, in fact, has greater affinity toward oxygen. As a result, when aluminum is exposed to air, the outer surface readily gets oxidized, forming aluminum oxide. This oxide skin has good bond with the parent metal and, thus, protects it from further oxidation.

Pure aluminum has low tensile strength of approximately 65 MPa (9427 psi) and Brinell hardness of about 20 HB. The mechanical properties of aluminum can be substantially improved by alloying. The principal alloying elements used are copper, manganese, silicon, magnesium, nickel, zinc and tin. The American Aluminum Association developed an identification system according to which aluminum alloys are divided into nine groups (Table 2-7).

According to the system, each alloy is specified by four digits, the first digit indicates major alloying element, second two digits indicate alloy ID and the final number following decimal point specifies type of product, in this case "0" indicates casting and "1" specifies ingot. Letters

"A" or "B" preceding alloy number signifies purity of alloy. Table 2-8 lists typical chemical composition of the most widely used cast aluminum alloys and their applications.

Depending upon the application, aluminum castings may be used as-cast or after heat treatment. Typical heat treatment of aluminum alloys is precipitation hardening, conventionally marked as T6, and aimed at improving mechanical properties and corrosion resistance. This heat treatment is based on limited solubility of the alloying element in aluminum at solid state and precipitation of a second phase during aging.

For example, in aluminum-copper alloy series 300, copper, above a temperature of 548°C (1018°F), is dissolved completely in liquid aluminum but, at room temperature, its solubility is significantly reduced with formation of the chemical compound $CuAl_2$. When this alloy is quenched and artificially aged (prolonged holding at 300–400°F for 3–6 hours) very fine particles of $CuAl_2$ are precipitated, which causes the strengthening of the alloy.

Typical mechanical properties of sand castings, made of the widely used aluminum alloy 356.0, after T6 heat treatment, are as follows:

- Minimum tensile strength 207 MPa (30 ksi)
- Minimum tensile yield 136 MPa (20 ksi)
- Minimum elongation 3%
- Brinell hardness 70–105

Table 2-7. Cast Aluminum Alloys Designation System.

Designation number	Primary alloying elements	Typical alloy-representative
1XX.X	Aluminum, 99% min and greater	100.0; 170.0
2XX.X	Copper	A201.0; A242.0
3XX.X	Silicon with added copper and/or magnesium	319.0; A356.0
4XX.X	Silicon	A413.0; B443.0
5XX.X	Magnesium	513.0; 520.0
6XX.X	Unused series	N/A
7XX.X	Zinc	710.0; 771.0
8XX.X	Tin	850.0; 852.0
9XX.X	Unused series	N/A

Table 2-8. Typical Chemical Composition of Some Commonly Used Aluminum Casting Alloys and Their Applications.

Alloy Designation Number	Chemical Composition, wt. %						Typical Applications
	Silicon	Iron	Copper	Manganese	Magnesium	Aluminum	
100.0	0.15	0.6–0.8	0.1	—	—	99.0	Rotors for electric motors
A206.0	0.05	0.1	4.0–5.0	0.2.0.4	0.15–0.35	balance	Pistons, pump housing
A356.0	6.5–7.5	0.20	0.2	0.1	0.25–0.35	balance	Sand and permanent mold cast automotive and aircraft parts
A380.0	7.5–9.5	1.3	3.0–4.0	0.5	0.1	balance	General purpose die castings

The automotive industry is the largest consumer of aluminum castings. Transmission housing, wheels, heat exchangers, suspension components and pistons and, recently, engine blocks for cars and trucks, and many other parts are cast of aluminum alloys. Their applications grow as new ways to save weight and gain fuel efficiency and performance. Cast aluminum alloys are also widely used to make a variety of cast parts for aircraft and marine engines and structures, and as a material for cast parts of small appliances, hand tools, lawnmowers, cookware, etc.

2.4.2. Copper Alloys

Copper alloys are heavy nonferrous alloys with a specific gravity of 7.47-9.14 g/cm³ (0.269-0.330 lb/in.³) and most are heavier than iron and steel. Similar to aluminum alloys, copper castings found their application because of excellent electrical and thermal conductivity and corrosion resistance. Pure copper is soft and relatively weak. It can be alloyed to improve the mechanical properties. The main alloying elements used are zinc, tin, lead and phosphorus.

The alloys of copper and zinc are called brasses. With zinc content up to 39%, copper forms a single-phase (alpha) structure. Such alloys have high ductility. The color of the alloy remains red up to a zinc content of 20%, but beyond that it becomes yellow. A second structural component called beta-phase appears between 39 and 46% zinc. It is actually the intermetallic compound CuZn, which is responsible for the increased hardness. The strength of brass gets further increased when small amounts of manganese and nickel are added. The cast brasses are used in plumbing fixtures, gears, bearings and hardware.

The alloys of copper with tin are called bronzes. They may contain up to 20% tin. With the increase of tin content in the alloy, bronze's hardness and strength increases, too. The ductility is also reduced with the increase in tin content above 5%. Today, the term bronze applies to a wide variety of copper-base alloys containing (besides tin) aluminum, phosphorus, lead, zinc and others. When aluminum is added (4 to 11%) the resulting alloy is termed as aluminum bronze, which has a considerably higher corrosion resistance.

Tin bronzes are used as a material for valves, bearings, piston rings and fittings. Lead is added to tin bronzes to balance machinability and mechanical properties. Due to excellent antifriction (bearing) properties, their primary application is as a bearing material that can be used with or without lubricant. Tin bronzes are comparatively costly compared to brasses due to the presence of tin, which is an expensive metal.

Some of the copper alloys with their compositions and applications are presented in Table 2-9.

2.4.3. Magnesium Alloys

Magnesium is one of the lightest structural materials with a density of about 1.8 g/cm³ (0.065 lb/in.³), which is 30% less than the density of aluminum alloys and 80% less than the density of steel. Table 2-10 lists chemical compositions and mechanical properties of some magnesium casting alloys used in the foundry industry.

The ASTM standard of magnesium alloys designation system consists of two letters representing two main alloying elements, for example, A = Aluminum; M = Manganese and Z = Zirconium, and two numbers corresponding to a rounded-off percentage content of the two alloying elements. Letters A, B, C or D following alloy number signifies the order in which ASTM registered the alloys.

Magnesium alloys can be cast by various methods such as sand casting, permanent mold casting or diecasting. The properties of as-cast components are comparable with each of these processes. The die casting alloys generally have high copper content so as to allow them to be made

Table 2-9. Typical Chemistry of Some Copper-Based Alloys and Their Applications.

UNS No.	Alloy	Copper	Tin	Zinc	Others	Applications
C81100	Copper	99.7	–	–	0.3 (impurities)	Tuyers for blast furnaces and cupolas.
C83600	Leaded red brass	85	5	5	5%Pb	Pipe fittings, water pumps, plumbing hardware
C90500	Tin bronze	87.5	10	2	0.5%P	Bearings & Bushings
C95400	Aluminum bronze	85	–	–	11%Al 4%Fe	Marine applications

from the secondary metals, to reduce the costs. The higher the copper content, the higher is the mechanical strength of magnesium wrought alloy components. Magnesium alloys can be readily welded by most of the traditional welding processes. A very useful property of magnesium alloys is their high machinability. They only require about 15% of power for machining, compared to low-carbon steel.

Because of their light weight and excellent mechanical properties, magnesium alloys are widely used in applications where the weight is important, for example, in electronics, aircraft, and aerospace industries and, lately, in light vehicles (seat frames, crankcases, inlet manifolds, wheels, etc.). For the same stiffness, magnesium alloys require only 37.2% of the weight of low-carbon steel 1025, thus saving in weight.

2.5. Heat Treatment

Heat treatment is one of the major methods used to modify structure and properties of cast components in solid state, or reduce stresses by application of controlled heating and cooling.

2.5.1. Heat Treatment of Ferrous Alloys

Previously, when a detailed description of the iron-carbon equilibrium diagram was presented (Fig. 2-4), it was noted that this type of diagram represents equilibrium conditions when all phase transformations occur at a slow cooling rate, allowing sufficient time for the reaction to take place. The heat-treatment methods that utilize relatively slow cooling rate and follow the iron-carbon equilibrium diagram are annealing, normalizing and stress relieving. Figure 2-19 illustrates the steel portion of the iron-carbon equilibrium diagram relevant for heat treatment of steels.

2.5.1.1. Annealing, Normalizing, Stress Relieving

Annealing is a controlled cooling process that involves heating of steel or iron castings above the austenization temperature (for hypoeutectoid steel, above the line GS; for hypereutectoid steel, to the region marked $A_{1,3}$), holding for a time needed for a complete transformation to austenite and subsequent slow cooling. Such cooling rate is achieved by leaving the castings inside the heat-treatment furnace without any further heat input. It is recommended to remove castings at about 430°C (800°F) and cool them in air.

If annealing is applied to hypoeutectoid carbon or low-alloy steel castings, the very slow cooling rate will

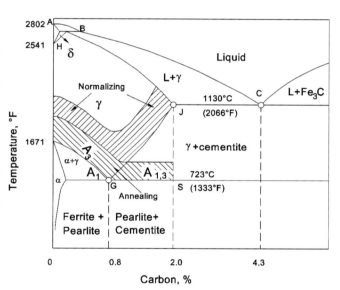

Fig. 2-19. Steel portion of an iron-carbon diagram relevant for heat treatment of steels.

Table 2-10. Typical Chemical Composition and Mechanical Properties of Magnesium Casting Alloys.

Alloy Number	Chemical Composition, %	Mechanical Properties			Casting Method
		Tensile strength, MPa (ksi)	Tensile Yield, MPa (ksi)	Elongation, %	
AZ91A	9Al; 0.7 Zn	270 (39)	165 (24)	5	Die casting
AZ91C	9Al; 0.7 Zn	234 (34)	70 (10)	3	Sand casting
AM60B	6 Al; 0.25 Mn	220 (32)	130 (19)	6	Die casting

produce a coarse pearlite-ferrite metallic matrix. This heat treatment practically eliminates residual stresses, reduces hardness, increases ductility and enhances machinability. Different annealing cycles are used in iron casting production. These cycles differ by temperature applied, holding time and cooling rate.

High temperature annealing at 900–950°C (1650–1750°F) is used for decomposition of iron carbide (cementite) in the process of conversion of white iron to malleable iron or for unalloyed gray or ductile iron to achieve a carbide-free metallic matrix. If fully ferritic microstructure is needed, the iron castings are heated above the austenization temperature, held at this temperature for a predetermined time followed by slow cooling through the eutectoid transformation temperature range, or held at this temperature for a time needed for a complete transformation of pearlite, and subsequently slow cooled to about 450–550°C (840–1020°F), and then removed from the furnace. If a pearlitic matrix is specified, castings are heated to the austenization temperature, held at this temperature for a predetermined time, followed by cooling in still or forced air.

The low-temperature annealing is recommended for gray and ductile iron castings, which as-cast microstructure does not contain iron carbide, but pearlite. This treatment cycle consists of heating to the eutectoid transformation temperature range of 730–760°C (1350–1400°F), holding at this temperature for a time needed for a complete transformation of pearlite, and subsequently slow cooled to about 450–550°C (840–1020°F) and then removing castings from the furnace. The applied annealing results in a ferritic microstructure, which has lower than pearlitic matrix tensile strength and hardness, but is easy to machine.

Normalizing is a controlled cooling process that involves heating of steel or iron castings above the austenization temperature, holding for a time needed for a complete transformation to austenite, and subsequently cooling in air at a more rapid cooling rate than annealing. The purpose of normalizing is to refine grain structure and improve tensile strength and ductility. Because of the faster cooling rate, the pearlitic structure obtained would be of uniformly fine grain size. This would result in higher tensile strength and hardness than what is possible by annealing. The mechanical properties achieved through normalizing depend to a great extent on the thickness of the section. In thick sections, the outer surface may be normalized, but the core would be annealed.

Stress relieving is employed to remove residual stresses and is typically done by heating castings up to 450–600°C (840–1100°F), holding at this temperature from 2 to 6 hours (depending on section sizes), and slow cooling. No phase transformation occurs at this temperature range.

2.5.1.2. TTT Diagrams and Hardening Methods

When a ferrous alloy is heated above the austenization temperature and rapidly cooled from this temperature by quenching, the new phase, called martensite with a BCT lattice structure, is formed. Heat treatment methods that involve high cooling rate represent non-equilibrium conditions and the phase transformations do not follow the iron-carbon diagram. These heat treatment methods follow the TTT (time-temperature-transformation) diagrams. The feature of the TTT diagram is that it shows phase transformation in time interval or, in other words, this diagram takes into account the cooling rate.

Time-Temperature-Transformation diagrams, because of the shape of the curves, are also sometimes called C-curves or S-curves. Figure 2-20 shows a typical TTT diagram for eutectoid steel, containing 0.8% C. The curve at the extreme left represents the time required for the transformation of austenite to pearlite to start at any given temperature. Similarly, the extreme right curve represents the time required for completing the transformation. In between the two curves are the points representing partial transformation.

The horizontal lines Ms and Mf represent the start and finish of martensitic transformation. Since austenite needs time for transformation to pearlite, super-cooled austenite would not have sufficient time for all of its carbon atoms to properly diffuse and form cementite. As a result, the carbon atoms would be trapped in the unit cell of iron. Since iron does not have enough interstitial space, the unit cell gets distorted with the extra carbon atoms. The distorted lattice structure is a body-centered tetragonal (BCT) or martensite. The degree of distortion depends on the number

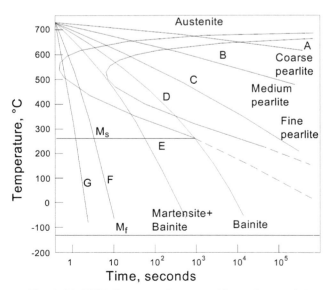

Fig. 2-20. TTT diagram of eutectoid steel containing 0.8% carbon.

of carbon atoms trapped in the cell. It is formed in steels when cooled rapidly at a high rate, which is approximately 500°C (932°F) per second for plain carbon steels.

Martensite has a needle-like structure. It is extremely hard and brittle. The maximum hardness of steel varies, depending upon the amount of carbon in steels. It is not possible to get any significant hardness improvements in low-carbon steels (less than 0.3% C). The maximum attainable hardness is reached by a carbon percentage of 0.7 to 0.8.

Cooling rates are employed to lower the austenitic temperature to room temperature and control the final microstructure of steel, which could be complete martensite, martensite with pearlite or complete pearlite. Also, the final grain size of pearlite produced could vary from very fine to coarse, thus giving rise to wide varieties of properties that could be expected of them.

As seen from the TTT diagram, all the retained austenite may not be transformed unless the temperature reaches the Mf temperature. This is generally below room temperature. The retained austenite (without transformation) can cause loss of strength or hardness, dimensional instability or cracking. In alloy steels, since the alloying elements decrease the martensite transformation's starting and ending temperatures, it may be necessary to cool the material to a lower temperature by the use of liquid nitrogen, to get the full hardness.

The curve A represents an extremely slow cooling rate, which gives rise to conditions conducive to grain growth, thus producing very coarse grains of pearlite in steels. The curve B, which shows a faster cooling rate than A, would give rise to medium-sized pearlitic grains. Similarly, the curves C and D, which represents faster rates than B but not so fast as to miss the complete transformation curve, produce complete pearlite, which is extremely fine and called bainite. The bainitic structure is somewhat between pearlite and martensite. The cooling rates are faster in curves E, F and G than in the rest and, thus, not all the austenite is converted to pearlite. The retained austenite below the Ms line is all converted into martensite and, thus, the final microstructure would be martensite and bainite. The amount of martensite formed increases as the cooling rate rises.

Using TTT diagrams, the final structure of a ferrous alloy part can be predicted and determined. For practical purposes, TTT diagrams may be complimented by hardness values on the right side of diagram, which allow to also predict the possible range of hardness for a specific microstructure.

The heat-treatment method that utilizes a TTT diagram is referred to as hardening by quenching. The hardening or quenching process involves first, heating to the austenitic range by properly soaking at a temperature that depends

on the section thickness and then, rapidly cooling the casting by dipping it into the quenching bath of water or oil, or salt solution in water called brine. The critical cooling rates required for getting the complete martensitic structure in steels depends on the carbon percentage: the higher the carbon, the lower is the cooling rate required. The comparative cooling rates with various cooling media are presented in Table 2-11.

Because of the severity of the cooling rate in brine (salt water), it is possible that distortions or cracks may appear in some components. Also, after quenching in salt baths, it is necessary to clean the components thoroughly, to minimize the corrosion. Oils have a lower cooling rate compared to water, thus reducing the risk of distortion. Also, the quenching capacity of oils is not subjected to much change in the temperature range from 20 to 150°C (70 to 300°F). The oils are more suitable for high-carbon steels and alloy steels. The main disadvantage of oil is the flammability.

When thick sections are involved in the hardening process, the interiors would experience somewhat lower cooling rates due to slower heat transfer through steel than from the surface. As a result, the hardness of the part during quenching gradually changes as the depth from the surface increases. The variation would be more for thick parts than the thin sections, as is illustrated in Fig. 2-21.

Table 2-11. Relative cooling rates of different cooling mediums used in heat treatment.

Cooling Medium	Relative Cooling Rate
Salt solution in water (brine)	1.20 to 1.30
Water	1.00
Oil	0.40 to 0.50
Forced air	0.03
Still air	0.02

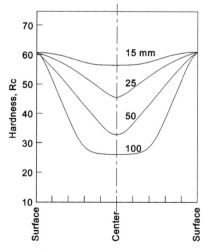

Fig. 2-21. Graph illustrating the variation of hardness in medium-carbon steel with 0.5% C, after quenching across bar sections with diameters 15, 25, 50 and 100 mm.

The depth and hardness achieved by quenching depends upon hardenability of a given alloy and should not be confused with hardness. Hardenability can be defined as the depth to which a certain hardness level can be obtained by the quenching process. High-hardenability steel would be able to be thoroughly hardened without too severe a quenching rate. Under standard conditions, it is possible to determine the hardenability characteristics of different ferrous alloys by the Jominy end-quench hardenability test. In this test, a standard specimen is heated above the upper critical temperature, and then placed into a special fixture, where one end is quenched with a stream of cold water. After cooling to room temperature, hardness is measured near the surface at regularly spaced intervals along the length of the specimen, and plotted as hardness versus distance from the quenched end.

Table 2-12 compares heat treatment temperature ranges for low-carbon and medium-carbon steels.

2.5.1.3. Tempering Methods

Martensite formed during the quenching process is extremely hard and brittle, and lacks the impact toughness required for some applications. Hence, a secondary heat treatment process, called tempering, is carried out on quenched parts to achieve the necessary toughness and ductility by marginally sacrificing hardness. This process also relieves the internal stresses, thus improving the ductility. Martensite, when heated during the tempering process, transforms into an equilibrium state of the structure called tempered martensite. This is a structure where cementite is finely dispersed in the ferrite matrix.

The tempering procedure involves heating the quenched steel to a temperature generally between 200 and 400°C (390 and 750°F), holding it for a while and then cooling, as shown in Fig. 2-22. Some low alloy steels are tempered as high as 650°C (1200°F). Tempering is

Table 2-12. Comparative heat treatment temperatures for carbon steels.

Type of Steel and Carbon Content	Quenching, °C (°F)	Normalizing, °C (°F)	Annealing, °C (°F)
Low–carbon steel, 0.1%C	x)	900–955 (1652–1751)	540–730 (1004–1346)
Low–carbon steel, 0.2%C	x)	900–955 (1652–1751)	540–730 (1004–1346)
Low–carbon steel, 0.3%C	855–900 (1571-1652)	870–915 (1598–1679)	675–745 (1193–1373)
Medium–carbon steel, 0.4%C	815–855 (1499-1571)	855–900 (1571–1652)	845–885 (1553–1625)
Medium–carbon steel, 0.5%C	800–845 (1472-1553)	845–900 (1553–1652)	830–870 (1526–1598)
Medium–carbon steel, 0.6%C	790–845 (1454-1553)	830–885 (1526–1625)	815–855 (1499–1571)

x) Hardening by quenching is not practical due to low carbon content

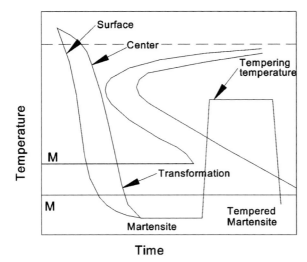

Fig. 2-22. TTT diagram illustrating tempering process.

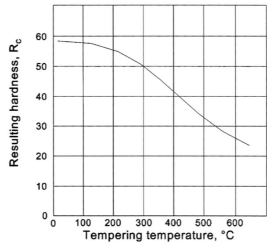

Fig. 2-23. Effect of tempering temperature on the hardness of quenched plain carbon steel.

a one-way process. If the hardness is to be regained, then the quenching process is to be repeated. The hardness of the steel finally achieved depends on the tempering temperature used, as in Fig 2-23. The higher the tempering temperature, the lower will be the final hardness. In the case of alloy steels, many of the alloying elements have the tendency for reduction in hardness due to the tempering process, particularly at low temperatures such as 200°C (390°F).

Austempering is a variation of the less-severe hardening process. In this process, the part is quickly quenched a little above the Ms temperature to just miss the nose of the cooling curve, and then held at the same temperature in a molten salt bath for a prolonged period. This is done so that austenite will be transformed under isothermal conditions to a less brittle structure called bainite (very fine pearlite). This temperature is selected based on the desirable final hardness. The bainite formed is stress-free and likely to cause less crack formation in the material.

This treatment is possible only for those steels that can be rapidly quenched without transformation. The properties obtained by austempering compare well with those of quenched and tempered steels, but with higher ductility and impact resistance. Similarly, ductile iron is austempered and the final product is called austempered ductile iron (ADI). Its heat treatment cycle is discussed earlier.

Martempering is similar to austempering but differs by cooling mode: the steel is heated to austenitic range, followed by rapid quenching (water bath) to a temperature above the Ms temperature. Thereafter, the material is maintained at constant temperature (oil or molten salt bath) such that the entire section is brought to a uniform temperature. As soon as the part attains uniform temperature, it is taken out of the bath and cooled in air. The air-cooling is sufficiently fast, such that martensite is formed. This provides relative stress free material without any distortion, and better mechanical properties compared to regular quenching and tempering process.

2.5.2. Case Hardening Methods

The heat treatment processes discussed previously were applied to the entire volume of the part, whereas case hardening or surface hardening processes are essentially used for improving the hardness of the surface only, while the core retains its original softness and ductility.

In many applications such as axes, shafts and gears, it is necessary to obtain the required high wear resistance and hardness only on the surface, while the core would remain soft and tough for absorbing any impact forces. For this purpose, the surface hardening methods are applied.

The surface hardening methods may be broken down into two groups:

- Methods that utilize local heating such as flame, induction or laser, and
- Diffusion methods in which the part surface is impregnated with carbon, nitrogen or with both.

Flame hardening is the simplest form of the case hardening process. The part is heated by means of a gas torch (oxygen-acetylene flame) followed by a water spray on the heated parts. The heat from the torch penetrates only to a small depth on the surface and, consequently, the material in the outer layers gets quenched to martensite and bainite. This process can achieve case depths up to 3 mm. Heating to about 200°C (390°F) for the purpose of stress relieving may follow this process. This process is suitable for any complex shape of the component such as crankshafts, large gears, cams, etc., with carbon percentages ranging from 0.3 to 0.6%. Though high-carbon steels can also be flame hardened, greater care is needed to avoid surface cracking.

Induction hardening is similar to flame hardening, but differs by source of heating that is achieved by electromagnetic induction. The part (such as crankshaft) is enclosed in the magnetic field of an alternating (10 kHz to 2 MHz) current conductor to obtain case depths of 0.25 to 1.5 mm (0.01 to 0.06 in.). The heated part is then quenched by water spray. The induction heat penetrates only the outer surface of the part and, as a result, the quenching process only hardens the skin. The whole process is very fast (from 5 seconds to a couple of minutes) and results in a hard outer surface (50 to 60 HRC), which is very wear resistant.

Laser hardening is using laser radiation to austenitize the surface of the part and then get it transformed to martensite/bainite/pearlite, depending upon the associated cooling rate achieved. A laser beam is scanned across the component, which causes the surface to heat rapidly. The surrounding material acts as an efficient heat sink, leading to rapid quenching and hardening phase transformations. As a result, a hardened surface layer is produced, while the desirable bulk properties, such as toughness and ductility, remain unaffected throughout the material. Components made from hardenable ferrous alloys are particularly suitable for laser hardening. Depending on the material, hardness values up to about 1000 HV can be achieved to a depth of around 1.5 mm through solid-state transformation.

Carburizing is carried out for low-carbon steels, which do not respond readily to the quenching process because of the low carbon content. In the process, carbon is introduced into the surface of the solid steel part by heating the part above the transformation temperature, along with a carbonaceous material.

In pack carburizing, the part is packed with charcoal or any other solid carbonaceous material in a sealed container and put in a furnace. The container is heated to a temperature between 800 and 950°C (1470 and 1740°F) and held for a period of 4 to 20 hours. During heating, the carbon diffuses into the outer skin of the part, resulting in a medium to high carbon steel structure in the surface of the part. The amount of carbon diffused into steel depends on the carburizing temperature and time. The case depth achieved is generally between 1 to 2 mm (0.04 to 0.08 in.).

In gas carburizing, carbon in gaseous form such as natural gas, propane or methane is used instead of charcoal. The process is very similar to pack carburizing. The main advantage of gas carburizing is better control of case depth than that is possible in pack carburizing.

In carburizing, because of the prolonged heating, grain size may be affected. The case carburized steel is to be further hardened by a secondary heat treatment process of quenching and tempering, depending on the desired application. Normalizing may also be done to refine the grain structure.

Nitriding is a case hardening process in which the part is heated in an atmosphere of nitrogen-bearing material. Nitrogen forms very hard nitrides with alloying elements contained in steels and irons, such as aluminum, chromium, vanadium and molybdenum, when they come in contact with nitrogen. This is made use of in the process of nitriding, where alloy steels are case hardened without any quenching process. The nitriding temperatures are in the range of 500 to 575°C (930 to 1065°F). The parts, which are already quenched and tempered, are put in a sealed container with ammonia gas and then heated to the nitriding temperature. The process is maintained for a duration of 8 to 40 hours (as high as 125 hours in some cases) for getting the necessary case depths. Because of the lower temperatures employed in nitriding, there are less possibilities of distortion and deformation than with any other case hardening process. Further, no finish machining is required.

Carbonitriding, also called *cyaniding*, is a case hardening process that involves the addition of carbon and nitrogen to the cases of carbon steels and alloy steels. This is achieved by heating the steel in contact with a molten bath of cyanide. The cyanide bath may consist of sodium cyanide, potassium cyanide, or potassium ferrocyanide, with inert salts such as sodium chloride and sodium carbonate, which provide the necessary fluidity to the cyanide bath. The bath is maintained at a temperature

between 750 and 850°C (1380 and 1560°F) and the contact time is between 30 to 60 minutes. This produces a reasonable case depth of nearly 0.15 mm (0.006 in.) and minimizes part distortion.

After the cyanide bath, the steel is quenched either in oil or a water-based quenching medium to produce the desired case hardness. If necessary, it may be followed with a low temperature tempering.

The carbonitriding process is faster than the carburizing process, but achieves lower case depths. It is generally employed for parts that do not require finishing after hardening. This process is not suitable for parts requiring high impact resistance, since nitrogen addition is detrimental for these properties.

2.5.3. Heat Treatment of Nonferrous Alloys

One of the principal methods by which the nonferrous alloys are heat treated is precipitation hardening. In this process, a second phase of the alloy is dispersed finely in the matrix of the first phase in solid state, thereby increasing the strength. The intermetallic compound present in a solid solution is generally hard, and its presence increases the hardness, even in a single-phase alloy. For example, in a copper alloy with zinc that forms the alpha solid solution, the hardness increases by about 39% when the zinc percentage is increased from 0 to 30%.

The precipitation hardening process is illustrated schematically using the example of an Al-Cu alloy equilibrium diagram in Fig. 2-24(a). As discussed previously, this alloy system represents alloys that are completely soluble at liquid state, but have limited solubility in solid state. From this diagram, it is known that, above the solidification temperature copper is completely dissolved in aluminum, but upon cooling to room temperature its solubility is significantly reduced to 0.02%.

In the example shown in Fig. 2-24(a), if an aluminum alloy with a copper content of 4%, which is within the soluble limit (up to 5.65% at around 548°C/1018°F), is heated to a temperature of high solubility (region α), all the copper will be dissolved in the aluminum. Rapid cooling, such as water quenching, will produce a supersaturated, thermodynamically unstable, solid solution of copper in aluminum. The precipitation hardening utilizes this phenomenon when the solid solution is supersaturated and unstable; when temperature or time is applied, the precipitation occurs.

The age hardening process that applies temperature higher than room temperature is called artificial aging.

If the precipitation process occurs at room temperature, it is called natural aging, but for some alloys it may take hours, days and even weeks or months.

The precipitation hardening process, schematically represented in Fig. 2-24(b), consists of two subsequently performed steps:

1. Solution heat treatment. The part is heated and soaked to put the second element or its compound with limited solubility, in this case CuAl$_2$, called copper aluminide, into solid solution, and then is cooled quickly (e.g., quenched in water) so that the single-phase structure is retained, even at the room temperature.

2. Age hardening. When this part is heated to a certain temperature and retained at that temperature for specified period, the precipitation of the second phase at a number of random locations throughout the solid solution takes place, thus increasing the strength of the alloy.

The hardness obtained is a function of precipitation temperature, since the size of the precipitating particles and their distribution controls the movement of dislocations. If the particles are too coarse, then they will not give rise to high strength. Hence, it is important to know the temperature and time to get an optimum size of the particles and their distribution, so that maximum strength can be obtained by the precipitation hardening process.

The precipitation hardening process is an important tool to increase the strength of aluminum, magnesium, copper and other nonferrous alloys.

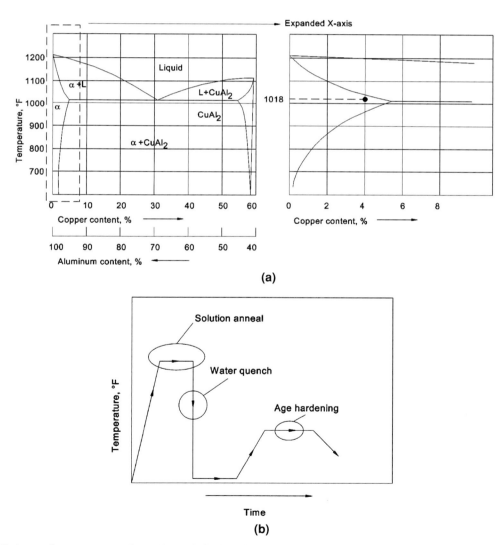

Fig. 2-24. Schematic representation of precipitation hardening on the example of Al-Cu alloy: (a) equilibrium diagram; (b) schematic of precipitation hardening.

References

1. *ASM Metals Handbook* Vol. 2. Properties and Selection: Nonferrous Alloys and Pure Metals; Vol. 4. Heat Treatment, American Society of Metals, Metals Park, 1979-81.

2. *Source Book on Copper and Copper Alloys*, American Society of Metals, Metals Park, 1979.

3. *Standards for Aluminum Sand and Permanent Mold Castings*, Aluminum Association, 2004.

4. Davies, D.J. and L.A. Oelmann, *The Structure, Properties and Heat Treatment of Metals*, Pitman Books, London, 1983.

5. Schleg, F.P., *Technology of Metalcasting*, American Foundry Society, Des Plaines, 2003.

6. *Iron Casting Engineering Handbook*, American Foundry Society, Des Plaines, 2004.

7. *Steel Castings Handbook*, Steel Founders' Society, Rocky River, 1980.

8. Lerner, Y.S., "Ductile Iron Use in Machine Tool and Hydraulic Components," *Foundry Management & Technology*, pp.108-115, 1995.

Review Questions

2.1 State the difference between steel and cast iron, with respect to their composition and microstructure.

2.2 Explain the details of the most common lattice systems found in metals. Give examples.

2.3 Briefly describe nucleation and grain growth in solidifying cast alloys.

2.4 Define strength. Explain the procedure for measuring the tensile strength of cast alloys.

2.5 Explain the behavior of low-carbon steels when they are tensile loaded.

2.6 Define the following as related to casting materials, and explain the principles of their measurement: a) Hardness; b) Ductility.

2.7 Summarize the Brinell hardness test (HB).

2.8 Explain how the impact toughness of cast alloys is measured.

2.9 Give the details of different tests available for hardness measurement. Compare their individual merits.

2.10 Compare the different methods available for measuring impact toughness of cast alloys.

2.11 Discuss residual stresses and how they affect the service performance of castings.

2.12 Explain what is meant by wear resistance.

2.13 Describe any one method by which the wear resistance is measured.

2.14 Define ferrite, austenite and cementite, and compare their properties.

2.15 Describe gray cast iron and outline major factors influencing its mechanical and service properties

2.16 State the reason why white cast iron is more brittle than gray cast iron.

2.17 Explain how malleable iron is made and specified.

2.18 Define ductile iron, its properties and applications.

2.19 Describe compacted graphite iron and methods for its production.

2.20 Give the details of austempered ductile iron and methods of its manufacture.

2.21 Define the composition of alloyed steel and give an example of its applications.

2.22 State how the properties of alloyed steels are affected by the following alloying elements: manganese, chromium, and tungsten.

2.23 Name any two commonly used nonferrous cast alloys, stating their composition and applications.

2.24 Highlight the advantages of aluminum alloys over ferrous alloys.

2.25 Give the composition of two copper-base alloys and their applications.

2.26 Explain the details of precipitation hardening. Describe its typical operation steps.

2.27 Define the effect of copper as an alloying element in aluminum alloys. Explain its behavior.

2.28 Outline the specific advantages of copper alloys.

2.29 Give a brief explanation of magnesium alloys.

2.30 State the ranges of composition for low-, medium- and high-carbon steels. Give at least two applications for each range.

2.31 Explain how carbon content influences the strength and ductility of plain carbon steels.

2.32 Define the necessity of heat treatment for steels. Describe the process of quenching.

2.33 Distinguish between the following:
- Quenching and tempering
- Normalizing and annealing
- Cementite and martensite

2.34 Give the reason why low-carbon steels don't respond to hardening by the quenching process.

2.35 Distinguish clearly between hardness and hardenability. Explain a method of measuring the hardenability of steel.

2.36 Explain why tempering follows the quenching process in the heat treatment of steels.

2.37 Describe the stress relieving of ferrous alloys.

2.38 Give the details of the case hardening processes that are normally used.

2.39 Is case carburizing done to high-carbon steels? State the reasons supporting your answer.

2.40 Briefly explain the difference between case hardening and conventional heat treatment processes such as annealing or normalizing.

2.41 Describe the following case hardening processes:
- Carburizing
- Nitriding

2.42 Specify the methods used for hardening low-carbon steels. Explain with reasons.

2.43 Explain briefly what you understand about the TTT curves.

FOUNDRY TOOLING

Objectives

Tooling is an important step in the production of sound, defect-free castings. After studying this chapter, the reader should be able to:

- Describe different types of patterns used in foundries
- Differentiate between pattern materials and their choices for various applications
- Design patterns from casting requirements
- Identify different types of cores used, based on casting geometry
- Discuss requirements of dimensional accuracy and its measurement

Keywords

Tooling, Parting Line, Pattern, Pattern Material, Metallic Pattern, Wooden Pattern, Shaped Plastic Material, Aluminum Alloys, Lost Wax Pattern, Molten Metal, Parting Line, Pattern Dimensioning, Match Plate Pattern, Master Pattern, Cast Steel, Sweep Pattern, Loose Piece Pattern, Follow Board Pattern, Core, Core Print, Shrinkage, Liquid Shrinkage, Solid Shrinkage, Shrinkage Allowance, Cope, Drag, Draft, Chaplet, Fillet, Density, Flask, Machining Allowance, Distortion, Gating System, Risering System, Core Box, Dimensional Accuracy, Dimension Tolerance, Casting Defects, Sand Core, Sand Mold, Coordinate Measuring Machine (CMM)

The casting manufacturing process begins with the design of a casting and selection of the most economical way to make a cast component. Typically, the foundry is dealing with the drawing of a finished/machined part. In this case, the foundry needs to transform it to the sketch of the casting and make the necessary tooling. Figure 3-1 illustrates the transformation of a machined part to a sketch of the cast component. In this drawing, solid lines indicate the contour of the machined part; the broken lines show cast surfaces. The abbreviations in this figure mean: PL – parting line; C – cope half of the pattern; D – drag half of the pattern; the symbol "X", which is placed crossing two small holes 7.5 mm (0.3 in.) diameter, indicates that these holes will not be cast.

In high volume and mass production, the designer develops the drawing of a casting and, after its verification and approval, passes it to the foundry. It is very important to ensure that the final casting design incorporates all the recommendations allowing for the production of sound, defect-free cast parts in the most cost-effective way.

In pattern designing, the following major steps are involved:

- Selection of pattern type and material
- Selection of the pattern parting line, which determines the casting's position in the mold during pouring
- Pattern dimensioning, i.e., addition of the shrinkage, machining and other allowances
- Addition of draft/taper on vertical faces of the pattern, allowing ease of removal from the mold
- Selection of core type, and provision of core prints
- Elimination of sharp corners by applying fillets and radii in intersections and junctions
- Elimination of the fine details that cannot be obtained by casting, and, hence, are to be obtained by further processing

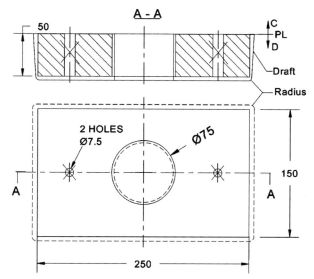

Fig. 3-1. Transformation of machined part drawing to a sketch of cast part (all dimensions in mm).

- Gating and risering systems design. *Note: Due to their significance, these topics are separated into Chapters 4 and 5.*

Dealing with the optimal casting design, the foundry is able to make the necessary tooling. Tooling for sand casting includes pattern equipment, coreboxes, flasks, chills (external and internal) and chaplets, and gages for quality control to check the accuracy of cores or mold assembly and the accuracy of finished castings. For permanent mold casting, for example, tooling includes a metallic mold with cooling and ejection systems, metallic cores or coreboxes to make sand cores, as well as gages for quality control.

3.1. Selection of Pattern Type and Material

The pattern is a replica or a prototype of the casting to be made by the casting process with some modifications, which will be discussed later.

3.1.1. Pattern Materials

The usual pattern materials for sand molding are wood, metal and plastics. Choice of these materials depends essentially on the size of the casting, type of molding process, number of castings to be made from the pattern, and the dimensional accuracy required.

Wood is the most commonly used pattern material, because of availability and low weight. It can be easily shaped, joined, and is relatively cheap.

One of the main disadvantages of wood is its absorption of moisture resulting in distortions and dimensional changes. A well-constructed pattern may be able to reduce the warpage to some extent. For this reason, proper seasoning and upkeep of wood is almost a prerequisite for large-scale use of wood as a pattern material.

Another disadvantage of wood is its low abrasion resistance, which is necessary to withstand the impact of molding sand. This makes wood a less suitable pattern material for large production runs, particularly, in machine molding.

The usual varieties of wood commonly used for making patterns are pine, mahogany, teak and walnut. Besides the wood, plywood boards of the veneer type as well as particle boards are also used for making patterns because of their availability in various thicknesses, higher strength and no need for seasoning. However, they can be used only in the making of flat type patterns with no complex contours, and for pattern plates.

Metallic patterns, because of their durability and smooth surface finish, are extensively used for large-scale casting production and for closer dimensional tolerances. Though many metals, such as cast iron, steel and brass, can be used as pattern materials, aluminum alloys are most commonly used. These are lightweight, can be easily worked, and are corrosion resistant. Table 3-1 compares advantages and disadvantages of various metallic pattern materials.

Most metal patterns are cast in sand or plaster molds from a master wood pattern provided with the double shrinkage allowance, which takes into account the shrinkage of the pattern metal as well as the shrinkage of the actual casting's alloy to be produced. (*This will be illustrated later in Example 3-2.*)

Plastics are also used as pattern materials because of their low weight, easier formability, smooth surfaces and durability. They do not absorb moisture and are, therefore, dimensionally stable and can be cleaned easily. The making of a plastic pattern can be done by machining or casting in sand or plaster molds. The most generally used plastics are cold setting epoxy resins with suitable fillers. Several of them don't shrink, and double-shrinkage allowances may not be required.

Table 3-1. Comparative Characteristics of Metallic Pattern Materials.

Pattern metal	Advantages	Disadvantages
Aluminum alloys	Good machinability High corrosion resistance Low density/weight Good surface finish	Low wear resistance and strength High cost
Gray cast iron	Good machinability High strength Good wear resistance Low cost	Corrosion prone High density/weight
Steel	Good surface finish High strength	Corrosion prone High density/weight
Brass and bronze	Good surface finish High strength High corrosion resistance	High cost High density/weight

Recently introduced into foundry practice, a new family of shaped plastics products is especially formulated for pattern modeling applications requiring high performance. These plastics outperform the properties, functionality and durability of traditional pattern materials. Being relatively cheap and available, these materials have the ability to hold precise tolerances, maintain outstanding dimensional stability even after exposure to humidity extremes, and produce excellent surface detail with solid, well-defined edges. They are easy to hand carve or cut on a CNC machine. To produce desirable design patterns or coreboxes, these plank or other shaped plastics are glued together and machined. Depending on properties, shaped plastics may be used to make prototype patterns as well as patterns for hand and machine molding and nobake coreboxes.

For very obvious reasons, the application of wood and plastic tooling is limited to molding and coremaking processes in which no heat is involved. The latter excludes use of these materials in heat-activated sand systems, such as in shell molding where pattern and corebox are preheated up to 250–300°C (482–572°F). Certain precautions must be taken if a plastic pattern or corebox is used for making chemically bonded molds and cores to be sure that the plastic material would not react with the sand mix components.

All previously discussed pattern materials are reusable, and are intended to be used many times. Their service life and performance may be significantly improved by applications of protective wear-resistant coatings.

Some special casting processes utilize heat-disposable patterns, also called lost patterns, which are used only one time. For example, in investment casting and in the lost-foam process, patterns are made of wax, plastics or plastic foams that can be melted or burned away inside the mold, without withdrawing. Polystyrene foam is the predominant pattern material used for this purpose. It is also used in rapid prototyping of tooling for these processes. This foam is very light and can be easily formed into any shape required. It can be used for a single casting or for mass production of castings. This material has a very low ash content and, hence, can be burned inside the mold with almost no residue.

The selection of suitable pattern material is based on the expected life of the pattern and coreboxes, which specify the number of castings produced before tooling equipment repair is required. Table 3-2 gives comparative values of pattern material choices, depending upon sizes of castings.

As can be seen, wood is a common pattern material in low-volume casting production. For high-scale production usually associated with machine molding and repeated impact of abrasive molding sand, metal or plastic materials exhibit significantly longer tooling life. In many cases, for very large castings, wood may be the only practical pattern material.

3.1.2. Types of Patterns

There are various types of patterns depending upon the complexity of the casting, the number of castings required and the molding procedure adopted.

Single-Piece Pattern or Loose Pattern

These are inexpensive and the simplest type of patterns. As the name indicates, they are made of a single piece as shown in Fig. 3-2. This type of pattern is used only in cases where the casting shape is very simple and does not create any withdrawal problems. It is also used for applications in small-scale production or in prototype development. The pattern is expected to be entirely in the drag half of the mold. One of the surfaces is expected to be flat, which is used as the parting line or parting

Table 3-2. Selection of Pattern Materials Based on Expected Tooling Life.

Number of castings produced before pattern equipment repair		
Pattern	Core box	Pattern Material
Small castings (under 600 mm/24 in.)		
2,000	2,000	Hard wood
6,000	6,000	Aluminum, Plastic
100,000	100,000	Cast iron
Medium castings (600–1800 mm/24–70 in)		
1,000	750	Hard wood
3,000	3,000	Aluminum, Plastic
Large castings (above 1800 mm/70 in)		
200	150	Soft wood
500	500	Hard wood metal reinforced

plane. If no such flat surface exists, the molding may become complicated and may require a follow board as explained later. These patterns are usually practiced in hand molding; ingates and risers may be cut manually or molded as separate loose pieces.

Split Pattern or Two-Piece Pattern

This is the most widely used type of pattern for more complex castings. When the contour of the casting makes its withdrawal from the mold difficult, or when the depth of the casting is too high, then the pattern is split into two parts so that one part is in the drag half of the mold and the other in the cope. The split surface of the pattern is the same as the parting plane of the mold. The two halves of the pattern are aligned by using dowel pins that are fitted to the cope half. These dowel pins match with the precisely made holes in the drag half of the pattern, allowing accurate alignment of the two halves as seen in Fig. 3-3. As in the previous case, split patterns are used in hand molding, and ingates and risers may be cut manually or molded as separate loose pieces.

Cope and Drag Pattern

These are similar to split patterns. In addition, the cope and drag halves of the pattern, along with the gating and risering systems, are attached separately to the metal or plastic or wooden plates, along with the alignment pins (Fig. 3-4). The cope and drag sides of the mold may be produced using these patterns separately, by two molders, and can be assembled to form a complete mold.

These types of patterns are widely used for high-volume production runs of small-to-heavy weight castings, requiring close tolerances. Typically, cope and drag patterns are employed in machine molding where high productivity and the best cost effectiveness are achieved.

Match Plate Pattern

These are extensions of the previous type. Here, the cope and drag patterns, along with the gating and the risering, are mounted on opposite sides of a single matching plate made of metal, plastic or wood, as shown in Fig. 3-5. On one side of the match plate, the cope flask is prepared and, on the other, the drag flask. After molding, when the match plate is removed, a complete mold with gating is obtained by joining the cope and the drag together.

Often, the complete pattern with match plate is entirely made of metal, usually aluminum, for its light weight and good machinability. But when dimensions are critical,

the match plate may be made of steel, with necessary case hardening of the critical wear points. The pattern and gating system are either screwed to the match plate, in the case of a flat parting plane, or are made integral, in the case of an irregular parting plane. When the cope and the drag patterns are similar, the pattern may be kept on only one side of the plate, and is used for making both the drag as well as the cope.

Match plate patterns are generally used for large-scale production of small- and medium-size castings. Multiple identical patterns or several patterns of different casting designs can be fixed to a single match plate, as it illustrated in Fig. 3-5. These patterns are used mostly for machine molding, and, despite the additional cost, are economically justified, because of increased productivity and dimensional accuracy of finished castings.

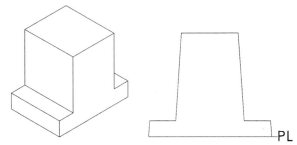

Fig. 3-2. Single piece pattern.

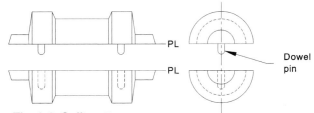

Fig. 3-3. Split pattern.

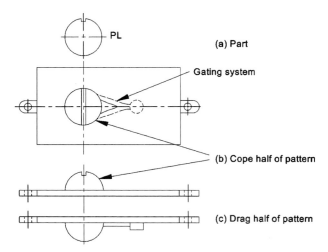

Fig. 3-4. Sketches of part (a) cope (b) and drag pattern (c).

Loose Piece Pattern

This type of pattern is used when the contour of the part is such that withdrawing the pattern from the mold is not possible. Hence, during molding the obstructing part of the contour is held as a loose piece. After molding is completed, first the main pattern is removed, and then the loose pieces are recovered through the gap generated by the main pattern (Fig. 3-6). Molding with loose pieces involves manual operations and, therefore is expensive and should be avoided where possible.

Follow Board Pattern

This type of pattern is adopted for mostly loose patterns having an irregular parting line. It is also used for those with some portions that are structurally weak and, if not supported properly, are likely to break under the force of ramming. Hence, the bottom board is modified as a follow board to closely fit the contour of the pattern and, thus, support it during the ramming of the drag. During the preparation of the cope, no follow board is necessary because the sand that is compacted in the drag will support the pattern. An example of this type of pattern is shown in Fig. 3-7. Molding with a

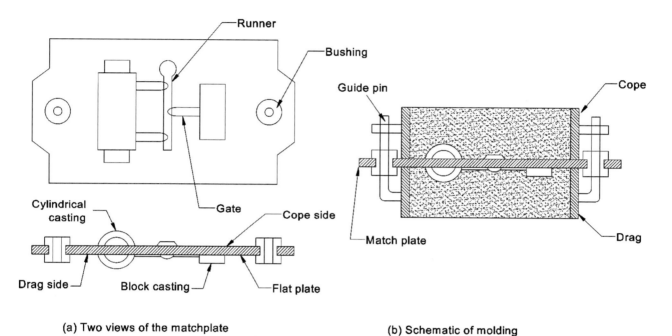

(a) Two views of the matchplate

(b) Schematic of molding

Fig. 3-5. Match plate pattern (a) and schematic of the molding (b).

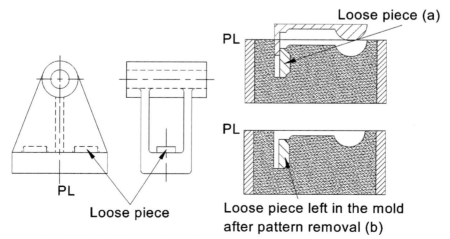

Fig. 3-6. On the right is shown pattern with loose pieces; schematic on the left illustrates loose piece pattern before (a) and after (b) pattern removal from the mold.

follow board pattern requires involvement of highly skilled professionals, which is generally expensive and, therefore, should be avoided, if possible.

Sweep Pattern

This is used to make the complete shape of the mold by means of a plane sweep, which is a template cut to the profile of the mold, and rotates about the vertical spindle. This type of pattern is used for generating large bell-shaped or cylindrical molds, such as shown in Fig. 3-8. Sweep patterns, along with the sweep molding technique, still are in use to make large ornamental bells, pots and some heavy gears, which are generally cast in pit molds. This eliminates the use of a full-size, costly, three-dimensional pattern, but the molding technique is manual and time consuming.

3.2. Pattern Design

3.2.1. Selection of Parting Line

The parting line determines the position of the casting in the mold and its location depends upon the shape of the casting. Selection of the best parting line is based on several considerations such as proper metal flow into the mold cavity, the possibility to minimize or eliminate cores and simplify molding, reduce risk of casting defects, provision of sufficient core support and venting, etc. The simplest parting line is that running through the centerline of the casting. The optimal solution is to design a casting with a parting line that is straight or as nearly straight as possible. A complex parting line increases the cost of tooling and, ultimately, the cost of the cast component.

3.2.2. Pattern Dimensioning

Dimensioning of the casting has the purpose to incorporate various allowances, such as shrinkage and machining allowances, to ensure that the finished casting is dimensionally correct.

3.2.2.1. Shrinkage Allowance

All metals, except perhaps bismuth, undergo expansion upon heating above ambient temperature and shrinkage or contraction when cooling. This is because of the interatomic vibrations, which are amplified by an increase in temperature, and reduced during cooling. However, there is a distinction to be made between different stages of shrinkage.

Risers are provided to feed the casting during solidification and compensate for volume contractions occurred as a result of liquid and solidification shrinkage. (*This will be explained in Chapter 5.*)

The shrinkage allowance is provided to take care of solid shrinkage. This occurs when metal cools down in the solid state from its solidification temperature to room temperature. This allowance is called patternmaker's or linear shrinkage. Table 3-3 gives approximate values of linear (patternmaker's) shrinkage for various foundry alloys cast in sand molds.

The actual value of shrinkage depends on various factors specific to a particular casting alloy, including its pouring temperature, mold materials, component size and its complexity (presence of cores), etc. For example, gray cast iron contracts to a lower degree than steel. Higher pouring temperature (above optimal)

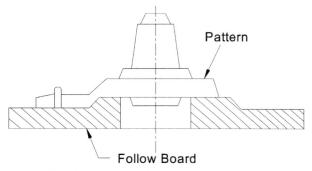

Fig. 3-7. Follow board with the pattern.

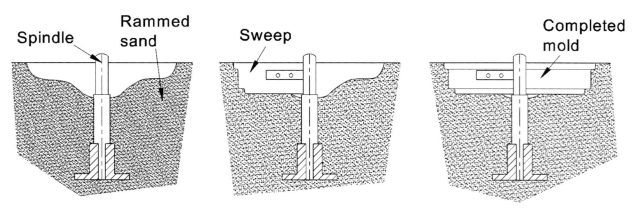

Fig. 3-8. Sweep patterns are used for making large symmetrical molds, such as church bells, in a pit mold.

always results in higher shrinkage. Using a more rigid mold, such as a permanent mold, restrains contraction. As a result, a different value of shrinkage allowance would be applied.

The value of contraction also depends upon the metallurgical transformation taking place during the solidification or heat treatment. For example, unalloyed white cast iron, typically used for making malleable iron castings, shrinks up to 20.0 mm/m or 2.0% because no graphite is formed during casting. However, when annealed, due to graphite precipitation, it grows by about 10.0 mm/m or by 1.0%, resulting in a net shrinkage of 10.0 mm/m or 1.0%. Similarly, in gray and ductile irons, the amount of graphitization (graphite precipitation) controls the actual shrinkage. When the degree of graphitization is more, like in high-CE cast irons, the shrinkage would be less and vice versa.

As a rule, when adding shrinkage allowance, all the dimensions are going to be altered uniformly unless they are restrained in some way. For example, a sand core at the center of the casting (Fig. 3-1) may restrain the casting from contracting, but the edges contract freely with no restraint. Thus, it may be desirable to provide a slightly higher shrinkage allowance for outer dimensions, compared to those that may be restrained or cored. The patternmaker's experience and a little bit of trial are to be used to provide the final pattern shrinkage values.

The shrinkage allowance is always to be added to the linear dimensions. In the case of internal dimensions (e.g., internal diameters of cylinders), the material has a tendency to contract toward the center and, thus, is to be increased. In patternmaking practice, a special shrink rule with special scales, where dimensions shown are actually longer by a measure equal to the shrinkage allowance for different alloys, is used.

The following examples illustrate practical steps involved in pattern dimensioning, taking into account shrinkage allowance.

Table 3-3. Pattern Shrinkage Allowances for Various Foundry Alloys Cast in Sand Molds.

Cast alloy	Pattern dimension, mm (in.)	Shrinkage allowance, mm/m (%)
Gray iron	Up to 600 (24)	10.0 (1.00)
	625 to 1200 (25 to 48)	8.5 (0.85)
	over 1200 (48)	7.0 (0.70)
Ductile iron		
Pearlitic	Up to 600 (24)	8.0–10.0 (0.8–1.0)
Ferritic	Up to 500 (20)	0.0–3.0 (0.0–0.3)
White cast iron	Up to 600 (24)	20.0 (2.0)
High alloy iron	Up to 600 (24)	11.0–13.0 (1.1–1.3)
Malleable iron	Casting section thickness up to 15 mm (0.6 in).	10.0 (1.0)
Plain carbon steel	Up to 600 (24)	21.0 (2.10)
	625 to 1800 (25 to 70)	16.0 (1.60)
	over 1800 (70)	13.0 (1.30)
		18–20 (1.8–2.2)
High alloy steel	Up to 600 (24)	
Aluminum	Up to 600 (24)	13.0 (1.30)
Copper	Up to 500 (20)	16.0 (1.60)
Brass	Up to 500 (20)	15.5 (1.55)
Bronze	Up to 500 (20)	15.5–22.0 (1.55–2.20)
Magnesium	Up to 600 (24)	13.0 (1.30)

Example 3-1

The casting shown in Fig. 3-9(a) is to be cast in plain carbon steel using a wooden pattern. Assuming only shrinkage allowance, calculate the dimensions of the pattern.

1. From Table 3-3, shrinkage allowance for this steel and given pattern dimensions is 21.0 mm/m or 2.1%.

2. Calculate dimensions of the wooden pattern by applying shrinkage allowance for:
   a. Dimension 200, allowance is 200 × 21.0 / 1000 = 4.20 mm
   b. Dimension 150, allowance is 150 × 21.0/ 1000 = 3.15 ≈ 3.20 mm
   c. Dimension 100, allowance is 100 × 21.0/ 1000 = 2.10 mm
   d. Dimension 80, allowance is 80 × 21.0/ 1000 = 1.68 ≈ 1.70 mm

3. The pattern drawing with required dimensions, taking shrinkage into account, is shown in Fig. 3-9(b).

As was mentioned earlier, double shrinkage allowance is provided on the master pattern, from which the metallic pattern for production runs is made. Theoretically, it would be done in two subsequent steps:

1. Add shrinkage allowance to compensate for linear contraction of the pattern material.

2. Add shrinkage allowance to compensate for linear contraction of cast material from which castings will be made.

Practically, for simplicity, the final shrinkage allowance value applied would be equal to the sum of the two allowances: the shrinkage of the pattern metal and a regular shrinkage of the casting alloy. This is illustrated in the following example.

Example 3-2

Calculate the dimensions of the wooden master pattern for the same low-carbon steel casting shown in Fig. 3-9(a), if this pattern is to be used for making the aluminum pattern.

1. From Table 3-3, shrinkage allowance for aluminum is 1.3% or 13.0 mm/m and for low-carbon steel and given pattern dimensions is 2.1% or 21.0 mm/m. The double shrinkage allowance is: 1.3% or 13.0 mm/m + 2.1% or 21.0 mm/m = 3.4% or 34.0 mm/m

2. Calculate double shrinkage allowance for:

- Dimension 200.0, allowance is 200.0 × 34.0 / 1000 = 6.8 mm
- Dimension 150.0, allowance is 150.0 × 34.0 / 1000 = 5.1 mm
- Dimension 100.0, allowance is 100.0 × 34.0 / 1000 = 3.4 mm
- Dimension 80.0, allowance is 80.0 × 34.0 / 1000 = 2.72 mm

The final dimensions of the wooden master pattern for making the production aluminum pattern are shown in Fig. 3-9(c).

3.2.2.2. Machining or Finish Allowance

The surface finish and dimensional accuracy achieved in different casting methods in many cases, particularly in sand casting, may not satisfy the part requirements, and generally, is concluded by subsequent machining. Hence, extra material, called machining or finish allowance, is to be provided on the surfaces of cast parts.

In general, machining allowance depends on the overall dimensions of the part, type of casting alloy, molding method, the finish required and, also, upon part location in regard to the parting line; the greater values apply to the surface located in the cope flask.

Table 3-4 gives some guidelines for the machining allowance selection for sand castings. Cast parts made by other processes, for example, by permanent molding, require less machining due to better surface finish and closer

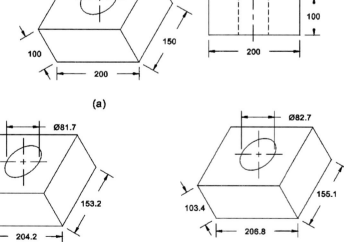

Fig. 3-9. Provision of shrinkage allowances for patterns in sand castings (all dimensions in mm).

dimensional tolerances. Castings made by special precision casting methods, such as or diecasting or investment casting, may require little or no machining at all.

Machining allowance is always added to the linear dimensions of the machined part drawing, besides holes where machining allowance is actually deducted from the whole diameter. This will be illustrated in the following example.

Example 3-3

Consider that the part shown in Fig. 3-9(a) is to be cast in plain carbon steel and that the entire casting is to be in the drag flask. Assuming only machining allowance, calculate pattern dimensions.

1. Choose machining allowance for cast steel from Table 3-4.
2. Calculate pattern dimensions:
   - Bore diameter is $80 - (2 \times 3) = 74$ mm (machining allowance is 3 mm)
   - Height is $100 + (3 + 6) = 109$ mm (machining allowance for cope side is 6 mm)
   - Width is $150 + (2 \times 3) = 156$ mm
   - Length is $200 + (2 \times 5.5) = 211$ mm

The final pattern dimensions after the addition of machining allowance are shown in Fig. 3-10.

Because provision of the machining allowance, which is to be subsequently removed by machining, is directly related to the overall cost of the cast part, it should be carefully examined before finalizing the casting dimensions. One way of reducing the machining allowance is to keep the entire casting in the drag flask, which also minimizes dimensional variation and prevents casting shift at the parting line.

3.2.2.3. Distortion Allowance

When irregular shaped castings, poured of certain alloys, solidify and contract, a high level of residual stresses, due to difference in their thermal gradients, is likely to occur. As a result, these castings are distortion or warpage-prone, which is considered as a deviation from original shape or the size of the cast part. The latter takes place in weaker sections, such as long flat portions, V-sections, U-sections or in a complicated casting,

which may have thin and long sections connected to thick sections, solidifying under conditions of restrained contraction. In general, the foundry practice should be aimed at reducing the distortion by applying proper casting design.

Alternatively, to compensate for distortion, the shape of the pattern itself may be intentionally distorted in the direction opposite to which it is expected. Typically, the foundry determines the correct distortion allowance on a trial-and-error basis.

3.2.2.4. Draft Allowance

At the time of withdrawing the pattern from the mold, the vertical faces of the pattern are in continual contact with the mold, which may damage the mold cavity, as shown in Fig. 3-11(a). To ease pattern withdrawal, the vertical faces of the pattern are always tapered from the parting line, as shown in Fig. 3-11(b). This provision is called draft allowance.

Table 3-4. Machining Allowances on Patterns for Sand Castings (all dimensions in mm).

Dimension, mm (in.)	Allowance, mm (in.)		
	Bore	Surface	Cope side
Cast iron			
Up to 300 (12)	3.0 (0.125)	3.0 (0.125)	5.5 (0.220)
301 to 500 (12 to 20)	5.0 (0.200)	4.0 (0.160)	6.0 (0.250)
501 to 900 (20 to 36)	6.0 (0.250)	5.0 (0.200)	6.0 (0.250)
Cast steel			
Up to 150 (6)	3.0 (0.125)	3.0 (0.125)	6.0 (0.250)
151 to 500 (6 to 20)	6.0 (0.250)	5.5 (0.220)	7.0 (0.275)
501 to 900 (20 to 36)	7.0 (0.275)	6.0 (0.250)	9.0 (0.360)
Non-ferrous			
Up to 200 (8)	2.0 (0.080)	1.5 (0.060)	2.0 (0.080)
201 to 300 (8 to 12)	2.5 (0.100)	1.5 (0.060)	3.0 (0.125)
301 to 900 (12 to 36)	3.0 (0.125)	2.5 (0.100)	3.0 (0.125)

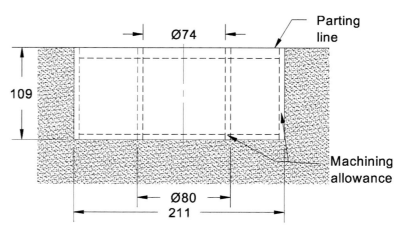

Fig. 3-10. Pattern after providing finish allowance (all dimensions in mm).

Draft allowance varies with the complexity of the casting. Commonly, inner details of the pattern require higher draft than outer surfaces. Table 3-5 is a general guide to the provision of drafts. The draft allowance given varies for hand molding and machine molding. More draft is needed to be provided for hand molding compared to machine molding. In machine molding, the actual draft given varies with the condition of the machine (new, rigid, properly aligned, etc. require less draft). One thing to be noted here is that draft is always provided on vertical surfaces as extra metal, over and above the original casting dimensions, as shown in the following example.

Example 3-4

Provide draft allowance to the wood pattern shown previously in Fig 3-10.

1. Using data from Table 3-5, choose draft angle for external and internal surfaces of wood pattern

2. Assuming a 0.75° taper for external details and 1.0° for internal details, calculate draft required for:
   - Bore diameter 74 mm, the taper required is 1.0° or $109 \times \tan(1) = 1.9$ mm; bore diameter after draft addition $= 74 - (2 \times 1.9) = 70.2$ mm
   - Height 109 mm, the taper required is 0.75° or $109 \times \tan(0.75) = 1.4$ mm
   - Similarly, length after draft addition $= 211 + (2 \times 1.4) = 213.8$ mm

After providing for draft allowance, the pattern drawing is as shown in Fig. 3-12(bottom).

It needs to be kept in mind that minimizing the draft allowance will lead to a reduced metal consumption, less machining, which, in turn, will reduce the cost of casting.

3.2.3. Cores and Coreboxes

Cores are used to cast holes or any shape of openings or cavities in the casting. There are essentially two types of cores, based on the type of sand used. Green sand cores are those that are obtained by the pattern itself during molding. Though this is the most economical way of making a core, the green sand, being low in strength, cannot be used for fairly deep holes and cavities. Also, a large amount of draft is to

be provided so that the pattern can be freely withdrawn as shown in Fig. 3-13. Dry (chemically-bonded) sand cores are those made by means of special core sands in a separate corebox, hardened, and then placed in the mold before pouring.

Core prints are attached to the core to support and secure it inside the mold cavity. Adequate sizes of core prints are provided to a pattern, which form recesses in the mold where the core is placed. Figure 3-14 shows an example of the provision of core prints for a flange-type casting, having a symmetrical parting line.

Table 3-5. Suggested draft values for patterns used in sand casting.

Pattern material	Height of the given surface, mm (in.)	Draft angle of surfaces, degrees	
		External surface	Internal surface
Wood	20 (0.8)	3.00	3.00
	21 to 50 (0.8 to 2.0)	1.50	2.50
	51 to 100 (2.0 to 4.0)	1.00	1.50
	101 to 200 (4.0 to 8.0)	0.75	1.00
	201 to 300 (8.0 to 12.0)	0.50	1.00
	301 to 800 (12.0 to 32.0)	0.50	0.75
	801 to 2000 (32.0 to 80)	0.35	0.50
	over 2000 (80)	--	0.25
Metal and Plastic	20 (0.8)	1.50	3.00
	21 to 50 (0.8 to 2.0)	1.00	2.00
	51 to 100 (2.0 to 4.0)	0.75	1.00
	101 to 200 (4.0 to 8.0)	0.50	0.75
	201 to 300 (8.0 to 12.0)	0.50	0.75
	301 to 800 (12.0 to 32.0)	0.35	0.50

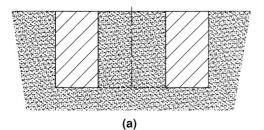

(a)

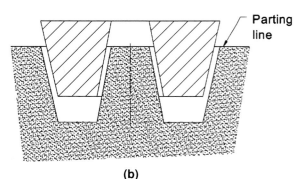

(b)

Fig. 3-11. Effect of draft on pattern withdrawal from the mold.

Depending upon the position, cores are classified as horizontal and vertical. Figure 3-15 illustrates two examples of horizontally positioned cores used to make an identical cavity: (a) is an unbalanced core with one core print, and (b) is a balanced core with two core prints. Note that the twin core design (b) allows not only a stabilized core position, but also spare mold space for additional cavity thus doubling productivity.

Figure 3-16 shows different designs of vertically positioned cores: (a) shows one with one core print (locked by a special holding plate in this case). The casting is poured through the ingates, located within the core print; (b) is a core with two core prints, and (c) is a drop core. In designing the coreboxes, care should be taken to consider the strength of the core. Before the

hardening process, the core is generally weak, and should be well supported. If the core is simple and strong in itself, no special precaution is required. But for slender and complicated cores, it may be necessary to leave the core in the corebox during the hardening process. Sometimes, flat or shaped plates, called dryers, are used to support the core after its removal from the corebox.

If a core is symmetrical, as shown in Fig. 3-17, it can be made in two equal parts and then assembled together by adhesives, or fastened. Care should be taken, while applying the glue, not to close the core vent holes made

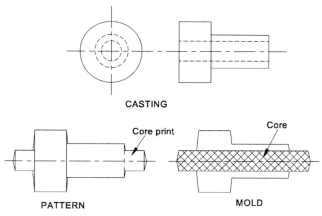

Fig. 3-13. Cross section of mold cavity (a) with green sand core (b).

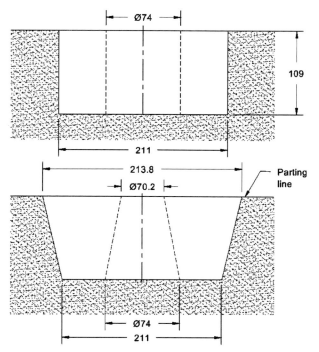

Fig. 3-12. Example showing how dimensions change after adding draft to the pattern (all dimensions in mm).

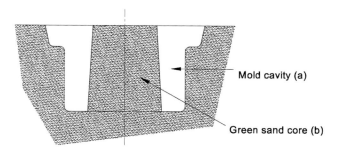

Fig. 3-14. Typical flange-type casting, its pattern and mold cavity with a core. Note: The core prints are attached to the pattern and to the core.

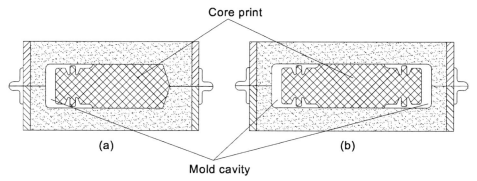

Fig. 3-15. Horizontally positioned dry sand core types, (a) unbalanced core with one core print; (b) balanced core with two core prints.

earlier for the gases to escape. When very large cores are to be joined, it may be necessary to use nuts and bolts. The bolt holes are generally covered with core plugs.

If the core is to be mounted in a particular orientation, then some specific provision should be made in the core prints so that the core can be placed in the mold in only one position, as illustrated in Fig. 3-18.

Coreboxes, like patterns, may be designed with single or multiple cavities. In some cases, complicated coreboxes may have loose pieces.

The materials used for making coreboxes are wood, metals or plastics, and its selection depends upon the necessary scale of production and size of castings, as well as expected tooling life (see Tables 3-1 and 3-2). (*More details on corebox design for core blowing machines are discussed in Chapter 6.*)

As was stated before, the core prints must provide secure and correct position of the core in the mold cavity. The size of the core prints is to be estimated, based on the specific casting alloy and core geometry, to take care of the weight of the core before pouring and the upward metallostatic pressure of the molten metal after pouring. The core prints should also ensure that the core is not shifted during the entry of the metal into the mold cavity.

The main force acting on the core when metal is poured into the mold cavity is due to buoyancy. The buoyant force can be calculated as the difference in the weight of

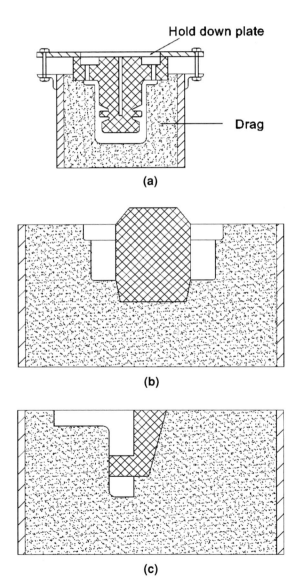

Fig. 3-16. Vertically positioned dry sand cores: (a) unbalanced core with one core print and special holding plate; casting is poured through the ingates located within the core print; (b) with two core prints; (c) drop core. Note: The (b) and (c) core designs are shown with drag half of mold removed.

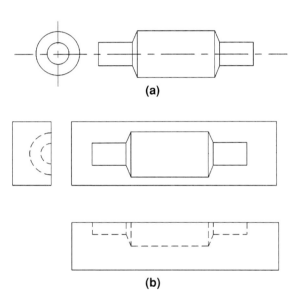

Fig. 3-17. Example of a typical symmetrical core for cylindrical casting (a) and core box used to make it (b). Note: The core is made into two equal halves assembled together.

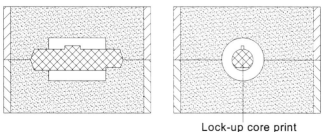

Fig. 3-18. Asymmetrical core location in the mold. Note: The right cylindrical core print has a partially flat surface allowing locking it in a particular position.

the liquid metal to that of the core material of the same volume as that of the exposed core. It can be written as:

$$P = V\,(\rho - d) \qquad (3.1)$$

Where:

P = buoyant force, N

V = volume of the core in the mold cavity, cm³

ρ = weight density of the liquid metal, N/cm³

d = weight density of the core material = 0.0165 N/cm³

Table 3-6 lists the weight density values of some foundry materials necessary for buoyant force calculations. The above equation would be valid for cases similar to the one illustrated in Fig. 3-19, which are more common, where V is given by 0.25 π D² H.

But for vertical cores, as those shown in Fig. 3-20, the buoyant force is given by:

$$P = 0.25\,\pi\,(\,D_1^2 - D^2\,)\,H\,\rho - V\,d \qquad (3.2)$$

Where:

H = core height

D = core diameter

As can be seen, buoyant force acting on a sand core will be increased with increasing density of the liquid cast alloy. As a result, the core print size for a given casting, for example, aluminum, would be smaller than that cast in copper alloy, iron or steel.

In order to keep the core in position, it is empirically suggested that the core print be able to support a load of 3.5 N/cm² (50 psi) of surface area. Hence, to fully support the buoyant force, it is necessary that the following condition be satisfied:

$$P \le 350\,A \qquad (3.3)$$

Where:

A = core print area, mm²

If the above were not satisfied, then it would be necessary to provide additional support by the use of chaplets, as described later. From the core print area, necessary core print sizes can be calculated.

The core print dimensions could also be verified using a practical recommendation to make the pressure acting on the core-bearing area (i.e., A, the core print surface area) to be less than 50 to 75% of the molding sand compression strength. Hence,

$$A > K\,\frac{V\,(\rho - d)}{\sigma} \qquad (3.4)$$

Where

V = total volume of the core including prints, cm³

K = 0.50 to 0.75

ρ = weight density of the liquid metal, N/cm³

d = weight density of the core material = 0.0165 N/cm³

σ = compression strength of the molding sand, N/cm²

A suggested guide for core print dimensions for different core positions, which were found suitable in cast iron practice for simple-shaped cylindrical castings, is given in Table 3-7. Note that in vertical core, the height of the bottom print may be shorter than the height of the upper print due to less buoyant force. The draft angles to be used for these core prints are given in Table 3-8 with reference to Fig. 3-21.

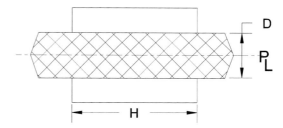

Fig. 3-19. Schematic for buoyant force calculations for horizontal core position.

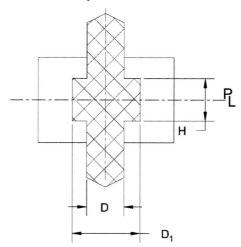

Fig. 3-20. Schematic for buoyant force calculations for vertical core position.

Table 3-6. Densities of Some Foundry Materials*.

Material	Average density	
	N /cm³	lb/ in.³
Aluminum	0.0265	0.0977
Copper	0.0878	0.3236
Magnesium	0.0171	0.0630
Zinc	0.0700	0.2580
Lead	0.1113	0.4102
Carbon steel	0.0771	0.2842
Gray cast iron	0.0680 to 0.0726**	0.2506 to 0.2676
White cast iron	0.0755	0.2783
Molding sand	0.0157	0.0579

* Density values for casting alloys are given for liquid state
** Density varies mostly depending on CE (carbon equivalent) values

The methods described above for calculation of core print sizes are empirical and give approximate values based on practical data. These may be optimized using solidification modeling methods and finite element analysis, which are discussed in Chapters 5 and 11, respectively.

3.2.4. Fillets and Radii

In order to eliminate stress concentration and subsequent cracks, all sharp corners and junctions of the casting must be provided with radii. In patterns and coreboxes, it is accomplished through applications of fillets of different materials. Typical radius depends upon size of intersections and casting method used and varies from 3 to 5 mm (0.125 to 0.200 in.).

Table 3-7. Core Print Dimensions for Horizontal and Vertical Core Positions.

Core diameter D, mm (in.)	Core length L, mm (in.)									
	<50 (2)		51– 150 (2.05 – 6)		151 – 300 (6.05 – 12)		310 – 500 (12.05 – 20)		500-750 (20.05 – 30)	
	vl	hl	vl	hl	vl	hl	vl	hl	vl	hl
up to 25 (1)	20 (0.8)	15(0.6)	25 (1.0)	25	--	40 (1.6)	--	--	--	--
26 – 50 (1.05 – 2)	20 (0.8)	20	40 (1.6)	(1.0)	60 (2.4)	45 (1.8)	70 (2.8)	60 (2.4)	--	--
51 – 100 (2.05 – 4)	25 (1.0)	(0.8)	35 (1.4)	35	50 (2.0)	50 (2.0)	70 (2.8)	70 (2.8)	100	90 (3.6)
101 – 200 (4.05 – 8)	30 (1.2)	25	30 (1.2)	(1.4)	40 (1.6)	55 (2.2)	60 (2.4)	80 (3.2)	(4.0)	100
201 – 300 (8.05 – 12)	35 (1.4)	(1.0)	35 (1.4)	40	40 (1.6)	60 (2.4)	50 (2.0)	90 (3.6)	90 (3.6)	(4.0)
301 – 400 (12.05 – 16)	40 (1.6)	30	40 (1.6)	(1.6)	40 (1.6)	80 (3.2)	50 (2.0)	100	80 (3.2)	110
401 – 500 (16.05 – 20)	40 (1.6)	(1.2)	40 (1.6)	50	40 (1.6)	110	50 (2.0)	(4.0)	70 (2.8)	(4.4)
		--		(2.0)		(4.4)		120	60 (2.4)	120
		--		--				(4.8)		(4.8)
		--		--						130
				--						(5.2)

vl = vertical length; hl = horizontal length.

Table 3-8. Draft Angles for Core Prints Shown in Fig. 3-21.

Core print length, hl or vl, mm (in.)	Draft angle, degrees	
	Vertical coreprint β	Horizontal coreprint α
< 20 (0.8)	15	10
21 to 50 (0.85 to 2.0)	10	7
51 to 100 (2.05 to 4.0)	8	6
101 to 200 (4.05 to 8.0)	6	5

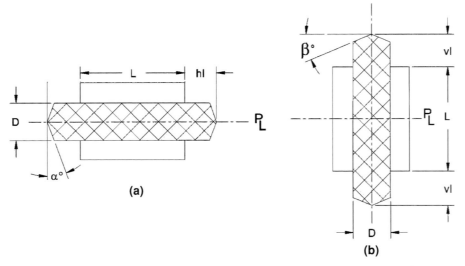

Fig. 3-21. Key symbols used for selection of core print dimensions for different core positions (Table 3-7) and draft angles (Table 3-8): (a) horizontal core supported on both sides; (b) vertical core supported by two prints. Note: The height of the bottom print may be shorter than height of upper print due to less buoyant force.

3.2.5. Elimination of Details

Often it is not possible to get very fine details on the surface, or very small holes, by sand casting. In such cases, it is desirable to simplify the casting process by eliminating those details and creating them during the machining process, as is shown in Fig. 3-1. In this example, two small holes with 7.5 mm (0.3 in.) diameter are crossed to show that the casting process will not make them.

The types of details that one would like to eliminate in the casting depend on the required accuracy, the capability of the chosen casting process, and the molding method employed. Figure 3-22 illustrates another example of a simplified design of an iron piston for a diesel engine; eliminating of some details, such as grooves for piston rings, make this part suitable for casting.

3.3. Flasks and Chaplets

A flask is a frame or container without bottom and top that holds the sand mold with the casting cavity. Commonly, the flask has two sections: drag (or bottom) and cope (or top). Proper matching of these sections is achieved by guide pins and bushings arrangement. Guide pins are typically placed into the drag, while bushings are located in the cope.

In flask molding, a flask, which stays with mold until it is shaken out, is called permanent or tight; if the flask is removed after the mold is prepared, it is called a snap flask. Sometimes, after snap flask removal, a metallic jacket may be placed around the mold to reinforce the assembled mold during pouring.

The shape of the flasks may be square, rectangular or circular, and they are made of metal (aluminum, iron or steel) or wood. The internal cavity of the flask may be designed with or without ribs of rigidity; these are aimed to provide

better support to the mold and prevent any deformation of the flask during molding that, in turn, increases dimensional accuracy of finished castings. Often, these rib designs follow the shape of the pattern, particularly, in those flasks utilized in specialized high-volume production molding lines.

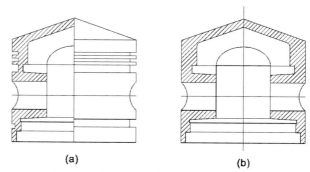

(a)   (b)

Fig. 3-22. Elimination of details on a casting to simplify molding.

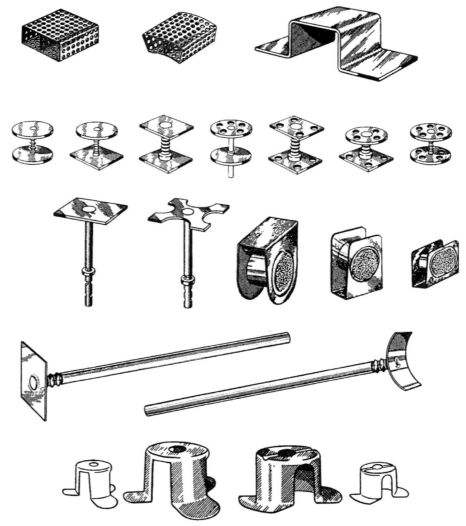

Fig. 3-23. Types of chaplets for supporting cores.

Chaplets are special spacers, mostly metallic, that are placed inside the mold cavity to support the cores, prevent their deflection, and ensure the desirable wall thickness in given cross sections. Some of the types of chaplets normally used are shown in Fig. 3-23, with an example of chaplet support in Fig. 3-24.

Chaplets are to be made of the same composition as the casting alloy so that the molten metal will provide enough heat to completely melt them and, thus, fuse with the parent metal during solidification.

Though the chaplet is supposed to fuse with the parent metal, in practice it sometimes may be difficult to achieve due to variables influencing the actual mold-filling temperature. That is why optimal cast alloy pouring temperature control, along with proper gating system design to prevent excessive metal cooling inside the mold, must be employed to avoid potential formation of a weak joint in the casting. The other likely problem encountered in chaplets is the condensation of moisture, which finally ends up as blowholes. To prevent this, the chaplets should be thoroughly cleaned of any dirt, oil or grease before they are placed in the mold.

As an alternative to metallic chaplets, rectangular and square-shaped chaplets made of polystyrene foam have been successfully introduced to the foundry industry. These chaplets are burned completely upon completion of mold pouring.

In order to calculate the required chaplet area, Ac, we need to know the value of the unsupported load. Referring back to the discussion on core prints (see Equation 3.3), it was suggested that:

$$P \leq 3.5\ A$$

Therefore, unsupported load = P–3.5 A

If the unsupported load is negative or equal to zero, no chaplet is required. But if it is greater than zero, the chaplet area required is 29 mm^2 (0.045 in.^{2}) for every Newton of unsupported load.

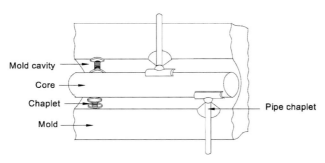

Fig. 3-24. Core supported by different types of chaplets.

Fig. 3-25. Coordinate measuring machine employed to verify castings and foundry tooling dimensions.

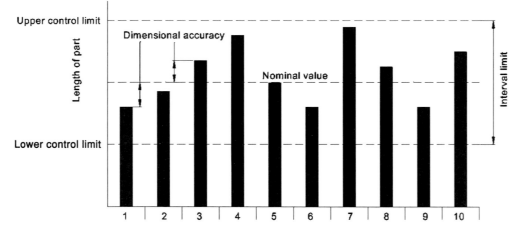

Fig. 3-26. Example of a casting's dimensional accuracy study using Statistical Process Control (SPC).

3.4. Dimensional Accuracy— CMM Applications

When casting design is completed, the necessary tooling will be made. Typically, before running the production, pilot runs will be made to verify casting quality and dimensions. Quality verification is intended to reveal potential casting defects, such as shrinkage, gas and slag porosity. Conventionally, nondestructive methods such as X-ray and ultrasound tests, followed by cutting a casting in problematic sections, are employed.

Dimension verification is aimed to measure all casting dimensions and make sure that shrinkage and machining allowances built into the pattern are correct. Dimensional accuracy specifies how close the dimension of the cast part is to the desirable dimension, and depends upon the casting method used and the part size.

For instance, in green sand casting, the dimensional tolerance limit for small-to-medium size castings is ± 0.75 mm (0.03 in.), while in diecasting of various alloys due to high mold rigidity and lack of mold wall movement, this value varies (depends upon the part size) in the range of ±0.125 to 0.250 mm (±0.005 to 0.01 in.).

A coordinate measuring machine (CMM) allows making dimensional measurements quickly and precisely. The computerized CMM (Fig. 3-25) does this by the use of a measuring tip (probe), attached to a mechanical arm with XYZ positions. The probe touches designated areas of the part to determine the exact dimension related to the entire part or area.

The software used allows importing computer-aided design (CAD) files for the creation of an inspection program. If no CAD file exists, an operator may have the option of entering data points or gathering dimensions from the actual part using a reverse engineering process to develop the inspection program or even create the drawing, which may be used to make a new pattern for the particular part.

After dimensions and quality verifications on the pilot run, the foundry will be running production lots of castings with the quantity of castings sufficient to determine dimensional variations using a statistical process control (SPC) technique. In this case, a dimensional accuracy study may be complimented with a process capability study to verify that the variation in dimensions (tolerance limits) is within desirable limits (Fig. 3-26).

Besides the castings' dimensions confirmation, CMMs are also widely used to verify dimensions of different foundry tooling for sand casting, as well as for measuring the dimensions of metallic molds for permanent casting and dies for diecasting.

References

1. Schleg, F.P.; *Technology of Metalcasting*, American Foundry Society, Des Plaines, 2003.

2. Jain, P. L., *Principles of Foundry Technology*, 2nd ed., Tata McGraw-Hill, New Delhi, 2003.

3. Titov, N. D. and Yu. A. Stepanov, *Foundry Practice*, Mir Publishers, Moscow, 1991.

4. Bradley, E.F., *High Performance Castings–A Technical Guide*, ASM International, Materials Park, 1989.

5. Johns, R., *Casting Design*, American Foundry Society, Des Plaines, 1987.

6. ASM: *Metals Handbook Vol.15, Casting*, American Society of Metals, Metals Park, 2008.

Review Questions

3.1 Explain the major steps involved in the design of patterns.

3.2 Describe the materials commonly used for making patterns.

3.3 Summarize the advantages and disadvantages of using wood as a pattern material.

3.4 Give a brief note on the advantages and disadvantages of using metal as a pattern material.

3.5 Identify the common materials used for making metallic patterns. Compare their characteristics.

3.6 Discuss the pattern materials more suitable for machine molding.

3.7 List the different types of patterns used for making sand castings.

3.8 Explain the concept of a loose piece pattern and the problems associated with its use.

3.9 Summarize the principles one should consider while selecting the parting plane for a sand casting.

3.10 Specify the various allowances added to the pattern dimensions. Explain their relevance.

3.11 Explain the concept of shrinkage allowance and how it is applied for pattern dimensions.

3.12 Explain the methods used to compensate for liquid and solidification shrinkage in castings.

3.13 Define draft, as used in patterns. Explain the application with an example having internal and external features.

3.14 Explain the reasons for the use of cores in sand castings.

3.15 Distinguish between a green sand core and a dry sand core.

3.16 Explain briefly the different types of dry sand cores used in castings.

3.17 Describe a core print. Explain methods used to specify its sizes.

3.18 Describe the use of chaplets in sand casting.

3.19 Give the details of dimensional accuracy of a casting and explain reasons why dimension verification is needed.

3.20 Write a brief note on the use of CMMs for foundry tooling dimensional verification.

GATING SYSTEMS

Objectives

Molten metal enters the mold cavity through the gating system. Its design is one of the major steps in tooling development that directly influence casting quality and proper mold cavity filling.

After studying this chapter, the reader should be able to:

- Explain the role of various elements present in a gating system
- Identify basic principles of gating system design
- Discuss fluidity of molten alloys and methods for its testing
- Choose the appropriate gating system for a given application
- Develop the concept of casting yield
- Design the gating system for different types of castings
- Choose various methods employed to trap slag in the metal flow systems in the molds

Keywords

Pouring Basin, Mold, Mold Cavity, Sand Mold, Horizontal Gating System, Vertical Gating System, Pouring Cup, Strainer Core, Core, Core Print, Sand Core, Sprue, Sprue Base, Tapered Sprue, Cope, Drag, Ingate, Step Ingate, Solidification Shrinkage, Pouring Temperature, Runner, Riser, Riser Neck, Casting Yield, Molten Metal, Molten Metal Flow, Fluidity, Mold Filling, Gating System Design, Metal Oxidation, Gray Iron, Pouring Time, Pressurized Gating System, Nonpressurized Gating System, Bernoulli's Theorem, Metallostatic Head, Cast Alloy, Steel Casting, Ductile Iron Casting, Choke Area, Top Pour Gating, Green Sand Mold, Permanent Mold , Shell Mold, Whirl Ingate, Molten Metal Filtration, Filtration Mechanism, Ceramic Foam Filter, Ceramic Cellural Filter, Cloth Filter, Scanning Electron Microscopy, Gas Porosity, Mold Erosion, Slag, Slag Inclusion, Slag Trap, Nonmetallic Inclusion, Stopper Plug, Insulating Sleeve, Refractory Material, Wettability , Mold Coating, Light-Weight Casting, Heavy-Weight Casting

4.1. Types of Gating Systems

As defined earlier, the gating system refers to a series of channels through which molten metal travels from the pouring ladle into the mold cavity, and fills it. Depending upon the casting's position in the mold, gating systems are classified as:

- Horizontal (Fig. 4-1)
- Vertical (Fig. 4-2)

Figure 4-1 illustrates a typical horizontal gating system used for casting alloys prone to solidification shrinkage. In this system, molten metal is poured from the ladle into pouring basin (pouring cup), and then flows into the sprue from which it flows into two runners, fills them and moves into two open-topside risers. In this example, risers, used to feed the casting during solidification, are part of the system, and molten metal feeds the casting through the riser neck, which plays the role of the ingate.

Figure 4-2 shows the vertical arrangement of a gating system used in a vertically-parted automatic, green sand

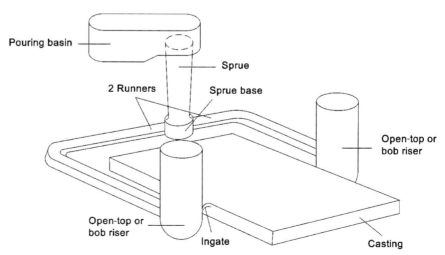

Fig. 4-1.Typical design of horizontal gating system with risers used for casting alloys prone to solidification shrinkage.

molding line and for shell molding. In this system, molten metal travels from the sprue into two horizontal runners, then moves through four vertical runners (two from each side of the horizontal runners, connected directly to the ingates, and finally flows into the casting cavities.

Considering molten metal flow in the gating system, two different types are distinguished:

- Laminar or smooth flow, with permanent stream velocity. This is preferable in any of the gating systems

- Transient or turbulent flow, with abrupt changes of stream velocity and direction. This type of flow creates metal oxidation, core and mold erosion, and should be avoided

Any gating system design aims at providing a defect-free casting. To achieve this, a properly designed gating system must fulfill the following major requirements:

- The molten metal should enter and fill the mold without turbulence, thus preventing metal oxidation that results in slag/dross defect occurrence and air entrapment, which, in turn, causes gas porosity

- The gating system should allow the separation of slag, eroded mold sand and other nonmetallic inclusions, by stopping them from entering the mold. With this purpose, the gating system may also incorporate a filtration element(s)

- The gating system should deliver an adequate volume of molten metal, with desirable temperature, into the mold cavity in the shortest time frame, thus preventing premature freezing of any gating elements

- The gating system design should provide the shortest and most economical path for delivering molten metal, increasing casting yield and permitting easy ingate removal after casting shakeout

In the selection of a properly designed gating system, the major factors, such as type of cast alloy poured and its solidification behavior, play an important role. By specifying the type of alloy, the foundry narrows the possible choice of system designs to its optimum, and takes it as a working prototype for further modeling and practical verification.

Before going into the mechanics of gating design, some of the functions and types of various gating system elements are discussed.

4.2. Elements of Gating Systems and Their Functions

4.2.1. Pouring Basin or Pouring Cup

In order to prevent mold erosion, the molten metal is not directly poured into the mold cavity.

Instead, molten metal from the ladle is poured into a pouring basin or pouring cup located on the top of the mold. This acts as a reservoir from which molten metal moves smoothly into the sprue. It also reduces the energy of the molten metal stream, falling down into the sprue from the pouring ladle, allowing smoother mold filling.

Figure 4-3 shows different designs of pouring cups used in the production of relatively light-weight castings. These cups are part of the mold and may have conical, semi-conical or square shapes. Pouring cups as well as sprues for high-temperature alloys, such as steel, that are poured at more than 1700°C/3100°F, and for heavy-weight castings, may be made of special refractory materials, and are embedded into the mold during molding. Graphite is also used as a material for pouring cups for casting of some reactive metals and alloys. When poured, these cups prevent molten metal reaction with the molding media, thus avoiding slag inclusions.

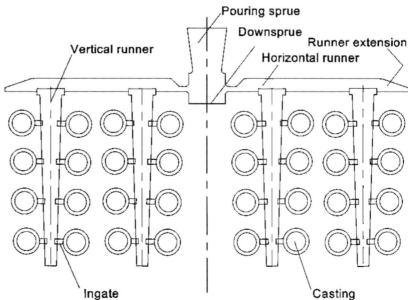

Fig. 4-2. Typical design of vertical gating system used in vertically parted sand automatic molding lines and shell molding.

Figure 4-4 illustrates two different pouring basin designs: (a), which is part of the mold and (b), made as an extension of the mold. The pouring basin, shown in Fig. 4-4(a), is cut into the cope portion of the mold directly, while the basin shown in Fig. 4-4(b) is made as a separate element of the gating system as a dry sand core. The latter design is also able to stop slag from entering the mold cavity by means of a special skimmer or skim core, as shown in Fig. 4-4(b). It holds back the slag and other inclusions, which float on the top, and allows only the clean metal underneath to flow into the sprue. One wall of the pouring basin is slightly inclined to allow absorption of the molten metal momentum, thus, avoiding the vortex formation when metal is poured on this face.

To prevent molten metal turbulence while entering the sprue, it is necessary that the pouring basin be deep enough, and the sprue entrance has a smooth radius. Experience shows that the pouring basin depth of 2.5 times the sprue entrance diameter is adequate for smooth metal flow and impedes vortex formation, as shown in Fig. 4-5.

It is important to keep the pouring basin full of molten metal during the pouring operation, otherwise a funnel is likely to form, through which atmospheric air and slag may enter the mold cavity.

Further provision should be made in the pouring basin so that constant conditions of flow are established. This can be also achieved by using a strainer core or filter, as shown in Fig. 4-6.

A strainer core, shown in Fig. 4-6(a), which is a ceramic screen with many small holes, restricts the flow of metal into the sprue and thus helps quick filling of the pouring basin and some slag separation. A ceramic filter, shown in Fig. 4-6(b), completely removes slag and dirt, since only clean metal is allowed to go into the sprue, and ensures a constant flow of metal.

The molten metal should be poured steadily into the pouring basin, keeping the lip of the ladle as close as possible. Pouring basins are most desirable for casting alloys which form troublesome oxide skins.

For heavy-weight castings, pouring basins with stoppers are used. The stopper plugs the sprue and prevents molten metal from going into it, until at least 75% of the pouring basin volume is filled with the molten metal. This allows better slag trapping and maintains constant metal height in the basin. The stopper may be made of graphite, which provides non-wetting properties, or of metal coated with a refractory wash.

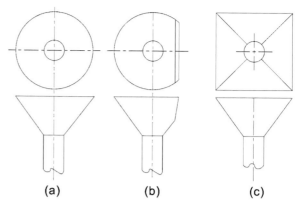

Fig. 4-3. Various pouring cup designs that are cut in the mold: (a) conical; (b) semi conical; (c) square.

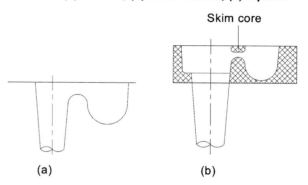

Fig. 4-4. Pouring basin designs: (a) cut in the mold; (b) made as an extension of the mold of dry sand or as a separately made core.

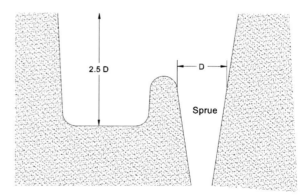

Fig. 4-5. Pouring basin design considerations.

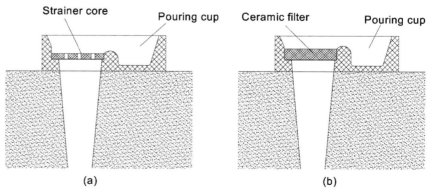

Fig. 4-6. Pouring cup with a strainer core (a) and ceramic foam filter (b).

For large and heavy castings, such as beds for machine tools and tables for heavy presses, two pouring basins with stoppers may be utilized to ensure proper and simultaneous mold filling. The advantages of pouring cups and basins that are cut in the mold are lower sand consumption and better casting yield.

4.2.2. Pouring Sprue

The sprue is a vertical channel through which molten metal is brought into the parting plane, where it enters runners and ingates to ultimately reach the mold cavity. The molten metal, when moving down the sprue from the top of the cope to the parting plane, gains velocity and, as a consequence, requires a smaller area of cross section for the same amount of metal to flow than it does at the top. If the sprue were to be a straight cylinder as shown in Fig. 4-7(a), it would not be full at the bottom, and some low-pressure areas would be created around the metal. Since the sand mold is permeable, atmospheric air would be sucked into this low-pressure area, which would then be carried to the mold cavity. To eliminate the problem of air aspiration, the sprue is tapered to gradually reduce the cross section as it moves away from the top of the cope, as shown in Fig. 4-7(b). This sprue design is commonly accepted in many types of gating systems for ferrous and nonferrous castings. But a tapered sprue is impossible to achieve in some horizontal automatic molding lines, in which the sprue is attached to the cope plate, creating a reverse taper sprue. The latter may cause gas and oxide types of casting defects. This problem can be partially alleviated by using strainer/choke cores or fiber screens or filters at the bottom of the sprue or in the runner.

4.2.3. Sprue Base or Sprue Well

The sprue base (well) is a reservoir for metal at the bottom of the sprue, also called downsprue, aimed to reduce the velocity of the molten metal and prevent mold erosion. The molten metal then changes direction and flows into the runner(s) with less turbulence in a more

uniform way. Sprue base shape may be round, rectangular or square with a flat bottom. Typical sprue base (well) designs are presented in Fig. 4-8.

A general guideline for sprue well dimensioning is that the sprue well area should be 3.5 times that of the sprue choke area and the well depth should be approximately equal to that of the runner. For a narrow and deep runner, the well diameter should be around 2.5 times the width of the runner in a two-runner system, and approximately twice its width in a one-runner system.

4.2.4. Runner

The runner is generally located in the horizontal plane (parting plane), which connects the sprue to the ingates, thus letting the metal enter the mold cavity. The runners are normally made trapezoidal in cross section. The approximate proportions are from square to rectangular, with the width twice that of the height of the runner.

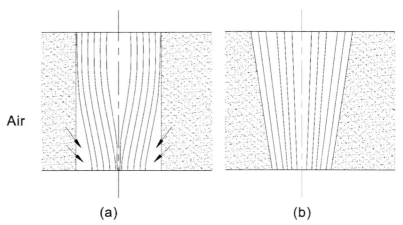

Air

(a)   (b)

Fig. 4-7. Metal flow in straight (a) and tapered sprue (b).

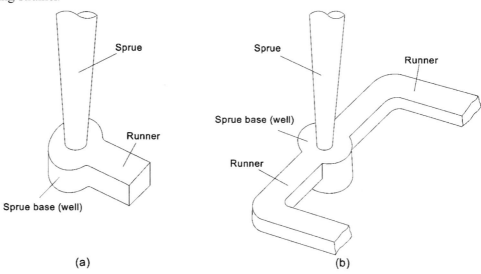

Sprue

Runner

Sprue base (well)

(a)

Sprue

Runner

Sprue base (well)

Runner

(b)

Fig. 4-8. Typical sprue base (well) designs: (a) one-runner system; (b) two-runner system.

It is a common practice for ferrous alloy castings to cut the runners in the cope and the ingates in the drag. The main reason for this is to trap the slag and dross, which are lighter and, thus, flow to the upper portion of the runners. But for aluminum alloy castings, it is recommended that the runners be placed in the drag and the ingates in the cope, so that the dross, which is heavier (3.99 g/cm³/0.1442 lb/in.³) than aluminum (2.70 g/cm³/0.0976 lb/in.³), is restricted. Also, the entry into the runners from the sprue base (well) should be made as smooth as possible in such castings; otherwise, the flow would tend to be turbulent and lead to dross formation when any change abruptly occurs in the cross-sectional area.

For effective trapping of slag, runners should flow full, as shown in Fig. 4-9(a). When the amount of molten metal coming from the downsprue is more than the amount flowing through the ingates, the runner would always be full, and slag trapping would take place. But when the metal flowing through the ingates is more than that flowing through the runners, the runner would be filled only partially, as shown in Fig. 4-9(b), and the slag would then enter the mold cavity.

4.2.5. Runner Extension

The runner is extended a little further after it encounters the ingate in both, horizontal as well as in the vertical gating system design, as illustrated in Fig. 4-2. This extension is provided to trap the slag in the molten metal. It is typically about 1.5 times the width of the runner.

4.2.6. Gates or Ingates

These are the openings through which the molten metal enters the mold cavity.

The shape and the cross section of the ingate should be such that it can readily be broken off after casting solidification, and also that it allows the metal to enter quietly into the mold cavity. Depending on the application, various types of gates are used in the foundry practice. The various types are: top, bottom, parting plane and step.

Top ingate is the type of gating system through which the molten metal enters the mold cavity from the top, as shown in Fig. 4-10. Virtually, molten metal is poured into the pouring cup, which plays the role of an open riser. Since the hotter metal is at the top, a favorable temperature gradient, promoting directional solidification, is achieved. Also, the mold is filled very quickly. But, as the metal falls directly into the mold cavity through its height, it is likely to cause turbulence and mold erosion. Also, because of turbulence, metal is prone to form dross and, as such, top ingate is not advisable for nonferrous alloys, as well as ferrous alloys that are likely to form excessive dross. To reduce the mold erosion, pencil ingates, or a strainer core, are provided in the pouring cup (Fig. 4-10a). The top pour

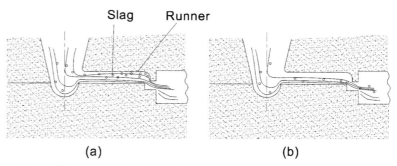

Slag   Runner

(a)   (b)

Fig. 4-9. Molten metal flow in the runner: (a) runner is full and traps slag inclusions; (b) runner is not full and slag inclusions are entering casting cavity.

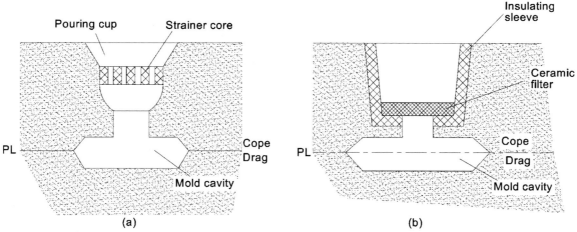

(a)   (b)

Fig. 4-10. Top gating system is a simplified type of gating that doesn't require sprue or runners: (a) with strainer core; (b) with insulating sleeve and ceramic foam filter.

gating system requires no additional sprue or runners, thus providing higher casting yield. It is suggested only for ferrous alloys and simple casting shapes that are essentially shallow in nature.

The capabilities of a top gating system to pour ferrous and nonferrous alloys are significantly extended with the introduction of direct pour top gating systems that incorporate an insulating sleeve with a ceramic foam filter (Fig. 4-10b).

Bottom ingate systems (Fig. 4-11) deliver molten metal from the bottom of the mold; as a result, metal enters the mold cavity slowly and will not cause any turbulence or mold erosion. Typically, this ingate is used in vertical pouring of sand, shell and permanent molds. An improperly designed bottom ingate may cause so-called jetting and metal oxidation. It takes a somewhat longer time for filling of the mold and also generates very unfavorable temperature gradients, compared to the top gating. Thus, the system may have to use additional padding of sections toward risers, and larger riser sizes to compensate for the unfavorable temperature distribution. Bottom gating may sometimes be preferable in conjunction with the use of side risers, since the metal enters the riser directly without going through the mold cavity.

Parting plane ingate systems (Fig. 4-12) are most widely used in sand castings. As the name implies, the metal enters the mold at the parting plane when part of the casting is in the cope and part in the drag. To ease ingate removal, the cross section at the area contacting with casting may be reduced, as shown in Fig. 4-12. However, if the drag portion of the mold cavity is deep, it is likely to cause mold erosion and aggravate dross formation and air entrapment when pouring nonferrous alloys. This can be somewhat reduced by making the ingate area larger, so that the molten metal velocity is minimized and it flows slowly along the walls into the mold cavity.

Step ingates (Fig. 4-13) are a design variation of parting line ingates. These can be used for some horizontally parted heavy and large sand castings, made by hand molding, as well as for small- and medium-size, vertically parted sand mold castings, employed in machine molding, and permanent mold and shell mold castings. The molten metal enters the mold cavity through a number of ingates, which are arranged in vertical steps. The size of the ingates is normally increased from top to bottom, such that the metal enters the mold cavity from the bottom-most ingate and then progressively moves to the higher ingates. This ensures a gradual mold filling without any mold erosion and turbulence.

4.3. Casting Yield

In designing a gating system, it is essential to choose a suitable type of gating system that considers the casting alloy, casting shape and size, and also takes into account the economical aspect such as total weight of the gating system, including risers.

In metalcasting, all the metal used while pouring does not finally end up as a casting. Typical routes the metal would take in a foundry are shown in Fig. 4-14. As can be seen, there are some losses in the melting due to burning some of the elements and materials. These losses may reach 6–10% of the total metal melted. Also, there is a possibility that some castings may be rejected because of the presence of various defects.

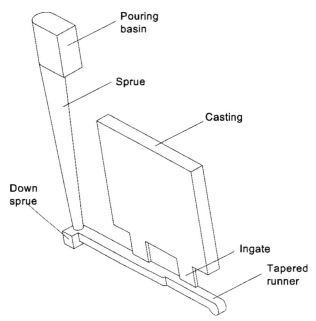

Fig. 4-11. Bottom ingate allows somewhat slower mold filling than top ingate, reducing turbulence and mold erosion. Improperly designed, it may cause so-called jetting actions and metal oxidation.

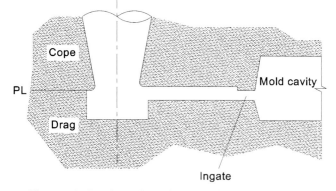

Fig. 4-12. Parting plane ingate. Note that the cross section of the ingate at the area contacting the casting is necked down to ease its removal at shakeout.

Upon completion of the casting process, the gating and risering systems are removed from the solidified casting, remelted and, along with scrapped castings, used again as raw material. Even when all gates and scrapped castings are remelted, the foundry still loses money on remelting costs and experiences inevitable metal losses during melting. To characterize the cost effectiveness of a given process and all the associated foundry operations, a term "casting yield" is used.

The casting yield, Y, is defined as the ratio of the actual casting weight, W, to the weight of metal poured into the mold, w, which includes the weight of the gating and risering system, and is expressed as follows (%):

$$Y = \% \ \frac{W}{w} \times 100 \qquad (4.1)$$

Casting yield is one of the major economic indicators of the foundry's operations. The higher the casting yield, the higher the economics of the foundry practice. Casting yield depends to a great extent on the casting alloys used and the complexity of the casting shape. Generally, those casting alloys that shrink heavily have lower casting yields. Also, massive and simple shapes have higher casting yield, compared to small and complex parts. Typical casting yields for different cast alloys are presented in Table 4-1.

4.4. Gating System Design

4.4.1. Basic Principles

In general, the major hydraulic laws that control liquid flow in a closed system may be applied to molten metal flow in the mold through the various channels of the gating system.

One of these laws is called Bernoulli's theorem. It states that at any point in a full system, the total energy head remains constant. The same stated in the equation form, ignoring frictional losses, is:

Table 4-1. Casting yield for some casting alloys.

Casting Alloy and Casting Description	Casting Yield Range, %
Steel	
heavy machinery parts	55 to 65
small castings	35 to 45
Ductile iron	
heavy machinery parts	55 to 65
small castings	45 to 55
Cast iron	
heavy machinery parts	65 to 75
small castings	45 to 55
Aluminum alloy	25 to 45

$$h + \frac{P}{w} + \frac{V^2}{2g} = \text{constant} \qquad (4.2)$$

Where

h = potential head, m

P = static pressure, Pa

V = liquid velocity, m/s

w = density of molten metal, kg/m³

g = gravitation constant, is equal 9.8 m/s².

Bernoulli's theorem may be interpreted in the application of metal flow into the mold in the following way: as the metal enters the pouring basin, it has the highest potential energy with no kinetic or pressure energies. But, as the metal moves through the gating system, a loss of energy occurs because of the friction between the molten metal and the mold walls. Also, heat is continuously lost through the mold material, though it is not represented in Bernoulli's equation.

Another law of fluid mechanics, which is useful in understanding the molten metal flow in a gating system, is the law of continuity, which states that the volume of metal flowing at any section in the mold is constant, if it is kept full. The same in equation form can be expressed as:

$$Q = A_1 V_1 = A_2 V_2 \qquad (4.3)$$

Where

Q = rate of flow, m³/s

A = area of cross section, m²

V = velocity of metal flow, m/s

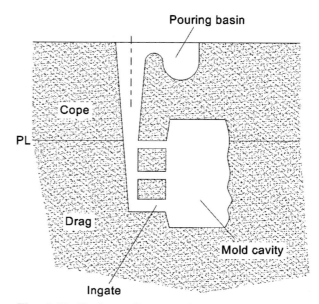

Fig. 4-13. Horizontally parted gating system with step ingate.

In application to the gating system, it means that any changes in the cross section of its components will result in changes in molten metal velocity. With decreasing cross section area, velocity is increased, and vice versa. It also means that if the cross section of a runner is larger than the sprue area, it will reduce the velocity of the molten metal stream and allow slag and nonmetallic inclusions to float up, and the runner would act as a scavenger for the system.

Applying the above equation of continuity along with the Bernoulli's equation also allowed optimization of the sprue shape. As mentioned previously, it was suggested that the sprue be tapered to reduce the aspiration of air due to the increased velocity as the metal flows down the sprue.

4.4.2. Fluidity or Fluid Life of Molten Metal

Dealing with the gating and riser design, it is absolutely important to know some specific casting alloy properties influencing system parameter selection. The term fluidity or fluid life is normally used in a foundry to designate the casting alloy's ability to stay fluid during mold cavity filling. The fluidity is a complex property, and there are a number of variables that affect it. Fluidity depends on the casting alloy's properties as well as the mold materials' properties.

The casting alloy's properties, which affect the fluidity to a great extent, are viscosity, heat content (degree of superheating), surface tension, freezing range and specific weight of the molten metal. The lower the coefficient of viscosity of the molten metal, the higher the fluidity will be, since the melt will be able to flow freely. Since the heat content and superheat of the molten metal decrease the coefficient of viscosity, it would also be responsible for an increase in the fluidity. Similarly, lower surface tension, which promotes wetting of the mold by the molten metal, would make the mold fill quickly, particularly in the narrow sections.

In general, the casting alloys, which have a narrow freezing range, have a higher fluidity than the wide freezing range alloys. In wide freezing range alloys, during the process of solidification, dendrites are spread over a much larger part of the mold and, thus, reduce the flow of the metal, decreasing the fluidity.

The mold properties that affect the fluidity of molten metal are the thermal characteristics, permeability and the mold cavity surface roughness. The way in which heat is transferred from the molten metal by the mold affects the ability of the metal to fill the mold cavity. For example, in a green sand mold, the fluidity would be lower since more heat is extracted by it than in a dry sand mold. The fluidity of molten metal in a mold that is coated with a refractory wash would be higher, compared to the one with no coating, due to slower heat transfer through the coating. Similarly, a higher permeable mold is conducive to better fluidity. Fluidity is significantly reduced when metal is poured in a permanent (metal) mold rather than in a sand mold, due to the higher thermal conductivity of the metallic mold. That is why proper preheating of metallic molds is required.

4.4.2.1. Fluidity Testing

Since fluidity depends on such a large number of diverse variables, it is not theoretically feasible to determine; therefore, practical testing is recommended. The most commonly used is the spiral fluidity test, shown schematically in Fig. 4-15. The casting poured into the mold is measured for the fluidity that is represented by the length of the solidified spiral.

The sand spiral mold should be made of the same sand composition used in the given casting process. If the fluidity test is intended to measure fluidity in a permanent mold, the mold for the fluidity spiral should be made of the same metal as the mold for the base process (Fig. 4-16). Before pouring, the metal fluidity mold should be coated with refractory material and preheated as are molds in the base process.

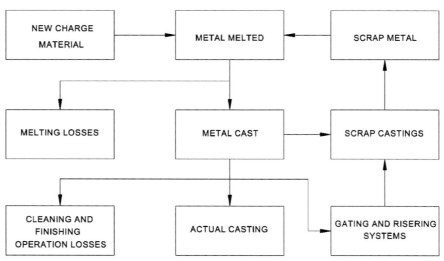

Fig. 4-14. Flow chart of metal utilization in the foundry.

Gray cast iron is the most fluid of all the ferrous alloys. The composition factor (CF) and the molten metal temperature (T) affect the fluidity of gray cast iron. Their combined effect on fluidity spiral length can be estimated by means of the following empirical relations:

Fluidity, cm = 37.846CF+0.228T–389.6   (4.4)

Fluidity, in.= 14.9CF+0.005T–155   (4.5)

Where

Composition factor CF=% C+0.25Si%+0.5P%

T=pouring temperature, °C for Equation 4.4 or °F for Equation 4.5

The graphical interpretation of the fluidity of sand mold poured gray iron as a function of the composition (CF), and the pouring temperature (T) are presented in Fig. 4.17.

Since the fluidity is affected by the pouring temperature, and to ensure the complete filling of the mold in a reasonable time, the mold pouring temperature is accordingly controlled. The pouring temperature should be a little above the melting temperature of the alloy, but with a sufficient enough superheat to account for the cooling of the molten metal from the time it is tapped from the furnace until it is poured into the mold. Recommended pouring temperatures for most of the casting alloys are given in Chapter 7, Melting Practices.

established generally by the practice at various foundries and by experiments. The general considerations for choosing a pouring time for gray cast iron may not be of much relevance for steels since they lose heat very fast and, therefore, the pouring time should be reduced. For nonferrous alloys, a longer pouring time would be beneficial, since they lose heat slowly and also tend to form dross if metal is poured too quickly.

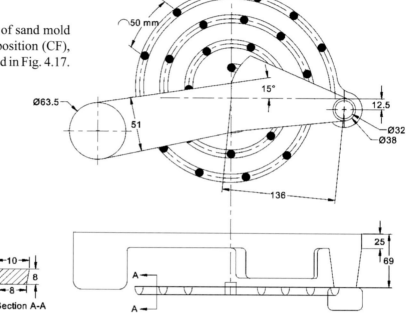

Fig. 4-15. Standard fluidity spiral design for sand casting (all dimensions are in mm).

4.4.3. Pouring Time

As mentioned earlier, one of the objectives for the gating system design is to fill the mold in the shortest time. The time for complete filling of a mold, termed as pouring time, is a very important criterion for the design of a gating system. Too long a pouring time requires a higher pouring temperature, and too short a pouring time means turbulent flow in the mold, which makes the casting defect prone. Thus, there is an optimum pouring time for any given casting poured of a given cast alloy.

The pouring time depends on the type of casting alloy, complexity of the casting, section thickness and casting size. The various relations used are not theoretically obtained, but

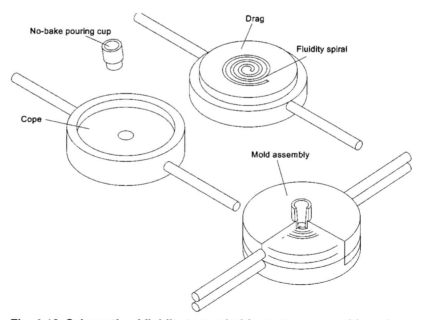

Fig. 4-16. Schematic of fluidity test spiral for permanent mold casting.

Because the thickness of a casting is affected, to a great extent, by the ratio of the surface area-to-volume of the casting, it is an important variable in calculating the optimum pouring time in addition to the weight of the casting itself. Normally, while considering the pouring weight of the casting, it may not be necessary to include the weight of the gating system, because the gating system is completely filled before metal starts entering the mold cavity. However, if the gating system is in comparable size to the actual casting, it is desirable to include its weight into the pouring weight calculation.

Following are some basic methods used to calculate the pouring time for different casting alloys:

- *Calculation of pouring time for a gray iron casting weighing less than 450 kg (1000 lb):*

$$\text{Pouring time}, t = K \left(1.41 + \frac{T}{14.59} \right) \sqrt{W} \ s \qquad (4.6)$$

Where

$$K = \frac{\text{Fluidity of iron in inches}}{40}$$

K = coefficient of fluidity

T = average section thickness, mm

W = pouring weight of the casting, kg

- *Calculation of pouring time for a gray iron casting weighting more than 450 kg (1000 lb):*

$$\text{Pouring time}, t = K \left(1.236 + \frac{T}{16.65} \right) \sqrt[3]{W} \ s \qquad (4.7)$$

Typical pouring time for a green sand gray iron casting weighing within 10–20 kg (22–45 lb) is approximately 6–10 sec; for comparison, for a casting weighing within 80–100 kg (175–220 lb), pouring time varies from 20 to 30 sec.

- *Calculation of pouring time for a steel casting:*

$$\text{Pouring time}, t = (2.4335 - 0.3953 \log W) \sqrt{W} \ s \ (4.8)$$

W = pouring weight of the casting, kg

- *Calculation of pouring time for a vertically parted shell mold ductile iron casting:*

$$\text{Pouring time}, t = K \sqrt{W} \ s \qquad (4.9)$$

Where

K = 2.080 for sections less than 10 mm (0.4 in.) thick

K = 2.670 for sections 10 to 25 mm (0.4-1.0 in.) thick

K = 2.970 for sections more than 25 mm (1 in.) thick

Typical pouring rates of different casting alloys in sand molds are given in Table 4-2. The calculated values from any of the above formula may be compared with data in Table 4-2.

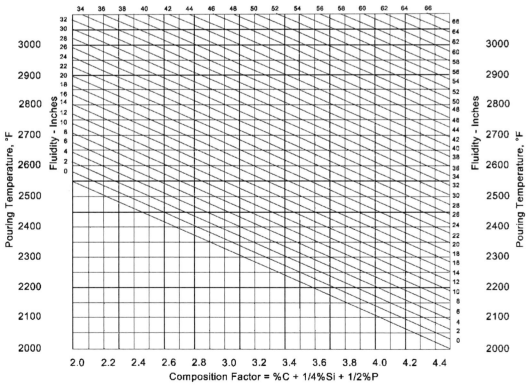

Fig. 4-17. Fluidity of gray iron as a function of chemistry (% of C, Si and P) and pouring temperature. [From Reference 5]

Example 4-1

Calculate the optimum pouring time of a sand casting, whose weight is 100 kg and wall thickness of 25 mm. Assume fluidity of iron is 32 inches. Calculate both for cast iron and steel.

Gray cast iron (Equation 4.6)

$$\text{Pouring time} = \frac{32}{40}\left(1.41 + \frac{25}{14.59}\right)\sqrt{100} = 24.988\ s \approx 25\ s$$

Steel (Equation 4.8)

$$\text{Pouring time} = (\,2.4335 - 0.3953\log 100\,)\sqrt{100} = 16.429\ s \approx 16\ s$$

4.4.4. Pressurized vs. Nonpressurized System

Having calculated the optimum pouring time, it is now necessary to establish the main control area. This meters the metal flow into the mold cavity so that the mold is completely filled within the calculated pouring time. This controlling area is called the choke area, and has the smallest total cross-section area of the gating system. The gating ratio refers to the proportion of the cross-sectional areas between the sprue, runner and ingates, and is generally denoted as:

Area of sprue: Area of runner(s): Area of ingate(s)

Depending upon choke location, gating systems are classified as:

- Nonpressurized system, in which the choke is located at the bottom of the sprue (Fig. 4-18a);
- Pressurized system, in which the choke is located at the ingates (Fig. 4-18b).

A nonpressurized gating system has total runner and ingate areas larger than the sprue area. In this system, there is no pressure existing in the molten metal flow, which helps reduce turbulence. When the metal enters the mold cavity through multiple ingates, the cross section of the runner should accordingly be reduced at each

runner breakup, to allow for equal distribution of metal volume through all the ingates.

The typical example of a gating ratio in this system is as follows:

Area of sprue: Area of runner(s): Area of ingate(s) = 1:2:3 or 1:3:4

The disadvantages of nonpressurized gating include possible air aspiration due to the fact that some elements may be filled partially. A tapered sprue is invariably used with this system. The runners are maintained in the drag

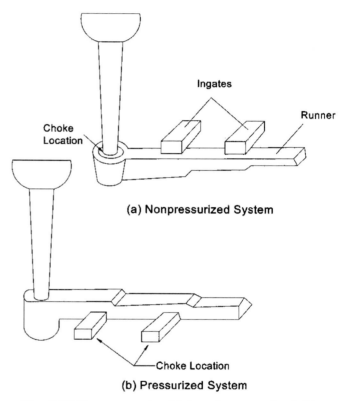

Fig. 4-18 Nonpressurized (a) and pressurized (b) gating systems.

Table 4-2 Typical Pouring Rates for Sand Castings.

Cast Alloy	Pouring Rate in kg/s (lb/s) for Castings Weight, kg (lb)			
	up to 10 (22)	10–50 (22–110)	50–100 (110–220)	100–500 (220–1100)
Gray Iron	1.1 (2.4)	1.5–2.0 (3.3–4.4)	3.0–4.0 (6.6–8.8)	3.5–6.0 (7.7–13.2)
Steel	1.2–1.4 (2.6–3.1)	1.9–2.5 (4.2–5.5)	4.0–5.0 (8.8–11.0)	4.5–7.0 (9.9–15.4)
Aluminum	0.25–0.3 (0.55–0.65)	0.5–0.7 (1.1–1.5)	1.0–1.3 (2.2–2.9)	1.2–2.0 (2.6–4.4)

while the gates are kept in the cope, to ensure that the runners are full. Casting yield is reduced because of the large volume of metal contained in the runners and gates. Nonpressurized gating systems are typically applied to alloys sensitive to oxidation, such as aluminum and magnesium alloys and, to some extent, to ductile iron and high-alloy steel.

A pressurized gating system normally consists of the ingates with a cross-sectional area that is the smallest in the system, thus maintaining a back-pressure throughout the gating system. Because of this, the molten metal is more turbulent and generally flows full and, thereby, can minimize the air aspiration, even when a straight sprue is used. When multiple ingates are used, this system allows all the gates to flow full. These systems generally provide a higher casting yield, since the volume of metal used in the runners and gates is reduced. Because of the turbulence and associated dross formation, this type of gating system is not used for light alloys, but is advantageously used for ferrous castings.

Gating ratio of a typical pressurized gating system is as follows:

Areas of sprue: Area of runner(s): Area of ingate(s) = 4:8:3 or 1.2:(1.1–1.3):1.0

4.4.5. Choke Area Calculation

The first step in the dimensioning of the gating system is selecting the type, pressurized or nonpressurized, which determines the choke location. After selecting the type of gating system, the appropriate gating ratio will be established and the choke area will be calculated. Knowing the choke area, the cross-sections of the other elements can be determined.

For a nonpressurized gating system, the choke is located at the bottom of the sprue; hence, the first element to be designed in this type of gating system is the sprue size and its proportions. For a pressurized gating system, the ingates are designed first, where the area of the choke would be the total area of the ingates.

The choke area can be calculated using the following equation:

$$A = \frac{W}{d\,t\,C\,\sqrt{2\,g\,H}} \qquad (4.10)$$

Where

A = choke area, mm^2

W = casting pouring weight, kg

t = pouring time, s

d = density of the molten metal, kg/mm^3

g = gravitational constant, mm/s^2

H = effective sprue height or metallostatic head or hydraulic head, mm

C = efficiency coefficient, which is a function of the gating system used

The effective sprue height (H) depends on the casting dimensions and the type of gating system used, and can be calculated using the following relations, as shown in Fig. 4-19.

Top gate, $H = h$ (Fig. 4-19a)

Bottom gate $H = h - \dfrac{c}{2}$ (Fig. 4-19b)

Parting gate $H = h - \dfrac{p^2}{2\,c}$ (Fig. 4-19c)

Where

H = height of sprue, mm

P = height of mold cavity in cope, mm

c = total height of mold cavity, mm

The efficiency coefficient of the gating system depends on the variations in design of its elements. Whenever a runner changes direction or joins with another runner or ingate, there is some loss in the metallostatic head, all of which, when taken properly into consideration, would give the overall efficiency of the gating system.

Ideally, the elements of a gating system should be circular in cross section, since this shape has lower surface area-to-volume ratio, which would reduce heat and friction losses. Moreover, streamlining the various gating elements would greatly increase the volumetric efficiency of the gating system and allow for smaller size gates and runners, which would increase the casting yield.

Average values of the efficiency coefficient are provided for typical gating systems in Table 4-3, which may be used for choke calculation.

Example 4-2

Calculate the choke area for the Grade 25 gray iron casting shown in Fig. 4-20 with the gating system.

1. Calculate the volume of the casting = 500 × 250 x 50= 6.25 × 10^6 mm^3

2. Calculate weight of the casting = 7.0 ×10^{-6}×6.25 × 10^6= 43.75 kg

3. Assuming a composition factor of 4.0 and a pouring temperature of 1300°C (2372°F), the fluidity, obtained from Fig. 4-17, is 22 inches.

4. Calculate the pouring time using Equation 4.6:

Pouring time, $t = \dfrac{22}{40}\left(1.41\ +\ \dfrac{43.75}{14.59}\right)$

$\sqrt{43.75} = 16.04\ \text{s} \approx 16\ \text{s}$

5. Calculate effective sprue height. Assuming a top gating system with 100 mm cope height, effective sprue height = 100 mm (Fig. 4-19)

6. Select efficiency coefficient, C, from Table 4-3, assuming that the gating system is pressurized and consists of two runners with four ingates; C = 0.73

7. Calculate choke area using equation 4.10, assuming the density of the liquid metal = $6.90 \times 10^{-6} kg/mm^3$

$$\text{Choke area, A} = \frac{43.75}{6.90 \times 10^{-6} \times 16 \times 0.73 \sqrt{2 \times 9800 \times 100}}$$

$$= \frac{43.75}{6.90 \times 10^{-6} \times 16 \times 0.73 \sqrt{2 \times 9800 \times 100}} = 387.855 \text{ mm}^2$$

8. Because in a pressurized gating system the choke is located in the ingates, the area of the choke calculated in 7 is the total cross section of four ingates each with area of 97 mm². Assuming rectangular cross sections for ingates, the ingate dimensions would be 16 × 6 mm.

4.4.6. Ingate Design

The following points should be kept in mind while choosing the positioning and size of the ingates:

- The ingate should not be located near a protruding part of the mold, to avoid the striking of vertical mold walls by the molten metal stream

- The ingates should preferably be placed along the longitudinal axis of the mold wall

- The ingates should not be placed near a core print or a chill

- The ingate cross-sectional area should preferably be smaller than the smallest thickness of the casting, so that the ingates solidify first and isolate the castings from the gating system. This would reduce the possibility of air aspiration through the gating system in case of metal shrinkage

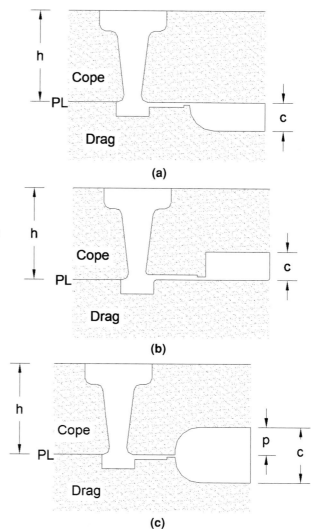

(a)

(b)

(c)

Fig. 4-19. Schematics for effective sprue height calculations for different gating system arrangements: (a) top, (b) bottom, (c) parting.

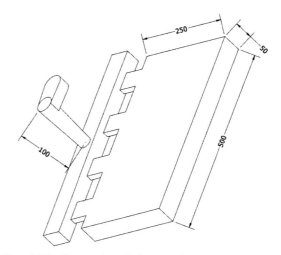

Fig. 4-20. Example of the casting for choke area calculation (all dimensions are in mm).

Table 4-3. Efficiency Coefficients for Various Types of Gating Systems.

Type of System	Nonpressurized	Pressurized
Single runner	0.90	0.73
Two runners with multiple ingates, no bends in runners	0.90	0.73
Two runners with multiple ingates, 90° bends in runners	0.85	0.70

In general, the ingates are made wider than the height (called aspect ratio), up to a ratio of 5. This facilitates easy removal of gating from the casting, after solidification. To simplify the ingate's removal, it may sometimes be preferable to reduce the area of actual connection between the ingate and the casting by means of a necking down, as shown earlier in Fig.4-12, or a V-notch made in a green mold, or by using a dry sand core for this purpose.

Small castings may be designed with a single ingate. However, large or complex castings require multiple ingates to completely fill all the sections of the castings effectively, as shown in Fig. 4-21.

In the case of multiple ingates, care has to be taken to see that all the ingates will be distributing the molten metal uniformly. If the runner system is designed with uniform cross sections, it is possible that more metals is likely to flow through the farthest gate from the sprue than through the other gates, particularly in the case of a nonpressurized gating system. To create a more uniform flow through all the ingates, the runner area should be progressively reduced (tapered) after each ingate, so that restriction on the metal flow would be provided, as is shown in Fig. 4-21(a).

For cylindrical castings, the sprue may be located on the axis of rotation with sufficient number of radial runners feeding the casting. An alternative arrangement is one where the sprue is located to one side of the casting and a runner is located around the periphery, with the properly positioned ingates, as shown in Fig. 4-21(b). In the case of thin castings, misruns are a problem; therefore, they should be poured as quickly as possible with a number of ingates all around the casting.

Example 4-3

Calculate the gating requirements for the casting shown in Fig. 4-22 to be cast in high-alloy steel.

1. Calculate the volume of the casting as a sum of the hemisphere, cylinder and flange volumes:

$$\text{Hemisphere} = \frac{4}{3} \times \frac{\pi}{2}(68^3 - 60^3) = 206,156 \text{ mm}^3$$

$$\text{Top cylinder} = \frac{\pi}{4}(58^2 - 30^2) \cdot 42 = 81,279 \text{ mm}^3$$

$$\text{Flange} = \frac{\pi}{4}(200^2 - 120^2)10 = 201,062 \text{ mm}^3$$

Total volume = 206,156 + 201,062 + 81,279 = 488,497 mm³

2. Weight of the casting = 488,497 × 7.80 × 10-6 = 3.81 kg

There are two castings in the mold and their weight 3.81 × 2 = 7.62 kg

$$\text{Weight of metal poured} = \frac{2 \times 3.81}{0.60} = 12.7 \text{ kg}$$

(Assuming a casting yield of 0.60)

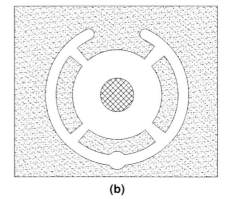

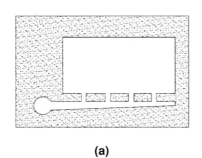

(a)   (b)

Fig. 4-21. Multiple ingates designed to induce uniform flow through all the ingates for various types of castings: (a) flat, rectangular; (b) hollow cylinder with central core.

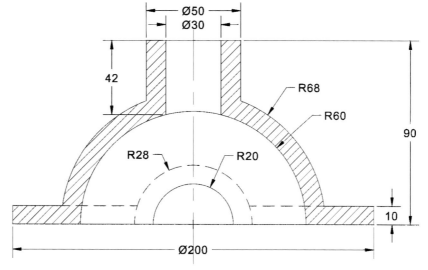

Fig. 4-22. Example casting for gating calculations (all dimensions are in mm).

3. Using Equation 4.9, calculate pouring time:

Pouring time $= (2.4335 - 0.3953 \cdot \log 12.70) \sqrt{12.70} = 7.12$ s

Pouring rate $= \dfrac{12.7}{7.12} = 1.784$ kg/s

4. Choosing parting ingates and two castings in the mold, the casting arrangement would be as shown in Fig. 4-23 and the effective sprue height is equal to 150 mm.

Assume that this is a nonpressurized gating system (the choke is located in the sprue) with one runner and two ingates. For this combination, the efficiency coefficient of the gating system from Table 4-3 is 0.90.

$$\text{Choke area} = \frac{12.7}{7.12 \times 0.90 \times 7.7 \times 10^{-6} \times \sqrt{2 \times 9800 \times 150}}$$
$$= 150.11 \text{ mm}^2$$

Choke diameter $= 13.82$ mm ≈ 14 mm

5. Calculate runner area and dimensions. Assuming a gating ratio of 1:2:2.

Runner area $2 \times \pi \times \dfrac{14^2}{4} = 307.88$ mm^2

Assuming a rectangular cross section, the runner dimensions would be approximately 12.5 x 25 mm.

6. Calculate ingates area and dimensions.

Each gate area $= 0.5 \times 307.88 = 153.94$ mm^2

Assuming an aspect ratio of 4 (the width to height ratio), the size of the gate is approximately 6 × 25 mm.

4.5. Slag Trap Systems

The presence of slag and other nonmetallic inclusions is one of the widespread causes of casting defects that are typical for both ferrous and nonferrous alloy castings.

There are several sources of nonmetallic inclusions: slag, dross and flux residues arise during melting; refractory particles from the furnace and ladle; oxides caused by turbulence in the gating system; and sand inclusions from the eroded mold or core.

In ductile iron, these nonmetallic inclusions are complicated by the inevitable presence of magnesium in the iron, which is very oxidizable and reactive. Magnesium oxides, sulfides, nitrides, silicates and various reaction products are the major constituents of the nonmetallic inclusions in ductile iron that can become defects.

In order to obtain sound casting quality, it is essential that the slag and other impurities be fully removed from the molten metal before it enters the mold cavity. Apart from the use of pouring basins with or without plugs and strainer cores, some other methods used to trap the slag in the gating system area are: runner extensions, whirl ingates and metal filtration.

4.5.1. Runner Extension

This feature is used by extending the runner beyond the ingate so that the momentum of the metal will carry it past the gates and into a blind alley, as shown in Fig. 4-2 and 4-22. If the gating system is properly designed, clean metal can be expected to go into the mold after complete filling of the runner extension. A runner extension having a minimum of twice the runner width is desirable.

4.5.2. Whirl Ingate

This design was employed successfully to trap the slag in steel castings (Fig. 4-24). This utilizes the principle of centrifugal action to throw the dense metal to the periphery and retain the lighter slag at the center. To achieve this action, it is necessary that entry area be at least 1.5 times the exit area so that the metal is quickly built up at the center. Also, the metal should revolve up to 270° before reaching the exit gate so as to gain enough time for separating the impurities. Sometimes, for more effective slag trapping, this gating may be designed as a centrifugal bob with more space at the top, allowing impurities to float up.

4.5.3. Metal Filtration in Gating System

4.5.3.1. Filtration Mechanisms

Molten metal filtration has become a common practice widely used by foundries to produce clean, defect-free castings. Depending upon the type of filter, there are

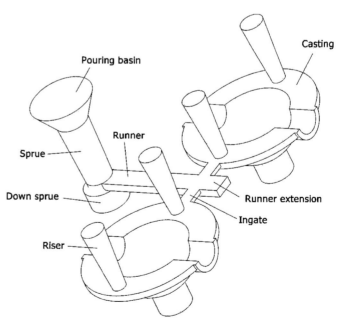

Fig. 4-23. Two castings with gating arrangement for example casting shown in Fig. 4-22.

three major categories of filtration, based on the mode of inclusion capture as is illustrated in Fig. 4-25. These filtration categories are: screening, cake and deep-bed

The screening type of filtration provides entrapping of only solid particles with sizes larger than the openings of the filter. When the filtering surface collects a certain amount of particles, the cake type of filtration occurs, which allows entrapping of smaller size particles. The long tortuous path inside a filter provides deep-bed type of filtration. This filtration mechanism allows elimination of both solid and liquid impurities, which are smaller than the surface openings of the filter.

4.5.3.2. Filter Classification

Currently, foundries use three types of filters: ceramic foam, ceramic cellular and woven refractory cloth. The filters have different impurity removal ability, thermal shock resistance, dimensional stability and cost.

Ceramic foam filters are classified depending upon their dimensional structure as coarse (No. 10), medium (No. 15) and fine (No. 25). With a decrease of the filter cell size, the active filtration surface area is increased but, simultaneously, a flow rate through this filter is decreased, which requires using larger size filters (Fig. 4-26).

The reticulated silicon carbide (SiC) ceramic foam filter has excellent thermal shock resistance up to 1565°C (2850°F) without creeping or melting. Also, it is chemically inert to resist any corrosive attack by both the molten metal and slag, and provides effective filtration of irons and nonferrous alloys. For higher pouring temperature carbon and alloyed steels, other materials, like zirconia (ZrO_2) with a thermal shock resistance of up to 2500°C (4532°F) are used.

These types of filters provide deep-bed filtration mode insuring effective filtration in 3-D level. Ceramic foam filters operate quite differently from a fiberglass or metallic screen filter. Fiberglass and metallic screens filter the molten metal by not allowing particles larger than the screen mesh to pass through the filter. The high internal surface area of the filter helps in the retention of the inclusions by gradually reducing the pore size of the filter; therefore, increasing the efficiency of the ceramic filter. This, in turn, increases the internal surface area of the filter.

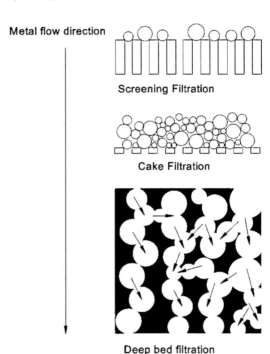

Fig. 4-25. Three major categories of filtration based on the mode of inclusions captured.

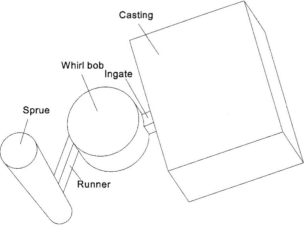

Fig. 4-24. Whirl ingate utilizes the principle of centrifugal action to throw the dense metal to the periphery and separate the lighter slag at the top and the center.

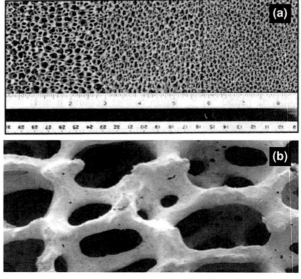

Fig. 4-26. Structure of ceramic foam filters: (a) dimensional structure; (b) SEM image of filter cell.

Figure 4-27 illustrates typical placement of a ceramic foam filter in the gating system of a horizontally parted sand mold, either in a horizontal (a) or vertical (b) position.

Latest studies have showed effectiveness of placing ceramic foam filters in each runner in multirunner gating system, particularly in aluminum casting.

In comparison with other types of filters, the reticulated ceramic foam filter can also effectively remove inclusion particles significantly smaller than the filter cell size due to the fact that the filter walls have good adhesive ability. In addition, a tortuous path inside the foam filter creates a continuous vortex flow of molten metal, essentially increasing the effectiveness of filtration. One disadvantage of a ceramic foam filter is the possibility of blocking the filter with previously captured inclusions.

Graphite-based, nonceramic, reticulated foam filters, developed for filtering molten aluminum alloys in both sand and permanent molds, provide significant advantages in performance and remelt characteristics compared with conventional silicon carbide- or alumina-based ceramic foam filters.

The graphite composition is more easily wetted by molten aluminum than are typical filter ceramics, so the metal head height required to prime the filter in the early stages of pouring may be reduced. Additionally, the low density and low thermal capacity of these filters reduce heat loss from the metal to the filter, preventing premature freezing and allowing feeding through the filter when used in direct pouring applications.

Because graphite-based filters do not contain abrasive ceramic components, the foundry has more freedom in application and placement—even very close to casting surfaces—since the filter can be removed by cutting or machining, without tool damage. With their low density (approximately 60% that of comparable ceramic foam filters), these filters float readily in remelt, so they can be easily removed by skimming.

Ceramic cellular filters with direct holes can be produced by pressing or extruding techniques. The extruded filter has holes with square cross-sections, each filter being formed by the slicing of a continuous extruded bar. The pressed filter has holes with round cross-sections as shown in Figure. 4-28, and is formed in one pressing operation, after which it is dried and fired.

The mechanisms of these filters are typically screening and cake type of filtration. The deep-bed filtration can occur only around the cell edges because the edge causes some vortex of molten metal flow. It activates the mixing and encourages micro particles to contact with the cell walls, which increases the chance of particles to adhere. The pressed filters have significantly more hot and cold

strength. Both pressed and extruded filters have a high metal flow rate, and small dimensional tolerance, which is especially important for automatic filter installation.

Lately introduced to foundry practice, the triangular-cell, extruded ceramic filter, shown in Fig. 4-29, possesses better filtration ability and improved cold strength, in comparison with a standard square-cell, extruded ceramic filter. The triangular structure of the filter decreases the hydraulic diameter, which is the ratio of the cell's cross-section area to its perimeter, which allows entrapping of inclusions of smaller size. In addition, the cell angle, 60° instead 90°, activates the "screening" and "cake" filtration due to smaller openings, and creates the prerequisite for "deep-bed" filtration due to increased capillary forces.

Woven refractory cloth filters (Fig. 4-30) are made from fibers of 97–99% silica (SiO_2) and have a various mesh (opening) sizes, from 1 to 3 mm (0.04 to 0.12 in.).They provide different flow rates and filtration effects. Cloth filters with a 1.5 to 2.0 mm (0.06 to 0.08 in.) mesh size are recommended for ductile iron and compacted graphite iron, as well as for nonferrous alloys. For steel, gray iron, malleable and white iron, cloth filters with 1.0 to 1.5 mm

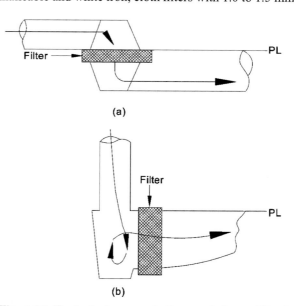

(a)

(b)

Fig. 4-27. Typical placement of ceramic foam filter in a gating system of horizontally parted sand molds: (a) horizontally positioned; (b) vertically positioned.

Fig. 4-28. A pressed ceramic cellular filter with round openings.

(0.04 to 0.06 in.) mesh size are found more useful. Some types of cloth filters can be resin-coated or framed. Resin-coated cloth filters have essentially better wettability. While framed filters are used for both horizontal and vertical orientations, the unframed cloth filters are typically used only for the horizontal positions in the gating system.

In any case, the cope ingates should be located above the runner system, to minimize entrapment of air and formation of dross inclusions downstream from the filter. Woven cloth filters can receive any degree of deflection during pouring and solidification, which is an undoubted disadvantage.

4.5.3.3. Inclusion Identification

Typically, to identify the type and chemical composition of inclusions trapped into filters, scanning electron microscopy (SEM) is used. The filters that are totally plugged with retained inclusions are sectioned, polished and analyzed, qualitatively, using SEM technique. Figures 4-31 through 4-36 illustrate the results of SEM and microchemical analyses of typical nonmetallic inclusions trapped in a ceramic foam filter during the pouring ductile iron.

Figure 4-31 is a typical SEM image of the retained dross inclusions. Figure 4-32 shows the microchemical analysis (MCA) of these retained dross inclusions. As can be seen, the inclusion material is primarily magnesium silicate. The analysis shows that the degree of loading filters with the dross defects increased with increasing residual magnesium content.

Another type of inclusion, trapped by filter, is slag-sand agglomerate shown in Fig. 4-33. Microchemical analysis of slag components (Fig. 4-34) indicated that the slag is composed primarily of fayalite ($2FeO.SiO_2$).

In some cases, accumulated slag inclusions have been identified as iron oxides attached to a graphite structure (Figs. 4-35 and 4-36). This combination of dross defect and the deteriorated graphite nodules adhering to them were present in ductile iron with increased residual magnesium content.

As can be seen, incorporating a ceramic foam filter into the gating system effectively removes various types of nonmetallic inclusions.

References

1. Schleg, F.P., *Technology of Metalcasting*, American Foundry Society, Des Plaines, 2003.

2. ASM: *Metals Handbook Vol. 15, Casting*, American Society of Metals, Metals Park, -2008.

3. Sandford, P., "DYPUR- the Direct Pouring Approach for Non-Ferrous Foundries," *Foundry Practice*, No. 217, April 1989, pp.15-17.

4. Pischel, R.P., "Direct Pouring of Aluminum. Improves Yields and Quality," *Foundry Management & Technology,* June 1993, pp. 40-44.

5. Hiene, R.W., C.R.Loper and P.C.Rosenthal, *Principles of Metal Casting*, McGraw-Hill, 1967.

6. Schmahl, J.R., L.S. Aubrey,"Filtration with Reticulated Silicon Carbide Foam: An Effective Means for Inclusion Removal in Gray and Nodular Iron Castings," *AFS Transactions*, Vol.101, 1993, pp.1011-1020.

7. Lerner, Y.S., L.S. Aubrey, "Development of an Improved Direct Pour System for Aluminum Casting," *Proceedings of First International Conference on the Gating, Filling and Feeding of Aluminum Casting,* October 10-13, 1999, Nashville, Tennessee, pp.148-158.

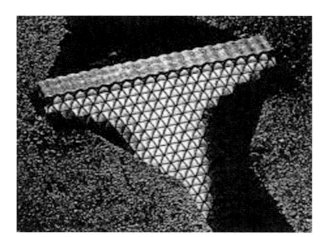

Fig. 4-29. Typical placement of a triangular-cell, extruded ceramic filter in the runner, prior to pouring the mold.

Fig. 4-30. Framed resin-coated refractory cloth filters with 1.0 × 1.0 mm (0.04 × 0.04 in.) mesh opening.

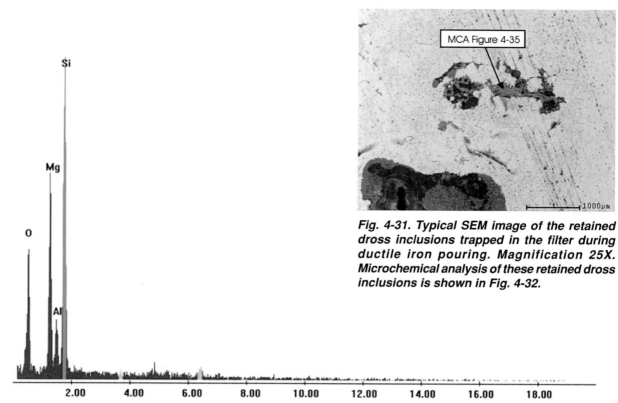

Fig. 4-31. Typical SEM image of the retained dross inclusions trapped in the filter during ductile iron pouring. Magnification 25X. Microchemical analysis of these retained dross inclusions is shown in Fig. 4-32.

Fig. 4-32. Microchemical analysis of retained dross inclusions trapped in the filter during ductile iron pouring (Fig. 4-31) indicating that the inclusion material is primarily magnesium silicate.

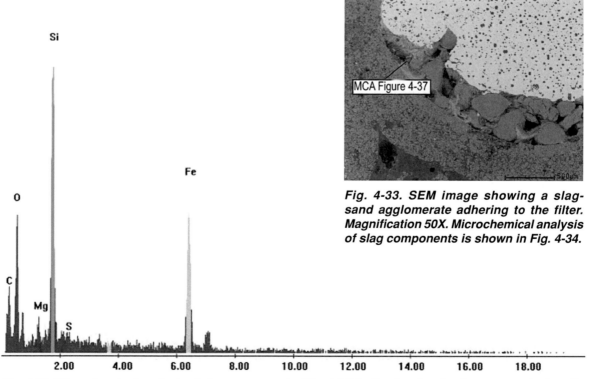

Fig. 4-33. SEM image showing a slag-sand agglomerate adhering to the filter. Magnification 50X. Microchemical analysis of slag components is shown in Fig. 4-34.

Fig. 4-34. Microchemical analysis of slag components (Fig. 4-33) indicating the slag is composed primarily of fayalite ($2FeO \cdot SiO_2$).

Review Questions

4.1 Define the various elements that comprise the gating system.

4.2 Describe the major requirements of a gating system in any casting.

4.3 Summarize the functions served by the pouring basin in a sand casting.

4.4 Sketch a pouring basin design with an arrangement for trapping slag.

4.5 Explain why the sprue should be tapered.

4.6 Describe the various methods available to a foundry engineer to reduce the momentum of the molten metal in the mold.

4.7 Describe the methods used to trap slag in a runner.

4.8 Explain the meaning of "gating ratio."

4.9 Describe the function of a runner extension in a gating system.

4.10 Give the details of the various types of ingates that are normally used.

4.11 Specify the advantages of the top ingate, and give its applications.

4.12 Compare the advantages and disadvantages of bottom and top ingates.

4.13 Discuss casting yield and explain its importance.

4.14 Define fluidity of cast alloys and methods for its measurements.

4.15 Explain the parameters that cause the pouring time of a given casting to vary.

4.16 Define choke area in castings. Explain how gating systems are classified based on choke location.

4.17 Discuss the criteria used for designing the pouring basin.

4.18 Differentiate between pressurized and nonpressurized gating systems with reference to the applications.

4.19 Discuss the reasons to use a nonpressurized gating system for the nonferrous metals.

4.20 Define the functions of stopper plugs used for pouring heavy-weight castings.

4.21 How are the ingate position and size determined?

4.22 Write a short note on whirl ingates.

4.23 Describe types of filters used for molten metal filtration.

4.24 Outline the advantages of ceramic foam filters in comparison to cloth filters.

4.25 Describe the technique used to identify the type and chemistry of nonmetallic inclusions in cast alloys.

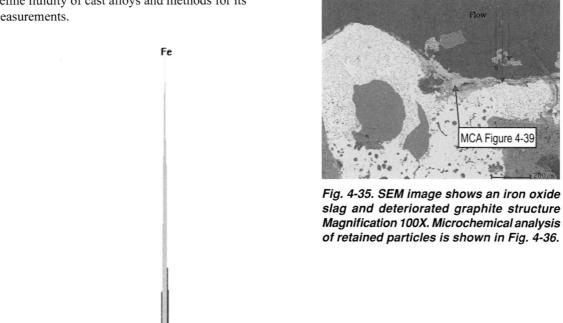

Fig. 4-35. SEM image shows an iron oxide slag and deteriorated graphite structure Magnification 100X. Microchemical analysis of retained particles is shown in Fig. 4-36.

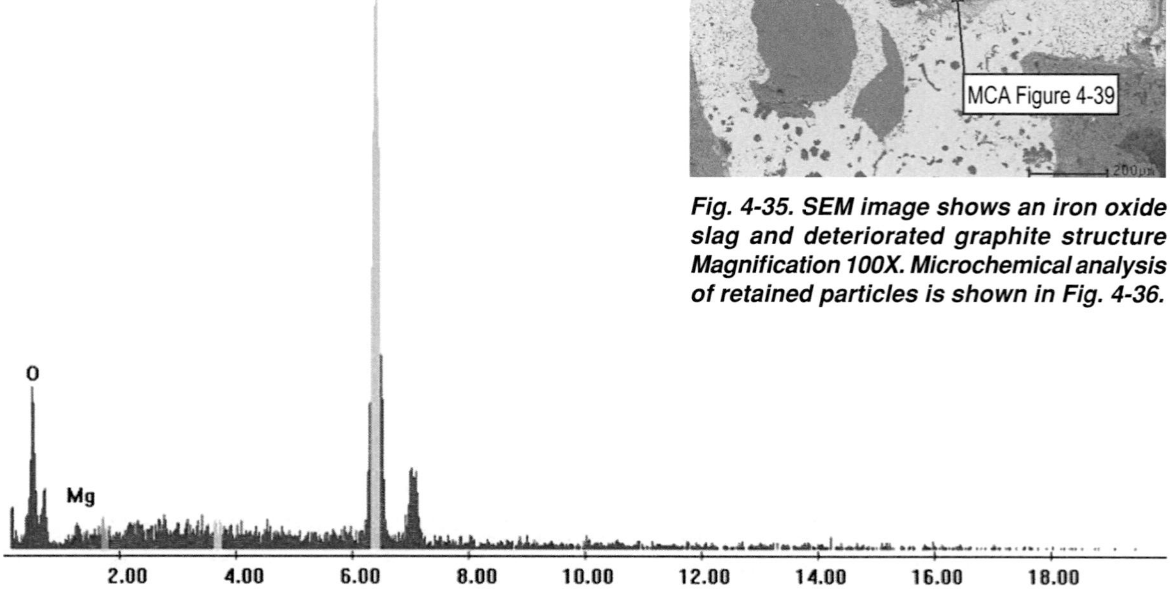

Fig. 4-36. Microchemical analysis of retained particles (Fig. 4-35) indicates the slag is composed predominantly of iron oxide.

Problem

4.1. Examine the drawing of the machined component shown in Fig. 4-37 to determine its suitability for the sand mold casting in gray iron Grade 25. Define the parting line, cope and drag parts, possible core and core prints locations. Design the gating system and give the details of the gating system elements with the calculated dimensions. This will be elaborated on in the Solutions manual.

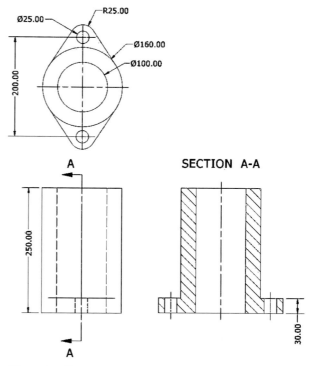

Fig. 4-37. Example casting for Problem 4.1.

RISERING AND FEEDING

5

Objectives

Risers serve to feed castings during solidification, compensate for volumetric contraction and prevent shrinkage-related defects. After studying this chapter the reader should be able to:

- Define solidification shrinkage and identify its major phases
- Explain directional solidification and measures to promote it
- Describe how alloy freezing range influences type of solidification shrinkage
- Design risers for specific applications using scientific principles
- Discuss how feeding distance may affect the effectiveness of risers
- Use chills and cooling fins to locally control solidification rate and reduce the casting defects
- Apply different feeding aids to obtain defect-free castings
- Utilize solidification modeling for optimization of casting process, scrap and cost reduction

Keywords

Solidification, Molten Metal, Mold Cavity, Casting, Green Sand, Solidification Temperature, Solidification Rate Enhancement, Direction Solidification, Liquid Shrinkage, Solidification Shrinkage, Solid Shrinkage, Volumetric Contraction, Solidification Time, Short Freezing Range, Long Freezing Range, Carbon Equivalent, Steel Casting, Shrinkage Void, Graphite Precipitation, Riser, Riser Neck, Gating System, Risering System, Hot Spot, Top Riser, Side Riser, Blind Riser, Open Riser, Hot (Live) Riser, Cold (Dead) Riser, Modulus Method, Casting Modulus, Shape Factor, Feeding Distance, End Effect, Feeding Aids, Chill, Water-Cooled Chill, Air-Cooled Chill, Copper Chill, Iron Chill, Cooling Fin, Riser Sleeve, Insulating Riser Sleeve, Exothermic Riser Sleeve, Insertible Riser Sleeve, Breaker Core, Casting Yield, Scrap, Cost Reduction, Solidification Modeling, Solidification Behavior, Numerical Modeling, Meshing The Model, Simulation, Sand Mold, Aluminum Alloy, Ductile Iron, Exothermic Compound, Thermal Conductivity, Mold Filling, Filling Time, Pattern, Mold Cavity, Nobake Sand Molding, Heat Transfer.

5.1. Casting Solidification and Shrinkage

Shrinkage is the volumetric contraction of the cast alloy upon its cooling in the mold, and changing from liquid to solid state and further cooling to room temperature. The casting alloy undergoes three subsequent stages:

- The first stage takes place in the liquid phase, when the alloy cools from its pouring temperature to the solidification temperature (liquidus). It is called liquid shrinkage. Its volume depends on the degree of superheat of molten metal over its solidification temperature. Increased superheating would lead to an increase in liquid shrinkage and overall solidification shrinkage. For example, heating molten steel over its solidification temperature will increase its volumetric shrinkage 1.6–1.8% per 100°C (212°F).
- The second stage, called solidification shrinkage, is liquid-to-solid shrinkage, which takes place when molten metal solidifies—cools from liquidus to solidus.
- The third and final stage of shrinkage, called solid shrinkage, occurs in the solid stage upon casting cooling from solidus to ambient temperature. This is also called patternmaker's or linear shrinkage, because it is taken into account as a shrinkage allowance while making the pattern.

The first two stages of shrinkage (liquid shrinkage and solidification shrinkage) directly influence the size of the riser and casting yield. The function of the riser is to compensate for all the volumetric changes as a source of molten metal supply during casting solidification.

Figure 5-1 schematically illustrates the sequence of solidification of a flange-type steel casting in a sand mold. Shown are the approximate locations of solidification zones, formed during different time intervals, which progressively move from mold walls toward the center. As time progresses, the metal starts freezing from all sides, trapping the molten metal inside. Further solidification results in volumetric shrinkage due to the change in temperature. At the end of solidification, shrinkage-related defects such as voids or porosity are likely to form in the casting, unless additional molten metal is fed into these places. These are termed hot spots, since they remain hot because metal is still staying liquid until the end of solidification.

Therefore, a reservoir of molten metal is to be maintained from which the metal can flow readily into the casting when the need arises. These reservoirs are called risers. While designing the riser for cast irons poured in a green sand mold, another factor needs to be taken into consideration: The riser should also compensate for volumetric changes caused by sand mold wall movement due to graphite precipitation. This phenomenon is called mold dilation.

The function of a riser is to feed the casting during solidification so that no shrinkage cavities are formed. The requirement of risers depends to a great extent upon the type of metal poured and the complexity of the casting. Table 5-1 gives the various solidification shrinkage values for typical cast alloys. As can be seen, different casting alloys have different shrinkage, hence, the risering requirements vary for the alloys.

In gray cast iron, because of graphitization (graphite precipitation) during solidification, an increase in volume takes place. The volumetric expansion would counteract the metal shrinkage, and no risers may be needed for some gray cast irons.

This, of course, depends on the degree of graphitization in gray cast iron, which is controlled by the carbon equivalent (CE). But for low-CE, high tensile strength grades of gray iron, as well as for ductile and malleable irons, aluminum alloys and steel, risering (sometimes elaborate), is required due to the volumetric contraction being very high.

When calculating the size of the riser, the solidification range or freezing interval of a given casting alloy needs to be taken into consideration. As stated in Chapter 2, all casting alloys solidify at a certain freezing range, which specifies the beginning and end of solidification on the phase diagram.

Depending on the range values, cast alloys are divided into three categories:

- Narrow or short range alloys
- Medium or intermediate range alloys
- Wide or long range alloys

The first two categories of cast alloys are prone to formation of large solidification shrinkage in the shape of voids, which may be easily compensated by risers. The ferrous alloys (cast steel and cast irons) and some aluminum alloys fall in this category.

The wide or long freezing range alloys produce large volumetric shrinkage and also small and dispersed shrink porosity, which is hard to feed. These alloys are copper-based and some are aluminum alloys. In these alloys, a riser doesn't eliminate shrinkage entirely, but evenly distributes it in the form of microporosity.

To make the riser effective, the metal in the riser should solidify last and the riser volume should be sufficient for compensating the shrinkage in the casting. In order to satisfy these requirements, large risers are generally used. But it proves to be a very expensive solution since risers eventually are cut off from the casting during finishing operations and remelted. The higher the riser volume and number, the lower the casting yield and the higher the cost of foundry operations.

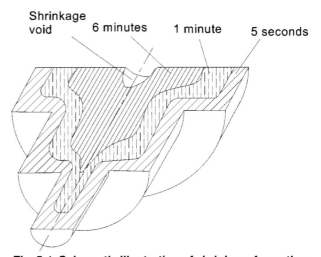

Fig. 5-1. Schematic illustration of shrinkage formation in a flange-type steel casting with locations of solidification zones during different time intervals. (Note: Solidification begins from the periphery and progresses towards the center with a formation of a shrinkage void.)

Table 5-1. Solidification Shrinkage of Various Casting Alloys.

Casting alloy	Shrinkage, (%)
Medium carbon steel	2.50 to 3.50
High carbon steel	4.00
Aluminum alloy (11 - 13% Si)	3.60
Aluminum bronze	4.10
Copper	4.10
Brass	4.92
Bearing bronze	4.50
Gray cast iron	1.80 to negative
Ductile iron	2.50-4.00
White cast iron	4.00-5.00
Magnesium alloy	4.00

To achieve the best results, the casting and riser should be designed to promote directional solidification. Figure 5-2 illustrates this concept of directional solidification in the example of a wedge-type casting. To accelerate further movement of solidification shrinkage toward the riser, additional tapering or padding may be used, as shown in Fig. 5-2(b).

The solidification of the metal starts at the remotest (thin section) area of the casting, and then continues to the thickest section and proceeds toward the riser. The solidification, when complete, finally results in the shrinkage cavity, which, in this case, is compensated by a riser.

5.2. Design of Risers

5.2.1. Riser Type and Shape

Depending on the position where a riser is attached to a casting, the riser is either a top riser, which is connected to the top of a casting, or a side riser, which is connected to the side of a casting. The top riser is the most conventional and convenient to make. But the position where it can be placed is limited.

A riser may also be referred to as an open riser when it extends to the top of the mold and is in contact with the atmosphere. An open riser readily loses heat to the atmosphere by radiation and convection. To reduce these losses, an insulation material with low thermal conductivity is often provided, or an exothermic mix is added on the top to help keep the riser in the liquid stage for a longer time.

A blind riser, is completely concealed inside the mold cavity, surrounded by molding sand, and does not extend to the top of the mold. Thus, it will lose heat slowly, keeping the metal in the riser hot for a longer time, and is more effective.

If a riser sits between the gating system and the casting, it is called a hot riser or a live riser. Positioning the riser in this manner allows the heat of the molten metal flowing through the riser to pre-heat the riser cavity, which reduces heat loss and keeps the riser liquid for a longer period of time. In horizontal molding, hot risers are usually side risers.

A cold riser, or dead riser, is not connected directly to the gating system. It receives its metal from the casting. As a result, a cold riser tends to solidify faster than a hot riser and is less effective. Cold risers often need to be a bit larger than hot risers to feed the same part. In horizontal molding, top risers are generally considered cold risers. Their effectiveness may be improved by applications of "feeding aids" that will be discussed later in subchapter 5.5.

Risers may be made in many shapes. A spherical-shaped riser, which has the lowest surface-to-volume ratio, would be the best fit for the riser because it will hold the metal in the liquid state longer. In practice, spherical risers are used mostly in vertically parted molds; in horizontally parted molds, their application is limited due to the necessity to have the riser diameter on the parting line.

A cylindrical-shaped riser is the most widely used. Typically, this riser has a hemispherical bottom that serves as an additional source of heat, allowing the riser to stay in the liquid state longer. To ensure proper metallostatic head, the ratio of height to diameter varies from 1:1 to 2:1.

5.2.2. Riser Dimensioning

5.2.2.1. Modulus Method

This method is based on Chvorinov's rule. The rule states that the solidification time of a casting, t_s, is proportional to the square of the ratio of volume, V_c, to surface area of the casting, SA_c. This ratio is called casting modulus, M_c

$$t_s = K \left(\frac{V_c}{SA_c} \right)^2 = K\, M_c^2 \qquad (5.1)$$

Where

t_s = solidification time, s

V_c = volume of the casting

SA_c = surface area of the casting

K = mold constant, depends on the casting and mold thermal characteristics.

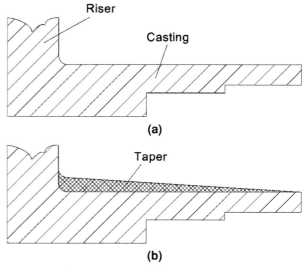

(a)

(b)

Fig. 5-2. Schematic representation of directional solidification concept on the example of wedge type casting (a). (Note: Solidification begins at the thin section, which is fed by a thicker section and, finally, riser compensates for shrinkage; (b) the same casting with additional taper (pad) to aid directional solidification.)

Casting Modulus $M_c = \dfrac{V_c}{SA_c}$ (5.2)

Since the riser is also similar to the casting in its solidification behavior, the riser characteristic can also be specified by the ratio of its volume, V_r, to surface area, SA_r, or by the riser modulus, M_r. To insure that the riser be the last to solidify, the solidification time of the riser, t_s, must be greater than the solidification time of the casting, t_c, or the modulus of the riser, M_r, must be greater than the modulus of the casting, M_c:

$$\dfrac{V_r}{SA_r} > \dfrac{V_c}{SA_c} \text{ or } M_r > M_c \qquad (5.3)$$

For steel castings, for example, the ratio of the riser modulus to the casting modulus varies from 1.1 to 1.2; for irons, from 0.8 to 1.2 depending upon CE. Figure 5-3 gives the formulas for moduli calculation of simple geometrical shapes. For calculating the modulus of a complex shape, it is useful to consider it as a combination of simple shapes.

Thus, in this method, the calculation of the riser size is simplified to the calculation of the modulus of the casting. It needs to be noticed that all contemporary CAD/CAM or solidification modeling systems allow for the calculation of the modulus of any complex shape of cast component at the design stage.

Example 5-1

Using the modulus method, calculate the size of a cylindrical riser (height and diameter equal) necessary to feed a steel block casting 25 × 25 × 5 cm (10 × 10 × 2 in.) with a top riser, casting poured horizontally into the mold.

1. Since casting is a block of 25 × 25 × 5 cm, it can be considered as a long bar with cross section 25 × 5 cm.

    From Fig. 5-3 Casting Modulus,
    $$M_c = \dfrac{25 \times 5}{2\,(25 + 5)} = \dfrac{125}{60} = 2.0833 \text{ cm}$$

2. Assume that modulus of the riser,
    $M_r = 1.2\,M_c = 1.2 \times 2.0833 = 2.5$ cm

3. Volume of riser $= \dfrac{\pi \cdot D^3}{4}$

Where

D = diameter of the riser.

The bottom end of the riser is in contact with the casting and, thus, does not contribute to the calculation of surface area.

$$\text{Surface area} = \dfrac{\pi D^2}{4} + \pi D^2$$

4. The modulus of such a cylindrical riser, M_r would be

    $M_r = 0.2\,D = 2.5$ cm

5. Calculate the riser diameter $D = \dfrac{2.5}{0.2} = 12.5$ cm

In steel castings, it is generally preferable to choose a riser with a height to diameter ratio of 1:1.

5.2.2.2. Shape Factor Method

This method was developed for carbon steel casting riser calculations and, instead of modulus, relates a shape factor, SF, of the given casting to the ratio of riser volume to casting volume. The shape factor is defined as:

$$SF = \dfrac{Length + Width}{Thickness} \qquad (5.4)$$

Casting Shape		Modulus, Mc
Plate	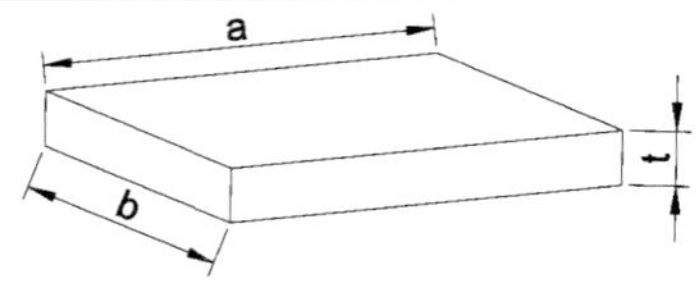 a, b, t	0.5 t (b > 5 t)
Long bar	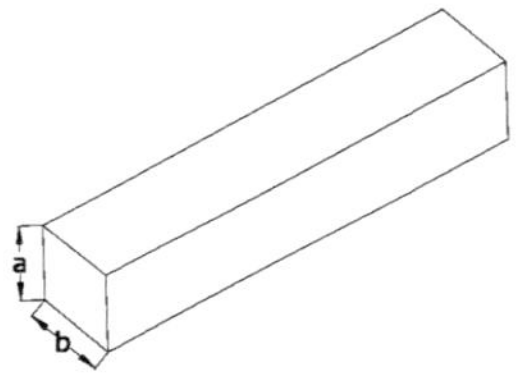 a, b	$\dfrac{ab}{2(a+b)}$
Cube	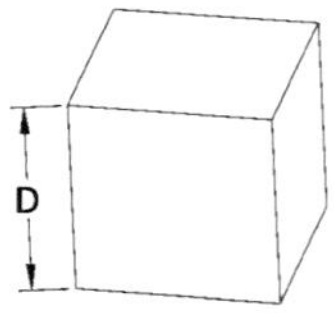 D	$\dfrac{D}{6}$
Cylinder	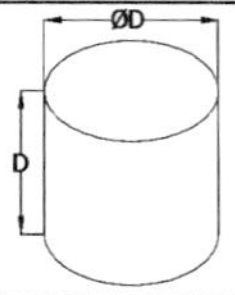 ØD	$\dfrac{D}{6}$
Sphere	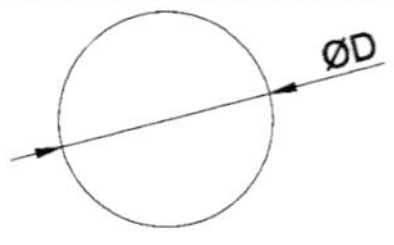 ØD	$\dfrac{D}{6}$
Hollow cylinder	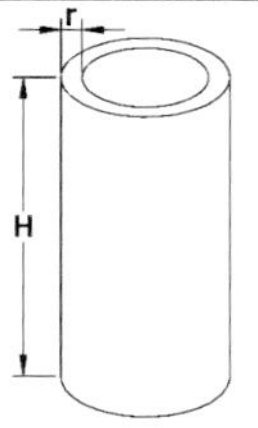 r, H	$\dfrac{rH}{2(r+H)}$

Fig. 5-3. Moduli of simple geometric shapes.

The length, width and thickness are computed from the maximum dimensions of the casting section. Then, the ratio of the riser volume to casting volume can be obtained from the graph shown in Figure 5-4 for carbon cast steels.

After finding the riser volume, reference may be made to Figure 5-5 to obtain the riser diameter and height for the given riser volume. It has been proven empirically that for side risers the height to diameter ratio is 1, and for top risers it is 0.5.

Example 5-2.

Recalculate the riser dimensions for the example 5.1 using the shape factor method.

1. Using equation (5.4) calculate the
$$\text{Shape Factor} = \frac{25+25}{5} = 10$$

2. Using the chart in Fig. 5-4, find the riser volume to casting ratio:

   Riser volume $V_r = 0.47$ x casting volume
   $= 0.47 \text{ x } 25 \text{ x } 25 \text{ x } 5 = 1468.75 \text{ cm}^3$

3. For a cylindrical riser of equal diameter and height

   a. $v_r = 0.25 \cdot \pi \cdot D^3$

   b. $D = \sqrt[3]{\dfrac{4 \cdot 1468.75}{\pi}} = \sqrt[3]{1870} = 12.32 \text{ cm}$

The same can also be directly read off of Fig. 5-5.

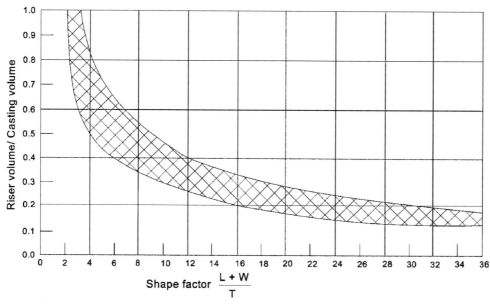

Fig. 5-4. Chart for riser volume selection using shape factor method.

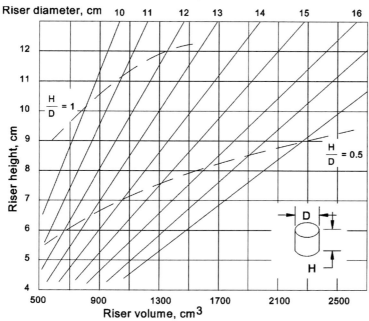

Fig. 5-5. Chart for riser dimension selection based on shape factor method.

5.2.3. Riser Neck Dimensioning

The riser neck connects the riser to the casting. There are two major dimensional parameters of the neck, which determine the riser's effectiveness in the system casting–riser: neck cross-section and length. These riser neck parameters must ensure directional solidification by allowing the riser to supply hot metal to the casting and remain liquid for as long as the section of the casting being fed.

Using the modulus method, this condition and, subsequently, effective feeding would take place if the modulus of the riser is greater than the modulus of the riser neck, which, in turn, should be greater than the modulus of the casting in the following ratio:

$$M_r > M_n > M_c = 1.2:1.1:1.0 \qquad (5.4)$$

Or the neck modulus M_n may be defined from the following equation as:

$$M_n = 1.1\, M_c \qquad (5.5)$$

If the neck size is too small, it may solidify before the casting itself and, thus, defeats the function of the riser. Too long a riser neck would also cause its premature solidification and cut off the directional solidification in the riser-casting system. Making the neck too large may create problems with riser removal and will reduce casting yield. Figures 5-6 presents another method to calculate the neck dimensions for various types of risers.

It is a normal practice to provide a thin ceramic or core material for the neck to reduce its cross section and ease riser removal. These cores are called "washburn cores."

5.3. Feeding Distances

While calculating the risering dimensions, it was assumed that the riser would be able to feed whatever the length of the casting may be. In reality, if the casting is long, the entire casting would not be sound because the riser would be unable to feed the entire length of the casting. This is particularly important for feeding bar- and plate-type castings. In cubical and spherical sections, the feeding would not be a problem.

If we consider a uniform diameter bar-shaped casting, with an end riser, solidification will occur slightly faster at the end of the casting away from the riser, because of more rapid heat transfer to the mold media. This phenomenon is called end effect. A comparable effect is noted at the edges of uniform thickness plate-shaped castings, and is referred to as edge effect. Figure 5-7 schematically illustrates shrinkage problems in cast carbon steel plates caused by excessive feeding distances and the riser's inability to feed the casting during solidification. In Fig. 5-7(a), no shrinkage will be found within the length of 2.5T (with T being the thickness of the plate), where cooling rate is high and solidification begins. When feeding distance exceeds optimal, it results in centerline shrinkage in plates with one, as shown in Fig. 5-7(a), or even two risers, as shown in Fig. 5.7(b).

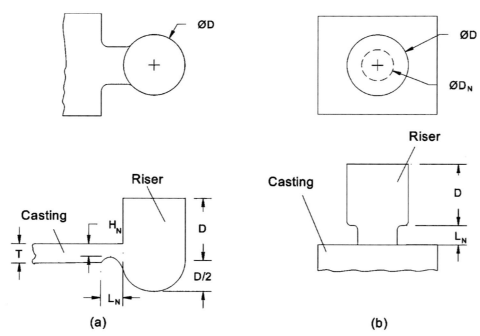

Fig. 5-6. Schematics showing riser neck (contact) dimensions: (a) side riser: $L_N \leq D/3$, $H_N = 0.6$ to $0.8\ T$, $W_N = 2.5\ L_N + 0.18\ D$; (b) top riser: $L_N \leq D/2$, $D_N = LN + 0.2\ D$.

5.4. Cooling Aids

Besides proper design of gating and risering systems, there are several methods used to control and modify solidification behavior of cast alloys. Within these methods, the most widely used are local cooling aids employing chills or cooling fins. Chills are metal inserts placed into the mold to accelerate heat transfer from potential hot spots (Fig. 5-8). Cooling fins are thin segments attached to problematic areas of a casting (Fig. 5-9). The latter helps to promote directional solidification when traditional methods are not possible to use due to limitations related to the casting design.

Chills are, essentially, large heat sinks that are provided in the mold to locally increase the heat extraction capability. Depending upon positioning, the chills can be of two types: external, or internal.

External chill inserts act as heat sinks and are a very precise and effective method to control solidification behavior in local areas of castings, by accelerating heat transfer from the potential hot spots. These chills are made of a material with higher thermal conductivity than the mold material. As well as enhancing directional solidification and helping eliminate shrinkage-related defects, they may also help reduce the level of residual stresses and associated hot tear defects in thin-thick wall junctions. The main advantage to using such inserts is that a wide selection of sizes, shapes, and materials becomes available. A positive effect of chills on microstructure improvement of iron castings and silicon-containing aluminum castings has also been reported.

The external chills are placed in the mold, adjoining the mold cavity at any required position. Providing a chill at the edge may not normally have the desired effect. Here, the temperature gradient is steeper at the end of the casting (the end effect), since the heat is removed from all sides, as shown previously in Fig. 5-7(a). However, if it were placed distant from the end of the casting, as shown in (Fig. 5-8(a), or between two risers, it would have maximum effect, as illustrated

in Fig. 5.8(b). The external chills, when placed in the mold, should be clean and dry to avoid gas porosity in the castings. Also, after placing the chills in the mold, particularly in the green sand mold, they should not be kept for a long time, since moisture may condense on the

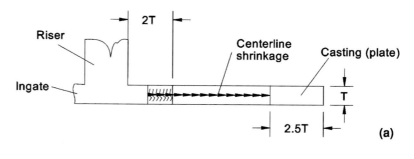

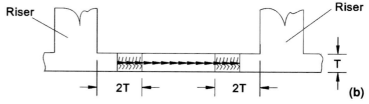

Fig. 5-7. Schematic illustration of shrinkage problems in cast carbon steel plates caused by excessive feeding distances and riser's inability to feed the casting: (a) with one riser; (b) with two risers.

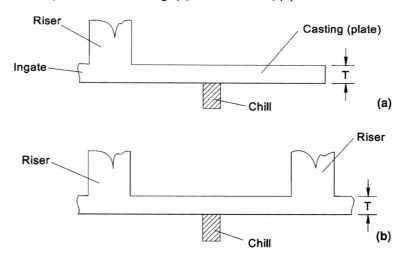

Fig. 5-8. Effect of chill on feeding distance in cast carbon steel plates: (a) with one riser; (b) with two risers.

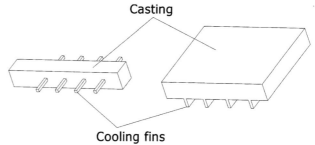

Fig. 5-9. Typical attachment of cooling fins to the problematic sections of the casting (hot spots) to locally accelerate heat removal.

chills causing blowholes in the casting. External chills should be removed once the casting is solidified during the mold shakeout. This increases the labor cost.

Internal chills are placed inside the mold cavity where an external chill cannot be provided. The chill material should approximately resemble the composition of the casting alloy for proper fusing. Cleanliness of internal chills is very important because they are surrounded on all sides by the molten metal. Because of the larger problems associated with the improper usage of internal chills, they should be used with precautions.

In iron casting, use of a chill provides a higher cooling rate, which is also likely to form a hard spot at the contact area with the chill and may, therefore, cause a problem if that area needs further machining.

For aluminum alloy sand mold casting, see Section 5.8 at the end of this chapter, which is a case study for the selection of cooling aids.

5.5. Feeding Aids

To increase the efficiency of a riser, it is necessary to keep the metal in the riser in a liquid state for as long a period as required so that it will feed the casting until it solidifies. This feeding promotes directional solidification, increases riser effectiveness and allows reduction of riser size, which, in turn, increases casting yield. The materials used for this purpose are called feeding aids. They can be either exothermic or insulating materials, called toppings, or in the shape of solid riser sleeves.

Exothermic material, when added at the top of the riser, generates temperatures up to 2095°C (3800°F) and releases heat over a short time, subsequently acting as heat insulators (through the reaction products) to the atmosphere, thus reducing the heat loss through radiation. The exothermic materials that can be used are graphite or charcoal powder, and thermite mixtures.

An insulating shield placed on the top of an open riser also reduces a considerable amount of heat loss by radiation, decreasing the size of the riser. For example, using an insulating shield, the solidification time of a 100 x 100 mm (4 x 4 in.) cylindrical riser for a steel casting increases from 5 minutes to 13.4 minutes, while for aluminum the same change was only from 12.3 to 14.3 minutes.

Riser sleeves (Fig. 5-10), either insulating or exothermic, are effectively used to reduce the heat transfer through the walls of the riser and, thus, improve the feeding of the casting. For example, the solidification time of a 100 x 100 mm (4 x 4 in.) cylindrical steel riser with insulating sleeve increases almost nine times, while for aluminum the same changes were only from 1.5 times.

For blind risers, it is recommended to use sleeves with a wedge formed into the top, which ensures atmospheric puncture of the skin of molten metal to allow more consistent feeding (Fig. 5-11). For top open risers, an optimum combination of riser sleeves around the cylindrical risers along with the top insulating shield or exothermic topping was found to be useful for all casting alloys.

Since the feeding aids keep the metal in liquid form in the riser for longer periods, for calculation purpose, the modulus of the riser needs to be reduced as compared to the conventional practice. The latter is taken into account by using a factor, f, called modulus extension factor (MEF), which represents the increase in the modulus of the riser:

$$M_{r'} = \frac{1.2}{f} M_c \qquad (5.6)$$

Fig. 5-11. Riser sleeve with the wedge formed into top of riser, which ensures atmospheric puncture of the skin of the molten metal to allow more consistent feeding. [Courtesy: Foseco Metallurgical, Inc.]

Fig. 5-10. Different types of riser sleeves for top and blind risers. [Courtesy: Foseco Metallurgical, Inc.]

Risering and Feeding

The implicit assumption in the above equation is that the insulation effect at the sides and the top is the same. If not, for example in the case of top risers, proper experimental data needs to be taken to get an average value of f. Typically, these values could be 1.8 for small insulating sleeves and 1.3 for large sleeves.

An economical analysis confirmed significant reduction in production cost by reducing riser volume. Improved casting yield and productivity for various castings alloys was achieved with the use of riser sleeves. One such example is the automotive cylinder head shown in Fig. 5-12(a) with insulated sleeve risers. Figure 5-12(b) shows a cutaway of riser sleeves.

In another example, various savings were reported by using insulated sleeve risers for a ductile iron tractor part weighing 156 kg. The use of the feeding aids resulted in a 26% yield improvement (from 48 to 74%), a 33% decrease in pouring time (from 36 to 24 seconds), an overall decrease in shrinkage defect rate, and a reduction in scrap (from 7.6 to 6.3%).

5.6. Grouping Castings

Grouping several castings around a single riser helps in increasing the casting yield, since the same riser will be able to feed more than one casting. Figure 5-13 illustrates two castings grouped on each riser. Also, by using riser sleeves, it is possible to reduce the risering requirement, as the heat from the sleeved riser would keep the metal hot for a longer period.

5.7. Solidification Modeling

Computer Aided Design (CAD), involving the analysis of stresses and deformations, has been widely used to optimize cast component design. Further progress has been made to simulate mold filling and casting solidification and the use of computer modeling systems for optimizing gating and risering systems and design.

The traditional method of designing casting processes, which is still in use in the majority of foundries, utilizes a combination of experience and a set of practical rules, similar to those described earlier, to develop an initial design of gating and feeding systems. Based on this traditional design method, the necessary tooling is constructed and test castings are poured. If the castings show presence of unacceptable defects, then the tooling is modified and new test castings are poured. This sequence may be repeated several times until sound castings are made. The trial-and-error method of process design is time consuming and costly.

As an alternative, a computerized solidification modeling system replaces the traditional trial-and-error

method, which is significantly shorter and very cost effective. Today, there are more than a dozen simulation software programs based on numerical modeling of the casting process by using mathematical models,

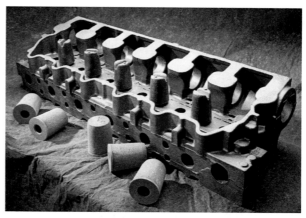

Fig. 5-12. Gray iron cylinder head cast with the use of five insertible sleeves. (Note: the breaker core is attached to the bottom of the sleeve.) [Courtesy: Foseco Metallurgical, Inc.]

Fig. 5-13. Grouping of castings to improve yield. [Courtesy: Finite Solutions, Inc.]

which simulate mold filling and solidification. Special foundry packages were developed to optimize gating and risering systems, simulate filtration of molten metal, and predict microstructure, mechanical properties and microsegregation in cast components.

In general, any solidification modeling process consists of the following major steps:

- Creating a solid 3-D model of the casting with gating and risering systems

  This may be done by importing the casting shape from a CAD file or creating a casting model using a design module available within the modeling software, and adding shapes of gating and risering systems, and, if necessary, chills, and riser sleeves. As an example, Fig. 5-14 shows a 3-D model of a casting with attached gating and risering systems, created using the CAD system.

- Selecting casting alloy and mold materials and their properties, available within the modeling software database

- Meshing the model Meshing is the process that breaks the model into small cubical elements, called nodes. The smaller the size and greater the number of nodes, the more accurate the modeling results will be. Figure 5-15 shows an example of a meshed casting with attached risers and riser sleeves.

- Running the simulation; analyzing and plotting its results

  As a result of modeling, the software will show the sequence of solidification. The system consists of casting, gating and risering system, hot spot locations, riser feeding, and areas of shrinkage, gas and other defects. Viewing mold filling simulations, it is possible to determine the temperature, metal velocity and pressure at any

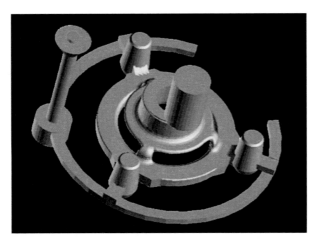

Fig. 5-14. This is a 3-D solid model of the casting with attached gating and risering systems, created using CAD system. [Courtesy: Finite Solutions, Inc.]

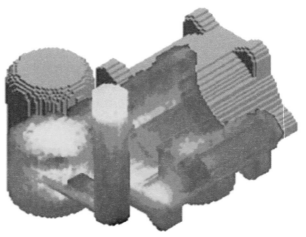

Fig. 5-16. Ductile iron casting mold filling. [Courtesy: Finite Solutions, Inc.]

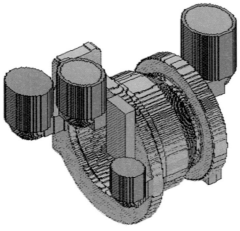

Fig. 5-15. Example of meshed casting with attached risers and riser sleeves. [Courtesy: Finite Solutions, Inc.]

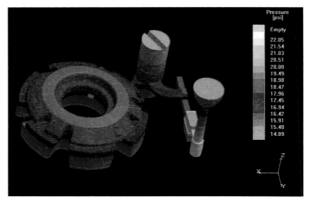

Fig. 5-17. Simulation of pressure distribution in the system riser-casting. (Note: the riser sleeve with the wedge is used to aid feeding.)

Risering and Feeding

point in the mold, casting, riser or chill. Figure 5-16 shows a fragment of the solidification modeling of mold filling of a ductile iron casting. It illustrates the sequence of metal flow from the sprue to the runner, then to the riser and, finally, to the casting. The mold is 58% full; iron temperature in the casting is 1320°C (2409°F). Figure 5-17 shows simulation of the pressure distribution in the system riser-casting. A riser sleeve with a wedge is used to aid feeding.

If modeling results show the presence of any potential problems, the foundry engineer, using the basics of gating and risering and knowledge of the given casting process and cast defect prevention methods, would correct the existing design. This correction would be an optimization of riser size, quantity or location, adjusting feeding distance or installation of additional riser(s) or riser sleeves or chills. As an example, Fig. 5-18 shows the modeling results of a casting, previously shown in Fig. 5-14, with the hot spot (shrinkage) located at the bottom of the flange from the side opposite to the top riser. As a result, the feeding system was redesigned and, instead of one big riser, two smaller size risers were installed, as shown in Fig. 5-19.

- Running the simulation of the new model

If the new simulation shows that the corrective measures eliminate problems, the optimized casting along with ingates and riser design is ready for making the necessary tooling. In the case of negative results, the simulation process is repeated. Figure 5-20 shows the modeling results of the new feeding system casting, previously shown with no hot spot (shrinkage), indicating that this risering arrangement ensures a sound casting.

Thus, utilizing the solidification modeling method allows the foundry to effectively use it for optimization of the casting processes. It needs to be noted that all aforementioned examples of simulation results apply to sand casting. But the contemporary modeling systems are capable of simulating not only sand casting of various casting alloys, but also all special casting methods such as permanent mold, low-and high-pressure die casting, investment and shell casting, continuous and lost foam casting.

The following case study illustrates practical applications of solidification modeling to predict the effect of chills vs. cooling fins, used to control solidification in local sections of aluminum sand mold castings.

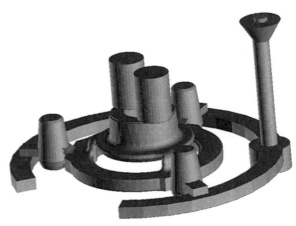

Fig. 5-19. Redesigned feeding system for part shown in Fig. 5-14. New design includes two smaller size risers. [Courtesy: Finite Solutions, Inc.]

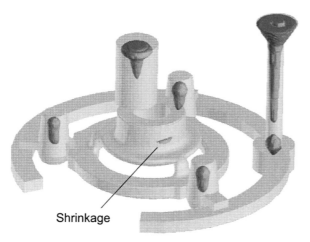

Shrinkage

Fig. 5-18. Modeling results of casting, previously shown in Fig. 5-14, with the hot spot (shrinkage) located at the bottom of the flange from the side opposite to the top riser. [Courtesy: Finite Solutions, Inc.]

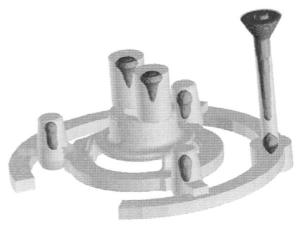

Fig. 5-20. Simulation results of redesigned feeding system showing no hot spot (shrinkage) in the flange, indicating that this riser arrangement ensures sound casting. [Courtesy: Finite Solutions, Inc.]

5.8. Case Study: Cooling Aid Selection for Aluminum Alloy Sand Mold Casting

The introduction reviews research conducted in the area of cooling aids and defines the objective of the study.

Introduction

Kim and Berry [Ref. 7] studied the effect of cooling fins on the acceleration of the solidification rate of pure lead, zinc and copper poured into nobake sand molds. Cooling fins with 10 mm (0.4 in.) thickness and variable length were attached symmetrically to both sides of 100 x 250 x 70 mm (4 x 10 x 2¾ in.) experimental plates. These researchers employed a pour-out methodology, in which a test casting was allowed to solidify for a given time and then the remaining liquid was decanted off, and the thickness of the solidified layer measured. Different solidification times for different metals were chosen: 1.5, 2, 4, 6 and 8 minutes for lead; 4, 6, 8, 10 and 12 for zinc; 1, 2 and 3 for copper. The fin effect was interpreted as increases in solidified area compared to those that had been solidified under similar conditions (temperature, time), but without fins. The fin effect was then expressed as the enhanced solidified area (A_f), divided by the width of the adjacent planar solidification front (S), and was plotted against the solidification time, expressed as the dimensionless ratio S/T, where T is the fin thickness. It was concluded that cooling fins have considerable potential for the local control of solidification rate.

Wright and Campbell [Ref. 8] studied the effect of cooling fins on solidification behavior of 100 x 100 x 20 mm (4 x 4 x ¾ in.) plates cast of pure aluminum in nobake molds. Two cooling fins were attached symmetrically to the thermal center on both sides of the plates. The solidification rate was measured directly by a K-type thermocouple placed in the thermal center of each experimental casting. Experimental results were compared with those obtained from SOLIDCast® software simulations. It was found that a cooling fin having a thickness 0.1 times or less of the half-plate thickness, and a length of four times the half-plate thickness, increases the local solidification rate by nearly ten times. A paper presented by Dimmick [Ref. 10] contains some examples of successful industrial applications of cooling fins, instead of chill inserts, in an aluminum sand casting foundry.

Despite the completely different mechanisms, both approaches (chills and fins) serve to reach the same goal: to locally increase the solidification rate at the problematic areas of a casting. Both approaches have technological and economical advantages and disadvantages. Both

approaches have found relatively wide applications in the metalcasting industry. However, in spite of this, there are no specific recommendations of cooling means selection, and their parameters have been published.

The problem addressed in this study was to find the relationship between cooling means parameters, i.e., overall number of attached fins or contact surface area and volume of a chill and their effectiveness. The objective was to develop the methodology allowing the use of one of the available cooling means (fins or chills) and vice versa with the same or similar effectiveness.

The research was conducted in two phases:

- Phase 1 compared cooling fins and internal chills effectiveness via solidification modeling
- Phase 2 validated the solidification modeling by physical experiments, which were conducted by pouring the aluminum alloy into sand molds

Employment of computer-aided modeling and realization of the rapid tooling concept allowed the research to be conducted in short period of time, with minimal material and energy expenses.

Phase 1. Comparison of cooling fins and chills effectiveness via solidification modeling

Methodology

Simulations of mold filling and casting solidification were conducted using SOLIDCast® software package with installed FLOWCast® module. SOLIDCast is based on the finite difference method (FDM) and operates with 3-D. Besides heat transfer calculations, the software simulates density changes and the movement of molten metal during solidification of the casting, taking into account gravity and dendrites crystal growth. The test

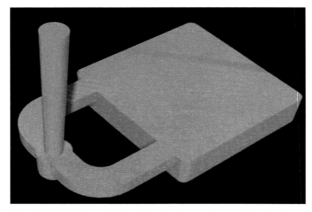

Fig. 5-21. 3-D model of the test casting with attached gating system.

casting used in the first phase of the study incorporates a 100 × 100 × 20 mm (4 × 4 × 0.75 in.) plate made of aluminum cast alloy A206 (Fig. 5-21).

According to cited recommendations, optimal geometry of cooling fins for an aluminum alloy sand casting of this size should be approximately 1 mm (0.04 in.) thick and 38 mm (1.5 in.) in length. In this work, for practical purposes, the thickness of fins used was increased up to 2.5 mm (0.1 in.). The length of the fins—38 mm (1.5 in.)—was selected based on the aforementioned recommendations. Since fin geometry was beyond the scope of the study, the only significant variables were the total number of fins and the mode of their attachment, from one or both sides.

Fourteen different configurations of fins were studied. Sets of one, two, three, four, five, six and seven fins were attached to one or both sides of the casting. In all sets having more than one fin on one side, the distance between the fins was kept constant and was equal to a half inch.

Two different materials of external chills (copper and iron) were studied. Chills were embedded into the wall of the mold, facing the mold cavity. Thus, the only significant variable parameters of the chills, besides their material properties, were their volumes (or weights), representing the heat capacity, and contact surface areas, influencing heat exchange between the chill and the casting.

For both chill materials, the same experimental matrixes were designed. Five chills, contact surfaces size 645, 968, 1290, 1613 and 1935 mm² (1.0; 1.5; 2; 2.5; and 3.0 in.²) and, subsequently, five chills, volumes 16,387; 24,581; 32,774; 40,968 and 49,161 mm³ (1, 1.5, 2, 2.5, and 3.0 in.³) were studied. For consistency, all heat transfer coefficients, air gaps, coating types, and thicknesses and other casting parameters were maintained identical.

Phase 1 Results and Analysis

The first series of solidification analysis was done for test castings with no cooling aids (fins or chills) in order to establish baseline data for further comparison.

It was determined that the thermal center (last freezing point) was insignificantly shifted from the geometrical center of the casting, due to the influence of the attached gating system. Solidification time, observed in the thermal center, was about 2.61 min. Figure 5-22 shows the relationship between the normalized solidification time and the number of fins. Hereinafter, a dimensionless factor entitled "normalized solidification time" is the ratio between the actual solidification time and the solidification time of the casting solidified with no cooling aids (base data).

As can be seen, the difference in solidification behavior appeared to be significant only when the solidification time in a local area (in the center of the casting) was considered. In this case, fins attached to both sides allow reaching greater improvement than the same quantity of fins attached to one side. Obviously, it is due to the simple fact that their junctions were closer to the test plate's thermal center. Figure 5-23 shows the relationship between the geometrical parameters of copper and iron chills, and the solidification time observed in the last freezing point or geometrical center of the test casting and mode of their attachment, from one or from both sides.

Also, while the area of iron chill's contact surface practically has no influence on the solidification time of test casting, the volume, representing heat capacity of the chill, is the only significant factor. However, both the factors considered influenced the solidification time in the center of the test casting. By reducing the contact surface area, along with keeping a constant volume of

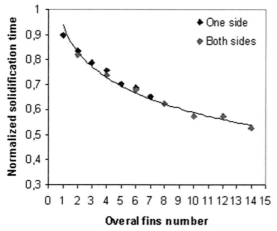

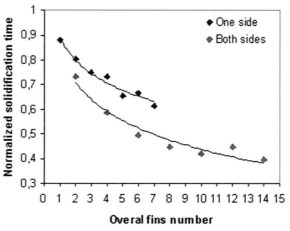

Fig. 5-22. Relationship between the number of attached fins and normalized solidification time observed in the last freezing point (left), and in the geometrical center of the test casting (right).

the insert, it is possible to achieve a substantial increase in the chill's efficiency in the local area of its attachment.

As shown in Fig. 5-23(a), copper chills significantly change the solidification parameters in the center and last freezing point of the test casting. In contrast to copper chills, variations in the iron chill's volume and contact surface area, as shown in Fig. 5-23(b), have not significantly changed the solidification time of the test casting. This difference between copper and iron chills is due to different thermal conductivity of these two materials. In the case of copper, due to high thermal conductivity, the whole chill is working, no matter what is the shape of the chill. In the case of iron, having relatively low thermal conductivity, the cross section of the chill, through which heat is transferred, becomes more important. For example, if the chill has a large volume, but small contact surface area, only part of the chill, which is closer to the casting, intensively

transfers heat from the solidifying casting, while the other end of the chill remains cold. Or, in other words, a certain part of the chill remains ineffective. In order to increase iron chill effectiveness, its contact surface must be relatively large with the volume-to-contact area ratio approximately 1:1.

Difference in the chill's thermal conductivity also influences the solidification rate enhancement achieved in the central area of the test casting. In the case of copper chills, contact surface area clearly influences the solidification time in the center: the less the area, the faster the solidification. In other words, if the contact surface of a copper chill is reduced while its volume remains the same, the cooling effect becomes stronger in the local area of the chill's location. The same relationships were observed for small-volume iron chills, but for large-volume chills, reduction of contact surface area led to reduction of chill effectiveness.

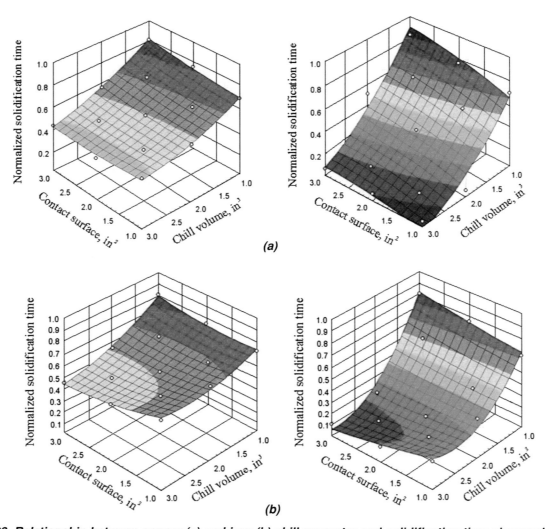

Fig. 5-23. Relationship between copper (a) and iron (b) chill geometry and solidification time observed in the last freezing point (left), and in the geometrical center of the test casting (right).

In order to quantify the relationships between solidification time of the casting and size of the fin set, as well as chill inserts (both copper and iron) parameters, a correlation analysis and nonlinear calculations have been conducted utilizing STATISTICA software. It was found that all relations can be expressed by the logarithmic approximation with high reliability for fins and copper chills (coefficients of determination (R^2) are 0.98 and 0.95, accordingly) and with acceptable reliability ($R^2 = 0.78$) for iron chills.

Achieved models have the following view:

$$\begin{cases} T = 0.930 - 0.144\,ln(N) \\ T = 0.769 - 0.313\,ln(V_C) \\ T = 0.747 - 0.216\,ln(V_I) \end{cases}$$

Where

T = the normalized solidification time, N = overall number of fins, V_C and V_I = volumes of copper and iron chills accordingly.

Pair-wise solution of equations of the given system provides the math expressions for choosing either a certain fin number or volume of chill having equal effectiveness, or volume of the chill as a function of the overall fin number with equal effectiveness:

$$\begin{cases} V_C = \dfrac{N^{0.46}}{1.67} \\ V_I = \dfrac{N^{0.67}}{2.33} \end{cases}$$

Similarly, the mathematical expression for replacing copper chills with iron chills and vice versa can be found from the expression:

$$V_I = \frac{V_C^{1.45}}{1.11}$$

Figure 5-24 graphically illustrates the effectiveness of copper and iron chills in comparison with different number of fins.

Basically, this diagram shows that both approaches are interchangeable. However, from a technological standpoint, chills are more flexible than fins. Incorporating cooling fins into a casting design will require additional cleaning and grinding operations for their removal and, hence, reduces casting yield and increases cost.

Analysis of experimental results shows that by applying chills with different contact surface areas different heat transfer effect can be achieved—concentrated or distributed. At the same time, it is not possible to achieve a strong concentrated effect by the application

of cooling fins. The only way to increase effectiveness of cooling fins is to increase the overall number of fins; however, fins must be uniformly located. The latter will not achieve the concentrated effect.

Neither iron chills, nor copper chills have an absolute advantage. Copper has greater thermal conductivity (223 versus iron's 26 Btu/hr·ft·°F), but iron has greater specific heat (0.11 versus copper's 0.092 Btu/lbm·°F). Thus, the iron chill has greater heat capacity than does copper with the same volume. However, because of the relatively lower thermal conductivity of iron that, in turn, results in relatively slow heat transfer through the iron chill cross section, not all heat transfer potential of an iron chill can be realized. Figure 5-24 can be used for comparison between iron and copper chills effectiveness, depending on their volume, and allows selecting optimal cooling means with equal effect.

As can be seen, for relatively small-volume chills, iron is the more appropriate material. Using copper appears to be beneficial only in cases when it is necessary and possible to use relatively large-volume chills, especially when strong and concentrated heat transfer effect is needed by placing relatively small contact surface, but large-volume chills.

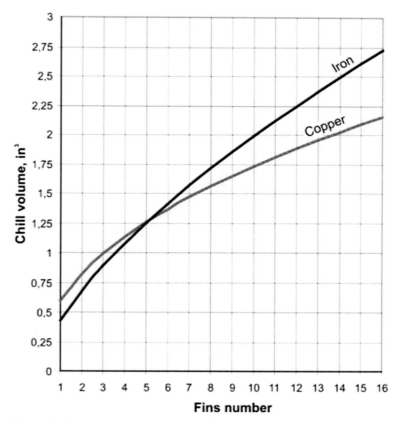

Fig. 5-24. This diagram compares effectiveness of cooling fins with copper or iron chill inserts and allows selecting optimal cooling means with equal effect.

Phase 2. Validation of solidification modeling via physical experiments conducted by pouring aluminum alloy into sand molds

Methodology

The test casting used in this phase incorporated two identical wedges, connected together. The test casting with attached gating system is shown in Fig. 5-25. The ingates were symmetrically attached to thin sections of the casting. No risers were used. This "inappropriate from the practical standpoint" gating system design allowed the generation of a hot spot in the center of the casting and concentrated shrinkage in that area. A pressurized gating system with ratio of approximately 2:3:1 was chosen, in order to maintain a relatively small cross section of the gates. A pattern for nobake sand molding was generated on Dimension 3-D-printer using the same

3-D CAD model used for solidification modeling. The 3-D-printer, based on fused deposition modeling (FDM), is an example of Rapid Prototyping (RP). In order to use a single pattern to make molds with different sets of attached fins, as well as with no fins, a specially designed composite pattern has been developed (Fig. 5-26).

The pattern consisted of three parts: main body with attached gate, runners and the bottom sprue; and two interchangeable pieces inserted in the center of the main body. Three variants of inserts were made: plain (for making the test casting with no fins), with one fin attached, and with three fins attached.

A 3-D model of the pattern has been created using ProENGINEER software package and then were converted to STL (standard triangular language) and transferred to the 3-D printer. The building process of pattern main body and both plain inserts took about 8 hours. The generated model is shown in Fig. 5-27.

The 3-D printer has sufficient geometrical accuracy; however, because of the layer-by-layer build principle, the surface of the generated pattern was not acceptable. In order to reduce the surface roughness, the pattern

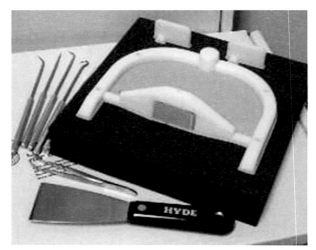

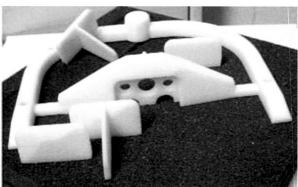

Fig. 5-27. RP-generated composite pattern as built (top) and after removing the support material (bottom).

Fig. 5-25. Test casting with attached pressurized gating system with ratios 2:3:1.

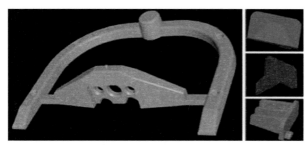

Fig. 5-26. CAD model of the composite pattern: main body (left) and three different designs of inserts (right) that could be attached from both sides of the pattern.

was coated with a special coating, and then ground with fine sandpaper. After that, the pattern was mounted on a wooden match board. Turned out of hard wood, the conical sprue was inserted into a special hole from the opposite side of the match board. After making several nobake molds, no defects were found on the RP-generated pattern.

The pre-alloyed ingots of certified A206 aluminum alloy were melted in a gas furnace. Molds were poured at about 760°C (1400°F) using 1 kg (2.2 lb) ceramic hand ladle (one mold at a time). Thermocouples were inserted into the thermal center of experimental molds and connected via a data acquisition system (containing an analog-to-digital converter) to a laptop computer equipped with special software.

Physical experiments were repeated via solidification modeling using the same approach described in Phase 1. All simulation parameters (filling time, initial temperature) were adjusted in ways to provide the most accurate representation of actual conditions of the physical experiment. In order to record the cooling curve during the simulation, pseudo-thermocouples were embedded into the model at the same point as in the actual experiments.

For each simulation, a mesh was generated with node size equal to 1.9 mm (0.075 in.). Such resolution provided appropriate accuracy and consistency of results.

Phase 2 Results and Analysis

Figure 5-28 shows experimental castings poured with different fins (gating system components are removed). As can be seen, all the poured molds were completely filled, including fin sections.

Figure 5-29 illustrates cooling curves, recorded in the center of the test casting during physical (a) and virtual (b) experiments.

Note that the application of fins led to a significant shift of the solidus point on the cooling curve in the direction of the time axis. Experimental and modeled cooling curves have different shapes; however the locations of solidification points are very close, and the deviation is inside 10% tolerance. This concludes that the results gained from the simulations were reliable.

Conclusions

Based on this case study, the following conclusions can be drawn:

1. In sand casting of aluminum alloys, both studied means of solidification rate enhancement show that cooling fins and external chills are partially interchangeable. From a technological standpoint, chills are more flexible, because by varying their geometrical parameters it is possible to achieve different cooling effects (distributed, as well as concentrated). At the same time, it is not possible to reach a highly concentrated heat transfer effect by applying cooling fins.

2. More expensive copper chills have no significant advantages in comparison with iron chills, unless use

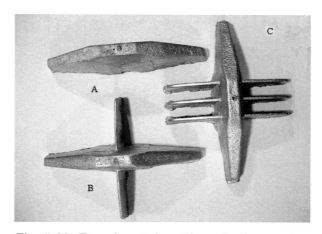

Fig. 5-28. Experimental castings (gating system components are removed) with: A) no cooling fins; B) one cooling fin attached from both sides; C) three cooling fins attached from both sides.

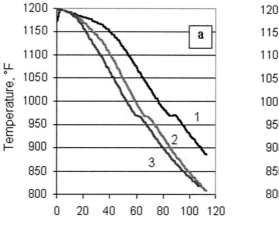
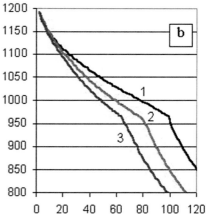

Fig. 5-29. Temperature in the center of test casting during the solidification of real casting (a) and the simulation (b): 1-test casting with no fins; 2-test casting with one fin on each side; 3- test casting with three fins on each side.

of relatively large chills is recommended. For relatively small chills, iron can be suggested as the optimal material. In order to increase iron chill effectiveness, its contact surface must be relatively large with a volume-to-contact area ratio of approximately 1:1.

3. Established relationships between the efficiency of different cooling means (fins, or copper and iron chills) allowed substituting one means by another, with no significant difference in its effectiveness.

4. The developed methodology for calculation of cooling means effectiveness, based on a combination of physical and virtual modeling, can be used to study solidification behavior of other alloys.

References

1. Schleg, F.P., *Technology of Metalcasting*, American Foundry Society, Des Plaines, 2003.

2. Bishop, H.F., E.T. Myskowski, W.S. Pellini, "A Simplified Method for Determining Riser Dimensions," *AFS Transactions*, Vol. 63, 1955, pp. 271–281.

3. Jain, P.L., *Principles of Foundry Technology*, 2nd ed., Tata McGraw-Hill, New Delhi, 1986.

4. *ASM Metals Handbook Vol. 15, Casting*, American Society of Metals, Metals Park, 2008.

5. Wallace, J.F. (ed.), *Fundamentals of Risering Steel Castings*, Steel Founders Society, 1960.

6. American Foundry Society/Cast Metals Institute: *Introduction to Metal Casting*, Handouts and Reference Materials, Schaumburg, IL.

7. Kim, M.H., J.T. Berry, "Some Experimental Observations of the Effect of Fins on Solidification of Pure Lead, Zinc and Copper," *AFS Transactions*, Vol. 97, 1989, pp. 329-334.

8. Wright, T.C., J.Campbell, "Enhanced Solidification Rate in Castings by Use of Cooling Fins," *AFS Transactions*, Vol. 105, 1997, pp. 639-644.

9. Kim, M.H., J.T. Moon, C.S. Lang, C.R. Loper, "Computer Simulation of Factors Influencing the Cast Fin Effect in Castings," *AFS Transactions*, Vol. 101, 1993, pp. 991-998.

10. Dimmick, T., "Cost Reduction Efforts Through Gating Techniques at Wisconsin Aluminum Foundry," 1st International AFS Conference on the Gating, Filling and Feeding of Aluminum Castings, 1999, pp. 271-292.

Review Questions

5.1 Define shrinkage in cast alloys and describe its major stages.

5.2 Explain the three categories of freezing ranges in cast alloys.

5.3 Outline the differences between an open riser and a blind riser.

5.4 Briefly explain the rationale of the modulus method for risering.

5.5 Discuss the concept of directional solidification using the modulus method.

5.6 Explain the differences between the shape factor method and the modulus method.

5.7 Describe the methodology for choosing the riser connection to the casting.

5.8 Distinguish between "end effect" and "edge effect".

5.9 Explain how excessive feeding distance affects shrinkage defects in castings.

5.10 Explain how a chill affects the feeding distance and prevents shrinkage.

5.11 Define the feeding aid methods available to increase the casting yield.

5.12 Describe cooling fins and their effect on the solidification of a casting.

5.13 Explain the difference between internal and external chills.

5.14 Discuss precautions one should take when choosing chills.

5.15 Illustrate, with an example, how grouping castings increases the casting yield.

Problems

5.1 Calculate the risering requirements for a sand mold cast steel roll of 100 mm (4 in.) diameter and 150 mm (6 in.) long. For riser volume reduction, economical riser removal and improving casting yield, consider the use of a riser sleeve with a breaker core at the bottom, similar to that shown in Fig. 5-10.

5.2 Two castings are molded in green sand. They differ in weight by a factor of 3.8 but they are both cubes. An experiment has shown that the lighter casting solidifies in 8.7 minutes. How much time would you estimate it would take for the heavier casting to solidify?

SAND MOLDING AND COREMAKING PROCESSES

Objectives

To prepare the mold cavity and cores, foundry sands of various properties and different techniques are used. After studying this chapter, reader should be able to:

- Discuss the various types of sands used in foundries and identify their properties
- Explain green sand composition and the equipment used to prepare it
- Identify various methods used for testing molding sand properties
- Describe various types of sand molds used
- Determine the moldmaking procedure and various equipment to be used for the purpose
- Applu coremaking procedure including the shell, nobake and coldbox processes
- Discuss the mold/core venting requirements
- Recognize the importance of various types of mold and core coatings used
- Describe the methods used for reclamation and recycling the foundry sand

Keywords

Molding Sand, Casting Solidification, Silica Sand, Naturally-Bonded Silica Sand, Thermal Expansion, Dry Sand, Synthetic Silica Sand, Olivine Sand, Zircon Sand, Chromite Sand, Fusion Temperature, Molding Sand, Spent Sand, Refractoriness, Green Sand, Binder, Clay, Clay Content, Core, Corebox, Molten Metal, Bentonite, Additives, Water, Core Blower, Core Blowing Machine, Blow Tube, Vacuum Cooling, Sand Cooling, Sand Rammer, Cope, Drag, Flask, Flaskless Molding, Split Pattern, Gating System, Gating Alloy, Ferrous Alloy, Non-ferrous Alloy, Casting Defects, Advanced Oxidation Process, Muller, Batch Muller, Continuous Muller, Sand Tests, AFS Standard Sand Specimen, Green Strength, Dry Strength, Sand Compression Strength, Moisture Content, Permeability, Compactibility, Mold Hardness, Friability Test, Thermal Conductivity, Lost of Ignition Test, Methylene Blue Clay Test, Sand Grain Size, AFS Grain Fineness Number, Ramming, Machine Molding, Jolt Molding, Squeeze Molding, High Pressure Molding, Sand Slinging, Hotbox Process, Shell Process, Coldbox Process,

CO$_2$ Process, Nobake Process, Phenolic Urethane Coldbox Technology, Venting, Mold Surface, Metal Penetration, Mold Coating, Core Coating, Sand Reclamation, Dry Sand Reclamation, Wet Sand Reclamation, Thermal Sand Reclamation, Mold Collapsibility, Sand Recycling

6.1. Foundry Sand

Foundry sand is the major component of all sand mixtures used in foundries for manufacturing molds and cores.

6.1.1. Types of Sand

The most used types of foundry sand are silica, olivine, zircon, and chromite, whose comparative properties are given in Table 6-1.

Silica sand forms the major portion of the molding sand used in the foundry because of its availability and low cost. Silica sand essentially consists of silicon dioxide (SiO$_2$), the rest are oxides of other metals such as aluminum, sodium, magnesium and calcium. These impurities should be minimized since they lower the fusion temperature of the silica sand, which varies from 1427°C (2600°F) up to 1704°C (3110°F). Ideally, the fusion temperature of foundry sand should not be less than 1450°C (2640°F) for cast irons and 1550°C (2820°F) for steels.

Silica sand, during heating and cooling, undergoes a series of polymorphic changes, accompanied by relatively high volumetric expansion, causing some specific defects directly related to this property, such as mold wall movement, scabs, etc. The main sources of silica sand are from river and lake sand deposits and from sandstone. They are used with or without washing.

Naturally-bonded silica sand contains up to 20% clay-based contaminants; this sand is suitable only for casting low melting temperature alloys. A majority of foundries use synthetic high-silica sand that has been washed to remove clay and other impurities, then dried, screened and classified to give a desired size distribution.

In the silica sand, all sizes and shapes of grains are mixed. The sand grains may vary in size from a few micrometers to a few millimeters. Shape of the grains may be round, sub-angular, angular and compounded (combination of previous shapes). Size and shapes of sand grains greatly affect the amount of binder material used and sand properties such as permeability and compactibility.

Olivine sand mainly contains two minerals: fosterite (Mg_2SiO_4) and fayalite (Fe_2SiO_4). Olivine that is highest in fosterite is suitable for foundry applications. It has less thermal expansion and higher thermal conductivity than does silica sand. Olivine is a versatile sand, and the same sand mixture can be used for a wide range of nonferrous alloys and steels. It is best suited for casting austenitic manganese steel, which is chemically reactive with silica sand.

Chromite sand is crushed from chrome ore; it possesses higher refractoriness and less thermal expansion than does silica sand. It is chemically stable, not easily wetted by molten metals, and has a high thermal conductivity. As a molding sand, it is mostly used to manufacture heavy steel castings requiring better surface finish.

Zircon sand is basically zirconium silicate ($ZrSiO_4$) and has the highest refractoriness and the lowest thermal expansion, compared to other sand. Other advantages are high thermal conductivity, high chilling power, high density and very low reactivity with molten metals. It is generally used to make precision steel castings, requiring improved surface finish, in sand and investment casting, as well as for mold and core coatings.

6.1.2. Sand Properties

The choice of molding sand is based on its processing properties. The properties that are generally required in molding sand are:

- ***Refractoriness***: The ability of the molding material to withstand high temperatures of the molten metal so that it does not cause fusion.

- ***Green strength***: The strength of a molding sand mixture at room temperature is termed as green strength. The molding sand should have enough strength so that the constructed mold retains its shape.

- ***Dry strength***: When the molding sand is dried, it is called dry sand, and its strength is called dry strength. When molten metal is poured into a green sand mold, the sand around the mold cavity is quickly converted into dry sand, as the moisture in the sand immediately evaporates due to the heat of the molten metal. At this stage, it should retain the mold cavity and at the same time withstand the metallostatic forces.

- ***Hot strength***: After all the moisture has evaporated, the molding sand reaches a high temperature, while the metal in the mold is still in the liquid state. At this stage, the strength of

Table 6-1. Comparison of Foundry Sand Properties.

Properties	Silica	Olivine	Chromite	Zircon
Color	White/light brown	Greenish gray	Black	White/Brown
Hardness (Mohs)	6.0–7.0	6.5–7.0	5.5–7.0	7.0–7.5
Dry bulk density (lb/ft³)	85–100	100–125	155–165	160–185
Specific gravity (g/cm³)	2.2–2.6	3.2–3.6	4.3–4.5	4.4–4.7
Grain shape	Angular/Round	Angular	Angular	Round/Angular
Thermal expansion at 1093 ℃ (2000 ℉), mm/mm (in./in.)	0.018 (0.018)	0.0083 (0.0083)	0.005 (0.005)	0.003 (0.003)
Apparent heat transfer	Average	Low	Very high	High
Range of fusion temperature, ℃ (℉)	1427–1710 (2600–3110)	1538–1760 (2800–3200)	1760—1982 (3200–3600)	2482–2549 (4500–4620)
High temperature reaction	Acid	Basic	Basic/Neutral	Slightly Acid
Wettability with molten metal	Easily	Not generally	Resistant	Resistant
Grain distribution	2–5 screens	3–4 screens	4–5 screens	2–3 screens
AFS Grain fineness number (GFN)	25–180	40–160	50–90	95–160

the sand that is required to hold the shape of the mold cavity is called the hot strength.

- *Permeability:* During the pouring and solidification of a casting, large amounts of gases are released from the mold. These gases are mostly generated by the molding and core sand mixtures and those that have been absorbed by the metal in the furnace, or air absorbed from the atmosphere and steam, and other gases. If these gases were not allowed to escape from the mold, they would be trapped inside the casting and cause defects. That is why the molding sand should be sufficiently porous so that the gases are allowed to escape from the mold. This gas evacuation capability of the molding sand is termed as permeability.

Besides these specific properties, the molding sand mixture should also have *plasticity* so that during the contraction of the solidified casting, it does not provide any resistance, which may result in hot tears or cracks in the casting. Molding sand should have good *thermal conductivity* so that heat from the casting can be quickly transferred and possibly reused.

When choosing the proper sand type for a given casting alloy, another physical characteristic, *thermal expansion* (increasing in linear dimensions with increasing temperature) also becomes important. As seen in Table 6-1, silica sand has the highest thermal expansion rate in comparison with other sand, which results in the occurrence of some mold-related defects and dimensional variations in castings.

6.2. Green Sand System

The main ingredients of any green sand molding mixture are foundry sand (new and returned), binder (clay) and water. Binder is a material that holds the grains of foundry sand together in molds or cores. Besides the binder, some other materials are also added to enhance the specific properties of molding sand.

Foundry Sand

Sand (new and returned) is the base ingredient of green sand mixtures. New, or reclaimed sand after cooling to at least 120°F (49°C), is added to the green sand system to compensate for the thermal destruction and loss of sand during the casting process; greater temperature has an adverse effect on sand properties, causing casting defects. The rate of new sand addition depends on the type of casting alloy poured. Table 6-2 contains general recommendations on new sand additions.

Clay

Because of its low cost and wide utility, clay is the most generally used binding agent mixed into molding sand to provide the necessary plasticity and strength. The most popular clay types used are bentonite and fireclay or kaolinite.

There are basically two types of bentonites; one with sodium, often called western bentonite, and the other with calcium, called southern bentonite. Sodium bentonites have better swelling capacity—volume increases some 10 to 20 times when exposed to sufficient moisture; high dry strength, which lowers the risk of erosion; better tolerance to variations in water content; and low green strength but high refractoriness (1150–1350°C/2100–2450°F).

In contrast, the calcium bentonites have low dry strength, but higher green strength. They have a lower refractoriness, about 980°C/1800°F. Calcium bentonite doesn't swell as much as sodium bentonite, but develops a green bond more readily, and the molding sand possesses better flowability and higher density. It is possible to improve the properties of calcium bentonite by chemically treating it with soda ash (sodium carbonate), which increases the sodium content.

Fireclay or kaolinite clay is highly refractory material that has a melting point between 1750 and 1787°C (3182 and 3249°F), providing high hot strength, but lowering plasticity and green strength. It is usually used in combination with bentonite, particularly for large heavy weight castings of ferrous alloys.

The clay chosen for molding sand should give it the requisite strength for the given application, taking into account the metal being cast and thickness of the casting. Normally, the naturally-bonded silica sand contains a large amount of clay and, therefore, can be directly used.

Table 6-2. Recommended Rates of New Sand Additions to Green Sand, Depending Upon Type of Casting Alloy Poured. [Source: AFS/Modern Casting]

Casting Alloy	New Sand Addition, kg/ton poured (lb/ton)
Aluminum	45.36 (100)
Brass/ Bronze	90.7 (250)
Iron	136.07 (300)
Steel	226.8 (500)

In other cases, the binding agent is added to the green sand mold mixture in the amount of 5–12%, often in the form of a preblended mixture of western and southern bentonites or fireclay with other additives.

Water

Clay is activated by water, which develops the necessary plasticity and strength. The process of adding water to activate clay in green sand is called tempering; the water added to produce the desirable moisture content is called tempering water. The amount of water used should be properly controlled. This is because a part of the water absorbed by clay helps in bonding, while the remainder, up to a limit, helps in improving the plasticity. Excessive amounts (free water) would decrease the strength and formability of green sand. The normal percentage of water used varies from 2 to 8%.

The advanced oxidation (AO) process, introduced recently into the green sand foundry practice, involves the addition of ozone and hydrogen peroxide, along with applications of high-powered acoustics, to recycle the clay and seacoal from dust collection systems. In this process, baghouse dust, which typically contains from 20 to 30% clay, is slurried with water. Intense acoustic energy then blasts apart the silica sand and clay particles. After that, gravity separates the lighter clay and seacoal from the silica fines in the black water clarifier. The advanced oxidant-treated slurry is then pumped back into the green sand system, reducing new sand, clay and additives. Foundries employing the AO system have reported significant reductions in their new sand, clay and seacoal usage, as well as a positive environmental effect resulting in reduced emissions and waste.

Additives

Besides the three main ingredients (sand, clay and water), many other materials also may be added to enhance the specific properties of green sand. Within the number of materials added to improve its properties, more frequently are carbonaceous materials (coal dust, also called seacoal, asphalt, fuel oil, and graphite), cellulose, cereal, iron oxide and silica or zircon flour.

Carbonaceous materials, such as seacoal or coal dust (finely crushed bituminous coal) *or other carbonaceous materials in the amount of 2–6% are* basically used in iron casting production to provide a better surface finish to the castings. When the material comes into contact with the molten metal it provides a gaseous envelope to keep the molten metal from fusing with the sand, thereby preventing metal penetration and scabbing, and ensuring good casting surface finish. Use of these materials increases green and dry strength, but reduces

permeability. *Carbonaceous* materials are not used in steel casting production, because of possible carbon pickup from the molding sand.

Cellulose additives (wood flour, ground walnut or pecan shells, oat and rice hulls) in the amount of about 2.0% max used in molding sand widens the range of water that can be added to get proper green strength. The cellulose content improves the collapsibility by slowly burning, and increases the permeability. It reduces expansion defects while improving the flowability of the molding sand, and helps maintain a uniform mold density. Too high a cellulose content makes the molding sand brittle, increases mold wall movement and produces castings prone to gas defect.

Cereal, which includes corn flour, dextrin and other starches, is added to enhance plasticity and increase green and dry strength. These additives are organic binding materials and may be used in molding sands as well as core sands. Besides increased resistance to deformation, their additions also reduce expansion defects such as scabs. A positive effect of these materials is found on the collapsibility of the sands. Typical amounts are 0.25–2.00%, excessive amounts may cause gas defects.

Iron oxide (up to 3% max) in molding sand improves surface finish, decreases metal penetration and reduces expansion-type defects. Iron oxide also increases green and dry strength, but decreases permeability while improving hot strength. It reduces collapsibility and makes the shakeout of the mold difficult. Excessive amounts of iron oxide may decrease refractoriness of the molding sand.

Silica or zircon flour increases green and dry compression strength and improves casting surface finish by increasing resistance to metal penetration.

6.2.1. Green Sand Preparation

One of the important requirements for the preparation of green sand is thorough mixing of its various ingredients to ensure their uniform distribution in the entire bulk of the sand mixture. During the mixing process, any lumps present in the sand must be broken up, clay should be uniformly enveloped around the sand grains and the moisture evenly distributed. Normally, equipment called a muller is used in foundries, to prepare the sand mixtures. There are essentially of two types of mullers: batch type and continuous.

As shown in Fig. 6-1, a *batch muller* consists of two wheels and equal number of plough blades, all of them connected to a single driving source. The wheels are large and heavy, and continuously roll inside the muller bowl. The plough blades ensure that the sand is continuously agitated. The combined action of these is a sort of kneading action, which uniformly distributes the clay and moisture throughout the sand mixture. The capacity of batch mullers may be 11–18 kg (25– 40 lb) for lab applications, while the industrial units range from 340 kg (750 lb) to 3.4 tons (7500 lb). Their production capacity range is from 15 to 150 t/hour (30,000 to 300,000 lb/hour).

A *continuous muller* (Fig. 6-2) consists of two bowls with wheels and ploughs. Sand, clay and water are fed through a hopper into one of the bowls. After getting mulled, the mixture moves into the second bowl, and then finally out, from where it goes directly to the molding machine hopper. A probe in the hopper signals the muller when the hopper is full, and the feed system automatically shuts down. If more sand is needed, the muller is already full of prepared sand and may be restarted immediately. Thus, well-prepared molding sand is continuously available for use. This equipment is generally used for large-scale production. The productivity of continuous mullers ranges from 15 to 500 tons/hour (30,000 to 100,000 lb/ hour).

Green sand mixtures may also be prepared in special mixing devices using high-speed turbine agitators (Fig. 6-3). In these high intensity mixers, the mixing tools rotate continuously with prebatched materials. Water is sprayed onto the aerated sand and uniformly dispersed throughout the sand-bentonite mix. Full homogenization of the sand and effective integration of water, bonding clay and additives is achieved. These devices are used in batch as well in continuous preparation of green sand.

The productivity of these mixers may be from 20 to 150 tons/hour (40,000 to 300,000 lb/hour) with batch capacity varying from 500 to 5000 kg (1100 to 11,000 lb), while the cycle time is about 100 seconds. Due to intensive

mixing, the mixing cycle in this type of device is shorter and the sand mix has more consistent quality.

High intensity mixers can also be designed with a vacuum system (Fig. 6-4), which provides sand cooling as well as mixing. Vacuum cooling is accomplished by reducing the boiling point of water to a desired sand temperature. Within the system, ingredients are prebatched into weigh scales and, after a short period of dry mixing, the sensor measures moisture content and sand temperature. These measurements are used in conjunction with feedback from the compactibility data supplied by the sand tester, to determine exactly how much water must be added for sand cooling, and to maintain the target compactibility. The water addition is metered in stages in accordance with a control algorithm, which accounts for initial sand temperature, moisture, compactibility and other programmable factors, to optimize performance for each individual foundry.

Fig. 6-2. Continuous muller. [Courtesy: Simpson-Gerosa Corp.]

Fig. 6-1. Batch muller. [Courtesy: Simpson-Gerosa Corp.]

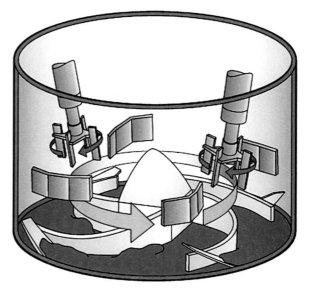

Fig. 6-3. High intensity sand mixer. [Courtesy: DISA Industries, Inc.]

The mixer/coolers are available for throughputs from 30–150 tons/hr for prepared green sand, yielding a light (53-lb/cu-ft bulk density), strong (up to 40-psi green compression strength) and flowable prepared sand. Depending on the return sand temperature and required green compression strength, a dump-to-dump cycle in the largest mixer typically takes as little as 150 sec (24 batches/hr).

All contemporary sand mixing equipment is supplied with an integrated control sensor system, providing automation of major operations: from precision weight control of sand mix components and additives to on-line quality control of sand mix properties.

6.2.2. Testing Green Sand Properties

After preparation, the molding sand should be properly tested to see that the requisite properties are achieved. These are standard and special tests specified in relevant AFS procedures. However, a brief review is made, here, of the general sand testing methods, and more details are given in the Lab & Safety Manual coupled with this textbook.

Sampling of Sand

The molding sand should be prepared exactly as is done in the shop on the standard equipment and then a representative sample of molding sand is taken and carefully put into an enclosed sample container, to safeguard its moisture content.

Moisture Content

Moisture is an important element of the molding sand, as it affects many properties. In a traditional test of the moisture of molding sand, a carefully weighed test sample of 50 g is dried at a temperature of 105–110°C (220–230°F) until all the moisture in the sand is evaporated.

The sample is then reweighed. The weight difference between wet and dry sand, in grams, when divided by the weight of wet sand multiplied by 100, would give the percentage of moisture contained in the molding sand.

Alternatively a Moisture Teller™ is widely used in foundry practice for measuring the moisture content. In this apparatus, the sand is dried by suspending the sample on a fine metallic screen and allowing hot air to flow through the sample. This method of drying completes the removal of moisture in a matter of minutes, allowing quick and consistent control at various points of sand usage.

Compactibility

In this test, the ability of molding sand to be compacted under applied force is measured using a standardized ramming instrument. Compactibility measures bulk density of the molding sand and, indirectly serve as an indicator of moisture content: with increasing moisture, compactibility increases, and vice versa.

This test is also used to make an AFS standard 50.8 mm (2 in.) diameter and 50.8 mm (2 in.) high test specimen, which is used for permeability and green strength tests. Since the permeability of sand is dependent, to a great extent, on the degree of ramming, it is necessary that the specimen be prepared under standard conditions. To get reproducible ramming conditions, a laboratory sand rammer is used along with a specimen tube (Fig. 6-5).

A measured amount of sand is placed in the specimen tube, and the sand is rammed three times. The specimen thus produced should have a height of 50.8 ±0.8 mm (2 ±0.03 in.). Usually, to produce this size of specimen, a sand sample of approximately 145 to 175 g would be required. As an alternative, a squeezer method of compactibility test may be used to prepare a standard AFS specimen by applying air pressure of 9.5 kg/cm² (140 psi).

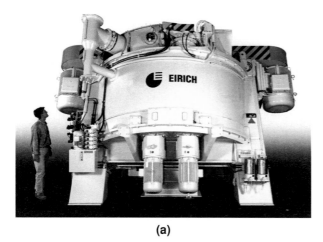
(a)

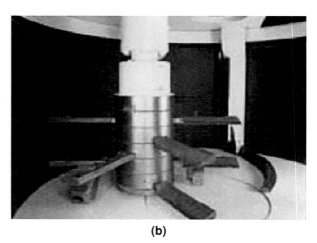
(b)

Fig. 6-4. High intensity vacuum sand mixer (a) and (b) variable speed mixing tool. [Courtesy: Eirich Machines, Inc.]

The Compacted Density of a standard AFS test specimen specifies the actual weight of the sand, in grams, required to produce the 50.8 mm (2 in.) diameter and 50.8 mm (2 in.) high specimen.

Permeability

The rate of airflow passing through a standard AFS specimen under a standard pressure is termed as *permeability*. It is a dimensionless measure of how fast air or other gases will pass through the molding or core sand during the pouring of molten metal. If the permeability number is too low, a significant amount of gas may remain in the mold or core, causing gas holes and porosity. Too high a permeability may cause metal penetration into the core or mold.

The standard permeability test measures the time taken by 2000 cm³ of air, at a pressure typically of 980 Pa (10 g/cm²), to pass through a standard sand specimen confined in the specimen tube of a permeability meter (Fig. 6-6).

Then, the permeability number, P, is calculated from the following equation:

$$P = \frac{V \times H}{p \times A \times T} \qquad (6.1)$$

Where

V = volume of air = 2000 cm³

H = height of the sand specimen = 5.08 cm

p = air pressure = 10 g/cm²

A = cross sectional area of sand specimen = 20.268 cm²

T = time in minutes for the complete air to pass through

Inserting the above standard values into the expression, we obtain:

$$P = \frac{501.28}{p \times T} \qquad (6.2)$$

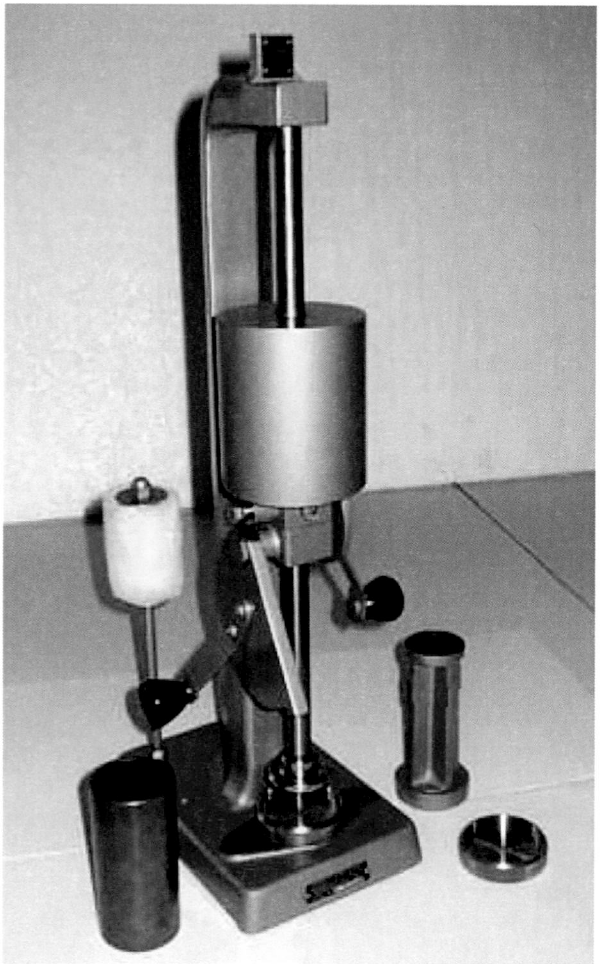

![Fig. 6-5 sand rammer]

Fig. 6-5. Sand rammer used for preparation of AFS standard test specimen.

Fig. 6-6. Permeability meter applies standard test regulations.

Sand Molding and Coremaking Processes

Contemporary permeability meters, such as shown in Fig. 6-7, allow reading the permeability number directly from the device, which also may be used for measuring permeability of actual molds and cores, by using special adapters.

The permeability test is conducted to evaluate not only green sand, but also for other molding and core sand mixtures.

Strength

The strength can be measured in compression, shear and tension. The sands that could be tested are green sand, dry sand or core sand. The compression and shear compression tests involve the use of the AFS standard cylindrical specimen that was previously utilized for the permeability test. Measurement of the strength of molding sands can be carried out on the universal sand strength testing machine (Fig. 6-8).

Green compression strength, or simply green strength, generally refers to the stress required to rupture the sand specimen under axial compressive loading. The sand specimen is taken out of the specimen tube and immediately (any delay causes the drying of the sample, which increases the strength) put on the strength testing machine, and the force required to cause the compression failure is determined. The green strength of molding sand for various types of castings generally varies in range from 0.07 to 0.28 MPa (10 to 40 psi).

Green shear strength or split tensile test uses a sand sample similar to the green strength test, but a different adapter is fitted into the universal machine, so that the loading will be made for the shearing of the sand sample. The stress required to shear the specimen along the axis is then represented as the green shear strength. The green shear strengths may vary from 0.010 to 0.050 MPa (1.45 to 7.25 psi).

Dry compression strength measures strength developed by the clay/water ratio of a specimen dried to zero moisture. Typically, it is carried out with the standard specimens dried between 105 and 110°C (220 to 230°F) for 2 hours. Since the strength greatly increases with drying, it may be necessary to apply larger stresses than in the previous tests. The range of dry compression strength found in molding sand is from 0.28 to 2.00 MPa (40 to 300 psi), depending on the sand type.

Dry tensile strength is typically tested to control properties of chemically-bonded sand. This test is made on dog-bone shaped samples.

Sand Grain Size

This test involves usage of the screen analysis to specify the sand grain size and distribution. In this test, from to 45 to 75 g of dried clay-free sand is placed on the top sieve of a sieve shaker, which contains a series of sieves, one upon the other, with gradually decreasing mesh sizes. The mesh sizes are standardized as shown in Table 6-3.

The sieves are shaken continuously for a period of 15 minutes. After the shaking operation, the sieves are taken apart and the sand left on each sieve is carefully weighed. The sand retained on each sieve, expressed as a percentage

Fig. 6-7. Electric sand permeability tester. [Courtesy: Simpson-Gerosa Corp.]

Fig. 6-8. Electronic universal sand strength testing machine. [Courtesy: Simpson-Gerosa Corp.]

Sand Molding and Coremaking Processes

of the total weight, can be plotted against the sieve number to obtain the grain distribution as in Fig. 6-9.

But more important is the AFS *Grain Fineness Number* (gfn), which is a quantitative indication of the grain distribution. To calculate the grain fineness number, each sieve has been given a specific multiplier as shown in Table 6-3. The percent retained on each sieve is multiplied by the respective multiplier, resultant product values are summed up, and the final result, rounded to one decimal place, gives the AFS gfn. By the above definition, the grain fineness number is the average grain size and corresponds to a sieve number through which all the sand grains would pass through, if they were all of the same size. This is a very convenient way of describing the grain size, and its value can be expected to be between 40 and 220 for those sands used by most of the foundries. Though the sand properties depend on both the grain size and the grain size distribution, gfn test remains a common sand testing method widely adapted in foundry practice. A typical example of the grain fineness number calculations is presented in Table 6-4.

Example 6-1

Calculate the AFS grain fineness number for the silica sand, intended to be used in an iron foundry, using data presented in Table 6-4.

Clay Content

The clay content in molding sand is determined by washing it off the sand. In this test, a 50–75 g sample of predried (105–110°C (220–230°F) for 1 hour) sand is placed in a wash bottle and washed in a solution of 475 ml of distilled water and 25 ml of a 2% solution of tetrasodium pyrophosphate (TSPP). After that, the sample is thoroughly stirred for a period of 5 minutes and diluted with fresh water, and is left undisturbed for 10 minutes, to settle. The sand settles at the bottom, and the clay particles washed from the sand float in the water. The water is siphoned off at 5-minute intervals until the water above the sand becomes clear, which is an indication that all the clay in the molding sand has been removed. Now, the sand is removed from the wash bottle, and dried by heating. The difference in initial weight of a sample and the dried sand, divided by the initial weight of a sample multiplied by 100, gives the clay percentage in the molding sand.

Methylene Blue Clay Test

This test is a chemical titration to determine the amount of active clay, which is capable to act as a bonding agent in green sand. The process involves introducing methylene blue

dye into the sand mixture. The dye reacts with clay in the sand via ion exchange, and the percentage of active clay in the sand can be calculated by endpoint determination.

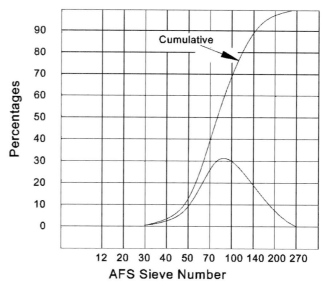

Fig. 6-9. Sand grain size distribution.

Table 6-3. AFS Sieve Numbers, Their Sizes and Corresponding Multiplying Factors.

AFS (ASTM E-11) Sieve size	Mesh opening (mm)	Multiplier
6	3.327	0.03
12	1.651	0.05
20	0.833	0.10
30	0.589	0.20
40	0.414	0.30
50	0.295	0.40
70	0.208	0.50
100	0.147	0.70
140	0.104	1.00
200	0.074	1.45
270	0.053	2.00
Pan	---	3.00

Table 6-4. Example 6-1 of Sieve Analysis and GFN Calculations.

Sieve number	Multiplier	Retained wt., g	Retained percent	Product (retained percent × multiplier)
40	0.30	2.495	5	1.50
50	0.40	13.972	28	11.20
70	0.50	23.952	48	24.00
100	0.70	6.986	14	9.80
140	1.00	2.495	5	5.00
		49.900	100	51.50

AFS GFN= 51.5 ≈ 52

The result of this test allows properly controlling clay content by its addition to a new sand mixture, and maintaining optimal clay content in the system. This test, along with green compressive strength, moisture content, compactibility, permeability, temperature and weight tests, are recommended to be performed on a daily basis. Tests on clay content, sieve analysis, combustibles and volatilibles testing (LOI) should be done on a weekly basis.

Loss on Ignition Test (LOI)

This test measures the combustible component content in the green sand system, primarily seacoal. Components that are burned off at a temperature below 482°C (900°F) are called volatile. Fixed combustibles are components that are burned off between 482°C (900°F) and 985°C (1800°F). The AFS test involves firing a 50 g predried sand sample at 985°C (1800°F), to determine the amount of carbonaceous material burned off. Knowing the LOI, the foundry can control and optimize the green sand mixture.

This test is also used to determine the quality of chemically-bonded reclaimed sand by measuring the amount of weight loss of the sand specimen, subjected to high-temperature exposure for an exact time period. The weight loss reflects the amount of resin burned off the sand grains, and allows proper calculation of new binder additions.

Mold Hardness Test

Mold hardness test is similar to the Brinell hardness test used on metals and alloys. In sand hardness testing, a handheld pocket-sized tester with a penetrator in the shape of a ball or a point (depending upon the density of the test object) is pressed into the surface to measure the resistance offered by the surface of a green sand mold or sample. The softer the mold surface, the greater the penetration into the mold.

Depending upon density of measured objects and penetrator employed, there are two common types of mold hardness testers:

- The scale "B" tester used for relatively softer molds typical for hand and squeeze molding (Fig. 6-10). It employs a 12.7 mm (0.5 in.) diameter steel ball loaded with a spring pressure of 980 g. Penetration is indicated on a reverse dial in thousandths of an inch. A mold offering no resistance to the point would have a zero reading; one having hardness capable of preventing any penetration would read 100. The lower number applies to soft molds, the higher applies to hard-rammed molds. Typical hardness of green sand molds varies from 40–50 (soft-

rammed mold) to 70–85 (hard-rammed mold) and sometimes to 85–100 (high-pressure/high-density mold).

- The scale "C" instrument is used to measure the surface hardness of high density green sand molds in the same manner as the "B" scale tester. It has a conical penetrator with a spring load of 1500 g. at full scale. The dial is calibrated from 65 to 100 hardness, spreading out higher readings for greater sensitivity in the range of high pressure molding. This tester is applied to evaluate hardness of molds made on automatic molding lines.

Electronic versions of these instruments are commonly used in foundry practice. For reliable results, in each case, the instrument must be used only on flat surface of mold or sample and applied at a 90 degree angle to the measured object's surface.

Other Property Tests

There are other sand tests to determine such properties as deformation, hot strength, thermal expansion (measures the behavior at high temperature by dilatometer), metal penetration, wet tensile, etc. These tests are used to supply information needed for a special molding method, or to prevent some specific casting defect.

The wet tensile test is designed to simulate what happens in the mold when the heat of the molten metal drives the moisture in the sand back, creating a wet layer or condensation zone. The test specimen is formed in the specimen tube and has a taper on one end, which fits into a lift-off ring that is subjected to heat. A tensile stress is then applied to the lift off ring, and the wet tensile strength, or the strength of the wet layer is measured. Wet tensile strength

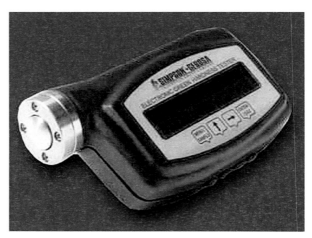

Fig. 6-10. Sand mold hardness tester. [Courtesy: Simpson-Gerosa Corp.]

is critical in some applications, because it represents the weakest layer in the mold, which may produce expansion defects such as scabs, buckles and rattails.

Some foundries perform other specialized sand tests such as friability (a measure of how easily the molding sand is abraded from a compacted sand surface) and moldability. Both tests use the same instrument, which is a device with a rotary screen that rotates over a catch tray. In the friability test, two compacted standard test specimens are placed in the rotating screen for one minute, and the weight percent of sand that abrades from their surface is measured. Generally, friability below 10% is considered acceptable. Molding sands that run over 10% friability are generally prone to erosion-, and inclusion-type defects, because the molding sand cannot withstand the erosive flow of the molten metal. The moldability test uses a loose mass of sand, which is rotated in the screen, and measures the stickiness or cohesiveness of the sand mass as a measure of how free-flowing it is. Free flowing sand in hoppers and on the pattern is important for higher moldability.

The details of these testing methods can be found in the references cited at the end of this chapter.

6.2.3. Variables Affecting Green Sand Properties

The properties of molding sand are dependent, to a great extent, on a number of variables. The important among them are:

- Sand grain shape and size
- Clay type and amount
- Moisture content
- Degree of compaction

Sand Grains

The shape and size of the sand grain would greatly affect the various molding sand properties. The sand grain size could be coarse or fine. Similarly the grain shape could be round or angular.

The coarse grains would have more void space between the grains, which increases the permeability (Fig. 6-11). Similarly, the finer grains would have lower permeability; however, they provide better surface finish to the casting produced. The distribution of the grain size also plays an important role. For example, widely distributed sand would have a different permeability than one with the same fineness number, but where all the grains have the same size. If the distribution has more fines, then it will have lower permeability. Conversely, if the distribution has more coarse particles (in excess of 30%), then the permeability will be higher.

Angular sand grains require higher amounts of binder. Round sand grains would have lower permeability compared to angular grains, because of the irregular shape of the latter.

The grain size also affects the refractoriness. The higher the grain size, the higher would be the refractoriness. The purity of sand grains also improves the refractoriness. For example, silica sand grains with a gfn of 30 to 45 may have fusion temperature up to 1650°C (3002°F). But finer grains and impurities in the sand, such as iron oxide and limestone, tend to lower the refractoriness by promoting fusion.

The strength of the molding sand is also affected by the grain size and shape. As shown in Fig. 6-12, the green compression strength increases with a decrease in the grain size, because finer grains provide a larger surface area for the binder to act.

Clay and Water

Besides the sand grains, clay and water have significant influence on major properties of the green molding sands. Comparative properties of molding sands with various clays are shown in Table 6-5.

During the sand mix preparation, clay is uniformly coated around the sand grains. The water then activates the clay and forms a strong bonding linkage throughout the molding sand. For this linkage to develop, there is only a certain amount of tempering water required, which is specified by the type and amount of clay present. Any additional amount of water increases the plasticity and dry strength, but reduces the green compression strength. There is

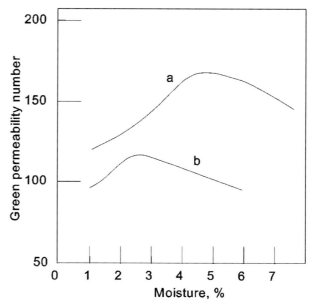

Fig. 6-11. Variation of permeability with sand grain size: (a) gfn = 55; (b) gfn = 78.

---

a maximum limit, up to which the green compression strength of molding sand with given clay content could be increased with increasing tempering water additions. Increasing the amount of clay increases the maximum strength, but requires higher water additions. These relationships are schematically illustrated in Fig. 6-13.

It was practically established that well-mulled green sand is characterized by a certain ratio between compactibility and moisture, where the compactibility is 10–12 times higher than the moisture number.

Degree of Compaction (Ramming)

Though the properties of molding sand depend, to a great extent, on its constituents, the molding procedure also makes a difference. The degree of ramming increases the bulk density of the sand and, subsequently, the mold hardness, and increases the green compression strength.

The permeability of green sand decreases with the degree of ramming, as shown in Fig. 6-14.

Table 6-6 shows some typical green sand properties that are desirable in various types of iron casting production.

6.3. Types of Sand Molds

In order to produce sound castings, sand molds are required to have some specific properties. Some of them are:

- It must be strong enough to withstand the temperature and weight of the molten metal.
- It must resist the erosive action of the flowing hot metal.
- It should generate minimum amount of gases during pouring of the molten metal.
- It should have good venting capacity to allow the generated gases to completely escape from it.

Table 6-5. Comparison of Green Sand Mold Mixture Properties with Various Clays.

Sand ingredients, wt %	Sodium Bentonite	Fireclay	Calcium Bentonite
Silica sand, AFS GFN 60	95	88	95
Clay bond	5	12	5
Moisture	2.5	3.0	2.5
Properties			
Permeability	110	60	108
Green compression strength, MPa (psi)	0.0765 (11)	0.0634 (9.2)	0.0972 (14)
Dry compression strength, MPa (psi)	0.6757 (98)	0.4688 (68)	0.3723 (54)

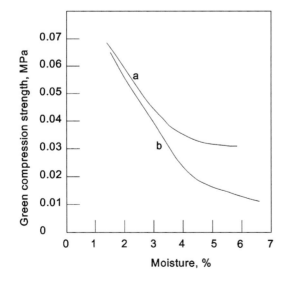

Fig. 6-12. Variation of green compression strength with sand grain size: (a) gfn = 78; (b) gfn = 36.

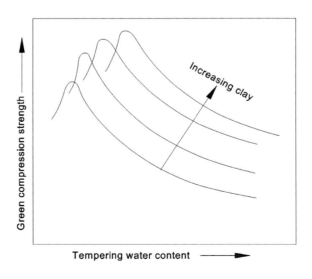

Fig. 6-13. Variation of green compression strength in clay-bonded sands with additions of tempering water for various clay content.

Sand Molding and Coremaking Processes

Molds that are used for sand casting may be broadly classified as green sand molds, dry sand molds and skin dried molds.

Green Sand Molds

Green sand molds are made of a freshly prepared green sand mixture, and metal is poured immediately. These are most commonly used and are adapted for rapid production, where the molding flasks are quickly removed prior to pouring. They require less floor space, as no storage is involved. Thus, it is the least expensive of all. Because of less strength and good collapsibility, the tendency for casting hot tearing is less in green sand molds. But mold erosion is common in these types of molds. The permeability of these molds should be properly controlled; otherwise, blowholes and gas defects are likely to form. Sometimes, two different sand mixtures are used in green sand mold production:

- Facing sand
- Backing sand

Facing sand is used next to the pattern to obtain cleaner and smoother casting surfaces.

Backing sand is normally the reconditioned foundry sand and is used for ramming the bulk of the molding flask. The molding flask is completely filled with backing sand after the pattern is covered with a thin layer of facing sand. Since the casting is not affected to any great extent by the backing sand, it usually contains the burnt facing sand, molding sand and clay.

Dry Sand Molds

These are green sand molds that are completely dried in an oven between 150 and 350°C (300 and 662°F) for 8 to 48 hours, depending on the binder in the molding sand. These molds have higher strengths than a green sand mold, and are generally used for medium-to-large castings. Better surface finish and dimensional accuracy can also be achieved in a dry sand mold. The main disadvantages are the likely distortion of

Table 6-6. Control Green Sand Test Data for Various Types of Castings.

Sand Property	Type of castings, applications, wt., kg (lb)/production line	
	Light and medium weight transportation castings, 2(4.4) to 90 (200) kg (lb) /DISAMATIC	Medium weight (GI) municipal castings, 23 (50) to 90 (200) kg (lb) /Horizontal Impact Molding Line
Moisture, %	2.7–2.9% (GI) 2.9–3.1% (DI)	2.9–3.2
Compactability, %	36–39 (GI & DI)	34–38
Green compression strength, MPa (psi)	0.248–0.262 (36-38)–(GI) 0.227–0.241 (33-35)–(DI)	0.248–0.255 (36–37)
Green shear compression strength, MPa (psi)	0.044–0.048 (6.5-7)–(GI) 0.041–0.044 (6-6.5)–(D)I	0.044–0.052 (6.5–7.5)
Dry compression strength, MPa (psi)	0.414–0.483 (60–70)–(GI) 0.448-0.517 (65-75) – (DI)	N/A
Sample Weight, g	161–162 (GI) 160–161 (DI)	157–158
Permeability, number	80–90 (GI) 66–73 (DI)	100–106
Total AFS Clay content, %	10–12 (GI) 11–13 (DI)	12–14
Methylene Blue Active Clay, %	8–8.3 (GI) 9–10 (DI)	9–10
Loss on Ignition (LOI), %	3.7–4.1 (GI) 4–4.3 (DI)	4–4.3
AFS grain fineness number, GFN	63–66 (GI) 66–69 (DI)	62–64
Friability, %	<10	<10
Wet Tensile, N/cm^2 x 10^{-3}	400–450 (GI) 430–470 (DI)	320–380

(GI)–Gray iron
(DI)–Ductile iron

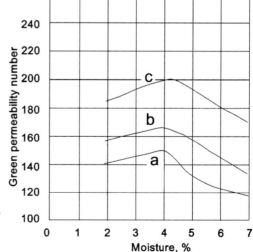

Fig. 6-14. *Change in the permeability of molding sand with the degree of ramming: (a) three rams; (b) six rams; (c) ten rams.*

---

the mold during the baking process; susceptibility to hot tearing of castings and longer production cycles. Also, this is more expensive than the green sand mold. Lately, almost all dry sand molds are replaced by the solid nobake molds or combination of nobake mixture used as a facing material and backed up with a green sand mixture.

Skin-Dried Molds

Though the dry sand mold is preferable for large castings, the complete drying process increases the cost. In the skin-dried molding process, a compromise is achieved by drying only the skin of the mold cavity with which the molten metal comes into contact, instead of the full mold. The skin is normally dried to a depth of 15–25 mm (0.6–1.0 in.), using either torches or by simply allowing the mold to dry at ambient temperature, for example, in pit molding. However, pouring of metal should be completed immediately after the drying process, so that moisture from the undried portion will not penetrate the dried skin. Infrared heating is lately applied for skin-dried mold curing, as well as for drying of coated molds.

6.4. Moldmaking Processes

Conventional moldmaking processes include hand and machine molding, used to make green sand or dry sand molds, and can be divided into two classifications: one that uses flasks, and the other, flaskless.

6.4.1. Hand Molding

Hand molding is used in the low-volume production of castings of various alloys. The typical procedures for making a hand-rammed green sand mold, using a split pattern, are described in the following steps (Fig. 6-15).

First, a bottom board is placed either on the molding platform or on the floor, making the surface even. The drag half of the molding flask is kept upside down on the bottom board, along with the drag part of the pattern, at the center of the flask on the board. The clearance between the pattern and the walls of the flask should be not less than 50 mm (2 in.). Necessary elements of the gating system are placed in the drag. The parting material (dry or liquid) is applied over the board and pattern, to provide a non-sticky layer. The flask is filled with freshly prepared molding sand of requisite quality, and is compacted with a hand rammer around the pattern. The ramming of the sand should be done properly so as not to compact it too hard,

which would make the escape of gases difficult, nor too loose, so that the mold would not have enough strength. After the ramming is over, the excess sand in the flask is completely scraped away using a flat bar to the level of the flask edges.

Now, using a vent wire of 1–2 mm (0.04–0.08 in.) diameter with a pointed end, vent holes are made in the drag to the full depth of the flask, as well as to the pattern, to facilitate the removal of gases during casting pouring and solidification. This completes the preparation of the drag. The finished drag flask is then rolled over to the bottom board, exposing the pattern. Using a slick or small trowel, the edges of the sand around the pattern are repaired.

Then, the cope half of the pattern is placed over the drag pattern, aligning it with the help of dowel pins. After that, the cope flask is placed on top of the drag, aligning with the help of the flask pins. The parting material is applied all over the drag and on the pattern. A sprue pin for making the sprue passage and a riser pin, if required, are placed at appropriate positions, and the flask is filled

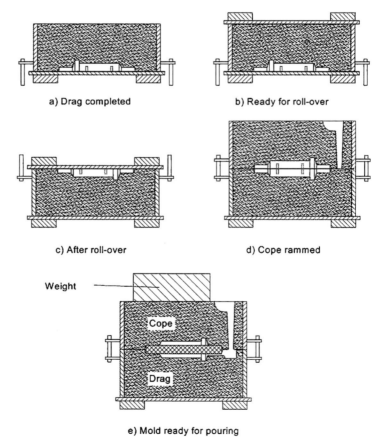

a) Drag completed

b) Ready for roll-over

c) After roll-over

d) Cope rammed

e) Mold ready for pouring

Fig. 6-15. Major steps in the green sand hand molding procedure using a split pattern: (a) the drag half is made; (b) the drag half with the board on the top is ready for roll-over; (c) the drag half after roll-over; (d) the cope half is completed; (e) assembled mold with the weight on the top of the cope.

with the molding sand. The sand is thoroughly rammed, excess sand scraped and vent holes are made all over in the cope, as in the drag.

Next, the pouring basin is cut on the top of the sprue and the sprue and the riser pins are carefully withdrawn from the top of the cope flask. The cope flask is separated from the drag half, and any loose sand on the cope and drag interface is blown off. After this, the cope and the drag pattern halves are withdrawn from the flasks. If necessary, runners and ingates are cut in the mold, carefully, without damaging the mold. Any excess or loose sand found in the gating system and mold cavity is blown away.

A dry sand core is prepared using a corebox. After suitable curing, it is placed in the mold cavity and the mold is then assembled and ready for pouring. Before pouring, mold weights are placed on the top of assembled mold, to prevent the cope from lifting off during pouring of metal.

6.4.2. Machine Molding

The advantages of machine molding include complete mechanization or automation of major operations—from ramming to separation of the pattern from the mold and mold assembly, more uniform mold density and more consistent casting quality, combined with high productivity.

In the machine molding process, there are six major methods used for ramming the sand around the pattern, to make a mold: jolting, squeezing, jolt-squeezing, impact-impulse, high density (high pressure) and sand slinging.

Jolt Molding

In the jolt molding method, the sand is first filled into the flask, generally from an overhead hopper. Then, a working table, along with pattern, flask and sand, is raised, either hydraulically or pneumatically, to a certain height, and then dropped onto the solid base of the machine. The resulting impact forces cause sand compaction around the pattern. This lifting and dropping process, or jolting, continues repeatedly until the required mold compaction is achieved. Compaction efficiency varies with the height of the drop and the depth of sand in the flask. The limiting capacity of a jolt machine is the total weight that the jolt cylinder is capable of lifting and letting fall.

A disadvantage of this type of molding is uneven compaction: the molding sand at the bottom experiences the highest force and, consequently, is packed well compared to the sand in the top layers.

Squeeze Molding

In squeeze molding, a plate, slightly smaller than the inside dimensions of the molding flask, is fitted into the flask already filled with the molding sand, as shown in Fig. 6-16(a). Uniform pressure is applied on the plate, by either moving it down or by moving the flask upward, to compact the sand uniformly. The sand next to the plate rams hardest, while the sand below is progressively less hard. The hardness achieved is also dependent upon the pressure applied to the squeeze plate. Since the hardness follows the contour of the squeeze plate, which is in contact with the sand, sometimes the plate is provided with a contour, as shown in Fig. 6-16(b), to match the pattern and obtain better and more uniform hardness of the mold. This compaction method is suitable for small castings molded in shallow flasks.

For tall, complicated shaped patterns, it is also recommended to use a diaphragm, as shown in Fig. 6-16(c), or squeeze plate equipped with many individual compensating heads, set at different squeeze pressures, as in Fig. 6-16(d), to provide a differential ramming force required for the contour of the pattern.

Jolt-Squeeze Molding

Jolt-squeeze molding is a combination of jolt and squeeze methods, which is more common in contemporary molding machines, because of more uniform ramming. Figure 6-17 shows typical jolt-squeeze molding machine.

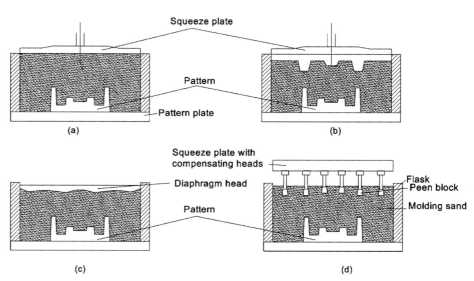

Fig. 6-16. Types of squeeze heads used for machine molding, (a) conventional squeeze plate; (b) profile squeeze head; (c) diaphragm squeeze; (d) compensating heads.

Impact-Impulse Molding

In impact-impulse molding, compressed air, typically of 0.28–0.52 MPa (40–75 psi) is used to blow sand into the flask and compact it. Due to good permeability of molding sand, the air pressure spreads evenly in the mold, resulting in consistent mold properties.

High-Density (High-Pressure) Molding

High-density (high-pressure) molding combines impact molding, used to blow sand into the flask, with additional high-squeeze pressure, which is equal to or greater than 0.689 MPa/100 psi, to make green sand molds with the highest hardness range of 85–100 on a mold hardness tester. Due to the mold's high density, castings made by this method have considerably better dimensional accuracy, with consistently uniform weight, surface finish and quality. This type of molding has virtually eliminated the problems of mold-wall movement in green sand molds. This phenomenon, typical for soft-rammed molds, is greatly increased with higher sand moisture content, lower mold density and surface hardness.

High-pressure molding practices have allowed lower moisture content in the molding sand, so that higher mold densities and rigidity can be achieved, and the volume of metal needed for feeding can be reduced. Currently, this molding method has been widely adapted for casting of most cast alloys. Disadvantages of the process include necessity of tighter sand quality controls and sophisticated equipment, maintenance, and operating procedures.

The largest flask molding line in the world for green sand molds was built for the flask dimensions of 3.0 × 1.8 × 0.5/0.5 m (10.0 × 6.0 × 1.7/1.7 ft.) and used for the production of steel parts for the railroad industry. The production line includes the sand preparation plant, molding machines, and mold cooling and shakeout systems.

Sand Slinging

Sand slinging (Fig. 6-18) uses centrifugal force to throw the green sand into the flask rapidly and with great force. The operator manipulates the slinger by moving the nozzle through the entire area of the flask, applying the sand in layers, and compacts it around and above the pattern.

The process is very fast and gives high uniform sand compaction. However, the initial cost of the equipment is high, compared to the other molding machines described, but it is cost effective in production of large ferrous alloy castings.

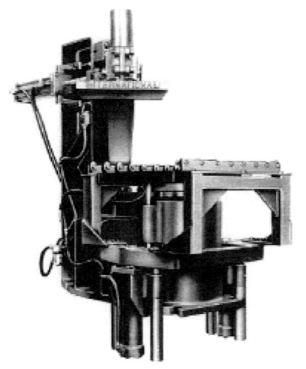

Fig. 6-17. Typical jolt-squeezing molding machine. (Source: Foundry Management and Technology.)

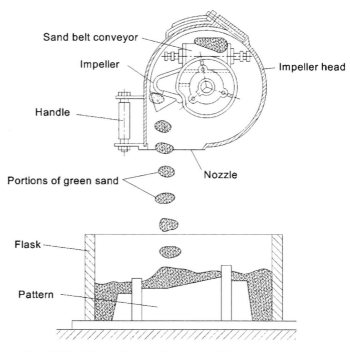

Fig. 6-18. Schematic of slinger molding.

Sand Molding and Coremaking Processes

6.4.3. Flaskless Molding

Flaskless molding is a highly productive molding method, employing sand blowing and sand squeezing actions. Molds are made in automated horizontal or vertical molding lines. Figure 6-19 illustrates the sequence of operations in vertical flaskless molding. The feature of this molding method is that the end surfaces of each halves of the mold contain impressions of the pattern, forming a mold cavity when two are joined together.

Referring to Fig. 6-19: in position (a), sand is blown into the molding chamber, which consists of two platens with patterns mounted on them; in position (b), sand is squeezed and one half of the mold is made; in position (c), the right platen swings out of the way, allowing the newly made half of the mold to be ejected from the molding chamber and join with the previously made half of the mold (at this position cores are set); in position (d), molten metal is poured into the assembled mold; in position (e), the new molding cycle begins.

The automatic flaskless molding line includes mold conveyors, automatic core setter and quick pattern plate unit, besides automatic molding machine, serving for fast replacement of tooling. The productivity of fully automated horizontal flaskless line may reach up to 500 molds (uncored) per hour. The necessity to install cores obviously reduces productivity.

6.5. Coremaking Processes

Cores are placed into the mold cavity to provide castings with cavities, passages or special contours. Cores may be classified by the material or binder from which they are made (green sand cores, dry sand cores, oil sand cores) or by their process (shell cores, sodium silicate/CO_2 cores, coldbox cores, etc.). In some cases, for differential cooling, cores are made from two materials: (top) from chromite sand with high thermal conductivity to chill the casting faster; (bottom) from silica sand, such as that shown in Fig. 6-20.

The coremaking technology uses numerous chemical binder systems that bond or cure the core through a chemical reaction during the foundry sand and binder mixing cycle. Other technologies may require gassing of the sand mixture, or heat being applied to the sand mixture, to complete the hardening process. The simplicity of the chemical binder systems usually makes their quality control less complex and sand mix properties more consistent.

The most widely used for coremaking processes are hotbox (heat-activated systems), coldbox systems and nobake (air-set) process, utilizing chemically-bonded self-setting sand mixtures. In low-volume production,

cores are made manually, using hand ramming, jolting or vibration for compaction. A coremaking machine, called a core blower, uses compressed air to fill the corebox cavity, and is used in high-volume production.

Figure 6-21 shows a single-station automatic core blowing machine used for horizontal parting line coreboxes. This machine allows for quick, 3–5 min changes of coreboxes and is intended to be used with the coldbox process. Figure 6-22 shows typical automotive application cores (cylinder head, exhaust manifold, etc.) made on a single-station automatic core blowing machine via coldbox technology.

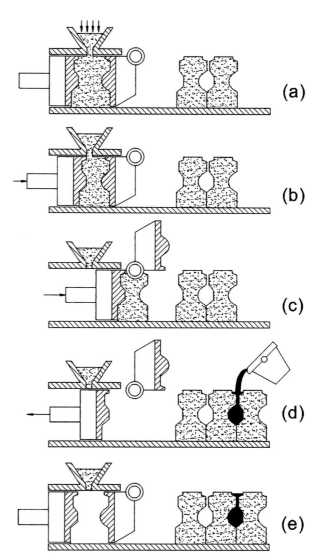

Fig. 6-19. Schematic of vertical flaskless molding: (a) sand is blown into the mold chamber, created by two halves of the pattern; (b) sand is squeezed and half of mold is made; (c) newly made half of mold is ejected from the molding chamber and joins with the previously made half of mold; (d) metal pouring; (e) new molding cycle begins.

The core blower, shown in Fig. 6-23, utilizes multiple-cavity coreboxes with vertical parting lines for making large cores, either by the coldbox or hotbox process. Cores are automatically ejected onto a conveyor belt.

6.5.1. Heat-Activated Processes

Oil Sand Process

One of the oldest heat-activated sand systems is a mix containing oil (natural or synthetic) mixed with sand, cereal and water. Small amounts of clay or other additives may be used to achieve specific properties.

The sand mix is rammed or blown into a corebox and the core is carefully removed from the corebox and placed on a flat or shaped metallic plate, called a dryer. The dryer, along with a core, is placed into an oven for baking. The oven temperature is set to 200–250°C (392–482°F), baking time is 1–3 hours, depending upon core size, type of oven and moisture content. Typically, gas or electric ovens are used for complete baking of oil sand cores.

Shell Process

Shell molding is a precision sand casting process used to produce castings with a superior surface finish and better dimensional accuracy than conventional sand castings. The process was developed and patented by Johannes Croning in Germany during World War II and is sometimes referred to as the Croning-process. The process is effectively used to make molds, as well as cores.

In the shell molding process, fine-grained, dry high-purity, clay-free, rounded silica sand (90 to 140 gfn) is coated

Fig. 6-21. Single-station automatic core blowing machine for horizontal parting line coreboxes. This machine allows quick 3–5 min change of corebox and is intended to be used with coldbox process. [Courtesy: Loramendi S. Coop.]

Fig. 6-22. Typical automotive application cores (cylinder head, exhaust manifold, etc.) made on a single-station automatic core blowing machine shown previously in Fig. 6-21. [Courtesy: Loramendi S. Coop.]

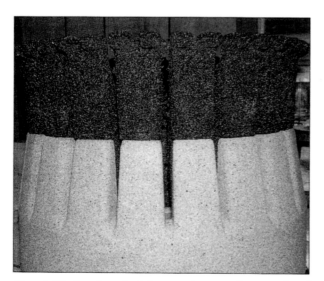

Fig. 6-20. Dual material core, top portion made of chromite sand to chill casting faster. (Courtesy: Modern Casting.)

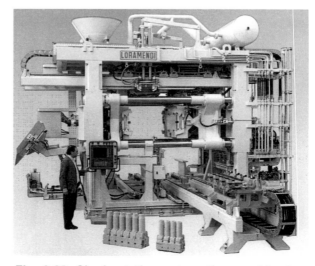

Fig. 6-23. Single-station automatic core blowing machine for vertical line coreboxes used for making large cores either by coldbox or hotbox process. [Courtesy: Loramendi S. Coop.]

The resin bond is developed while the coated sand is in contact with a metal pattern or corebox heated up to 250–300°C (482–572°F). The process allows making a thin shell, being in the section of only 10 mm (0.4 in.) thick. The synthetic resins used in shell molding are essentially thermosetting resins, which harden irreversibly by heat. The resins most widely used are phenol formaldehyde resins. Combined with sand, they develop high strength and resistance to heat. Typical sand compositions for shell molding are given in Table 6-7.

Additives, such as coal dust or iron oxide, may sometimes be added into the sand mixture, to improve the surface finish and avoid thermal cracking during pouring. Lubricants, such as calcium stearate or zinc stearate, may also be added to the resin sand mixture, to improve the flowability of the sand and permit easy release of the shell from the pattern.

The first step in making the shell mold or core is preparing of the sand mix or the coating of the sand with resin. During the coating process, heated sand is mixed with a phenolic resin, then the resin melts and coats the sand.

Since the sand-resin mixture is to be thermally cured at temperature about 250–300°C (482–572°F), only metal tooling (patterns with the associated gating and coreboxes) is used. The material used for making the tooling is gray cast iron, mainly because of its easy availability and excellent dimensional stability at the temperatures involved in the process.

There are various methods used to make molds and cores by the shell process; namely, the dump method and the blow method.

Dump method is one of the oldest methods of making shells. In this method, the metal pattern or corebox is

heated to a temperature of 200–300°C (390°F–570°F) and a silicone release agent is sprayed on its surfaces. The heated pattern or corebox is securely fixed to a dump box, as shown in Fig. 6-24(a), wherein the coated sand in an amount larger than required to form the shell of necessary thickness is already filled in. Then the dump box is rotated as shown in Fig. 6-24(b) so that the coated sand falls on the heated pattern or corebox. The heat from the tooling melts the resin adjacent to it, locking the sand grains in place, thus forming a thin shell.

When the desired thickness of the shell is achieved, as shown in Fig. 6-24(c), the dump box is rotated backwards by 180 degrees and the excess uncured sand falls back into the box, leaving the formed shell

Table 6-7. Typical Shell Sand Compositions for Various Casting Alloys.

| Casting Alloy | Shell sand composition, % | | | |
	Silica Sand	Zircon Sand	Resin	Additives
Low-carbon and alloy steels	63	30	5	2
Medium- and high- carbon steel	--	96	3	1
Gray cast iron	60	35	4	1
Brass and bronze	90	--	6	4
Aluminum alloys	95	--	4	1
Magnesium alloys	--	95	4	1

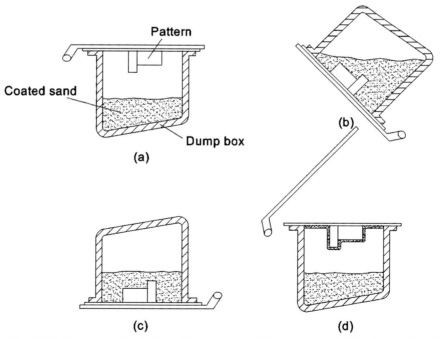

Fig. 6-24. Dump method of making shell molds or cores: (a) the heated pattern or corebox is securely fixed in the dump box; (b) the dump box is rotated 180 degrees and sand mix falls on the pattern or corebox; (c) sand mix is left on the pattern or corebox until desirable shell thickness is obtained; (d) the dump box is rotated back 180 degrees and the excess sand falls back into the box, leaving the formed shell intact with the pattern or corebox.

---

intact with the pattern as in Fig. 6-24(d). After the cure cycle is completed, the shell is mechanically separated from the pattern or corebox by ejector pins (operating through the tooling), and the unit is ready for the next run.

The average shell thickness achieved depends on the temperature of the pattern and the time the coated sand remains in contact with the heated pattern. Figure 6-25 shows typical shell thicknesses that can be obtained with various pattern temperatures and contact times. The actual shell thickness required depends on the pouring metal temperature and the casting complexity.

Blow method utilizes compressed air to deliver the shell sand to the pattern or corebox. The rest of the operations are similar to the dump method. Typically, fully automatic machines are used to make cores or molds.

Before pouring, molds are assembled, incorporating cores, if required, using adhesives applied to the mold joint surface. Pressure is usually practiced at the closing stage to improve adhesion and minimize joint line growth.

It is recommended that the shells be supported during and after pouring and put in a metal container (Fig. 6-26). This reduces the tendency of shells to distort or crack, which would diminish the quality of the castings. Dry sand, metal shot or granular refractory materials are used for supporting shell molds. Vacuum may be used to extract gas developed during pouring.

Shells have excellent breakdown at the shakeout stage resulting in lower cleaning and cleaning costs. A thermal process in which the sand is heated to eliminate the residual organic materials may reclaim shell mold sand. After cooling and screening, the sand can be recoated again with resin.

Advantages of the shell process include lower capital investments in comparison with mechanized green sand molding, low sand-to-metal ratio, elimination of mold coatings and high casting surface quality.

As disadvantages, the process requires relatively expensive materials and is limited in the size and weight range of castings made. In addition, the shell process generates harmful fumes, which must be effectively extracted.

The latest developments in shell molding technology resulted in significant reduction of resin content (up to 2%) in the mold and core mixtures, which noticeably reduced emissions and improved working conditions

6.5.2. Coldbox Processes

In the coldbox process, foundry sand is mixed with liquid binder and cured by a vapor or gas catalyst that is passed through the sand at the ambient temperature. Several different coldbox systems are currently used, employing various binders and gases as catalysts.

Typical representatives of these processes are the CO_2 process, using inorganic sodium silicate binder and carbon dioxide as a catalyst, and phenolic urethane binder using an amine vapor catalyst. In addition, there are other resin systems that may utilize gases like CO_2 and SO_2 (sulfur dioxide).

Figure 6-27 illustrates a 4-position fully automated coremaking machine incorporating coldbox technology. This Windows®-based PC control unit allows four different cores to be made simultaneously, with an average machine cycle of 7 seconds and an average tooling change time of 3 minutes.

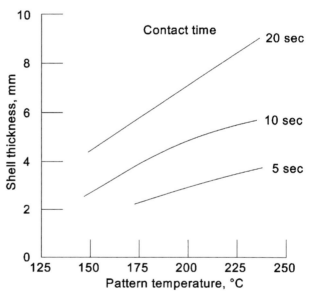

Fig. 6-25. Shell thickness as a function of pattern temperature and contact time.

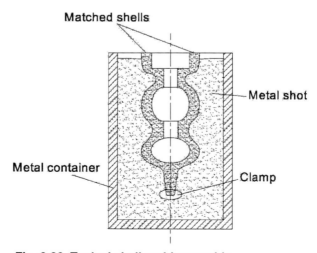

Fig. 6-26. Typical shell mold assembly.

6.5.2.1 Sodium Silicate/CO₂ Process

The concept of the coldbox process, in which a mold or core hardens in contact with the pattern or corebox at ambient temperature, emerged when the sodium silicate/CO_2 process was introduced to the foundry industry in the 1950s. The sodium silicate/CO_2 process utilizes odorless and relatively inexpensive sodium silicate as a binder and CO_2 gas (carbon dioxide) as the catalyst, which converts the sodium silicate to silica gel, resulting in a hardened mold or core.

Sodium silicate, as a binder, is compatible with all foundry sands (silica, zircon, olivine, or chromite) and does not contain nitrogen, sulfur or phosphorus; therefore, the danger of their pickup by the molten metal is eliminated and they are compatible with the green sand molding system. The latter is important when the process is used in coremaking, because the core material will be discharged into the green sand system at shakeout.

Typically, between 3 and 5% of sodium silicate, based on sand weight, is required to develop desirable sand mixture properties. The mixed sand has a reasonably good bench life, if it is not exposed to the atmosphere. In this case, the sand mix reacts with CO_2 gas contained in the atmosphere, and begins to cure. The sand mixture has very little green strength, but is improved by small additions of clay or dextrin, which also ease casting shakeout and decoring.

Patterns may be made of wood, plastic or metal, and the sand requires only minimum compaction. Commonly, a combination of light ramming with vibration provides the necessary degree of compaction for molds, while cores may be blown. The sand is hardened with CO_2 gas by using special nozzles or through the vents in the pattern or corebox. Before assembly and prior to pouring, the molds or cores are usually coated with a refractory wash to improve casting surface finish.

The major problems of the sodium silicate/CO_2 process are deterioration of molds and cores during storage. This is due to their sensitivity to humidity, and poor collapsibility, associated with the inorganic silicate bond. In addition, the process requires strict control of the CO_2 gassing stage to avoid over gassing, which leads to poor shelf life. Castings made by this process have more accurate dimensions and a smoother finish.

6.5.2.2. Phenolic Urethane/ Amine Process

Another coldbox technology, called phenolic urethane coldbox binder (PUCB) system, uses a two-part organic binder, consisting of a phenolic resin, dissolved in an organic solvent (part 1), and a polymeric isocyanate component, dissolved in a similar solvent (part 2). An amine gaseous catalyst is used to cure the core or mold (Fig. 6-28).

The resin chemistry for this process is essentially identical to that used in the nobake process, the only difference is in the part 1 solvent composition. Figure 6-29 illustrates a typical coremaking process, utilizing coldbox technology and a core blowing machine.

Fig. 6-27. Four-position, fully automated coremaking machine incorporating coldbox technology allows making four different cores simultaneously. [Source: Foundry Management and Technology, Laempe+Reich Co.]

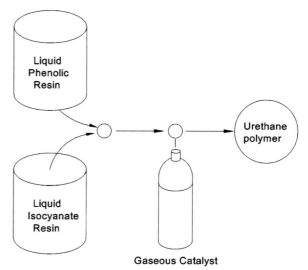

Fig. 6-28. A schematic of simplified curing reaction mechanism of the PUCB process.

First, silica sand is mixed with the binder (parts 1 and 2) in a certain proportion and put into the blowing head of the blowing machine. Then the sand mixture is blown into the corebox, and the gas catalyst is introduced through vents in the corebox, to harden the contained sand mix. The solid urethane polymer bonds the sand grains together and gives it desirable strength. The catalyst gas cycle is followed by an air purge cycle that forces the amine gas through the sand mixture and removes residual amine from the hardened core. It is recommended that the exhaust from the corebox be chemically scrubbed to remove the amine.

The PUCB process can be used with all types of foundry sand commonly used for coremaking. There are some variables, such as sand temperature and moisture that influence the properties of PUCB. The sand temperature must be between 20 and 25°C (70 and 80°F). A lower temperature can reduce mixing efficiency and increase cure times and higher temperatures reduce gassing cycles and the amount of catalyst required, but shortens the bench life of the coated sand mix. Maximum sand moisture content of 0.2% is acceptable for the process at room temperature (20°C/70°F), but when the sand temperature rises to 30°C (90°F), the moisture content of the sand must be kept at less than 0.1 % for the process to function properly.

All types of sand-mixing equipment, either batch or continuous, can be used with the PUCB process. For ferrous alloy castings, the addition of 0.75–1.5% binder, consisting of equal parts of part 1 and part 2 components, is used on washed and dried sand. For the aluminum, magnesium, and other low pouring temperature cast alloys, binder level may be reduced to 1% or less to improve collapsibility.

Certain sand additives can be used with the PUCB system to eliminate some specific casting defects. For example, iron oxide additions can effectively eliminate subsurface pinhole porosity and substantially reduce core veining (a surface defect appearing as veins or wrinkles on the casting surface due to sand cracking at elevated temperature). The organic resins and solvents in the PUCB system make it high in carbon content, which creates a reducing mold atmosphere during casting and significantly improves casting surface quality.

6.5.2.3. Resin/CO2 Process

Introduced in the 1990s, this process uses a water-based alkaline phenolic resole resin, containing less than 0.05% free phenol and less than 0.1% free formaldehyde. The binding system is activated when gaseous CO_2 passes through the sand mixture. Typically, binder is added to the silica sand at the rate of 1.5–2.2%. At a gas flow rate

between 200 and 400 liters per minute, CO_2 consumption is approximately 2% to the weight of sand. Cores and molds are made similarly to any previously described processes. Figure 6-30 shows a ductile iron valve body made using the resin/CO_2 process core. As seen, the internal cavity is free from gas porosity and veining defects.

Another significant advantage of this process is greatly improved environmental conditions, due to reduced emissions, in comparison with other resin-based systems.

6.5.3. Nobake Sand Systems

In the nobake (air-set) process, dry, clay-free foundry sand is mixed with a resin binder and liquid catalyst, which cures the resin with a controlled, predictable rate at ambient temperature without usage of external

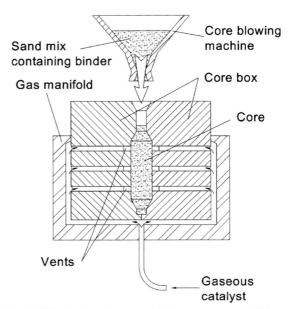

Fig. 6-29. Typical coremaking process, utilizing coldbox technology and core blowing machine.

Fig. 6-30. Ductile valve body cast with core made by resin/ CO_2 process. The internal cavity is free of gas porosity and veining defects. [Courtesy: FOSECO Metallurgical, Inc.]

Sand Molding and Coremaking Processes

heat. In one widely used nobake system, called the phenolic urethane system, the binder consists of a phenol formaldehyde resin dissolved in a special blend of solvents (part 1) and a polymeric isocyanate also dissolved in solvents (part 2).

Liquid amine catalyst added to the mix regulates the speed of reaction between parts 1 and 2. Typically, a mix of part 1 and 2 is used in a ratio of 40–60% (part 1) to 60–40% (part 2). Total binder addition (part 1 + part 2) is 0.8–2% of the weight of sand, depending upon sand mix applications. Catalyst content is based on the weight of binder additions and varies from 8 to 12%.

The curing process begins immediately after mixing sand with the binder and catalyst, and should be used immediately. In nobake systems, the rate of cure greatly depends upon the operating temperature, optimum being within the range of 20–25°C (70–80°F). This will reduce the amount of catalyst as well as binder consumption. Reduction of sand temperature may slow down the curing process, while increasing temperature will speed it up and may cause bench life problems.

The most widely used nobake preparation systems use high-speed continuous mixers from which the sand mix may be directly placed into the flask and over the pattern. Proper care, such as cleaning, to ensure that no sand mixture is left in the mixer, and periodical calibration should be routine procedures. Molds or cores can be produced by any compaction method for different weight and production rate, ferrous or nonferrous alloy castings.

6.5.4. Corebox Design Features for Core Blowing

Typical corebox design used in coldbox technology for core blowing machines includes a vented cavity, blow holes through which the sand enters the cavity, and ejector pins. Depending on the core complexity and process used, coreboxes may be designed with one or multiple cavities, having a horizontal or vertical parting line.

In a horizontally parted corebox, sand is distributed more evenly; therefore, more complex shaped cores can be made than in vertically parted coreboxes. The disadvantage of horizontally parted corebox construction is that some vents are frequently plugged with sand, because sand is blown directly onto the corebox.

In a vertically parted corebox, sand is blown parallel to the parting line, thus eliminating the vent plugging problem, but this design is limited to simple, mostly cylindrical shaped cores. The latter makes these coreboxes cheaper than horizontally parted boxes.

Vents are placed throughout the corebox to let the gas into and out of the corebox. The input vents supply the gas, and the exhaust vents draw the gas through the core. The size and shape of the core determine the number of input and output vents. A general rule of thumb would be to space vents no greater than 50 mm (2 in.) between their centers.

Typical corebox material is cast iron or mild steel, which are almost comparable in abrasive wear characteristics, and allows using these materials for approximately 150,000 blows. Stainless steel, however, has better wear resistance, but is more expensive. Urethane plastic is fairly inexpensive and easy to machine, but normal usage is not more than 50,000 blows. Coreboxes made of plastic can also be coated with metal. Metal coatings can effectively double the life of the tooling. For additional strength, plastic coreboxes can be used with metal frames or mandrels, allowing tooling to be used on equipment with higher clamp pressure.

The blow tubes, which are the channels or entry points where the sand mix from the core blower enters the corebox through the blow holes, are usually made from nylon or urethane plastic or medium-carbon steel thick-walled tubings. Blow tubes should be as large as possible. The larger the blow tubes, the less chance of clogging them with hardened lumps of sand. Large diameter tubes with adequate tube area per cavity allow using lower blow pressures. Preferable blow pressure ranges from 35 to 45 psi (0.24 to 0.31 MPa). Lower blow pressures reduce the velocity of the sand against the box surface and its wear, and decreasing the amount of resin wipe-off from sand grains at the point of impact. In addition, the lower the velocity, the longer the corebox will last.

Ejector pins are used to eject the core from the corebox and pickup arms are provided to simplify core-handling operations.

6.6. Mold and Core Venting

During pouring and solidification of castings, a significant amount of gas is evolved from metal, mold, core, coating and binder. Often, the permeability of sand is not enough to relieve all gases from the casting and avoid their adverse effect on casting quality, and gas-related defects such as pinholes, blowholes and scabbing may result. It needs to be kept in mind that the permeability of molds made using high pressure is significantly reduced due to higher mold density and hardness.

The gases generated within the mold can develop backpressure (pressure buildup), affecting not only the pouring time and mold filling with possible mold lifting and mold runouts resulting in production of castings with misruns (denotes an irregularity of the casting surface), but also creating unsafe working conditions during pouring. That is why proper venting of cores and molds is necessary to improve casting soundness and insure safety.

Core venting is particularly important, because the major portion of the core is directly exposed to molten metal, and areas where gases may escape are usually limited due to complex core configuration. Figure 6-31 shows a typical sand mold and core venting system. As seen, some core vents located on the areas directly exposed to the molten metal are plugged, while the others going through the core prints are open and connected to parting line mold vents, creating an integrated system of passages for gases to escape.

Vents in cores and molds can be formed by rods or wire, by drilling or by scratching. Vents passing through baked or nobake cores, or through the mold parting line, may be made using flexible textile tubing, which is placed in the core or mold during its production, where it remains during pouring.

In automatic molding, vents may be mounted on the pattern, making vertical or horizontal passages from core prints, in the gating system or onto a squeeze plate, eliminating manual operations and increasing production economics (Fig. 6-32).

6.7. Mold and Core Coatings

Mold and core coatings, also referred to as refractory coatings or washes, are paints specially developed to protect mold and core surfaces from direct contact with molten metal, and to prevent metal penetration into the sand grains; thus ensuring a good casting finish. These coatings are designed to withstand the high temperatures of molten metal, and act as a barrier between molten metal, and the core or mold surface.

A typical foundry coating is a suspension of a high-temperature mineral or refractory in a liquid carrier, either water or alcohol. Water-based coatings have the lowest cost, are nontoxic and nonflammable, but heat is required to dry the coating. It may be done in circulating air or infrared or microwave ovens. Another drawback of water-based coatings is that they may reduce the tensile strength of cores made of urethane nobake or coldbox sand mixtures, increasing

potential for core breakage. Because of this and the problem of getting the moisture out of the deep pockets of molds or cores, alcohol is preferred as a carrier for this purpose.

Alcohol-based coatings are recommended if fast drying is required and if flammability is not a problem. All containers containing alcohol-based coatings must be kept covered when not in use, properly grounded and kept away from heat, sparks and an open flame. The use of 99% isopropyl alcohol is recommend; the use of 91% alcohol can cause some coatings to thicken and lose suspension or interfere with drying.

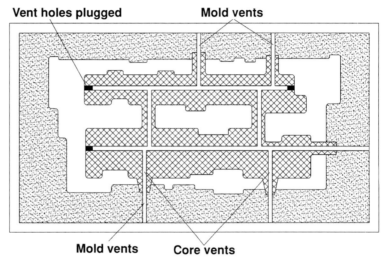

Fig. 6-31. A typical sand mold and core venting system. This is a top view of the drag half (parting line) while cope is removed.

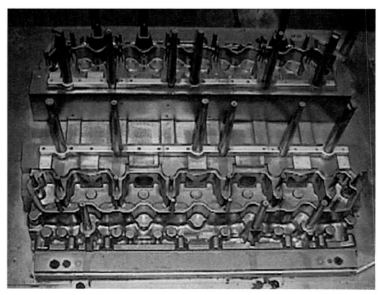

Fig. 6-32. Metal pattern for automatic molding with attached venting system.

After being applied to the core or mold surface, the liquid carrier is removed by evaporation (with or without heat) and a layer of refractory is left on the sand surface. This layer or barrier can prevent or minimize the penetration of molten metal into the sand, can reduce or prevent burn-on and erosion of the sand, and generally improve the quality of casting surface. As a result, the cost of cleaning and finishing operations and total cost of the castings will be reduced.

In sand mold practices, purely carbonaceous materials such as seacoal, finely powdered graphite or proprietary compounds are applied on to the mold cavity or to core surface by spraying, swabbing, dipping or painting. The proprietary washes are available in powder, paste or liquid form. The powder needs to be first mixed with carrier and other components and then applied, while paste and premix liquid requires only dilution, and can be used straight away.

6.8. Sand Reclamation and Recycling

6.8.1 Sand Reclamation

Sand reclamation refers to the process in which used foundry sand (mix of molding and core sands) is treated by application of the mechanical, chemical or thermal means to restore its original properties. The reclamation of spent foundry sand is a complex problem driven not only by economics of foundry operations, but also by environmental regulations controlling certain hazardous elements in disposed sand.

Conventional sand molding processes consume a significant amount of sand to produce castings. The total sand consumption depends upon the molding process used, casting size, weight and complexity, and differs for the alloys cast. For example, the typical sand-to-liquid metal ratio for iron castings is 5:1, or in other words, to pour one ton of castings, the foundry needs to use approximately 5 tons of sand.

Currently, not every foundry reclaims its sand, but disposes of it. At the same time, the cost of new sand and disposal of spent foundry sand continues to rise along with the costs of meeting environmental compliance regulations. Eventually, foundries may not be allowed to dispose of spent sand at any cost. However, a significant cost-saving potential, along with environmental impact, exists if spent sand would be reclaimed.

Reclamation Methods

Before it is reclaimed and reused, spent foundry sand, coming from shakeout, undergoes a series of operations,

performed in the following sequence:
- Crushing of sand lumps to original grains or small particles
- Magnetic separating of metal particles (core rods, nails, spills)
- Sieving the sand to control its grain size
- Sand cooling prior to blending with the new sand

This process, called primary sand reclamation or reconditioning, doesn't remove binder residuals. If binder residuals need to be removed, a special process, called secondary reclamation, is applied. Green sand can be reused multiple times without significant refinement. The sand is screened to remove fines (dead clay is also removed as fines). New sand and required additives are added to account for those lost, and then the sand is reused.

Chemically-bonded sand used for coremaking and molding is not so easily reused. However, many methods have been developed to recover foundry sand, with mixed success. These methods aim to remove residual binders and contaminants from the sand grains so that the sand can be reused without affecting the quality of the molds and cores. The selection of the methods depends largely on the type of metal cast, the binders used, and the desired reuse.

Following are three major types of secondary sand reclamation techniques involving further processing of foundry sands: Dry Sand Reclamation, Wet Sand Reclamation and Thermal Sand Reclamation.

Dry Sand Reclamation

Dry sand reclamation utilizes mechanical and pneumatic scrubbers to remove binders from the used sand.

In mechanical scrubbers, sand is fed into a rotating drum where centrifugal forces throw it against a vaned ring, and then against the drum walls. As a result, friction forces move each sand grain through a sand-to-metal or sand-to-sand interface to remove binder and other impurities. Attrition alone cannot remove all residual binders, but works well with nobake binders.

Pneumatic scrubbers use air to propel sand between baffles, rubbing and impacting each sand grain, thus removing the binder. This technique is particularly effective for removing clay from molding sands and binders in systems that are not baked.

Dry reclamation (attrition) scrubbers may produce large quantities of fines or dust. Being captured by a properly maintained emission collection system, it contributes to the total volume of solid waste. If reused sand contains a lot of fines, sand permeability is decreased.

For more effective removal of binder, heat may be added to process spent sand in dry reclamation units. The combination of sand attrition and binder combustion completely removes binders from sand grains.

Wet Sand Reclamation

Wet sand reclamation uses water to separate and remove sand binders. First, the water forms a slurry, then mixing and scrubbing actions are used to produce the friction needed to remove the binder. Clay-bonded systems work well with water reclamation processes because the clays are very soluble in water. Sodium silicate sand binders can also be removed using wet reclamation. Other less soluble chemical binders cannot be effectively dissolved in water. The drawback of the process is that organic resins that dissolve in water, and other water-soluble impurities, can cause significant water contamination. Wet sand reclamation is too expensive due to the high volume of waste water (one ton of water per ton of reclaimed sand) and strict environmental regulations. In addition, the sand, after being soaked in a water bath, needs to be dried before reuse.

Thermal Sand Reclamation

Thermal sand reclamation uses heat in rotary kiln, multiple-hearth furnaces, or fluidized bed units, to burn and remove binders and contaminants from clay and chemically-bonded sand. This process is called calcination, and the equipment used for this purpose is called a calciner.

In one of the systems used for reclamation of clay-bonded sand, the previously screened sand is fed at a controlled rate into the calciner by a variable-speed drive motor on the conveyor. The calciner, which is a natural gas, direct-fired, horizontal rotary   unit, applies heat (above 760°C (1400°F) to the sand, long enough to burn the clay, breaking its adhesion so the clay can be separated from the sand grains.

Introducing secondary combustion air through an air lance enhances the effectiveness of the process. Lance air is preheated with recovered heat from the rotary cooler and then is blown into the calciner's solids bed to oxidize the organic binders. Introducing secondary combustion air aids the complete oxidation of the binder and avoids the production of fixed carbon, or "coke," by creating an oxidizing zone at the lance. The internal heat generated by the combustion of organic materials within the bed allows the sand to reach calcination temperature quicker, and effectively extends the calcination zone. After calcination, the sand is processed through a rotary cooler, where the sand is cooled to desirable temperature and waste heat is recovered.

The disadvantage of the process is possible changing of sand composition and thermal cracking of the sand grains. That is why a good temperature control system is needed for the equipment as well as for the reclaimed sand. Otherwise, thermally treated sand may not be usable.

Infrared energy can also be used to thermally treat sand. This method allows maintaining more of the sand's original composition, while still destroying binders. External blowers push the sand through fluidized beds, allowing the sand to directly contact the infrared radiation, which breaks down the binders. The electric sand reclamation units do not produce the combustion products associated with traditional thermal reclamation processes. In foundry practice, a combination of thermal and dry (mechanical) methods is effectively used.

Process Control

The most important quality tests of reclaimed sand are screen analysis, temperature control and LOI tests. For green sand, the clay test is also significant.

Potential problems include:

- Buildup of fines with higher LOI caused by an improperly working classifying (screening) system
- High LOI with the increase in fines results in incomplete binder removal, usually associated with improperly working reclamation unit
- High sand temperature caused by high metal pouring temperature or low sand-to-metal ratio, or high ambient temperature that cannot be effectively reduced by an adequate sand cooling system

6.8.2. Sand Recycling

After several uses, about 10% of the mold and core sand in the form of fine aggregate, which cannot be reclaimed, must be removed from the sand preparation system. The most effective option for discarded foundry sand reuse is recycling. Many industries use sand as a raw material in their processes. As foundry sand is usually not hazardous, it can serve this purpose. Markets for spent foundry sand include manufacturing of cement, concrete, asphalt, bricks and tiles, flowable fill (permeable, low-strength concrete), road fill and landfill cover. A lot of potential for foundry sand use is in highway construction.

References

1. *AFS Mold and Core Test Handbook*, 3rd Ed., American Foundry Society, Des Plaines, 2000.
2. Baker, S.G., "Building the foundation to green sand," *Modern Casting*, August 2005, pp. 26-29.

3. Clegg, A.J., *Precision Casting Processes*, Pergamon Press, 1991.

4. Kotzin, Ezra, "Venting… a lost art," *Modern Casting*, March 1998, pp. 40-42.

5. *ASM Metals Handbook, Vol. 15, Casting*, American Society of Metals, Metals Park, 2008.

6. Schleg, F., *Technology of Metalcasting*, American Foundry Society, Des Plaines, 2003.

Review Questions

6.1 Explain the importance of permeability in molding sands.

6.2 Describe what properties of molding sand are desirable, from the standpoint of sound castings.

6.3 Define the ingredients of molding sand.

6.4 Explain the different additives used in molding sand.

6.5 Describe the methods used for green sand preparation.

6.6 Explain the method of determining the moisture content in molding sand.

6.7 Discuss the procedure to prepare the standard sand test specimen for testing the strength or permeability.

6.8 Describe the method used for determining the permeability of any molding sand.

6.9 Explain the grain fineness number. Give the procedure for determining this number for molding sand.

6.10 Show graphically how the green strength of sand varies with moisture content.

6.11 State the detriment caused to the mold properties if the molding sand contains (a) too much clay, (b) too much moisture.

6.12 Discuss the role of clay in molding sand. Identify the method adopted for determining the clay content in molding sand.

6.13 Explain how the shape and the size of sand grains affect the permeability and green strength of molding sand.

6.14 Explain the relevance of the facing sand toward the casting quality. Describe the difference between facing and backing sands.

6.15 Distinguish between green sand molds and dry sand molds, from the point of view of (a) process and (b) application.

6.16 Define a skin dried mold. Explain its applications.

6.17 Explain the hand molding procedures.

6.18 Describe a sand slinger and its applications in making of molds

6.19 Explain the action of a jolt molding machine.

6.20 Give the details of different types of machines available for molding.

6.21 Define flaskless molding. Describe its major operations.

6.22 Discuss different processes that are available for coremaking.

6.23 Explain the shell process for making cores and molds.

6.24 Explain the sodium silicate/CO_2 process for making cores.

6.25 Differentiate between coldbox and nobake technology used in coremaking.

6.26 Discuss the need for mold and core venting.

6.27 Write briefly about mold and core coatings and their methods of application.

6.28 Describe design features of coreboxes intended to be used with a core blowing machine.

6.29 Explain the need for sand reclamation.

6.30 Define recycled sand and give the applications where can it be reused.

Problems

6.1. A 50-g sample of silica sand is weighed after washing and drying and found to weigh 41.6 g. What would be the clay percentage in this sand sample?

6.2. The silica sand sample, when sieved through the standard sieves, was found to retain the following amounts of sand on the respective sieves:

Sieve No.	12	20	30	40
Retained Wt., g	0.73	1.26	1.03	1.44

	50	70	100	140
	2.20	3.57	5.77	14.15

	200	240	Pan
	11.13	3.98	4.67

Plot the cumulative grading curve and calculate the grain fineness number.

6.3. The zircon sand has produced the following results on sieve analysis:

Sieve No.	70	100	140
Retained Wt., g	0.02	0.51	22.60

	200	270	Pan
	24.01	2.69	0.18

Calculate the grain fineness number and explain its uses.

6.4. The olivine sand has been found to contain the following size grading:

Sieve No.	40	50	70
Retained Wt., g	0.5	17.45	20.15

100	140	200	270	Pan
8.40	1.65	1.05	0.40	0.40

Calculate the grain fineness number. If the above sand has a fusion temperature of 1700°C (3092°F), what are the applications in which this sand could be beneficially used?

6.5. Calculate the permeability number of a sand specimen if it takes 1 min 15 s to pass 2000 cm^3 of air at a pressure of 6 g/cm^2 through the standard sample.

MELTING AND POURING PRACTICES

Objectives

Melting of foundry alloys constitutes an important component in ensuring the proper characteristics of castings. After studying this chapter the reader should be able to:

- Recognize broad varieties of furnaces used for melting cast alloys
- Decide on the different types of melting furnaces that could be suited for ferrous alloys
- Discuss inoculation methods used in iron melting practice
- Choose the appropriate magnesium treatment technique to produce ductile iron for a given foundry
- Explain the various types of melting options for nonferrous alloys
- Select from a range of equipment for pouring molten metal into the molds
- Utilize different methods for controlling the quality of molten metal

Keywords

Furnace, Melting, Tapping, Batch Melting, Tap-and-Charge Melting, Continuous Melting, Charge Mix, Charging, Molten Metal, Coke, Scrap, Alloying Elements, Graphite Flake, Flux, Charge Preheating, Cupola, Tuyeres, Gray Iron , Ferrous Alloy, Nonferrous Alloy, Refractories, Magnesite, Basic Refractories, Acid Refractories, Neutral Refractories, Slag Basicity, Hot Blast Cupola, Cold Blast Cupola, Recuperative System, Iron Melting, Crucible, Induction Coreless Furnace, Induction Melting, Channel Induction Furnace, Ferroalloys, Ferrosilicon, Furnace Lining, Sintering of Lining, Iron Inoculation, Preinoculation, Postinoculation, Ladle Inoculation, In-Stream Inoculation, Masteralloy, Wire Inoculation, In-Mold Inoculation, In-Filter Inoculation, Gray Iron, Ductile Iron, Nodulizer, Deoxidation, Magnesium Treatment, Magnesium Recovery, Pyroeffect, Pure Magnesium, Magnesium Masteralloy, Rare Earth Metals, Ladle, Sandwich Process, Plunging Process, Treatment Converter, Tundish Ladle, Tundish-Converter, Cored Wire Magnesium Treatment, Flow-Through Magnesium Treatment, Electric Arc Furnace, Steel Melting, Crucible Furnace, Reverberatory Furnace, Aluminum Alloys Melting, Degassing, Fluxing, Grain Refinement, Gas Diffuser, Thermal Efficiency of Melting Furnace, Melt Loss, Pouring, Pouring Ladles, Automatic Pouring, Pouring Manipulator, Traveling Pouring Station, Automatic Ladling System, Pressurized Induction Pouring Furnace, Electromagnetic Pouring System, Laser Sensoring System, Vision-Based Pouring System, Quality Control, Chemistry Control, Thermal Analysis System, Spectrometry, Temperature Measurements, Noncontact Thermometer-Pyrometer, Slag, Slag Control, Gas Control, Reduced Pressure Test, Cleanliness Testing of Molten Aluminum, Iron Solidification Structure, Chill Control, Hydrogen Content, Microstructure, Filter, Castability, Iron Carbide, Chill Wedge.

After molding, melting is the major operation that controls the quality of the castings. Theoretically, melting is a process in which metal changes its state from solid to liquid by applying heat. Practically, many more operations are involved in molten metal processing of ferrous and nonferrous alloys.

Common to any melting process are the following three procedures:

1. Charging or placing materials to be melted in the melting furnace; these materials are called charge materials. A typical charge mix consists of fresh (new) raw materials (pig irons for ferrous alloys or prealloyed ingots for nonferrous alloys), purchased scrap, foundry returns (gating systems and scrap castings), alloying elements in the form of pure metals or alloys and slag-forming materials, called fluxes, used to dissolve and remove impurities.

2. Melting, during which metal refining and chemistry adjustments are made.

3. Tapping or molten metal withdrawal from the melting unit into the transfer or pouring ladle.

There are three methods involved in the melting practice of foundry alloys:

- *Batch operation*, in which the entire furnace is emptied and then recharged; each batch is called a heat. This melting mode can be used in any type of furnace.

- *Tap-and-charge operation*, in which a portion, typically between 50 and 75% of molten metal, is tapped and recharged with equal quantity of charge mix. This type of operation is also called a hot heel. It helps preheat the next charge and accelerate its meltdown. This method is mostly utilized in the induction melting of irons and in the crucible or reverberatory furnaces melting practice of some nonferrous alloys.

- *Continuous melting operation*, in which charging, melting and tapping procedures are done continuously, for example, in cupola melting, steelmaking and vacuum refining of specialty steels and superalloys.

When a second furnace is used to hold and maintain a certain molten metal at temperature, it is called a holding furnace and the process is called a duplex-process. For example, in iron melting practice, a common duplex-process may be either a cupola with a channel type induction holder, or an induction furnace with an induction channel holder. To protect the molten metal surface against reaction with the atmosphere, special compounds or toppings are used. These compounds also insulate the molten metal and reduce heat loss during prolonged holding or pouring.

7.1. Melting Furnaces

There are a number of furnace designs available for melting foundry alloys. Their choice depends on the technical considerations such as amount and type of alloy to be melted, required temperature, quantity of molten metal needed, and type of charge materials, along with economics of the installation and operations and environmental requirements.

Table 7.1 shows melting temperatures and the heat required for melting some foundry metals. As can be seen, the melting requirements differ greatly for various metals.

The variety of melting furnaces generally used in the

foundry industry to melt cast metals and alloys may be classified, based on the source of heating, as:

- Electrical (arc, resistance or induction)
- Fuel-fired (solid, oil or gaseous)

Another classification may use design features of furnaces that identify them as hearth, rotary, crucible, channel or reverberatory. Some of the more commonly used melting furnaces include cupolas, crucible furnaces, electric (induction, resistance and arc) furnaces, and reverberatory furnaces.

The cupola has been the most widely used furnace for melting cast iron. This is because of the low cost involved in its operation. However, less control of the final iron quality and the necessity of meeting stringent emission regulations caused significant construction changes and increased operation and maintenance cost. The latter brought about a new generation of modern, but costly, cupolas, economically justified only in high-volume consumption of molten cast iron.

With the development of induction melting, induction furnaces are being increasingly used in view of the better chemistry and temperature control of molten metal and lower melting losses. For the same purpose, the induction furnaces have been widely used for melting of small-to-medium sized steel castings. For heavy steel castings, the electric arc furnaces are generally suitable for melting. Rarely, are they used in iron melting practice.

Table 7-2 shows the efficiency and melt loss for various melting furnaces [Ref. 12]. Electric resistance furnaces are generally used for melting and holding nonferrous alloys.

7.1.1. Refractory Lining

Lining Materials

Data on refractoriness of some foundry sands was presented in Chapter 6 (Table 6-1). Most of these materials are also used as refractory for lining of melting

Table 7-1. Melting Temperatures and Heat Required for Melting Cast Metals.

Cast Metals	Melting Temperature, °C (°F)	Mean Specific Heat, Cal /g°C (Btu/lb-°F)	Latent Heat of Fusion, Cal /g (Btu/lb)	Heat required for melting 1 kg (2.2 lb), kJ (Btu)
Iron	1537 (2799)	0.141 (0.141)	65.0 (117)	1168 (1107)
Nickel	1453 (2647)	0.131 (0.131)	72.1 (130)	1084 (1027)
Copper	1083 (1981)	0.105 (0.105)	48.9 (88)	674 (639)
Aluminum	660 (1220)	0.237 (0.237)	92.7 (167)	1022 (969)
Magnesium	650 (1202)	0.289 (0.289)	85.6 (154)	1122 (1063)
Zinc	420 (788)	0.101 (0.101)	26.3 (47)	285 (270)

furnaces and pouring ladles. Table 7-3 compares some high temperature properties of refractory materials widely used in foundry practice.

Melting furnaces are refractory-lined, mostly to protect the steel shell against heat, abrasion and oxidation. In ferrous alloy melting practice, the lining material has an additional and very important function: to control sulfur and phosphorus contents. The process aimed to remove sulfur is called desulfurization. Phosphorus is removed by the process called dephosphorization. To remove these elements, basic-type fluxes should be used so that the lining material will be able to withstand the detrimental effect of basic slags.

Commonly, refractory materials, used for lining of melting furnaces, are divided into three groups (acid, basic or neutral) depending upon their reactivity with the slags formed during the melting process.

The first group, acid refractories, consists of materials, such as silica (SiO_2), fireclay (alumino-silicate); refractory bricks made of fireclay can withstand temperature up to 1600°C/2900°F), mullite (alumino-silicate) and zircon, which contains SiO_2 in different amounts. These refractories do not react with acid slags, but are very reactive with basic slags. The latter means that, in acid ferrous alloy melting, sulfur and phosphorus contents cannot be removed because the basic type of slags produced as a result of these reactions would destroy the acid lining. The acid refractories mostly are low cost materials used in iron melting and aluminum melting.

Table 7-2. Comparative Efficiency and Melt Loss for Different Melting Furnaces [Ref. 12]. [Courtesy: Modern Casting]

Melting Furnace	Casting Alloy	Melt loss	Thermal efficiency
Cupola	Iron	3–12%	40–50%
Direct arc	Steel	5–8%	35–45%
Immersion	Zinc	N/A	63–67%
Electric reverberatory	Aluminum	1–2%	59–76%
	Zinc	2–3%	59–76%
Gas crucible	Aluminum	4–6%	7–19%
	Magnesium	4–6%	7–19%
Gas reverberatory	Aluminum	3–5%	30–45%
	Zinc	4–7%	32–40%
Gas stack melter	Aluminum	1–2%	40–45%
Induction	Aluminum	0.75–1.25%	59–76%
	Copper base	2–3%	50–70%
	Magnesium	2–3%	59–76%
	Iron	1–2%	50–70%
	Steel	2–3%	50–70%

Table 7-3. Some High Temperature Properties of Refractory Materials.

Refractory material and it chemical notation	Average melting temperature, °C (°F)	Coefficient of linear expansion, $\times 10^{-6}/°C$ ($\times 10^{-6}/°F$)
Fused Silica (>98%SiO_2)	1710 (3110)	0.5 (0.28)
Mullite ($Al_2O_3.SiO_2$)	1810 (3290)	6.0 (3.33)
Alumina (Al_2O_3)	2020 (3668)	9.5 (5.28)
Magnesia (MgO)	2800 (5072)	13.5 (7.50)
Zircon ($ZrO_2. SiO_2$)	2482 (4500)	4.5 (2.5)
Zirconia (ZrO_2)	2650 (4802)	4.0 (2.22)
Silicon Carbide (SiC)	~ 2700 (4892)	3.5 (1.94)
Graphite	~4200 (7592)	-

The second group, <u>basic refractories</u>, consists of magnesia, which is magnesium oxide (MgO), magnesite, which is magnesium carbonate ($MgCO_3$) and dolomite, which is calcium magnesium carbonate ($CaMgCO_3$). These materials contain high amounts of MgO or CaO (calcium oxide), they can withstand damaging effect of basic slags and dross, they have high fusion temperature, but are more costly.

The third group, <u>neutral refractories</u>, includes such materials as alumina and chromite that have average fusion points of 2020°C (3668°F) and 1980°C (3596°F) respectively, as well as graphite, which can withstand temperatures up to 4200°C (7592°F). These neutral refractory materials, as their name implies, do not react with either acid or basic slags or dross and can be used in melting of any alloys if economically justified.

Slag Basicity

The refractory used in the furnace determines the type of flux used and, subsequently, the type of slag produced. To characterize slag reactivity, the term slag basicity, B, is commonly used, and is calculated from the following equation:

$$B = \frac{(CaO\% + MgO\%)}{(SiO_2\% + Al_2O_3\%)} \qquad (7.1)$$

If B > 1, the slag is considered basic; if B < 1, the slag is acid type.

If the furnace is lined with an acid type of refractory, the slag should also be acid with a high percentage of SiO_2. Otherwise, the slag will attack and destroy the lining, because at high temperature, acid SiO_2 and basic MgO or CaO, contained in basic slag, can react and form calcium or magnesium silicates:

$$SiO_2 + CaO = CaSiO_3 \quad \text{or} \qquad (7.2)$$
$$SiO_2 + MgO = MgSiO_3 \qquad (7.3)$$

Both $CaSiO_3$ and $MgSiO_3$ have a low melting point, leading to refractory deterioration and drastic reduction of lining material life.

Depending upon furnace size and technical requirements, refractory materials can be used in the form of ramming mixes, sintered dry granular mixes, plastic mixes, bricks or precast nozzles or crucibles.

7.2. MELTING OF FERROUS ALLOYS

7.2.1. Cupola Melting of Cast Irons

Cast irons can be melted in cupolas, electric induction and arc furnaces. This section will center on cupola melting.

The cupola is one of the oldest types of melting equipment used for cast iron melting. It is estimated that cupolas generate almost 50% of the current worldwide iron production. In the USA, cupola-operated foundries make about five million tons of castings for the automotive industry, farm machinery, piping and municipal applications.

7.2.1.1. Cupola Construction

The cupola is a cylindrical, vertical, steel shaft-type melting furnace in which the metallic charge material melts in direct contact with the fuel. Coke, gas or other carbon-bearing materials are used as fuel in cupolas. The cupola (Fig. 7-1) consists of a cylindrical steel shell with a refractory-lined interior. After closing the drop doors (located at the bottom) a proper sand bed is prepared. This rammed sand bed provides the necessary refractory bottom for the molten metal and the coke during cupola operation.

Right above the sand bed is the tapping hole, which is initially closed with a plug until the molten metal is ready for tapping. In a rear-slagging cupola, the slag hole is situated above the metal tap hole, in a position opposite

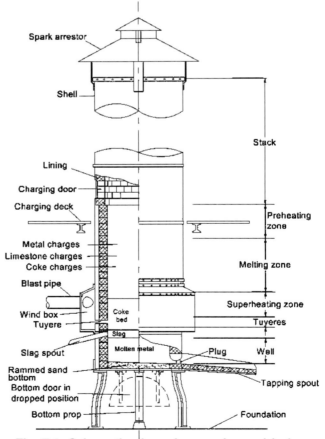

Fig. 7-1. Schematic view of a cupola used in iron melting practice.

to it. The slag generated during the melting process is discharged through the slag hole or spout. In a front-slagging cupola, slag and molten iron are continuously discharged through the same taphole and separated in a small basin in the spout. Above the slag hole, is the windbox, which is connected to the air blowers supplying the requisite air at a given pressure and quantity. The air blast enters the cupola through the openings called tuyeres.

In small-size cupolas, the tuyeres are arranged in one row; most medium and large cupolas are provided with two or even three rows of tuyeres; for example, two rows of tuyeres, specifically spaced apart from each other with the blast equally divided between them. The benefit of increased rows of tuyeres is that the iron tapping temperature is increased by about 40–50°C (104–122°F) at a given coke consumption. In contemporary cupolas, tuyeres are slightly protruding toward the center of the shaft, are water-cooled and made of copper (Fig. 7-2).

At the charging deck, a charging door is located, through which the charge consisting of coke, flux and a mix of metallic materials is fed into the cupola. In medium- or large-production foundries, cupolas are furnished with a mechanized charging system (Fig. 7-3). In this system, incoming materials, brought by railroad cars, are stored in hoppers (for metals) or in bins (for coke and flux), from where they are moved to weighing hoppers, then placed into charging buckets and finally charged into the cupola.

Modern cupolas are water-cooled; the cooling system may be internal, where water is circulated between the inner and outer shell or external, in which a water stream flows along the outer shell, creating a water curtain.

Conventional cupolas are refractory-lined internally to protect the steel shell against heat, abrasion and oxidation. Overall lining thickness in the melting zone ranges from approximately 100 to 300 mm (4 to 8 in.); in the charging zone, the cupola is lined with cast iron brick to withstand the mechanical impact of charge materials. The refractory lining above the charge door is not as thick as in the melting zone, since it is not exposed to much heat.

The type of lining material used depends upon the desired cast iron chemistry. For conventional gray irons, acid lining, such as fireclay brick or block, is commonly used. This lining may be repaired by patching with a monolithic ramming mixture, using a pneumatic gun to blow a mixture of clay and ganister (containing water) which becomes entrained in the stream as it exits the mixing nozzle.

A basic lining (magnesite or dolomite) is recommended if the molten iron is intended for ductile iron production, in which the sulfur content before magnesium treatment is restricted. This lining costs several times more than an

Fig. 7-2. Side view of a blast air windbox with water-cooled tuyeres in a continuously-operated hot blast cupola with melting rate of 40 t/h (88,000 lb/h).

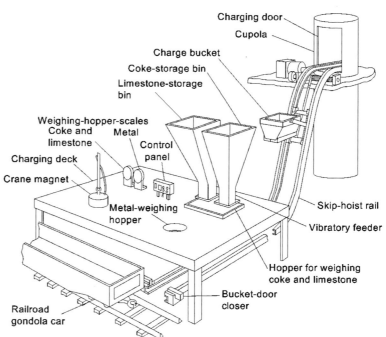

Fig. 7-3. Mechanized charging system for cupola installation. [Source: ASM Handbook, vol.15]

acid lining. In the conventional melting practice of cast iron, a pair of cupolas is used; while one is melting, the other is repaired.

7.2.1.2. Cold and Hot Blast Cupolas

Depending on the air blast temperature, cupolas are classified as cold-blast and hot-blast. In a cold-blast cupola, air, injected through the tuyeres, has an ambient temperature. In an advanced design variation of the cupola, called a hot-blast cupola, the incoming air is preheated with the help of the recuperative system utilizing heat of generated gases coming out of the stack, which preheats the incoming air to a temperature of 400–500°C (750–930°F).

In the latest hot-blast cupola designs, the recuperative system is additionally equipped with a gas combustion device in which outgoing gases (such as carbon monoxide) are burned to produce an additional amount of heat. This source of energy can boost heat input to the cupola by as much as 50%. The heat from these sources is directed into the heat exchanger, developing blast air temperatures up to 550–700°C (1020–1300°F)

Figure 7-4 shows the recuperative system of a continuously operated hot-blast cupola with a melting rate of 40t/h (88,000 lb/h).

The main advantage of a recuperative system, besides the environmental impact, is that for the given iron temperature, the amount of coke required by the cupola may be reduced. This, in turn, reduces the contact of the metal with the coke and air, thus reducing the carbon and sulfur pickups as well as oxidation losses. These cupolas are used for the production of low sulfur ductile-base iron using a basic lining and basic fluxes.

The emission control system in a modern cupola, designed to meet environmental regulations, is a complex and costly system. Because of the additional equipment and the extra care needed for operation and maintenance, the hot-blast cupolas are used only in foundries that require large amounts of molten metal, operating on a long campaign (time between shutdowns) in a continuous basis. Contemporary cupolas can operate continuously without repair as long as six months, producing between 25 and 125 tons of molten iron per hour; their inner diameter can vary from 1 to 3 m (3 to 10 ft), and height may reach up to 12.2 m (40 ft).

7.2.1.3. Charging and Operations

The charge materials used in cupolas consist of coke, metal charge and flux. Coke is typically added in the amount 8–12% of metal charge, depending upon the size and operation parameters. Coke should have a proper

chemistry (less than 0.8% sulfur, over 90% carbon and less than 8% ash), sufficient strength and abrasion resistances, and must be screened to desirable size to remove small particles, which limit air distribution and may cause overloading of the emission system.

The metal charge needed to produce cast iron essentially consists of pig iron, cast iron scrap that includes foundry returns (ingates, risers, internal scrap), steel scrap and ferroalloys. Steel or iron turnings are used in the form of briquettes; thin steel punchings or cans must be compressed into bundles. Ferroalloys are added to compensate for elements such as silicon and manganese that might be lacking in the charge. The proportions of these components depend on their chemical compositions and on the final chemistry of the cast iron desired.

Fig. 7-4. Recuperative system of hot blast continuously-operated 40 t/h (88,000 lb/h) cupola installation.

Melting and Pouring Practices

The fluxes are added in the charge to remove the oxides and other impurities present in the metal. The flux most commonly used is limestone ($CaCO_3$) in a proportion of about 2 to 4% of the metal charge. Some of the other fluxes that may also be used are dolomite, sodium carbonate and calcium carbide. The flux is expected to react with the oxides and form compounds that have a low melting point and also are lighter. As a result, the molten slag is floating on the top of molten iron and, thus, can very easily be separated and removed.

To operate the cupola, first, the drop doors at the bottom are closed and a sand bed with a gentle slope towards the tap hole is rammed. Then, a coke bed of suitable height, typically to a level 1000–1500 mm (40–60 in.) above the tuyeres, is prepared and ignited. When the coke bed is properly ignited, layers of metal charge, flux and coke are consecutively fed into the cupola through the charge door, maintaining the necessary proportions and rate of charging. The charge is then allowed to soak in the heat for a while, and then the air blast is turned on. Within about 5 to 10 minutes, the molten metal is collected near the tap hole. Further operations depend on the type of cupola tapping operation: intermittent or continuous.

In *intermittent* tapping, both, metal and slag holes are plugged until enough molten metal is collected in the well of the cupola, and the slag is drained off through the slag hole before opening the metal tap hole. This type of operation is suitable mostly for relatively low-volume metal consumption. Most large, highly productive cupolas operate in *continuous* tapping mode, with an open tap hole where molten iron flows either into a forehearth (refractory-lined unheated reservoir) or through the launder (refractory-lined channel) into the holding furnace. The forehearth serves for storing molten metal and chemical composition adjustments. The molten metal collected in the forehearth or holding furnace, is then tapped into the pouring ladles and transported to the molds where it is poured with a minimum time loss.

In general, the operational parameters of a cupola depend upon its diameter, type of air blasts used and metal-to-coke ratio. Table 7-4 shows how melting rate, air blast rate and pressure, as well as charge mix components, would be changed in cupolas having different diameters and metal-to-coke ratio.

Air blast enrichment with oxygen at a rate of 2–4% is found to be the most effective measure for improving metal tapping temperature at the start up of a cupola operation, or following shutdown periods. The continuous use of oxygen (if economically justified) results in higher molten metal temperatures and carbon pickup at the same coke level, or reduces coke consumption for a given tapping temperature. The cupolas may be used alone as a principal melting unit or in a duplex-process: cupola-induction holding furnace or electric arc holding furnace.

Table 7-4. Typical Cold Blast Cupola Operational Parameters.

Diameter of melting zone, m (ft)	Melting rate, t/h, Metal to coke ratio		Air Blast Rate m³/h (ft³/h)	Air Blast Pressure kPa (psi)	Typical charge content, kg (lb)		
	10:1	8:1			Coke	Metal portion	Flux (limestone)
0.50 (1.6)	1.97	1.57	1,340 (47,320)	10.20 (1.48)	20 (44)	200 (440)	7 (15)
0.60 (2.0)	2.84	2.46	1,940 (68,510)	10.50 (1.52)	28 (62)	284 (626)	9 (20)
0.80 (2.6)	5.11	4.36	3,450 (121,830)	11.20 (1.62)	51 (112)	510 (1124)	17 (37)
1.00 (3.3)	7.99	6.83	5,380 (189,990)	11.70 (1.70)	80 (176)	800 (1764)	26 (57)
1.20 (3.9)	11.50	9.79	7,750 (273,690)	12.70 (1.84)	115 (254)	1150 (2535)	38 (84)
1.40 (4.6)	15.60	13.33	10,600 (374,340)	13.40 (1.94)	157 (346)	1570 (3461)	52 (115)
1.60 (5.2)	20.44	17.41	13,800 (487,340)	14.40 (2.09)	200 (440)	2040 (4497)	67 (148)
1.80 (5.9)	25.88	22.05	17,450 (616,240)	15.40 (2.23)	260 (573)	2590 (5710)	85 (187)
2.00 (6.6)	31.95	27.22	21,550 (761,030)	17.20 (2.49)	320 (705)	3200 (7055)	106 (234)

7.2.1.4. Chemical and Charge Calculations

The combustion of carbon (C) in coke generates temperatures up to 1650–1675°C (3000–3100°F), which melts the metallic charge. This reaction is shown in equation 7.4.

$$C + O_2 = CO_2 \text{ (oxidizing zone)} \qquad (7.4)$$

Upon moving up through the coke, carbon dioxide reacts with C forming carbon monoxide:

$$CO_2 + C = 2CO \text{ (reduction zone)} \qquad (7.5)$$

Outgoing hot gases heat the above-located layers of the charge mix thus reducing their meltdown time. Produced droplets of molten iron, about 4–6 mm (0.2–0.25 in.), are filtered through the coke, absorb the carbon (carburized) and sulfur (sulfurized), and slightly oxidize above the tuyeres and, finally, fall and collect at the bottom on the cupola. Because of oxidation, the chemical elements may gain or lose during cupola melting.

Typical range of chemical composition of cupola melted iron is as follows (wt %): 3.2–3.8 C; 1.5–3.0 Si; 0.2–1.0 Mn; up to 0.15%S and up to 0.25 %P. Note. For special gray irons, P content can be intentionally increased up to 0.8%. In general, increasing P up to certain limits, significantly improves fluidity of molten iron that plays an important role in thin and ultra-thin gray iron castings production, i.e., automotive and tractor piston rings, etc. At the same time, increased P in gray iron forms low temperature iron-phosphate eutectic, called steadite, which is useful for wear resistance, but detrimental to machinability, mechanical properties and quality of castings by promoting shrinkage and metal penetration.

For proper control, it is very important in the foundry to know the final composition of the molten metal obtained. The chemical elements in the final cupola melt analysis are essentially the sum total of what is contained in each of the charge ingredients, with some losses or pickup. Out of the various elements, the ones that are the most important for cast iron are carbon, silicon, manganese, sulfur and phosphorous

As the charge comes through the coke bed, the metal, depending on the temperature and the time when the metal is in contact with the coke, picks up some amount of carbon. Thus, it may be reasonable to assume a pickup of about 0.15% carbon. Silicon is likely to be oxidized in the cupola and therefore, a loss of 10% of total silicon contained in the charge is expected. To compensate for the silicon loss, ferrosilicon or silicon carbide bricks can be added.

Manganese is also likely to be lost in the melting process. The loss could be of the order of 15–20%. Loss of manganese in the final analysis can be made up by the addition of ferromanganese. Similar to carbon, sulfur is also likely to be picked up from coke during melting. The pickup depends on the sulfur content of the coke, but a reasonable estimate could be from 40 to 60%. There are no changes in phosphorus content.

Example 7-1 illustrates typical estimation of the final chemistry of the gray cast iron produced with the following charge mix compositions and proportions.

Example 7-1

	Carbon	Silicon	Manganese	Sulfur	Phosphorus	% In charge
Pig iron 1	3.50	2.50	0.40	0.01	0.40	40
Pig iron 2	3.20	1.50	1.00	0.02	0.60	35
Gray iron scrap	3.20	2.50	0.50	0.10	0.40	25

First, estimate the total amount of elements present in 1 ton (1000 kg) of charge, assuming carbon pickup as 0.15%, sulfur pickup as 0.05%, silicon loss as 10% and manganese loss as 20%, and then calculate final chemistry of iron (Table 7-5).

The foundry can control the iron chemistry by actually trying various mixes of charge materials available at a given foundry, to obtain the most economical melt. For this purpose, some foundries are using their own, or supplied by furnace's manufacturer, computerized programs that calculate the final chemistry based on the addition rate of every charge component and its cost.

7.2.1.5. Latest Developments

Among the latest developments, which have drastically improved cupola operations and effectiveness, the following are the most important:

- Computerized control, monitoring and interfacing of major cupola operation parameters (air blast, charging and emissions)

- Automated systems for metallic and nonmetallic charge assembly, delivery and loading into the cupola

- Tuyere injection system, utilized for coke breeze and other carbon-containing waste materials and for alloys and ferroalloys

- Cokeless cupola, using natural gas as a fuel, minimizes pollution and enables the melting of iron with low sulfur, suitable for ductile production

For years, cupola melting was extensively used because of low operational cost and high production rate. With implementation of all latest innovations, the cost of new modern cupolas and their maintenance significantly rose. The latter, along with tightening environmental regulations requiring strict emission control, led to the declining cupola usage in favor of induction melting, which generates less emissions and ensures more precise chemistry and temperature control.

7.2.2. Induction Melting of Iron

Depending upon the construction and applications, there are two types of induction furnaces:

- Coreless induction furnace, which is used primarily for melting of cast alloys

- Channel or core induction furnace, which is used as a holding furnace

7.2.2.1. Coreless Induction Furnace

The coreless induction furnace (Fig. 7-5) is a box-type furnace, consisting of a refractory crucible, surrounded by a hollow water-cooled copper coil. When alternating electric current is applied to this induction coil, it first generates a magnetic field around the coil, and then produces a secondary magnetic field in the charge material that heats and, eventually, melts it. As a result of interference of these two opposing magnetic fields, a strong electromagnetic stirring effect is generated. The intensity of stirring is determined by the size of the furnace, the power put into the metal, the frequency of the electromagnetic field and the type and amount of metal in the furnace. Due to this effect, charge materials become quickly immersed in the melt, producing a homogeneous metal with precise chemistry and temperature, and low oxidation losses.

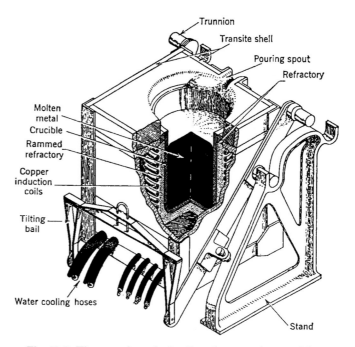

Fig. 7-5. The coreless induction furnace is used for melting all grades of irons and steels as well as many nonferrous alloys.

Table 7-5. Computation of Cupola Melted Iron Chemistry.

Charge materials	kg	%	Carbon, %		Silicon, %		Manganese, %		Sulphur, %		Phosphorous, %	
			in material	in charge	in material	in charge	in material	in charge	in material	in charge	in material	in charge
Pig iron 1	300	30	3.5	3.5×0.30 = 1.05	2.5	2.5×0.30 = 0.75	0.4	0.4×0.30 = 0.120	0.01	0.01×0.30 = 0.003	0.25	0.25×0.30 = 0.075
Pig iron 2	350	35	3.2	3.2×0.35 = 1.12	1.5	1.5×0.35 = 0.525	1	1.00×0.35 = 0.35	0.02	0.02×0.35 = 0.007	0.35	0.35×0.35 = 0.1225
Cast iron scrap	250	25	3.2	3.2×0.25 = 0.80	2.5	0.25×0.25 = 0.625	0.5	0.50×0.25 =0.125	0.1	0.10×0.25 = 0.025	0.25	0.254×0.25 = 0.0625
Steel scrap	100	10	0.2	0.2×0.10 = 0.02	0.2	0.20×0.10 = 0.02	0.6	0.60×0.10 =0.06	0.02	0.02×0.10 = 0.002	0.03	0.03×0.10 = 0.003
Total	1000	100										
Total in charge, %				2.99		1.92		0.655		0.037		0.263
Change in cupola				+0.15		-0.192		-0.131		+0.05		
Estimated composition, %				3.14		1.728		0.524		0.087		0.263

The chief advantage of this type of furnace is the fact that the heat source is isolated from the charge, and the slag and flux get the necessary heat directly from the charge instead of the heat source.

However, the stirring effect of the electric current would cause fluxes to be entrapped in the melt if they are mixed along with the charge. Therefore, flux is generally added after switching off the power to the furnace. Then sufficient time must be allowed for the oxides to be removed by the flux (as slag) before transferring the metal for pouring. The stirring effect allows utilizing low-cost raw materials, such as metal turnings or other small size returns or chips, and at the same time, achieving better control of temperature and composition. Due to the same effect, ferroalloy and alloying element additions can be made to the melt to correct iron chemical composition.

A disadvantage of the stirring is that it causes the refractory lining of the furnace to wear gradually away through the action of the moving metal on the furnace walls. This gradual wear requires that furnaces be relined periodically.

Currently, foundries are using the most economical medium-frequency (150–700 Hz) induction coreless furnaces, where capacities may vary in the range from 0.1 to 100 ton (220 to 220,000 lb).

The coreless induction furnace is commonly used to melt all grades of steels and irons as well as many nonferrous alloys in all kinds of production: low to mass production. They are found to be particularly useful in the small, low-production rate foundries operating on a batch basis. That means a number of sand molds are prepared and kept ready for pouring before the molten metal is prepared. This process may take a few hours or shifts depending upon the size and type of the foundry. Thus, it necessitates melting only as needed.

7.2.2.2. Channel Induction Furnace

The channel induction furnace, illustrated in Fig. 7-6(a) and (b), is a vertical or horizontal type refractory-lined vessel in which the channel encircles a laminated steel core and coil assembly. The electric circuit formed by the core and coil is completed when the channel is filled with molten metal. Once the channel is filled with molten metal, power is applied to the copper coil. This produces an intense electromagnetic field, which causes the electric current to flow through and further heat the molten metal in the channel. Hotter metal leaving the channel circulates upward, raising the temperature of the entire bath.

Because the local heating takes place only in the channel of these furnaces, metal superheating and dissolution rates of additives used in iron melting, such as carbon and ferroalloys, are limited. The channel induction furnaces are used mostly as holding or duplexing units in the cast iron melting practice.

These furnaces operate only in a tap-and-charge mode, where molten metal is added into the bath after some of its portion is tapped out, to keep the induction channel fully filled with molten metal. Because these furnaces serve mostly for molten metal holding, they are simpler in design and have better electrical efficiency than coreless induction furnaces, but require greater attention to the proper selection of refractory lining material for the channel and monitoring of the lining condition, to prevent plugging. The channel induction furnaces are built in capacities up to 200 ton (440,000 lb).

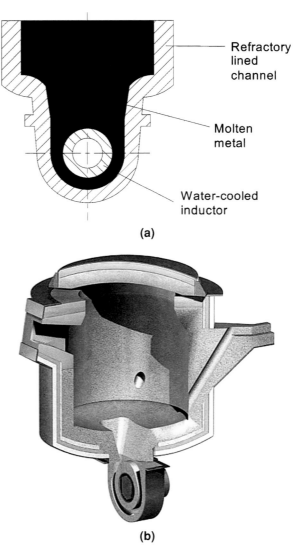

Fig. 7-6. Vertical type channel induction furnace used mainly for holding and duplexing cast irons: (a) cross-section; (b) actual view.

7.2.2.3. Charging and Chemical Calculations

Due to the ability to accurately control chemistry and temperature and high flexibility in cast alloy changes, induction furnaces are widely used in iron melting practice. Another advantage is the possibility of utilization of steel scrap up to 70% in the charge mix. It is estimated that current induction melting contributes to nearly 40% of all domestic iron production.

Charge Calculations

For mostly hypoeutectic (C.E. < 4.3%) compositions of gray iron, the charge mix may consist of any materials and their proportions such pig iron, cast iron returns, cast iron turnings, steel scrap, carbon material, called carbon riser, and ferroalloys additions.

For mostly hypereutectic or eutectic compositions of ductile iron, the charge mix may consist of the previously-mentioned materials in which sulfur and phosphorus content is restricted. Residual carbide-promoting elements, such as boron, chromium, titanium and vanadium, must be limited to specification levels. Besides these, controlling the very small amounts of tramp (harmful) elements, preventing graphite nodule formation and promoting flake graphite (i.e., aluminum, antimony, arsenic, lead, zinc), in the charge mix materials for ductile iron is also very important. All of these things can have a negative effect on castings properties and performance.

Ferroalloys and alloying elements, as well as carbon-containing materials, are added into the melt to adjust the final chemistry. Economic and technical considerations dictate optimal usage of different charge materials in each given foundry. The following examples only illustrate possible variations in charge makeup for gray and ductile irons.

Example 7-2

Charge calculation for gray iron Grade 30, melted in 3000 kg. (6600-lb) capacity coreless induction furnace.

Required chemical composition: C = 3.2–3.4%, Si = 2.1–2.3%, Mn = 0.6-0.9%

Charge Materials	%	Carbon, %		Silicon, %		Manganese, %	
		in material	in charge	in material	in charge	in material	in charge
Pig iron (foundry grade)	40	3.50	3.5×0.4=**1.40**	3.20	3.2×0.4=**1.28**	0.60	0.6×0.4=**0.24**
Gray iron returns	30	3.20	3.2×0.3=**0.96**	2.10	2.1×0.3=**0.63**	0.70	0.7×0.3=**0.21**
Steel scrap	30	0.20	0.2×0.3=**0.06**	0.20	0.2×0.3=**0.06**	0.60	0.6×0.3=**0.18**
Total without melting loss	100		**2.42**		**1.97**		**0.63**
Melting loss		10.00	**0.242**	10.00	**0.197**	10.00	**0.063**
Total with melting loss			**2.178**		**1.773**		**0.567**
Carbon raiser (recovery 1.00)	1.14	98.50	**1.12**	--	--	--	--
Ferroalloys additions FeMn70 (recovery 0.8) FeSi75 (recovery 0.9)	0.327 0.632			75	**0.427**	70.00	**0.183**
Estimated composition			2.178+1.12=**3.30**		1.77+0.427=**2.2**		0.56+0.183=**0.75**

Chemistry Adjustments

Carbon

Need: 3.3 - 2.178 = 1.122 %; carbon raiser recovery -- 1.0

Addition of carbon raiser: $\dfrac{1.122}{0.985 \times 1.0} =$ **1.14%** or by weight $\dfrac{3000 \times 1.14}{100} = 34.2 kg$ (**75.24 lb**)

Silicon

Need: 2.2 - 1.773 = 0.427 %; FeSi75 (75%Si) recovery -- 0.9

Addition of FeSi75: $\dfrac{0.427}{0.75 \times 0.9} =$ **0.632%** or by weight FeSi75 $= \dfrac{3000 \times 0.632}{100} = 18.96$ kg (**41.71 lb**)

Manganese

Need: 0.75 - 0.567 = 0.183 %; FeMn70 (70 %Mn); recovery -- 0.8

Addition of FeMn70: $\dfrac{0.183}{0.8 \times 0.7} =$ **0.327%** or by weight FeMn70 $= \dfrac{3000 \times 0.327}{100} = 9.81$ kg. (**21.58 lb**)

Example 7-3

Charge calculations for ferritic ductile iron Grade 65-45-12, melted in 3000 kg

(6600-lb) capacity coreless induction furnace.

Required chemical composition: C = 3.6–3.8%, Si = 1.6–1.8% (before inoculation), Si = 2.6–2.8% (after inoculation), Mn = 0.2–0.3%, S ≤ 0.02%, P ≤ 0.03%

Charge Materials	%	Carbon, %		Silicon, %		Manganese, %	
		in material	in charge	in material	in charge	in material	in charge
Ductile returns	50.00	3.70	1.85	2.60	1.3	0.23	0.115
Special pig iron	30.00	4.25	1.275	0.09	0.027	0.01	0.003
Steel scrap	20.00	0.20	0.040	0.20	0.040	0.50	0.100
Total without melting loss	100.00	--	3.163	--	1.365	--	0.218
Melting loss		10.00	0.316	10.00	0.1365	10.00	0.022
Total with melting loss			2.844		1.2285		0.196
Carbon raiser*	0.869	98.50	0.856	--	--	--	--
FeSi75 addition, (recovery 0.9)*	0.7			75	0.4715		
FeMn70 addition (recovery 0.8)*	0.104						0.058
Estimated composition		--	3.7	--	1.7	--	0.25

Charge Materials	%	Sulfur, %		Phosphorus, %	
		in material	in charge	in material	in charge
Ductile returns	50.00	0.008	0.004	0.030	0.015
Special pig iron	30.00	0.020	0.006	0.022	0.0066
Steel scrap	20.00	0.020	0.004	0.030	0.0057
Total without melting loss	100.00	--	0.014	--	0.0273
Melting loss		--	--	--	--
Total with melting loss					
Carbon raiser*	0.869	0.050	0.0004	--	--
FeSi75 addition, (recovery 0.9)*	0.7				
FeMn70 addition (recovery 0.8)*	0.104				
Estimated composition		--	0.0144	--	0.0273

* The chemistry adjustment method used is the same as previously described in Example 7-2.

Charge Preheating

Charge preheating is common in induction melting because it allows increasing productivity, reducing smoke emissions of burning oils, paint and lubricants, as well as removing any moisture from the scrap, and creating safer working conditions. The latter is particularly important for furnaces using the tap-and-charge method in which a portion of molten metal is tapped out and replaced by the same amount of charge mix. In this case, charge preheating is a must to prevent the potential hazard of placing wet charge materials into a furnace with a heel of molten iron.

Figure 7-7 shows a charging and preheating system used in induction melting operations. In this design, the charge materials are placed on the flow-feed conveyer and then on the preheater conveyor that moves them through the gas preheater and then feed directly into the furnace.

7.2.2.4. Refractory Lining Installation

In iron melting, the coreless induction furnace is typically lined with an acid refractory such as silica. The lining life varies from 4 to 6 months depending operations parameters and the furnace size.

In a typical refractory installation procedure (Fig. 7-8) dry granular silica-based refractory material (99.2% SiO_2), combined with the sintering (bonding) agent, boric acid (H_2BO_3), is rammed between the bottom and walls of the furnace and a specially made steel lining form. This form is disposable, because is used only one time and then is melted out with the first heat that sinters the lining.

First, a ceramic blanket cloth is installed to insulate the water-cooled coil and a fused alumina-based refractory mix (Al_2O_3) is applied to the inside face of the furnace coil. Then, the bottom of the furnace is rammed with a silica-based refractory. Before applying this refractory, ground detection wires are installed in an upward position. Other sensors, to monitor lining temperature and thickness (wear), are also installed in the sidewalls of the furnace. Then, the lining form is set up and the sidewalls are lined using a vibration technique.

After the new lining has been installed, it is sintered. For this purpose either a starting block or special charge mix is loaded inside the steel form and the furnace temperature is raised at the rate of 93°C (200°F) per hour until a temperature of 1038°C (1900°F) is obtained. Then, the furnace is held at this temperature for at least four hours to ensure proper refractory curing. After this, the temperature is increased more rapidly up to 1593°C (2900°F) at the rate of 204°C (400°F) per hour, and the furnace is held at this temperature for at least three hours to finish the total sintering and generation of

new lining. Typically, the whole sintering process may take 20 to 24 hours.

The conventional manual lining procedures of induction furnaces are labor-intensive and require adequate safety gear. In addition, applications of low-cost silica lining as a primary refractory for iron induction melting increase workers' exposure to hazardous silica dust. A new refractory installation system (Fig. 7-9) allows automating the process and improves the working conditions. Once the bottom is completed, the furnace form is placed and centered, and a rotary material feeder automatically dispenses the dry refractory mix into the annular space between the furnace wall and form.

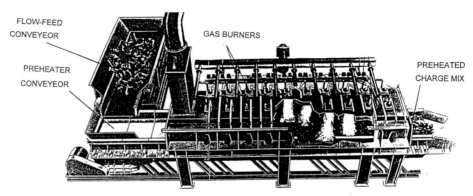

Fig. 7-7. Charging and preheating system for a coreless induction furnace.

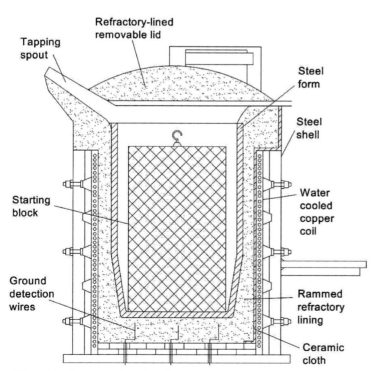

Fig. 7-8. Schematic of refractory installation in a coreless electric induction furnace.

Fig. 7-9. Automatic unit for refractory relining of coreless induction furnace. [Source: Foundry Management & Technology and http:www.gradmatic.com.]

Melting and Pouring Practices

During operation, compaction is accomplished by lowering a hoist-hung vibration tool. Due to better and consistent material distribution, the density of the lining is increased, which, in turn, extends the lining life and increases tonnage per furnace campaign. Similarly, a basic type of refractory mixed with a bonding agent may be applied and then sintered using the same technology.

7.2.2.5. Induction Furnace Automation

The newly developed automation system for iron induction melting with built-in melt control provides operator assistance for the complete melting cycle, based on operator-entered charge weight and the kilowatt hours per ton needed to reach the desirable pouring temperature. The system controls the melting cycle and turns the power supply off or lowers it to hold power when the cycle is complete.

During preheating, the system turns on the furnace at a certain time at a reduced power level designed to preheat the lining. This allows the operator to initiate full melting operations at the start of the production shift, reducing labor cost and extending lining life.

The system also controls the sintering process of the lining with up to eight operator-entered steps. Each step includes a heating rate, target temperature, and hold time and maximum sinter temperature deviation. During the first stages of the sintering process, temperature data is captured from thermocouples that measure the temperature of the lining form. This data stream ends when the thermocouples reach their failure temperature.

As the cycle progresses, a chart on the screen displays the temperature set points, maximum deviation and temperature from the thermocouples. The Windows™-based operating system displays and operates on a touch-sensitive, flat-panel video screen. The system is able to not only record, display, store and print the real-time information on electric parameters, but also allows using this data for optimizing and diagnostic purposes.

7.2.3. Iron Inoculation

Generally, inoculation refers to the iron melting practice of adding various alloys, mostly silicon (Si)-based, to the molten iron, to promote graphitization during solidification, which increases cell count and reduces dendrite size. Lately, inoculation has become one of the major metallurgical operations in the production of quality iron castings.

In gray cast iron, inoculation promotes small, uniformly dispersed, Type A graphite flakes and minimizes chill by inhibiting primary iron carbide formation. In ductile iron, inoculation prevents the formation of iron carbide as well as increases the number of nodules and improves their shape. Proper inoculation practice results in reduced shrinkage, improved fluidity, better machinability and reduced residual stresses.

Quality procedures used to test the solidification structure (chilling tendency) in cast irons and inoculation effects are described later in Section 7.5. The most widely used are ferrosilicon-based inoculants containing from 50 to 75% silicon and moderate amounts of calcium and aluminum. Table 7-6 lists typical chemistry of some commercially available ferrosilicon-based inoculants recommended for use in iron melting practice.

The need for greater chill control in thin sections initiated the development of special ferrosilicon-based inoculants containing increased amount of aluminum, barium (Ba), bismuth (Bi), strontium (Sr), rare earth metals (REM) and other chemical elements that effectively reduce the amount of iron carbide in light sections of the castings poured with a low carbon equivalent iron. Reduced inoculation fade also is reported from the use of some inoculants, particularly those containing combinations of Ba, Bi and REM.

For gray irons, the inoculant additions are at the rate of 0.1–0.3%. In ductile iron production, the inoculant addition rate depends upon the desired metallic matrix and casting section size. Because the undercooling of ductile iron is greater than gray iron, higher inoculant additions are recommended at the rate of 0.3–1.0%. Higher inoculant additions are ineffective because of possible dissolution problems, their accumulations in the ladle, filter plugging, dross defects and risk of over-inoculation.

There are a variety of inoculation methods and techniques used in current cast iron melting practice. Inoculation may occur in the ladle or while the molten iron is poured into the mold. Ductile iron inoculation may be done either after or during magnesium treatment (see Section 7.2.4.). The choice of inoculation method is particularly important in thin-wall casting production, where parts must not only be free of iron carbide, but also free from slag inclusions. In this case, the combination of different inoculation methods is used to ensure proper results.

One of the major problems of the iron inoculation process is that its effect is not permanent. It has a tendency to fade, over time, with more than half of its effect lost in the first 5–7 minutes after the inoculant addition. In gray iron, inoculant fade (or fading of inoculation effect) resulted in the presence of iron carbide (chill) and undercooled graphite, rather than Type A graphite. In ductile iron, fading of inoculation effect is considered as decreased nodule counts and increased iron carbide formation. Many factors influence fading of inoculants: their chemical composition, iron carbon equivalent (CE), holding and pouring temperatures, etc.

Among the factors affecting an iron's nucleation potential is the oxygen (O_2) content in the molten iron. The deoxidization of irons will increase graphitization of an iron by providing oxides or silicate particles that serve as heterogeneous nuclei for the graphite formation.

Preinoculation or preconditioning is sometimes necessary for the production of consistent quality thin- and ultra-thin wall iron castings, particularly powertrain components for automotive, tractor and other industries.

For this thin- and ultra-thin wall ductile iron casting production, foundries are using 75% ferrosilicon (FeSi75) or silicon carbide (SiC), as preinoculation agents. These agents are added to the charge mix in the furnace, as the first operation in multi-step inoculation procedures. In ductile iron practice, preinoculation with SiC provides better magnesium recovery, which can lead to less chill tendency, reduced shrinkage and high castability, where residual magnesium content is at the same level as in iron preinoculated with FeSi75.

7.2.3.1. Ladle Inoculation

Ladle inoculation is the simplest and most flexible method to inoculate iron, being used while the iron is tapped from the furnace into the pouring ladle. In order to ensure proper inoculant dissolution and to utilize the stirring effect, inoculants are typically added to the metal stream once the ladle is at least 20–25% full. Inoculant should not be added to the bottom of an empty ladle prior to tapping, due to the risk of the inoculant being encapsulated in liquid slag and/or its oxidation.

There are three major methods of inoculant addition to the ladle, which are illustrated in Fig. 7-10:

- Gravity feeding of granular inoculant into the stream
- Air assist injection of fine inoculant particles into the stream
- Wire inoculation technique injects wire, containing inoculation grade FeSi75, into the molten metal stream

7.2.3.2. Late Inoculation

Late inoculation or post-inoculation involves inoculant addition either to the metal stream, while the iron is poured into the mold, or directly into the mold cavity. Late inoculation is mostly applicable to foundries utilizing automatic or mechanical pouring systems. The use of these pouring systems implies that treated iron is stored in holding furnaces at high temperatures for

Table 7-6. Chemical composition of some ferrosilicon-based inoculants widely used in iron melting practice.

Inoculant	Chemical composition, %										
	Si	Al	Ca	Ba	Zr	Sr	Ti	Mn	Bi	Ce/REM	Fe
Ferrosilicon FeSi75	72-78	0.8-1.2	0.8-1.2	-	-	-	-	-			Balance
Ferrosilicon Containing Aluminum	70-78	2.0-3.5	0.5-1.5	-	-	-	-	-	-	-	Balance
	70-75	3-4.5	0.5-1.3								Balance
Ferrosilicon Containing Barium	74-79	0.8-1.2	0.8-1.3	0.8-1.3	--	--	-	-	--	--	Balance
	60-77	1.5 max	0.5-2.0	0.5-2.0			0.15max	0.3 max			Balance
	60-65	0.8-1.5	1.0-3.0	4.0-6.0			--	8.0-12			Balance
Ferrosilicon Containing Strontium	74-79	0.6 max	0.1 max	--	--	0.8-1.2	--	--	--	--	Balance
Ferrosilicon Containing Bismuth	72	0.9	1.5	--	--	--	--	--	1.0	--	Balance
	69-75	0.75-1.25	1.7-2.2	0.4-0.6					0.4-0.6		Balance
Ferrosilicon Containing Cerium/REM	70-78	0.5-2.0	0.5-2.5	--	--	--	--	--	--	0.2-2.5/ 0.2-1.5	Balance
	70-75	0.8-1.2	0.8-1.2	--						1.75-2.25	Balance
Ferrosilicon Containing Magnesium	70-76	0.05-4.0	0.75-1.5	--	--	--	--	--	--	--	Balance
Ferrosilicon Containing Titanium	50-55	0.75-1.5	5-7	--	--	--	9.0-11.0	--	--	--	Balance
	52-59	0.9-1.2	0.5-1.5	--	--	--	10.0-12.0				Balance
Ferrosilicon Containing Zirconium	73-78	<0.5	<0.1	--	1.5-2.0	0.8-1.2	--	--	--	1.8-1.2	Balance
	77-82	1.0-1.5	1.0-1.5	--	2.8-3.5	1.2	--			--	Balance

long periods of time, reducing any previous inoculation effect. In some cases, however, late inoculation (in-stream and in the mold) may be used in conjunction with manual pouring.

Advantages of late inoculation include virtual elimination of fading and significant reduction of inoculant addition rates. However, improper late inoculation may cause some serious problems, such as the possibility of undissolved inoculant appearance in the casting and nonuniform inoculant distribution. The late inoculation techniques may be categorized into three groups:

The first group involves the addition of powdered inoculant (gravity fed or air-blown) into the metal stream during pouring into the mold. This technique is also called in-stream inoculation. This method requires a fine-sized inoculant with proper chemical analysis and low oxygen content. Figure 7-11 presents a schematic of a typical automatic in-stream inoculation technique utilizing compressed air as the inoculant carrier.

In this unit, finely sized inoculant from the hopper reaches the dispensing mechanism and then, prompted by the molding line "push" sequence, is injected by dry compressed

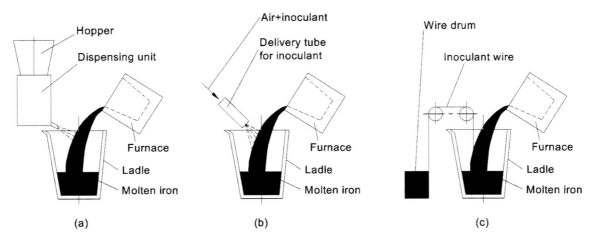

Fig. 7-10. Ladle inoculation methods: (a) gravity feeding of granular inoculant into the stream; (b) air-assisted injection of fine inoculant particles into the stream; (c) wire, containing inoculation grade FeSi75, is injected into the stream.

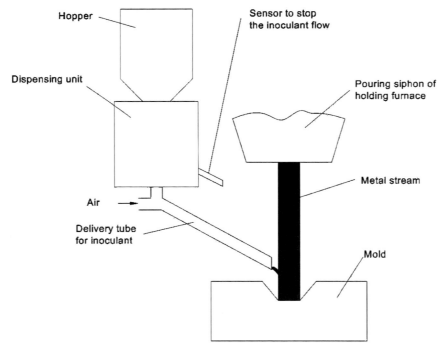

Fig. 7-11. Schematic of in-stream inoculation technique utilizing compressed air as inoculant carrier.

Melting and Pouring Practices

air into the stream as the metal is poured into the mold. Sensors are used to stop the inoculant flow. When manual pouring is used, the inoculant may also be gravity fed into the metal stream as it enters the mold. In this case, a sensor-operating mechanism, dispensing inoculant from the hopper as the pouring ladle tilts, activates the inoculation system. The feed tube position must be synchronized with any lateral or vertical ladle movement.

As discussed, in-stream inoculation usually is coupled with automated pouring on automatic molding lines. Inoculant addition in in-stream inoculation units is measured either by flow rate (grams/sec) or by fixed mass (grams/mold). Both methods are usually calibrated to a target weight percent addition of 0.05–0.25%, typically 0.15–0.20%. Conventionally, fine- granular (20 x 100 mesh) FeSi75 is used as an inoculant, but some foundries use a special in-stream sized 0.2–0.7 mm (30 x 70 mesh) inoculant with higher manganese content (3–5% Mn) and zirconium additions. These foundries claim that, due to the absence of finer sized dust particles, the inoculant is less abrasive to the dispensing mechanism components than a resized FeSi75, and the higher manganese and zirconium contents assist inoculant dissolution. Due to improved solution characteristics in iron, trace-inoculating elements are distributed more uniformly and consistently. It is also common to use REM-containing inoculants, for instance, FeSi75 with up to 2% REM, at the addition rate 0.1–0.3%.

However, air-assisted inoculant injection is sometimes inefficient due to inevitable losses of inoculant, when the metal stream does not catch it, and a portion of inoculant may be wasted and mixed with the mold material.

The second late inoculation group employs a cored wire inoculant in the basin of a pressurized induction holding furnace (Fig. 7-12). The essence of this method is that FeSi75- containing cored wire, 5–10 mm (0.2–0.4 in) in diameter, is injected into the molten iron located in the pouring siphon (spout) of the pressurized induction holding furnace, just prior to pouring the mold.

The injection angle may vary from 75° to 90°. Based on ductile iron practical experience, some foundries recommend the use of double wire injection and maintain the temperature of molten iron in the holding furnace at 2555–2595°F (1402–1424°C), with the typical inoculant addition varying from 0.05 to 0.1%. The low additions are usually due to the addition being one part of an inoculation program, which then will follow by effective in-mold inoculation. A potential problem of adding inoculant to the molten iron directly at the autopouring spout or siphon is that it may aggravate an already significant problem of dross buildup, particularly in the areas with poor mixing.

The third technique is in-the-mold inoculation, which involves the placement of the inoculation alloy directly into the gating system, such as in a pouring basin, in the sprue well area or in suitable chambers in the running system (Fig. 7-13). Inoculants used for this method may be in the form of crushed material, fine granular material bonded into pellets, or as pre-cast slugs or blocks.

As in the case of any late inoculation, alloy dissolution rate is an important factor. The pre-cast and bonded alloys are designed to dissolve at a controlled rate throughout the entire pouring cycle. Figure 7-13(a) illustrates the in-mold inoculation technique utilizing an inoculant block placed in the sprue well area. As the metal enters the mold cavity, inoculation material gradually dissolves in the stream, resulting in an effective inoculation process. Figure 7-13(b) shows inoculation in the reaction chamber located in the runner. The metal enters the mold through

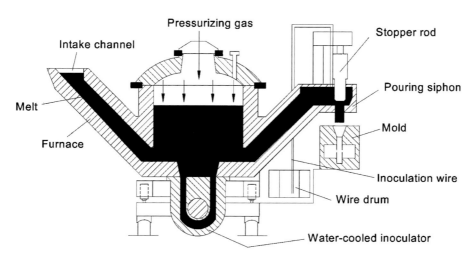

Fig. 7-12. Wire inoculation in the pouring siphon (spout) of pressurized induction holding furnace.

the sprue, flows over the inoculant placed in the reaction chamber and, as it is being inoculated, fills the mold cavity. Typically, crushed inoculant alloy of 20–70 mesh in size is used for this application, and the recommended addition rate varies from 0.05 to 0.1%.

For efficient in-mold inoculation, the reaction chamber design must permit a regular iron flow over the alloy to facilitate its gradual dissolution and minimize the amount of undissolved residues that could reach the mold cavity. To prevent undissolved inoculant particles from entering the casting, recommended practice involves combining in-mold inoculation technique with effective in-mold filtration, either cloth or ceramic filters.

Another possible solution of in-mold inoculation is the positioning of an inoculant block into the pouring basin of the mold (Fig. 7-14). In the design, shown in Fig. 7-14(a), the block is anchored in the base of pouring basin and is dissolved during the pouring.

The slag trap of the pouring basin prevents the penetration of undissolved inoculant into the mold cavity. In the case where a high amount of iron is poured, a stopper may be used. The stopper delays the mold cavity filling, so that inoculant in the pouring basin has enough time to dissolve and be distributed evenly in the iron.

Figure 7-14(b) illustrates the late in-mold inoculation technique, which employs an inoculant floating in the pouring basin. The cylindrical or cubic block of inoculant is placed into the pouring basin before the mold is poured. Partial dissolution of inoculant ensures the effective late inoculation of iron. The block size must be such that, even after partial dissolution, it would be greater than the diameter of the sprue. This, along with the slag trap, prevents the block from falling into the sprue and mold cavity.

7.2.3.3. In-Mold/In-Filter Inoculation

Recent developments in the in-mold inoculation technique are attempting to place the inoculant inside filters. There are several technical solutions developed to utilize in-filter inoculation technology. In one of these

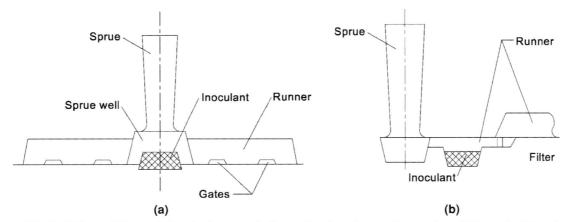

Fig. 7-13. In-mold inoculation techniques in the gating/running system using: (a) inoculant block placed in sprue well area; (b) granular inoculant placed in the reaction chamber in the runner.

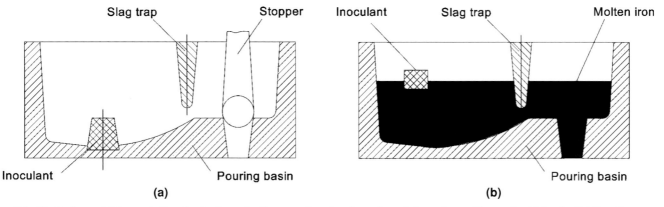

Fig. 7-14. In-mold inoculation technique in the pouring basin using: (a) anchored inoculant block; (b) floating inoculant block.

Melting and Pouring Practices

designs, the inoculation alloy, in the form or shape of fine granules, crushed particles or tablet, is placed in a small cavity formed in the middle of a ceramic cellular filter by its two halves, as is shown in Fig. 7-15.

In a more effective inoculant-filter design, shown in Fig. 7-16, an agglomerated treatment block is placed into the open cavity of a ceramic foam filter. Figure 7-17 illustrates the typical installation of the newly developed filter-inoculant assembly (black) in the runner of a gating system.

During pouring, the metal flow dissolves the inoculant, and the filter prevents undissolved alloy from reaching the mold cavity. The treatment block has a cylindrical shape and can be produced by casting or from fine-grained raw material by pressing, sintering or bonding.

This approach has a lot of technical and economic advantages. Using this technique practically eliminates chill due to preventing fading of inoculant, simultaneously providing effective filtration, which improves mechanical properties and machinability. It also allows the production cycle to be reduced and automated and, as a result, reduces operating cost.

7.2.3.4. Method Selection

There is no inoculation method that is universally suitable for all types of cast iron production. Each method has it own advantages and limitations. Any of the methods outlined or their combination can be used. The choice of the inoculation method depends upon the melting practice at the given foundry, but final selection must be justified based on reliability of the technique(s), performance level of the material, and value to the overall casting production.

Following is some practical information regarding the various inoculation applications:

- In thin- and ultra-thin wall iron casting production, preinoculation with silicon carbide (SiC) or 75% ferrosilicon (FeSi75) is recommended as a first step in multi-step inoculation treatment, followed by ladle inoculation, then post- or late inoculation, which may, in turn, include two subsequent operations: in-stream inoculation and/or in-mold inoculation.

- Ladle inoculation technology is characterized by a fairly high inoculant addition amount and may be utilized in both low- and high-volume

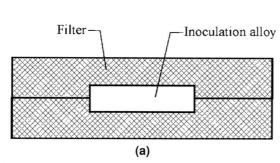
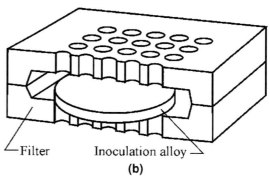

Fig. 7-15. In-filter inoculation technique employing crushed (a) and tablet shaped inoculant (b) placed into the cavity of ceramic cellular filter.

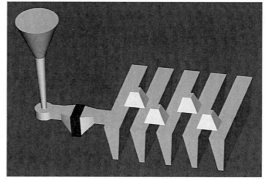

Fig. 7-16. In-filter inoculant assembly in which agglomerated treatment block is placed into open cavity of ceramic foam filters.

Fig. 7-17. Typical installation of the filter-inoculant assembly (Fig. 7-16) into the mold cavity prior to iron pouring.

casting production. The major problem of this technique—inoculant fading—can only be partially addressed by the use of special inoculants containing elements, such as Ba, Bi, Ca, Sr, and or REM, which slow down fading of the inoculant.

- Air-assisted injection of inoculant and wire inoculation techniques virtually eliminate inoculant fading and its negative impact on the solidification structure and properties of iron. These methods are efficient only in high-volume production in conjunction with automated molding and pouring systems. Air-assisted injection of inoculant is sometimes not very efficient, due to inevitable losses of inoculant, when the metal stream does not catch it, and a portion of inoculant may be wasted and mixed with a mold material. One of the potential problems of adding inoculant to the molten iron directly to the autopour spout or siphon may aggravate an already significant problem of dross buildup, particularly in the areas with poor mixing.

- For manual pouring, the gravity feeding of inoculant into the stream prior to entering the mold may be a good solution. Generally, the utilization of these techniques is cost–effective due to the low level of inoculant required in a single treatment.

- The in-mold inoculation technique, employing placement of the inoculation alloy in the form of premade blocks, inserts or crushed inoculants directly into the gating system, is also a very effective post-inoculation method that eliminates inoculant fading and may be used successfully in low- and high-volume production. To prevent undissolved inoculant particles from entering the casting, an inoculant-filter technique is recommended.

- In-mold/in-filter inoculation technique practically eliminates chill due to preventing fading of inoculant, simultaneously providing effective filtration, which improves mechanical properties and machinability of irons. It also allows reducing inoculant consumption, automating the production cycle and, as a result, reduces the operational costs.

7.2.4. Magnesium Treatment

Ductile iron is made by the special treatment of molten cast iron with spheroidizing or nodulizing material.

During this treatment, graphite changes its form from flake to nodular or spheroidal. The treatment process is a key operation in the production of ductile iron that ensures predetermined microstructure, mechanical and engineering properties of castings. Today, magnesium (Mg), pure or in the form of a masteralloy, is the most effective nodulizing agent used by the foundry industry to produce quality ductile iron castings.

However, the usage of magnesium for treating molten iron has a number of difficulties caused by the specific physical properties of Mg. This includes low melting and boiling temperatures ($650°C/1202°F$ and $1107°C/2025°F$, respectively), low density (1.738 g/cm^3/0.0628 lb/in.^{3} vs. 7.0 g/cm^3/0.25 lb/in.^{3} of molten cast iron density (average values) and low solubility in molten iron (about 0.001% wt at $650°C/1200°F$).

As a result, the introduction of magnesium or Mg-containing alloy into molten iron is typically accompanied by significant flame and fume, called pyroeffect, which makes the magnesium treatment process highly violent and unsafe. The latter causes significant magnesium losses due to magnesium burning and, hence, reductions of residual magnesium content in the solidified castings.

Certain magnesium losses are also incurred due to magnesium reaction with elements contained in base iron: first, with sulfur, and second, with oxygen. The first reaction, desulfurization or reduction of sulfur content with formation of magnesium sulfide is defined as:

$$Mg + S \rightarrow MgS \qquad (7.6)$$

The second reaction, deoxidation or reduction of oxygen with formation of magnesium oxide is as follows:

$$2Mg + O_2 \rightarrow 2MgO \qquad (7.7)$$

An additional possible loss of magnesium may result from a reaction with the silica (acid) lining:

$$2Mg + SiO_2 \rightarrow Si + 2MgO \qquad (7.8)$$

In addition, during extended holding before pouring or prolonged pouring, residual magnesium content in treated molten iron gradually decreases or fades. Fading is a time-dependent factor that manifests itself as graphite shape deterioration and nodule count reduction, causing a significant drop of ductile iron mechanical properties. All these factors have a great impact on magnesium recovery and the economic aspects of magnesium treatment.

In general, magnesium recovery (Mg_R) depends upon several factors, such as the treatment method, sulfur content in the base iron to be treated, iron temperature, type and size of nodulizing material, quantity of iron being treated, tapping rate, etc., and may be calculated as:

$$Mg_R = \frac{0.76 \cdot \Delta S + Mg_{res}}{Mg_{add}} \cdot 100 \text{ %} \qquad (7.9)$$

Where

ΔS equals the difference between the sulfur content in the base iron and the treated metal, wt %;

Mg_{res} equals the residual magnesium, wt %;

Mg_{add} equals the magnesium addition, wt %.

Sometimes, when the sulfur content in the base iron is low and the magnesium consumption for desulfurization may be neglected, equation 7.9 may be simplified:

$$Mg_R = \frac{Mg_{res}}{Mg_{add}} \times 100\% \qquad (7.10)$$

The methods developed for magnesium treatment aim to minimize magnesium losses, maximize and stabilize magnesium recovery, and ensure safe and environmentally friendly working conditions. These methods use different approaches to introduce magnesium or its alloys into molten iron: from simple plunging bells to special types of ladles or devices and to the in-mold treatment technique. Each method uses appropriate treatment alloy and has certain advantages and disadvantages.

The magnesium treatment methods currently used by the foundry industry may be broken down into two groups depending upon the type of magnesium additions employed:

1. Methods utilizing pure magnesium
2. Methods utilizing Mg-containing masteralloy

In turn, Mg-containing masteralloys are broken down into two subgroups depending upon their density in relation to density of molten iron: 1) light masteralloys and 2) heavy masteralloys. Accordingly, different treatment methods are employed for each of these subgroups. Table 7-7 lists the typical chemical compositions of Mg-containing treatment alloys used in ductile iron casting production.

7.2.4.1. Treatments Using Pure Mg

These methods use pure magnesium in the form of ingots, briquettes, pellets or powder as a treating agent and utilize special equipment or devices to control the reaction rate and to maximize magnesium recovery.

Table 7-7. Typical Chemical Composition of Ductile Iron Treatment Alloys (Nodulizers) Used in Foundry Practice.

Treatment Alloy	Chemical Composition, %							
	Mg	Si	Ca	Al	Ce or REM*	Cu	Ni	Fe
Pure magnesium	99.98	0.008 -	-	0.005	-	-	0.002	0.005
Magnesium ferrosilicon	3-3.5	44-48	0.8-1.3	1.25max	-	-	-	Balance
	5-6	44-48	0.8-1.3	1.25max	-	-	-	Balance
	8-10	44-48	0.8-1.3	1.25max	-	-	-	Balance
Cerium grade magnesium ferrosilicon	4.7-6.2	44-48	0.8-1.3	0.8-1.2	0.5-0.7	-	-	Balance
	5-6	44-48	0.8-1.3	1.25max	0.3-1.2	-	-	Balance
REM grade magnesium ferrosilicon	3-3.5	44-48	0.8-1.3	1.25max	1.5-20	-	-	Balance
	5-6	44-48	0.8-1.3	1.25max	0.5-1.3	-	-	Balance
Nickel-magnesium	5-15	-	-	-	-	-		Balance
Nickel-iron-magnesium	4-4.5	-	-	-	-	-	32-36	Balance
Nickel-silicon-magnesium	13-15	26-32	-	-	-	-	3-5	Balance

* REM- rare earth metals

Treatment with pure magnesium has a number of common advantages. First, the desulfurizing can be carried out in the same ladle before or during treating. Thus, the base iron can be melted in any melting furnace, including cupola. Second, in contrast to Mg-containing masteralloy, the absence of calcium or aluminum in the treatment additions allows decreasing slag buildup during the holding and pouring of treated iron. Finally, if the foundry uses a significant amount of iron returns and the silicon balance is a problem, the usage of pure magnesium is an excellent alternative to FeSiMg masteralloy, to avoid the undesirable addition of silicon.

However, usage of pure magnesium has some disadvantages. For instance, to improve magnesium recovery and minimize the pyroeffect, relatively complicated equipment and devices requiring essential investments need to be used. Due to significant undercooling, and absence of elements controlling the chill rate and metallic structure, it is necessary to apply sufficient inoculation before or during the pouring of iron.

Plunging Method

The plunging method (Fig. 7-18) was one of the earliest techniques used for ductile iron production since its invention.

In this method, the plunging bell, containing pure magnesium, or Mg-masteralloys or Mg-impregnated coke, is plunged into the molten iron. The plunging bell may be made of refractory-coated steel pipe, graphite or ceramic material. During the treatment, the plunging bell with nodulizing material is held deeply below the melt surface to provide more uniform distribution of magnesium in treated iron and to improve magnesium recovery, which does not exceed 30% while using pure magnesium and may reach up to 50% when 5–6% FeSiMg masteralloy is utilized. In order to ensure better safety and proper environmental conditions, it is recommended to use tall and narrow ladles with a cover.

There are obvious advantages that still allow usage of the plunging method by foundries. First, this method may utilize a wide range of nodulizing materials; second, its ability to treat iron with a relatively high sulfur content and, finally, its simplicity. The disadvantages of this method include considerable temperature losses ($\geq$ 200°F/93°C), as a result of plunging of a large and cold plunging bell with nodulizer, and significant pyroeffect. In addition, due to the plunging bell's extreme working conditions (heat shock, impact and high temperature erosion), it is often not reusable or requires repair and, after a few treatments, needs to be replaced.

Pressure Ladle

Further improvement of the plunging method has eliminated usage of a plunging bell. In this process, a refractory-coated magnesium billet or ingot is plunged into the ladle with molten iron. This is used in production of ductile iron pressure pipes. Magnesium recovery in the process of utilizing low-sulfur base iron varies in the range from 35 to 45%. Temperature losses are similar to those of the plunging method with significantly less pyroeffect.

The pressure ladle (Fig. 7-19) is a pressure vessel, where pressure is created by the magnesium vapor. In this ladle, molten iron is placed under the movable pressure chamber head with the cover having a rubber gasket in the area of contact with the ladle. Then, the pneumatically or hydraulically operated cover tightly closes the pressure ladle, leaving the central hole for the pressure head. Next, the hydraulic rod with the sealing head plunges the

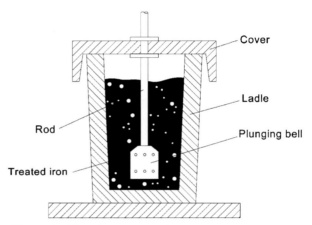

Fig. 7-18. Plunging magnesium treatment.

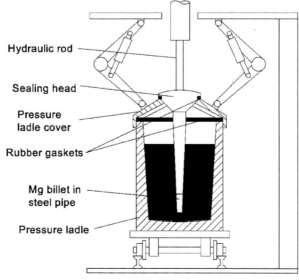

Fig. 7-19. Pressure ladle used for magnesium treatment.

magnesium billet into the ladle and finally seals it. The billet is secured in the steel pipe to retard reaction between molten iron and magnesium, until the ladle is sealed completely. While iron is reacting with magnesium, the pressure inside the ladle increases and returns to the initial level with the end of reaction. The remaining pressure is released when the cover is lifted, and the ladle with a treated iron is ready to pour.

The major disadvantages of pressure ladles are: significant temperature losses (52–82°C/125–180°F) of treated iron, relatively high cost of equipment and necessity of regular maintenance during operation.

Treatment Converter Method

Within treatment methods employing pure magnesium, treatment converters are more widely used.

A treatment converter (Fig. 7-20) is a tilting cylindrical vessel, lined inside with a refractory material. The converter is furnished with a perforated reaction chamber, located at the bottom of the treatment vessel, above the molten iron surface when the converter is in a horizontal position, to avoid premature magnesium contact with the molten iron.

While the converter is in a horizontal position (as shown in Fig. 7-20a), a measured amount of pure magnesium pigs is charged into the reaction chamber via the charging door. After loading the reaction chamber, molten iron is tapped into the converter through the spout having a pneumatically operated cover. The treatment occurs when the converter is tilted into a vertical position (Fig.7-20b). Molten iron enters the reaction chamber through the holes and reacts with magnesium. The magnesium vapors increase pressure in the reaction chamber, pump out treated iron promoting intensive mixing of magnesium with the rest of the iron. The reaction rate

depends on the diameter of holes and does not exceed a couple of minutes. The whole treatment cycle depends on the vessel's capacity and varies from 15 minutes for a converter capacity up to one ton, to 30 minutes for a capacity above 3 ton (6600 lb). When the treatment is completed, treated iron is tapped (Fig. 7-20c) into a pouring ladle or is transferred into a holding furnace, and the converter returns to the filling position to prepare for the next cycle.

To insure safety and environmental conditions, it is recommended to operate the converter in an area with proper ventilation. Treatment in the converter makes possible the use of cupola-melted base iron, which contains a considerable amount of sulfur (up to 0.15%), by providing effective desulfurization. Magnesium recovery in a converter is typically about 50–55%. The converter sizes vary from 1540 to 22,000 lb (0.7 to 10 tons), as well as their integrated equipment (forklift, swivel, monorail and crane converters), and may be fully automated.

The disadvantages of this method include considerable investment, a relatively long treatment cycle and the requirement of strong postinoculation, typically, in-stream inoculation for the automated holding-pouring systems.

Cored Wire Method

The cored wire process (Fig. 7-21) is a treatment method utilizing Mg-containing wire introduced into molten iron by a special feeding device gradually delivering wire into the closed ladle. The wire is a long, low-carbon steel tube filled with Mg-containing alloy and other additives required for the treatment process. The magnesium alloy may contain from 9 to 92% of magnesium in any form: from pure magnesium powder to its mix with additions of FeSi, calcium carbide or rare earths in any combinations, or up to 30% Mg FeSiMg masteralloy. Typical treatment

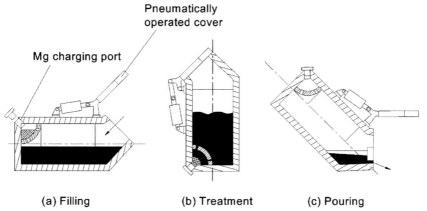

Mg charging port

Pneumatically operated cover

(a) Filling   (b) Treatment   (c) Pouring

Fig. 7-20. Treatment converter capacity for ductile iron production varies from 0.7 to 10 t (1640 to 22,000 lb).

weights range from 1100 lb (0.5 ton) to 60,000 lb (5 tons) in foundries with continuous molding lines; and up to 600,000 lb (50 tons) can be treated for large-casting producers. Best results are obtained for treatment ladles with the ratio height/diameter equals two, but the ratio of one is well acceptable for the large treatments.

The cored wire process is automated, allowing precise control of residual magnesium content due to exact wire addition, and flexible for the capacity, base iron sulfur content, and temperature ranges. Magnesium recovery is increasing with decreasing magnesium content in the wire, and it is normally in the range from 30 to 50%. This method is tolerant to base iron containing up to 0.09% sulfur due to the use of high Mg-containing alloy. The temperature losses are relatively low: 32–54° C (90–130°F).

The possible disadvantages include excessive wire consumption, slag buildup and high cost, when this process is used for treating high sulfur-base iron. Together with insufficient agitation, the latter may reduce metal cleanness. In addition, this iron needs strong inoculation after treatment. Finally, the cored wire station requires a good ventilation system. In spite of the relatively high cost of the device and wire, this method has an established position in the foundry industry and may be considered as an alternative to other methods.

7.2.4.2. Treatment Methods Using Mg Masteralloys

All Mg-containing masteralloys can be classified as light and heavy, depending on their density in comparison with molten iron. According to the features of each type of masteralloy, different treatment methods are used, which allows achieving the desirable magnesium recovery and economics.

The most commonly used light magnesium masteralloys are silicon-based, and heavy masteralloys are nickel- or copper-based magnesium alloys (see Table 7-7). For commercial production of ductile iron, these masteralloys may contain additions of aluminum, calcium, barium, cerium or other rare earth elements.

The addition of cerium or rare earths not only neutralizes contaminants in iron that impede graphite nodulizing, but also improve magnesium recovery. These contaminants, such as aluminum, antimony, arsenic, lead and zinc may be present in the charge mix components in very small amounts, as trace elements, harmful enough to interfere with formation of nodular graphite and cause further deterioration of mechanical properties.

The presence of calcium or aluminum, both graphitizing elements, provides nucleation during nodulizing and reduces chill. However, it should be taken into account that aluminum may cause pinholing in ductile iron. Calcium causes excessive slag buildup that makes it an undesirable element for the holding furnace. The magnesium content is a very important characteristic of Mg masteralloys. With increasing magnesium content, magnesium recovery in molten iron decreases while the pyroeffect increases.

Typical light FeSiMg masteralloy contains 3.0–10.0% Mg, 43–48% Si, 0.8–2.00% Ca and up to 2.5% Ce or REM. Nickel- or copper-based masteralloys may contain from 5.0% to 15% Mg, the rest is Ni or Cu. In some cases, the part of nickel can be replaced by 32–36% Fe or 26–33% Si with a view to economy. Nickel- or copper-based Mg masteralloys have a density higher than molten iron. This fact allows eliminating any special means preventing masteralloy from floatation. Nickel and copper act as strong pearlite stabilizers as well as light graphitizers, minimizing variations in mechanical properties between thin and thick sections of castings.

Light masteralloys require using the appropriate treatment methods for improving magnesium recovery, by keeping treatment alloy below the molten iron surface up to its full dissolution and, thus, minimizing Mg losses and reducing the pyroeffect. Within these methods, the most widely used are in-ladle, flow-through and in-mold treatment processes.

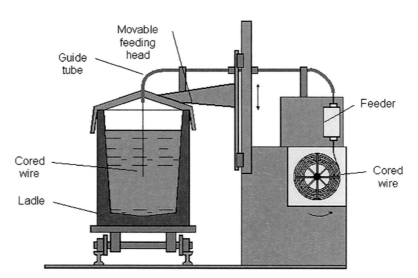

Fig. 7-21. Cored wire magnesium treatment process utilizing a steel tube filled with various types of powdered nodulizing materials.

In–Ladle Treatment Method

The open ladle method is currently used for treating molten iron, mostly with heavy Mg-masteralloys. In this method, the measured quantity of treatment alloy, sometimes mixed with inoculant, is placed at the bottom of an empty ladle. Inoculation, in this case may be done simultaneously with Mg treatment or during pouring (late inoculation). While the ladle is filled with iron, the treatment alloy is melted by the molten iron and mixes with it. The usage of heavy Mg- masteralloy helps to avoid typical problems of light masteralloys, such as the alloy floating up and significant pyroeffect. While using heavy alloys, ladle design is not so important as well as the filling time. The Mg recovery is reported in the range of 50–70%. However, nickel- and copper-based masteralloys are relatively expensive and typically used to produce mostly pearlitic grades of ductile iron. Otherwise, the usage of heavy masteralloys for Mg treatment becomes less cost effective. In addition, the reuse of ductile iron returns treated by heavy masteralloys is limited due to possible buildup of Cu and Ni content.

Sandwich Method

The sandwich method (Fig. 7-22) is an improved modification of an open ladle technique. In this process, FeSiMg (5–6% Mg) masteralloy is placed into a pocket at the bottom of the ladle and covered with steel punchings or iron turnings. The cover material delays the magnesium reaction with molten iron simultaneously preventing the masteralloy from floating up and causing undesirable premature oxidation. In addition, the decreased temperature above the masteralloy, due to melting the cover material, improves the magnesium dissolution. The use of ladles with a height to diameter ratio of 2:1 or higher is recommended.

The major advantages of this method are simplicity and low cost, while magnesium recovery in the range of 30–50% can be achieved. Temperature losses are relatively low and for a well-preheated ladle are about 110–140°F/43–60°C. The sandwich method is flexible and can be used for different sizes of ladles. The disadvantages of this method include the necessity to use low sulfur-base iron, unstable magnesium recovery, and relatively high pyroeffect.

The modified sandwich method employs an open-ladle technique and specially developed treatment compound based on magnesium ferrosilicon. The treatment compound consists of granular 5% magnesium ferrosilicon mixed with granular 75% ferrosilicon and inert additives (magnesia, graphite) in a ratio of 1 (5% Mg FeSi) to 1 (75% FeSi and inert additives), while total addition of the treatment compound to the weight of metal in the ladle is 2%. This treatment compound is placed into a special pocket at the bottom of the ladles with a capacity of 3 to 5 tons, and covered with iron turnings. Iron tap temperature is within the range of 1460–1480°C (2600–2696°F). After filling the ladle, during 1.5–2 minutes, only slight "boiling" of iron is observed. Residual magnesium in the treated iron is in the range of 0.048–0.052% to ensure the required nodularity rating and mechanical properties within the ASTM A-536 specification for grade 65-45-12. The magnesium recovery averages between 60 and 65%. In comparison with the traditional sandwich method, this treatment method has better magnesium recovery and is environmentally friendly because it is eliminating the pyroeffect.

Tundish Method

The tundish method is a further improvement of the sandwich method and aims to reduce the oxygen level inside the ladle, by applying a special cover. This cover is designed in the form of a pouring basin (Fig. 7-23) with a hole to fill the ladle with molten iron and provide a permanent flow rate. A special dividing wall or chamber is located at the bottom of the ladle to separate the area with nodulizing material and the part to be filled first, to avoid premature masteralloy dissolution. A covering material is also required, though, generally, in smaller amounts than used in the sandwich method.

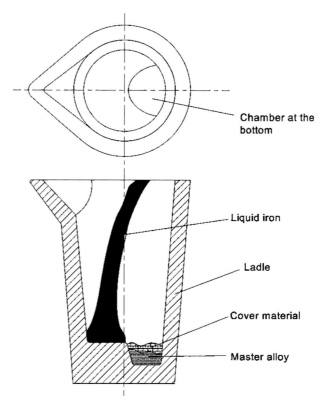

Chamber at the bottom

Liquid iron

Ladle

Cover material

Master alloy

Fig. 7-22. Schematic of sandwich process used for magnesium treatment in open ladle.

In the early designed tundish ladle with a fixed cover, as shown in Fig. 7-23(a), the treatment alloy is placed into the ladle through a special charging pipe with a removable cap. Molten iron is poured in and poured out through the narrow orifice, sized to provide the required filling time. However, excessive slag buildup may block the pouring out of the treated iron. In the improved tundish ladle with a fixed cover design, as shown in Fig. 7-23(b), the treatment alloy is placed into the ladle through a controlled venting orifice, which is also used as the pour-out spout and deslagging port, due to a larger diameter of the orifice. To prevent blowback from the tundish orifice, a relief valve is installed.

The teapot tundish ladles shown in Fig. 7-24 are designed to ease slag removal. After placing the treatment alloy, shown in Fig. 7-31(a), the cover cap is closed, clamped, and ladle is filled through an enlarged opening in a teapot spout, eliminating the need for a pouring basin. The disadvantage of this design is that molten iron in the spout cannot be treated, because the metal is filled and poured through the same teapot spout. The double teapot tundish ladle, shown in Fig. 7-24(b), eliminates this problem, providing treatment of all iron passing through the reaction chamber.

The latest developments in the tundish method design are aimed to improve its technical characteristics and decrease the maintenance cost. Some of these modifications allow eliminating or automating the cover removal during the treatment cycle. The design with a permanently fixed cover does not allow timely maintainance, which is certainly the disadvantage of this design. The semi-permanently fixed cover (bolted-on or wedge-clamped) solves this problem only partially. One of the latest designs utilizes the concept of the lifting cover.

The tundish ladle with the lifting cover (Fig. 7-25) combines the accessibility of an open ladle and the major advantages of the tundish method, such as high

magnesium recovery and safety. Lifting covers can be either integrated to the ladle with a separate lifting lug or constructed as a fully removable cover by using, for instance, a forklift truck.

In order to reduce the excessive use of a crane and simplify handling, the tundish ladle was placed on a platform of a 4-position rotating turntable, as illustrated in Fig. 7-26. The turntable rotates between each position in a preset time. The process begins on position IV, where treatment alloy is placed in the pocket on the bottom of the previously emptied treatment ladle.

After that, the turntable rotates 90 degrees to the position I, where the cover with the help of a pillar swings toward the ladle, lowers on its top and closes the ladle. In this position, molten iron from the melting or holding furnace is tapped into the ladle and fills it through the pouring orifice. When magnesium treatment is accomplished, the cover is lifted and swung aside, and the ladle of treated iron is brought to position II for deslagging, after which

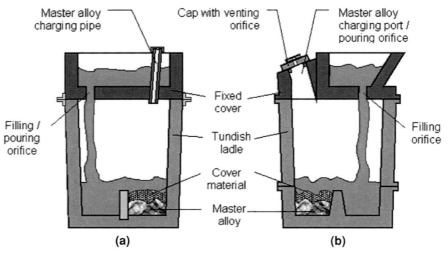

Fig. 7-23. The tundish process uses a ladle with fixed cover: (a) old design; (b) new design.

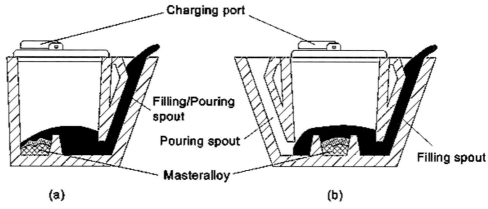

Fig. 7-24. Teapot tundish ladle designs: (a) single spout; (b) double spout.

Melting and Pouring Practices

it is brought to position III for tapping into the pouring ladle. The turntable arrangement of the tundish method allows improved technical and economic aspects of the process as well as its environmental conditions.

The tundish-converter, shown in Fig. 7-27, is another modification of this method, which is virtually a combination of a conventional tundish ladle and an Mg-treatment converter. This device contains a reaction chamber attached to the bottom of the ladle to hold pure Mg or Mg-containing alloys. Molten iron is tapped through the tundish cover and then through the orifices, located at the bottom, enters the reaction chamber and reacts with the nodulizer loaded into the reaction chamber before tapping.

Inoculant may be added into the stream during tapping into the pouring ladle or during pouring of molds. A crane or monorail delivery system also allows the use of the tundish-converter as a transfer ladle to tap ductile iron into a pouring ladle or autopour. According to users of this unit, low capital expenses and simplicity in maintenance, along with relatively high Mg recovery (up to 40%), combined with the advantages of using pure magnesium, make the tundish-converter a cost-effective alternative to more complicated Mg-treatment devices such as treatment converters.

A number of common advantages are the reason for wide industrial usage of the tundish process that currently accounts for about 30% of world ductile iron production. Magnesium recovery in the tundish process may reach up to 75%. The low cost of tundish ladles is accompanied with high environmental safety. Using FeSiMg masteralloy containing 5–7% Mg, it is possible to operate these ladles without venting. The tundish process is reported for treating up to 22,000 lb (10 t) of molten iron. Finally, iron treated in tundish ladles possesses a good inoculating ability.

A few disadvantages are related to the deslagging problem requiring less than 0.02% sulfur content in the base iron to decrease slag buildup. The temperature losses vary from 125°F (52°C) to 180°F (82°C) depending upon the ladle capacity. The amount of charging iron should be controlled due to the inability to visually check the ladle filling.

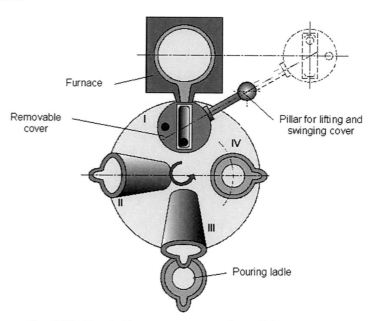

Fig. 7-26. Turntable arrangement of tundish magnesium treatment process.

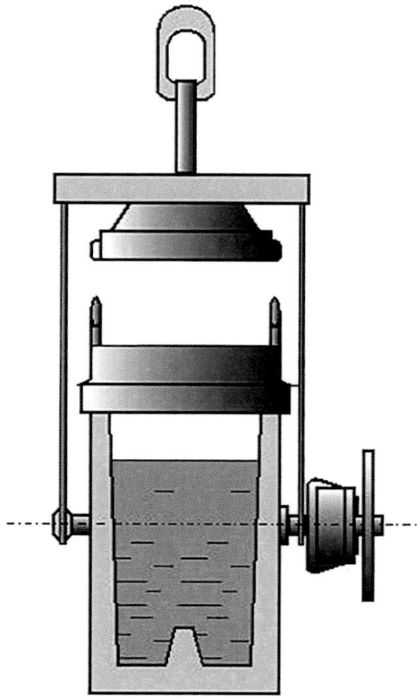

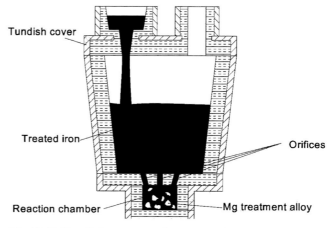

Fig. 7-27. Tundish converter for magnesium treatment of iron.

Fig. 7-25. Tundish ladle with lifting cover.

In-Mold Treatment Process

In this process (Fig. 7-28), the FeSiMg masteralloy with a relatively low Mg content of 3-5% is placed into the reaction chamber of each mold during mold assembling. Molten iron is treated by passing it over the reaction chamber that is a part of running system of the mold. All parameters of the treatment process such as temperature and flow rate of molten iron, geometry of reaction chamber and gating system, size and type of masteralloy must be predetermined and strictly controlled to provide successful treatment.

The in-mold process allows achieving magnesium recoveries of 70–80%, simultaneously providing an effective inoculation, because the iron is treated directly in the mold before solidification. Temperature losses are minimized as well as the pyroeffect.

A high risk of impurities in the castings is a major disadvantage of this process. To reduce slag buildup and

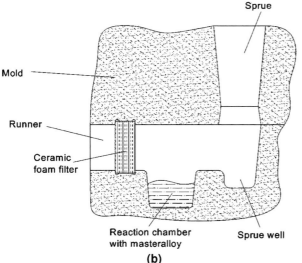

(a)

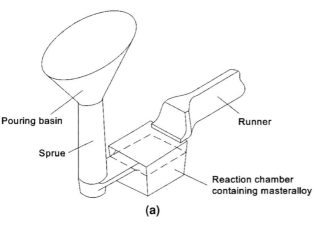

(b)

Fig. 7-28. Schematic of original in-mold process (a); the same, employing ceramic filter for slag trapping (b).

its delivery into castings, an extremely low-sulfur base iron must be used (less than 0.010%), and in-mold filtration is recommended as is shown in Fig.7-28(b). Because each mold represents a discrete treatment process, it must be considered as a bath or heat, and special quality control procedures are required to check for nodularity, especially in safety parts. Finally, due to the location of the reaction chamber inside the mold, casting yield and foundry economics are reduced. The in-mold process, in combination with automated holding/pouring systems, is used in mass production of some automotive parts.

Flow-Through Treatment Process

This method is virtually a modification of the in-the-mold process and employs a special reaction chamber, which is external in regard to ladles or molds. There are several types of external chamber designs, but all of them employ the same idea of dynamic passing of molten iron through the treatment chamber containing MgFeSi-masteralloy. Figure 7-29 illustrates a typical design of a flow-through treatment device. This unit is located between the source of molten iron, such as a coreless induction furnace, and target ladle, such as the transfer ladle.

Before treatment, Mg-containing masteralloy is charged into the reaction chamber through the charging orifice, which is further sealed, limiting the access of oxygen. Molten iron is tapped into the pouring basin, fills the reaction chamber containing the masteralloy, and is treated while it is passing through the reaction chamber, by gradually involving and dissolving particles of masteralloy. The diameter of the output orifice controls the iron flow, which is very important to achieve the best results. Masteralloys containing 3-6% Mg are typically used to reduce the reaction violence. The use of base iron with very low sulfur content (less than 0.02%) minimizes the amount of slag and improves magnesium recovery. The inoculant may be added into the reaction chamber or into the ladle.

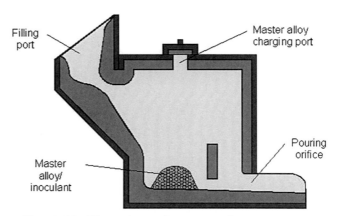

Fig. 7-29. Flow-through magnesium treatment process.

Melting and Pouring Practices

This process has certain advantages such as a relatively high magnesium recovery (60–70%), and the absence of smoke eliminates the necessity of a ventilation system. The device is not expensive, but highly productive, allowing treating one ton of iron in 1–1.5 minutes. Depending on the treatment bath, the temperature losses vary from essentially low to a sensible level of 125–160°F/52–71°C. This device requires minimum maintenance, mostly deslagging of the pouring basin and reaction chamber. With a number of advantages, the necessity of keeping sulfur content on the predetermined low level might be a disadvantage. In addition, the need of using masteralloy with low magnesium content increases its total consumption, which may have a negative effect on overall process economics.

Treatment Method Selection

The wide variety of available magnesium treatment methods makes the selection of an optimal method for a given foundry difficult. In general, this decision is to be made based on the overall analysis of many factors, such as type of melting furnace and sulfur content in the base iron, as well as advantages and disadvantages of each treatment method: magnesium recovery, productivity, temperature losses, necessity of special equipment or devices and their maintenance, safety and environmental impact. The following case studies illustrate examples of practical applications of some previously discussed methods.

Example 7-4

Foundry A is a jobbing green sand foundry making gray iron parts in the weight range of 45–450 kg (100–1000 lb) for agricultural and construction equipment markets. The base iron is melted in a cold blast cupola with a basic lining and duplexed with coreless induction furnaces. Every other day the foundry needs to make 2–3 heats of ductile iron. For these specific production conditions, a wire core injection machine for magnesium treatment has been recommended and installed as shown in Fig. 7-30.

Treatment is done in a 909 kg (2000-lb) ladle in a special treatment chamber. After treatment, a crane carries the treated iron to the pouring area. Pretreatment sulfur is 0.06–0.08%, and magnesium recovery is 32–38%.

Example 7-5

Foundry B manufactures steel shell-molded and investment castings. Melting is carried out in three 450-kg (1000-lb) capacity coreless induction furnaces. Because of market demands, the foundry decided to begin ductile iron production utilizing existing moldmaking equipment, but modernize its melting department. For this purpose, two additional 450-kg (1000-lb) capacity induction furnaces were added to satisfy increased demand for molten metal, and a flow-through Mg-treatment device was installed on rails to be able to move from one furnace to another as shown on Fig. 7-31.

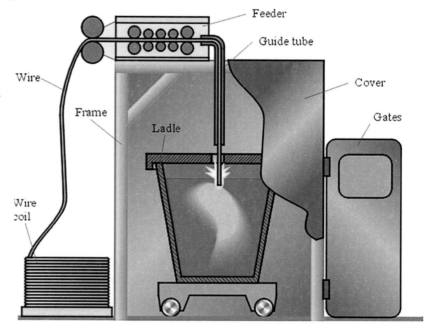

Fig. 7-30. A typical layout of magnesium treatment station utilizing magnesium cored wire.

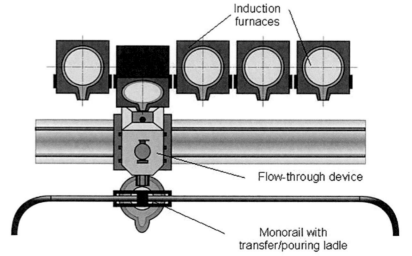

Fig. 7-31. Ductile iron production line consisting of five coreless induction furnaces, movable flow-through device, and monorail-operated transfer/pouring ladle.

Melting and Pouring Practices

155

Figure 7-32 illustrates a typical arrangement of an induction furnace, flow-through Mg-treatment device and pouring ladle. A 5.5% FeSiMg masteralloy consumption varies in the range of 1.6– 1.8% to the total weight of the melt. Depending upon casting wall thickness, temperature losses during treatment are in the range of 150–175°F/65–80°C; magnesium recovery is 62–66%.

The entire treatment process from the beginning of treatment—tapping iron from the furnace into the treatment unit—does not exceed one minute. The suggested layout provides the use of only one flow-through device for the whole production line and is found to be cost-effective for the given foundry conditions.

7.2.5. Melting of Steel

7.2.5.1. Electric Arc Furnace

Direct arc electric arc furnaces are mainly used in the steel melting practice. Some foundries may also use them for melting iron. The modification of this furnace, coupled with vacuum, has found its application in the melting of highly oxidizing titanium alloys. The direct arc furnace is a dish-shaped, refractory-lined, steel shell, having a bottom and swing roof with three vertically installed graphite electrodes protruding through it.

In this furnace (Fig. 7-33) the charge material is heated and melted by means of an electric arc formed between the charge material and the vertically positioned electrodes, and by the radiant energy evolved by the arc.

The bowl-shaped bottom of the furnace, called the hearth, is lined with refractory bricks and granular refractory material, and is usually water-cooled in larger size furnaces. The top of the furnace is covered with a movable roof, through which the graphite electrodes enter the furnace. The roof can be swung aside, off the furnace, for charging. Typically, an arc furnace has three cylindrical electrodes. Each electrode consists of sections

with threaded couplings, allowing addition of new sections upon their wear. The electrodes are automatically raised and lowered by a positioning system, regulating the arc parameters.

The tapping spout is located at the front of the furnace. The access door—used for making necessary additions, observing the process, removing slag and taking samples—is located at the back of the furnace. The furnace has a tilting mechanism allowing it to be tilted forward for metal tapping or backward for deslagging. During tapping or deslagging operations, the furnace roof with the electrodes remains attached to the furnace

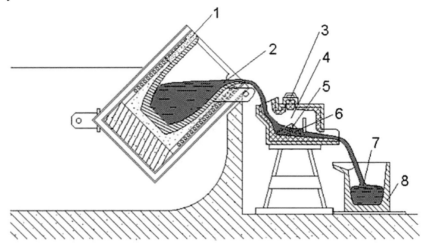

Fig. 7-32. The schematic showing tapping of base iron from the induction furnace through the magnesium treatment device directly into the pouring ladle: 1-coreless induction furnace; 2-base iron; 3-charging window; 4-reaction chamber; 5-FeSiMg treatment alloy; 6-inoculant; 7-treated iron; 8-ladle.

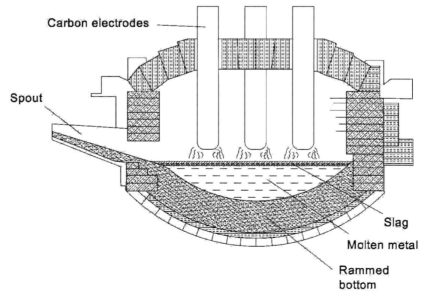

Fig. 7-33. Direct arc electric furnace, used mostly in steel melting practice. Their capacity varies from 1 to 400 t (2200 to 880,000 lb).

shell. An operation control panel allows monitoring of major melting parameters as well as total and per-heat energy consumption.

The furnace may be lined with acid or basic refractories. Arc furnace capacity ranges from approximately one ton (2200 lb) used in foundries for iron melting, and up to about to 400 ton (880,000 lb) used in steel melting. Typically, for the 90-t (198,000-lb) capacity furnace, the whole process from the tapping of one heat to the tapping of the next (the tap-to-tap time) takes about 60–70 minutes. The modern furnace installation allows reducing tap-to-tap time to 35–40 minutes. Typical arc furnace energy consumption in steel melting is in the range of 350–370 kWh/ton (600–630 Btu/lb). Thermal efficiency is between 55 to 65%.

7.2.5.1.1. Charging and Operations

The electric arc furnace can operate in a batch-melting mode, producing batches or heats of molten steel or in the tap-and charge cycle, when a portion of the heat is tapped out and the furnace operates with a heel of molten metal.

In acid melting, an acid type refractory, mostly silica, is used as the lining material, and the slag is acid. It means that sulfur and phosphorus cannot be removed during the melting process. The latter sets up specific requirements to the initial content of these elements in the charge mix: typically 0.05% max of each element. The charge mix may consist of up to 100% steel scrap (foundry returns, turnings and purchased scrap).

In basic melting, steel melts in a furnace lined with a basic type of refractory (magnesite or dolomite) and the nature of slag is basic. The basic lining allows the removal of sulfur and phosphorus, with the help of fluxes such as limestone or lime. A typical charge mix consists of 75–80 % steel scrap (foundry returns and purchased scrap), 5–15% low sulfur pig iron and 2–4% flux. The melting practice in electric arc acid and basic operations is mainly similar and consists of the following procedures.

The first step is loading the charge mix into large buckets and transporting them to the furnace; then the roof is swung off the furnace, buckets are opened and the furnace is charged. The charge may be preheated to improve furnace efficiency. After charging, the roof is swung back over the furnace, the electrodes are lowered onto the charge mix, an arc is struck, and meltdown starts.

At the end of meltdown, melt refining is performed to reduce carbon content. This process, called a carbon boil, is initiated by introducing iron ore (iron oxide) or gaseous oxygen. Modern furnaces are furnished with an oxygen lance or wall-mounted oxy-fuel burners, which are used to accelerate scrap meltdown and may also be used for carbon boiling.

Initially, oxygen reacts with elements, such as iron, silicon, aluminum, manganese and calcium, forming oxides that flow into the slag. All of these reactions are exothermic (i.e., they generate heat) and supply additional energy to aid in the melting of the charge. During the oxidation period, which begins immediately after charge meltdown, in furnaces having basic lining, sulfur and phosphorus are also actively removed. This is due to reaction with basic flux, and their reaction products flow into the slag. Then, oxygen burns carbon, producing carbon monoxide (CO), which causes a vigorous melt bubbling action, resulting in nitrogen and hydrogen removal from the steel and a more uniform temperature and chemical element distribution.

Because of carbon loss due to oxidation, its initial content in the charge is intentionally maintained in excess of the final level set by specification: 0.1–0.15 % for acid melting and 0.2–0.4% for basic melting. At this time, a melt temperature and a chemistry control sample is taken. Knowing the bath chemistry allows determining the necessary chemistry adjustments by increasing the amount of oxygen to be blown, to burn the excess carbon or, in case of carbon deficiency, adding carbon-containing material and ferroalloys.

Before tapping, the addition of deoxidizers, such as aluminum in the form of ferroaluminum, or silicon in the form of ferrosilicon or silicomanganese, which stop carbon boiling, commonly referred to as "blocking the heat" or "killing" the steel, is made. After final alloy additions, the melt temperature is raised to desirable temperature and the molten steel is tapped. Final deoxidation and alloy additions are made into the stream as molten steel is being tapped into the ladle. Slag-forming compounds are also added to the ladle, so that a slag cover preventing melt temperature loss and oxidation can be formed prior to transfer to the pouring station.

7.2.5.2. Electric Induction Furnace

Steel melting in induction coreless furnaces, particularly in small capacity furnaces, is widely used to melt all grades of carbon and alloy steel due to the ability to change alloys frequently and produce small batches of alloys with exact specifications. That is why investment casting foundries use induction furnaces as the main melting equipment. For high-alloy steel melting, these furnaces may be furnished with a cover and protective atmosphere of neutral gas, such as argon, aimed at preventing alloying element oxidation and loss as well as gas pickup.

While the equipment used to melt steel is very similar to iron melting, there are some differences involved in producing quality steel. There are many similarities in melting steel in induction furnaces and electric arc furnaces. In induction furnace, as well as in electric arc furnace, acid and basic refractories are used where applicable; in the melting of alloy and stainless steel, alumina refractory is exclusively used. The difference is that, typically, no intense carbon boiling is involved, because direct blow with the oxygen lance is not used. Some foundries employ a semi-refining process, in which, as a source of oxygen, iron ore (taconite pellets) in the rate of 1.5–2.0% is added to the charge. This creates only slight boiling during meltdown, resulting in lower carbon loss and reduced oxidation of the other elements.

Because of the limited refining of molten steel in an induction furnace, higher grades of scrap with controlled chemistry are required. Other operations, such as blocking carbon burning, chemistry adjustments and deoxidation are identical to steel melting in arc furnaces.

7.3. Melting of Nonferrous Alloys

7.3.1. Crucible Furnace

These furnaces are the oldest and simplest melting units used in the nonferrous foundry melting practice for a variety of alloys in small quantities. Typically, crucible furnaces are classified according to the method of molten metal removal from the crucible:

- Stationary tilting furnace, in which the molten metal is tapped into the pouring or transferring ladle by tilting the crucible along with the furnace.

- Stationary, bowl-type furnace, in which the metal is ladled from the crucible to the mold or transferred to the holding unit.

- Movable furnace, in which the crucible with the molten metal is removed from the furnace and then poured into the mold or tapped into holding furnace. The crucible may be removed from the furnace manually or mechanically.

Movable furnaces may use gas or an induction coil for melting. In movable coreless induction furnace design, as shown in Fig. 7-34(a), called a push-out furnace, the crucible is seated on a vertically oriented hydraulic ram, which moves the crucible up and down, and the induction coil is stationary. In another design shown in Fig. 7-34(b) called a lift-coil furnace, the coil is moved about crucible. Handling of movable furnaces requires special safety precautions while removing the crucible from the furnace and pouring from it.

In the crucible furnace, the charge mix is placed in a refractory crucible made of carbon-bonded silicon carbide. The heat is applied to the crucible, thus there is no direct contact between the source of heat and the metal

charge. This type of melting is very flexible, since it suits a variety of nonferrous casting alloys. Degassing and any metal treatment can be completed in the crucible before it is removed for pouring. Melt quality and temperature are controlled reasonably well.

Gas and electric crucible furnace capacities vary from 45 to 1360 kg (100 to 3000 lb). These furnaces are tilt or stationary models and are constructed from a 6 mm (¼ in.) rolled steel shell with 20 mm (¾ in.) steel top plates. Modern gas furnaces provide uniform heat transfer using full proportioning burner control systems with a full combustion safety train that includes UV (ultraviolet) flame monitoring.

Electric resistance crucible furnaces (Fig. 7-35) are typically furnished with high-temperature nickel-chromium alloy heating elements that provide good

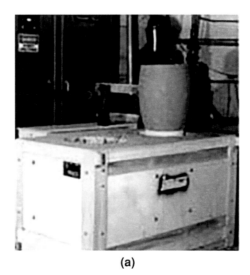

(a)

(b)

Fig. 7-34. Movable crucible type coreless induction furnaces: (a) double push-out; (b) lift-coil. [Source: Foundry Management & Technology]

service life and are repairable in the case of accidental metal splashing.

Contemporary electric resistance crucible furnaces are furnished with a computerized control panel with element temperature protection. Degassing and filtration furnaces may use gas or electricity for heating and can be interconnected to the existing melting furnace. Filtration furnaces are supplied with roll-off lids for easy filter changing and cleaning.

Modern, fully automated and integrated melting systems are intended for continuous delivery of high-quality molten aluminum to highly productive automotive casting lines. One system, used to supply molten aluminum to a lost foam engine casting line, consists of a high-efficiency gas melting furnace and an electric furnace used for degassing and filtration, which are connected by a launder transporting system.

Another system delivers molten aluminum at 800°C (1472°F) from a 23,405 kg/h (51,491 lb/h) capacity furnace to the molding lines making engine blocks, engine heads and wheels through a 122 m (400 ft) heated launder.

Heated launders are designed to provide continuous metal transfer from the melting furnace to the holding furnace, or directly to the pouring station, with uninterrupted metal flow and minimum heat losses. Molten aluminum may be transferred safely and quietly from 3 to 122 m (10 ft to over 400 ft) with this system. Cylindrical, operated lift lids provide easy access to skimming and cleaning. Heat is supplied by high output electric nickel-chromium or silicon-carbide elements. The advantages of this launder system are that they ensure contained metal transfer for worker safety and clean plant environment. Additionally, cover gas purges reduce metal oxidation, preserve metal quality and prolong refractory life. Use of highly insulated precast refractory liner construction allows easy replacement with minimum production delays and more energy efficient operations.

Capacity of furnaces in molten aluminum processing systems range from 90 to 90,910 kg (200 lb to 200,000 lb).

7.3.2. Reverberatory Furnace

These furnaces may utilize various types of heating: gas or electricity or both (dual-energy type) and differ greatly in design from horizontal to vertical arrangements. In a typical furnace design (Fig. 7-36), a gas-fired flame heats the roof and sidewalls, heat radiates from the refractory, and finally melts a charge mix.

Fig. 7-35. Low-capacity electric resistance crucible furnace used for melting and holding aluminum alloys. [Source: Foundry Management & Technology]

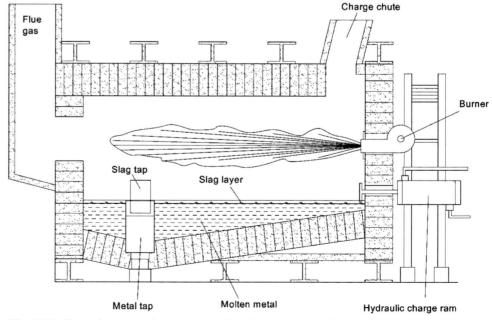

Fig. 7-36. Reverberatory furnace used in aluminum foundry.

The reverberatory furnaces are generally used for melting large volumes of nonferrous alloys, for example aluminum, to supply holding furnaces coupled with pressure diecasting machines. Capacity of these units varies from 2270 to 90,910 kg (5000 to 200,000 lb). These furnaces are simple in maintenance and have relatively low capital cost, but their thermal efficiency is at about 40%. Melting capacity of radiant electric melting and holding furnaces varies in sizes from 680 to 27, 270 kg (1500 to 60,000 lb) with the melt rates from 90 to 1360 kg/h (200 to 3000 lb/h).

7.3.3. Aluminum Alloy Melting Problems

Aluminum alloys can be melted in a wide variety of furnaces: from crucible gas-fired or induction heated to reverberatory furnaces. Typical charge materials are ingots that already have the prealloyed chemistry, scrap and foundry returns. There are two major problems commonly seen in the melting practice of aluminum alloys.

First, molten aluminum is very susceptible to hydrogen absorption, causing gas porosity, which results in loss of mechanical properties and pressure tightness in the castings. Hydrogen is the only gas that is soluble in molten aluminum. The solubility of hydrogen gas increases as the temperature is raised. Moisture is the major contributor of hydrogen that reacts with molten aluminum. This reaction is defined as follows:

$$3H_2O + 2Al \rightarrow 6H + Al_2O_3 \qquad (7.11)$$

Sources of moisture and, hence, hydrogen are the furnace atmosphere and refractory, charge materials, sand mold, furnace tools (skimmers), etc. As a preventive measure, dry charge materials and furnace tools must be used, and excessive melting and tapping temperatures, as well unnecessary melt agitation, should be avoided.

Second, melt oxidation is a problem due to aluminum and other alloying elements with a high affinity to oxygen. These elements are magnesium, calcium, titanium and strontium. Oxides or dross formed during melting significantly reduce properties and integrity if they remain in the solid casting.

To insure high melt quality, hydrogen and nonmetallic inclusions must be removed prior to pouring. Employing a special operation, called degassing, allows the removal of hydrogen, oxides and other impurities. These are effectively removed by treating the melt with inorganic salt fluxes, which form high fluidity, low melting temperature slags that flow to the top and are easily skimmed.

Degassing became a standard melt treatment practice employed in many aluminum foundries. One of the simplest degassing methods is the straight lance

technique, in which a graphite or ceramic pipe, connected to a source of gas such as nitrogen or argon, is immersed into the melting or holding furnace or ladle, producing gas bubbles. Hydrogen diffuses into the bubbles since the partial pressure of hydrogen in the melt is greater than the partial pressure of hydrogen in the bubbles. Small bubbles have a greater surface area than larger bubbles of the same total volume, and are more effective in degassing. The large purge gas bubbles produced by a straight lance are not very effective for degassing.

Another technique, the rotary degassing system (Fig. 7-37 and Fig. 7-38), proves to be more effective by producing smaller bubbles. One of the advantages of this

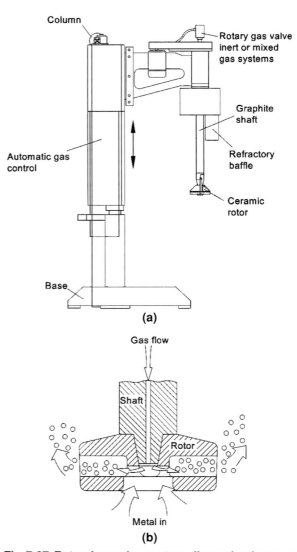

Fig. 7-37. Rotor degassing system allows simultaneous degassing with flux injection and is very effective in aluminum alloys melting practice: (a) principle components; (b) schematic, showing ceramic rotor, attached to the shaft, in action. [Courtesy: Foseco Metallurgical]

Melting and Pouring Practices

technique is that flux may be injected simultaneously with the degassing when gas is used as a carrier for different types of fluxes.

Fluxing the aluminum melt allows maintaining metal cleanliness and prolongs furnace refractory life. When flux is injected as a part of the degassing process, it better removes dross due to inclusion floatation. In addition, fluxes economically recover metallic aluminum contained in dross. Untreated dross may contain 80 wt% or more metallic aluminum, which can be returned to the melt. Prior to casting, spent flux and its residuals must be completely skimmed off the melt. Failure to do so can lead to entrainment of flux inclusions in the castings produced.

Common in aluminum melting, grain refinement is a necessary operation aimed at forming fine equiaxed grains structure during solidification at the expense of dendrites. One of the practical and very effective methods used is the addition of small amounts of trace elements, in the form of masteralloys called modifiers, into the melt prior to pouring. A typical grain refiner used in aluminum melting practice is a titanium-boron (Ti-B) alloy, containing 3–10%Ti and 0.2–1.0%B.

Benefits of grain refinement in the foundry operation include improved feeding, reduced porosity and hot tearing and increased pressure tightness. In addition, mechanical and high-temperature properties are better and more consistent, particularly after heat treatment. The advantages during the subsequent processing stages include improved machinability and better appearance in polished and anodized coatings.

Liquid aluminum filtration helps to remove the oxides and other nonmetallic inclusions more completely if it is done twice: first, when melt is tapped out of the furnace following the degassing operation and second, in the mold, using ceramic filters.

7.4. Pouring of Cast Alloys

The molten metal from the melting or holding furnace is tapped into ladles at requisite intervals and then either transferred to another operation, like degassing in aluminum alloy practice, or directly poured into the molds. Pouring of metals is one of the most important operations in the casting production, since molten metals have a relatively high sensitivity to holding time. As the metal is tapped into the ladle and held there, it looses a large amount of heat to the surrounding atmosphere by radiation. Table 7-8 gives average data on the expected temperature drop of molten iron in conical ladles of variable capacity.

As seen in the large ladles, there is a relatively small drop of temperature due to the larger heat content, whereas in the small ladles the drop is substantial. Hence, more speed in operation of the small ladles is desirable, particularly in manual operations.

Because the actual pouring temperature of the melt as it enters the mold would be different from that of the

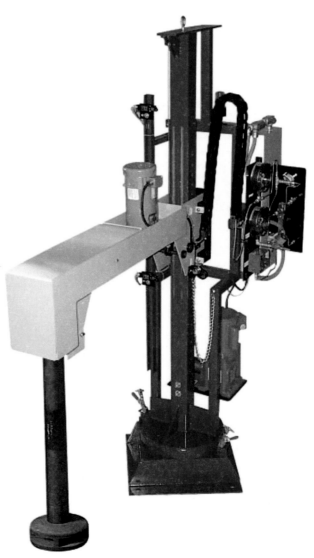

Fig. 7-38. Actual view of the rotor degassing system. [Courtesy: Foseco Metallurgical]

Table 7-8. An Average Data on Expected Temperature Drop Of Molten Iron in the Conical Ladles with Variable Capacity.

Ladle Capacity, kg (lb)	Expected temperature drop, °C/min (°F /min)
50 (110)	20–40 (11–22)
150 (330)	10–15 (5.5–8.3)
300 (660)	5–7 (2.8–3.9)
1000–2000 (2200– 4400)	2–3 (1–1.7)
3000–4000 (6600–8800)	1.5–2.5 (0.8–1.4)

temperature when it was actually tapped from the furnace, it is necessary to account for this drop in the tapping temperature of the cast alloy from the melting or holding furnace. The actual alloy pouring temperature into the molds should satisfy optimal data recommended for given alloy and casting section size (Table 7-9).

Excessive holding may cause not only temperature losses, but also chemistry changes, as it takes place in iron melting, resulting in fading of inoculation and nodulizing effects. Besides specified precise chemical composition and temperature, molten iron must be poured at the proper rate to ensure adequate metallostatic head pressure in the mold.

These conditions require special pouring techniques and methods. The pouring methods presently used in the foundry can be broken down into two groups:

- Equipment and devices utilize ladles. This group includes hand-held and manually-operated pouring ladles suitable for low-volume production.

- Ladleless systems comprise more advanced pouring equipment with progressively reduced levels of human involvement, ranging from mechanical to fully automated. The latter reflects the trend to develop new environmentally friendly pouring techniques and technologies that minimize or totally eliminate human involvement.

Automated ladles and ladleless pouring systems allow the stabilization of the pouring process parameters, vastly improving casting production economics, safety, and working conditions in the foundry. However, the installation and handling cost of such equipment appears to be a limitation for a majority of small foundries.

Therefore, in currently operating foundries, it is very common to see all varieties of manual, mechanical and automatic pouring devices and equipment.

7.4.1. Pouring Ladles

Ladles, ranging from small hand-held to large automatically or mechanically-operated units, are the most common pouring and transfer equipment used in any type of castings production. Depending upon the shape of ladles, there are two major groups used for pouring castings: conical and drum-shaped ladles (Fig. 7-39).

A conical ladle is a steel receptacle with the capacity varying from 100 kg to 30,000 kg (220 to 66,000 lb) and up. They are lined with refractory and usually have an open top and pouring lip or nozzle for pouring convenience. Typically, such ladles are secured in a steel ring with two trunnions, and equipped with pawls that prevent overturning during transferring. The downside of these ladles includes relatively high temperature losses, considerable rates of emissions during transfer and pouring, and a higher possibility of producing casings contaminated with slag inclusions because of excess exposure to the atmosphere, and oxidation. Conical ladles can be equipped with a special teapot device, as seen in Fig. 7-39(b), which restrains slag inside the ladle. But for steels, to separate the slag effectively, the metal is to be poured from the bottom with the help of the bottom-pour

Table 7-9. Approximate Range of Pouring Temperatures of Various Casting Alloys in Sand Molds Depending Upon Castings Wall Thickness.

Casting alloy	Casting wall thickness, mm (in.)	Pouring temperatures, °C (°F)
Gray iron	< 4 (0.16)	1450–1400 (2640–2550)
	4–10 (0.16–0.40)	1430–1340 (2610–2440)
	10–20 (0.40–0.80)	1400–1320 (2640–2410)
	20–50 (0.80–2.0)	1380–1300 (2520–2370)
	50–100 (2.0–4.0)	1340–1250 (2440–2280)
	100–150 (4.0–6.0)	1300–1230 (2370–2250)
	> 150 (6.0)	1280–1220 (2340–2230)
Ductile iron	< 4 (0.16)	1450–1430 (2640–2610)
	4–10 (0.16–0.40)	1430–1400 (2610–2550)
	10–20(0.40–0.80)	1410–1380 (2570–2520)
Malleable iron	< 4 (0.16)	1480–1450 (2700–2640)
	4–10 (0.16–0.40)	1450–1400 (2640–2550)
	10–20 (0.40–0.80)	1430–1360 (2610–2480)
Carbon &low alloy steel	10–60 (0.40–2.40)	1675–1575 (3050–2870)
Aluminum alloys	5–40 (0.20–1.60)	710–760 (1310–1400)

ladle, as seen in Fig. 7-39(c). The bottom-pour ladle has an opening in the bottom that is fitted with a refractory nozzle. A stopper rod, suspended inside the ladle, pulls the stopper head up from its position, thus allowing the molten alloy to flow from the ladle.

With drum-shaped ladles, as in Fig. 7-39(d), temperature losses are significantly lower than in conical designs, but they typically have limited capacity up to 3400 kg (7500 lb). In this ladle, the molten metal is poured into the mold through the nozzle by tilting the ladle. The drawback to using these ladles is their difficulty to clean and reline.

For some conical ladles, replaceable shanks (one-piece teapot shaped liners) with ceramic webs for slag separation are employed. The disposable, preformed insulating linings require no preheating and can reduce energy cost, while improving casting quality and working conditions. Pouring ladles for low- and medium-volume production are tilted manually by special tilting wheels or handles. While they are easy to maintain and less expensive, they are labor intensive.

7.4.1.1. Mechanically-Operated Ladles

Pouring ladles with a motorized, gear-tilting option and mechanical transfer system are typically employed for medium- and high-volume production. Depending on the type of metal, molding equipment and production rate,

ladles may be transferred and teamed by a monorail, seen in Fig. 7-40(a), or overhead crane, seen in Fig. 7-40(b), or fork-truck, pictured in Fig. 7-40(c). Ladles carried by roller conveyor are usually used as transfers and are teamed with other devices.

In some cases, pouring is done by a more complicated combination of several mechanized systems that transport, position and tilt the ladle. One effective system used for this purpose is a manipulator, which is a manually-controlled device that helps an operator move the ladle from the melting furnace after tapping and pouring molds as shown on Fig. 7-41.

The manipulator features several axes of movement of the manipulating arms carrying the ladle, while the operator manually pushes it in a horizontal direction. The latter allows an operator to pour molten metal quickly, precisely and safely. A common manipulator is an overhead trolley, which can be electrically or hydraulically powered. The arm can also be mounted on a stationary floor pillar. Manipulating arms are mostly hydraulic. Lifting control is done by a lever or push button, and the hydraulic arm is driven up and down. Designed to eliminate hand-held ladles and manual operations, this system allows reducing temperature losses, increasing productivity and safety in pouring small quantities of metal in investment and permanent mold castings.

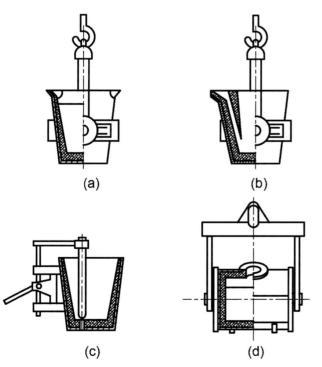

Fig. 7-39. Type of ladles used to pour or transfer molten metals: (a) conical; (b) conical with teapot spout; (c) conical bottom pour with a stopper rod; (d) drum-shaped.

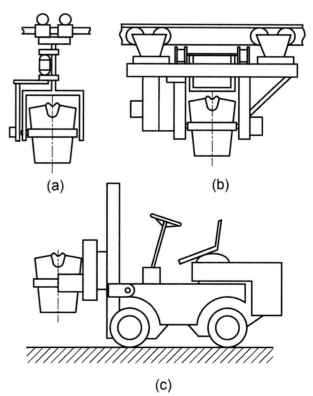

Fig. 7-40. Ladles may be transferred by different means: (a) monorail; (b) overhead crane or (c) fork lift.

The traveling pouring station (Fig. 7-42), used for iron pouring on straight molding lines with different rates of production, is a typical design of a mechanically-operated pouring device, where the ladle is transferred and teamed by two different mechanized systems. One system combines a traveling gear and a hydraulic ladle-tilting mechanism, set on the base stand, to move a standard conical ladle with a capacity of up to 10,000 kg (22,000 lb) or a drum-shaped ladle of up to 3400 kg (7500 lb) along the molding line, and tilts. The other system uses powered roller conveyors to exchange an empty ladle for a full one.

The operator, who handles all transfer and pouring operations, also controls pouring time, molten iron temperature and metal quantity. However, low consistency of pouring weight reproduction and molten metal quality (mainly nonuniform temperature), plus the worker's continued involvement in the pouring cycle, has limited the application of these pouring units.

7.4.1.2. Automatically-Operated Ladles

The use of automatically-controlled devices for the transporting and teaming of ladles provides a correctly-performed pour, and almost entirely eliminates human involvement in all stages of the pouring process. This ultimately increases productivity and reduces cost. The automatically-controlled ladle also may be coupled with automatic molding lines and associated machines, stabilizing the pouring process and improving quality control and working conditions.

A typical example of these pouring machines, intended for mass production, is an automatically-operated, specially-designed tundish ladle (see next paragraph) with a controlled stopper rod. The automatic tundish ladle with controlled stopper rod (Fig. 7-43) comprises the tundish-ladle set on the support frame and hydraulically-activated position system driving the tundish ladle along the molding line.

The tundish ladle is a steel shell lined with refractory and equipped with a thermal insulating cover. The ladle is divided into intake and pouring chambers by a removable refractory dam that separates slag from the poured iron. The size of tundish ladles may vary from 1000 kg to 3000 kg (2200 lb up to 6600 lb), mostly depending on the weight of castings. The controlled stopper rod, located

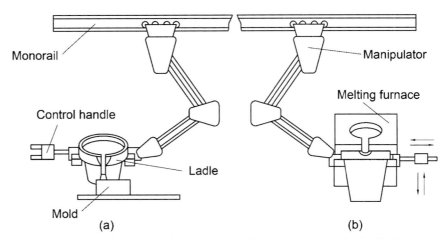

Fig. 7-41. Manually operated manipulator is used to move the ladle from the melting furnace after tapping (a) and to pour molds (b).

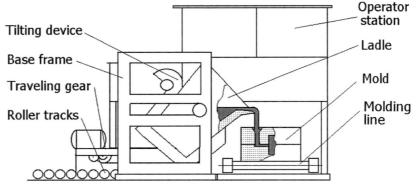

Fig. 7-42. Traveling pouring station used for iron pouring on straight molding lines.

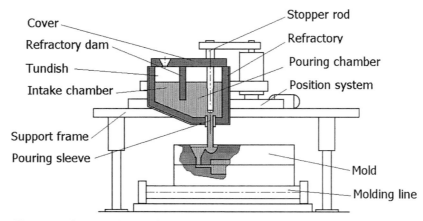

Fig. 7-43. Automatic tundish-ladle with a stopper-controlled rod.

Melting and Pouring Practices

in the tundish's pouring chamber, regulates the molten iron flow by opening and closing the hole in the pouring sleeve located at the bottom of the ladle. The level of molten iron in the pouring cup of the mold is controlled by intelligent sensors, either visual camera or laser sensor.

The specific features of this system help minimize the effect of slag formation, although it does not have a power element for molten metal superheating. The metal, therefore, must be handled in batches to reduce temperature loss while the pouring rate is kept high. This system is used mainly in conjunction with automatic sand molding lines. One very successful application of this unit was for pouring relatively low-weight ductile iron castings on vertical flaskless molding lines. Refilling of the tundish ladle every 5–7min with a fresh portion of Mg-treated iron reduces temperature losses and prevents ductile iron fading.

The automatic ladling system (Fig. 7-44) utilizes small ceramic pouring ladles (cups) for transferring over short distances and pouring small amounts of molten metal. This system is widely used in diecasting of aluminum alloys.

The ceramic pouring cup, set on the arm, picks up, from a holding furnace, a sufficient amount of molten metal for the entire pour of one mold and then pours it into the mold. A servomotor drive system allows smooth movement of the arm, by simultaneously rotating the ladle. A computer controls the pouring process parameters with special preinstalled programs for arm manipulation, which allows the pouring system to work without control sensors. All information on the pouring process is provided to the operator station, allowing the operator to make adjustments outside the working area.

This ladling/pouring system supplies precisely-dosed molten metal at a constant temperature into the mold, without operator involvement. Ceramic cups can be removed and changed without special tools, but the unit's use is limited because it is designed only for low-weight castings. Another limitation of this system is a break in the pouring process while the holding furnace is recharging.

7.4.2. Ladleless Pouring Systems

The increased productivity of automatic molding lines has initiated the development of precisely dosing automatic ladleless pouring systems having capabilities adequate to the molten metal consumption of the molding line. These pouring systems are electric holding/pouring furnaces, which require no ladles for molten iron dispensing. They are equipped with additional devices that create special forces, such as compressive, tilting or electromagnetic, to move molten metal up to the mold. The application of these systems is effective because they are flexible enough to handle different casting weights and allow for uninterrupted pouring.

Pressurized pouring furnaces with a controlled stopper rod are the most widely used ladleless pouring systems in the highly productive iron foundries. A typical design of this unit (Fig. 7-45) includes the induction channel pouring furnace. The furnace has a lined vessel, one intake and one pouring channel, and a water-cooled inductor that is positioned vertically or horizontally at the bottom of the vessel, to serve as a heating element.

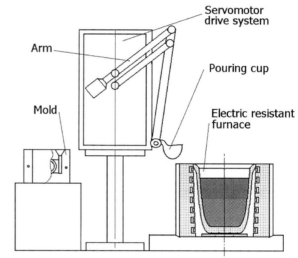

Fig. 7-44. Automatic ladling system is widely used in diecasting of aluminum alloys.

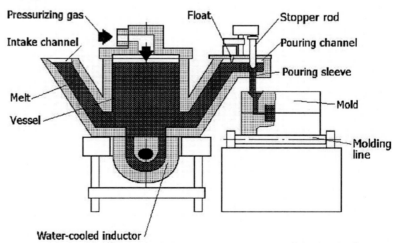

Fig. 7-45. Pressurized induction channel pouring furnace with stopper-controlled rod used in high volume production iron foundries.

As the pressurizing gas (nitrogen or dry air) flows into the chamber above the melt, molten iron is forced into the pouring channel. During the pouring process, a float regulates the pressure of gas inside the vessel, so that the molten iron in the pouring channel stays at a certain, constant level. A laser sensor or video camera (see next section) then measures the level of molten iron in the pouring cup of the mold and sends a command to close the pouring sleeve and start moving the molding line. It also controls the automated inoculation process. Typically, a pressurized pouring furnace is used in a duplex-process as a secondary unit to hold and pour irons, when the base metal is melted in a cupola or coreless induction furnace. This pouring system is capable of delivering precisely-dosed molten metal at a uniform temperature, to help produce slag-free castings.

In recent years, pressurized pouring furnaces have demonstrated high practical performance and have been successfully incorporated into gray and ductile iron casting production, offering optimal conditions for holding and pouring. These furnaces are mostly induction channel pouring holders, with capacities varying from 1000 kg to 20,000 kg (2200 lb to 44,000 lb).

Short transfer distances between the melting furnace and the pressurized pouring furnace provide minimal temperature loss by shortening the contact time of the molten metal with air. Combined with the automatic sand molding lines, this integrated automatic pouring system ensures flexibility, repeatability of pouring weight and casting quality. It is used in mass production foundries.

An electromagnetic pouring system comprises the channel induction furnace combined with an electromagnetic unit (pump), which produces a force capable of moving molten metal (Fig. 7-46). The pouring furnace consists of a steel vessel inner-lined with refractory bricks. Molten metal is charged through the intake hole at the top of the vessel. When the furnace is charged, the intake hole is covered with a thermal insulating cover to prevent temperature loss and contact of metal with air.

An electromagnetic induction unit is attached to the bottom of the furnace, and can be operated in two different modes: preheating or pouring. While in the pouring mode, the molten metal is electromagnetically forced into the pouring pipe, up to the pouring channel of the furnace and dispensed into the mold. Sensors that also command the unit to change the mode of operation may assess the level of molten metal in the mold's pouring cup.

The electromagnetic pouring system is suitable for any type of production and is usually coupled with molding lines. Currently, electromagnetic pumps are used for transfer and nonturbulent, low-pressure filling of sand, permanent and semipermanent molds, mostly of nonferrous alloys (aluminum, magnesium and zinc). The pump can also be used as a dosing or metering device for filling of molds via gravity.

The system provides a noncontact transfer of the molten metal and is flexible for a wide range of casting weights, is safe and environmentally friendly. However, the practical applications of this or similar furnace designs have shown frequent clogging in the pouring pipe or channel. Some attempts to use this system to pour ductile iron without a protective atmosphere have failed because of considerable slag buildup in the channel.

A properly selected pouring method is essential because it significantly influences the quality and cost of castings, the casting yield, safety and labor intensity of production. A variety of factors go into the decision, including the type of cast alloy, casting weights and the scale of casting production. Economic justification of castings produced by any chosen method will be further evidence of pouring process effectiveness.

7.4.3. Automatic Pouring Control Systems

Since repeatability of pouring weight for each individual mold is one of the major requirements for automatically-operated molding lines and machines, precise computerized systems have been designed to control this parameter. Depending upon the type of operation, two major systems may be used: laser sensor or video camera. These sensors allow metalcasters to shift from time-based pouring to sensor-based control of the stopper rod in automatic pouring devices.

Laser Sensor

The laser sensing system, illustrated in Fig. 7-47(a), is typically used in straight sand molding lines. The major elements of this system are line laser generator, which

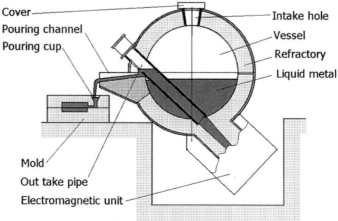

Fig. 7-46. Electromagnetic pouring system.

shines a beam of infrared light on the metal surface, and receiver, which picks up the reflection of this beam. The generator and receiver are placed at opposite ends of the pouring device. Using a triangulation technique, the distance between the sensor and the metal level is computed. As the molten metal in the pouring cup reaches a certain level, the laser sensor gives the command to stop pouring and start the movement of the pouring conveyor.

The improved 3-D laser system consists of a line laser generator that paints a laser line across the pour cup. On the opposing side, a sensor uses its view of the line to determine the iron level in the cup. By using this direct measurement method (no interpretation), the pour stream is ignored and an accurate real-time level reading can be obtained. For cup detection and automatic positioning, the 3-D laser is fitted with a single-point laser. The 3-D laser system is recommended for all applications with vertically-parted molding lines, small pour cups and high production rates.

Video Camera

The video camera, seen in Fig. 7-47(b), monitors the molten metal in the pouring cup and can be used with any type of pouring equipment and molding lines. The camera is inserted into an air-cooled protection container and works with an electronic shutter that operates at a speed of 1/8000 sec. Because the molten iron emits bright light, the contrast between the metal in the pouring cup and the dark mold surface is clear. A computer digitizes information from the pouring cup and processes it, establishing the metal level in relation to the mold surface. As the computer receives information that the pouring cup has reached a certain level, it gives the command to stop pouring. This camera also supplies a video image of the actual pour to the unit's control panel, so the operator can actually see the level of the metal in the pouring cup.

A vision-based system is capable to accurately pour into pouring cups as small as 2.5 times the pouring nozzle and is recommended for use on vertically and horizontally parted molding lines pouring cast irons and copper alloys. A newly introduced line sensing system combines a line laser with a vision camera offering the benefits of more precise control of pouring weight and flexibility.

7.5. Quality Control in Melting

Quality control (QC) in the melting process is aimed at verification of the major requirements to the quality of molten metal, which are mostly common for all alloys.

7.5.1. Chemical Composition Control

From previously studied material (see Chapter 2 Casting Alloys) it is known that mechanical (e.g., strength, hardness, ductility), physical (e.g., thermal or electric conductivity) as well as chemical (corrosion resistant) and service (wear resistance) properties of a casting depend on its structure and chemical composition. The structure of a solidified cast alloy can be modified by a heat treatment, however, only remelting can change alloy chemistry. Therefore, proper chemistry is the basis of required properties of a casting. Currently, three techniques for quick chemistry evaluation are widely used in metal casting:

1. Thermal analysis system
2. Optical emission spectrometry
3. Carbon and sulfur determinator

A thermal analysis system (Fig. 7-48) analyzes the casting alloy solidification curve (the freezing temperature and the amount of energy released at each freezing point) and refers this data to the chemical composition of the alloy.

Fig. 7-48. Thermal analysis instrument analyzes casting alloy solidification curve (the freezing temperature and the amount of energy released at each freezing point) and refers this data to the chemical composition of the alloy.

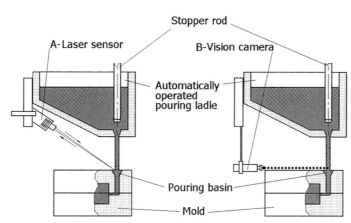

Fig. 7-47. Control systems used in automatic pouring, illustrated in the example of automatic tundish-ladle with a stopper-controlled rod: (a) laser sensor; (b) video camera.

In iron melting practice, it is employed to provide, with reasonable accuracy, information on carbon equivalent and carbon content as well as calculated silicon content.

This test is done prior to tapping to ensure that the chemistry is in accordance with the melt specification. In this test, a sample of liquid metal is taken from a furnace or a ladle and poured into a sand cup with a thermocouple and a small portion of tellurium at the bottom of the cup. Tellurium, one of the strongest carbide stabilizers, causes the iron to solidify as a white iron with a fully carbidic structure without graphite. This allows more accurate determination of the given iron's solidification curve parameters and, based on this data, calculation of the carbon equivalent, carbon and silicon content.

During the metal's solidification, data from the thermocouple is transferred into the computer-based core of the thermal analysis system, where the cooling curve (Time-Temperature diagram) is compiled and analyzed by special software. Beside the chemical composition, the cooling curve describes metal solidification behavior and can be used to predict final properties. For example, in gray iron, an advanced thermal analysis system is used to predict chill and ferrite/pearlite content; in ductile iron this instrument is used to predict shrinkage, nodularity and nodule count.

In nonferrous metallurgy, thermal analysis systems are also widely used. For example, in aluminum alloy casting production, thermal analysis commonly used for grain refinement and silicon modification measurement, as well as for hydrogen and porosity prediction. In copper melting, it is used for phosphorus content determination.

Optical emission spectrometry is a second tool for rapid chemical composition analysis. This technique is widely used in all types of foundries. The main advantages of these systems are high accuracy and quick operation that allows within a few minutes to obtain complete analysis of major and trace elements. The analysis takes only a few minutes from the moment of pouring the test sample to printout of the element content.

In contrast with thermal analysis systems, spectrometers, seen in Fig. 7-49(a), deal with solid metallic samples. In the case when quick analysis of an iron in a furnace or in a ladle is needed, the test sample of metal must first be poured and solidified. For accurate analysis, the test piece of iron must be free of graphite (free carbon). Pure carbidic (white) structure can be reached by rapid solidification in special copper molds.

The obtained test sample must be rough ground on one side; this side should be flat and clear for correct chemistry evaluation. The ground flat surface of the sample is placed against the spark stand where it is flooded with argon, and a rapid series of high-current sparks are produced (Fig 7-58(b)). A large quantity of the sample surface is evaporated and emits light (photons).

The emission is passed to the spectrometer optical system, where it is dispersed into its spectral components. Each separated element has a specific wavelength of emission, and the emission intensity is proportional to the element concentration. Wavelengths are used for element identification, and the intensities of emission are used for composition evaluation. Results of analysis are reported as a computer printout within a minute.

The carbon and sulfur determinator is a microprocessor-based instrument that can perform rapid wide-ranged measurements to simultaneously determine the carbon and sulfur content in ferrous and nonferrous metals. This instrument is widely used in iron and steel foundries.

7.5.2. Temperature Measurement Control

Testing for temperature measurements is done to make sure that molten metal is superheated above the melting point, to ensure that it will remain molten and flow into and within the mold for a sufficient length of time. These tests are typically done in the furnace, before tapping, and in the ladle, during pouring. The instruments commonly used are:

(a)

(b)

Fig. 7-49. Spark source optical emission spectroscopy is a major technique for direct analysis of metals and cast alloys. The analysis takes only a few minutes from the moment of pouring test sample to printout the elements content: (a) spectrometer; (b) spark stand.

Melting and Pouring Practices

- Contact (immersion) thermocouples, as seen as Fig. 7-50(a1) and (a2), with ceramic protective shields or replaceable tips for quick changes, which measure metal temperature by immersion into the melt. The melt technician takes a temperature reading using immersion thermocouples in an induction furnace, shown in Fig. 7-50(b).

- Noncontact thermometers, such as pyrometers (Fig. 7-51) measure molten metal temperature without contact in the range of 600 to 3000°C (1100 to 5500°F). A variable focus system allows focusing from 1 m (39 in.) to infinity with a digital display of the target temperature and data printing.

7.5.3. Gas and Slag Control

Certain procedures are aimed at reduction of slag inclusions, oxides and gas porosity, associated with melting operations. In ferrous melting practice, gases such as oxygen, hydrogen and nitrogen tend to be dissolved in the molten stage and are controlled by using a special instrument, called a gas analyzer, which measures gas content. In aluminum melting practice, hydrogen control and a degassing operation to reduce its content are mandatory.

Gas diffusers, also known as porous plugs, have been used in steel ladle metallurgy to allow gas purging of steel melts before pouring the metal into molds. The purging step degasses the melt and produces cleaner steel, resulting in a reduced scrap rate in castings. Recently [Ref. 11], porous plugs have been applied for induction melting of steels, irons and aluminum alloys to deliver inert gas directly to the melt. The latter allows lowering scrap rates, improving furnace campaign life and overall efficiency of the melting process.

For a gas diffuser to function safely and effectively, a number of factors have to be considered. The refractory material selected must be able to resist penetration when in contact with liquid metals. The design must ensure that the gas diffuser is able to deliver small quantities of inert gas to the induction furnace melt in a controllable manner. Also, it must be compatible with the induction furnace lining materials. The gas diffuser must be easy to install and operate, and it must be able to last for the life of the induction furnace lining. Ultimately, it must be cost effective, too.

The standard range of gas diffusers for induction furnaces are made with high alumina refractories. Pressed and fired permeable alumina diffusers are designed specifically for aluminum applications. Pressed and fired permeable magnesite diffusers are recommended for general ferrous foundry applications.

Diffusers should be installed in the center of the furnace base, or as close as possible to the center. The furnace must have a gas supply to connect to the gas diffuser, and there must be a suitable gas-flow control system. Such a system may be as simple as a pressure regulator on an argon-gas bottle with an inlet needle valve and flow meter. Or, it may be as sophisticated as a PLC package linked to a computer-controlled process control system.

The induction furnace lining must be sintered before the gas diffuser is used, so that the gas can pass through the lining without disturbing it. Using a gas diffuser early in the melting process is not recommended; it's necessary for adequate sintering to take place first. Experience indicates that the best results are obtained from introducing gas to the diffuser during the third melt and onward.

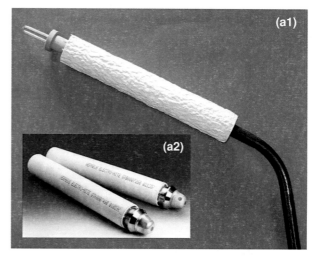

Fig. 7-50. Contact (immersion) thermocouple with ceramic protective shields or replaceable tips for quick changes, which measure metal temperature by immersing into the melt (a1) and (a2), and melt technician taking temperature reading in an induction furnace (b). [Courtesy: Heraeus Electro-Nite]

Gas flow is turned on at "full melt" and the flow is increased until a gentle bubbling motion is seen on the surface of the melt. This is generally at a rate of around 10 liters/minute for a one metric-ton melt. Gas expands as the temperature rises, so there may be more bubbling as the temperature increases prior to tapping. Gas flow can be reduced at this stage to 6–8 liters/minute. Gas purging should be continued for the duration of the melt, right up to the point of tapping.

7.5.3.1. QC and Cleanliness Testing in Al Foundries

To define hydrogen gas content, a reduced pressure (vacuum) test (RPT) is widely used (Fig. 7-52a). In this apparatus (Fig. 7-52b), equipped with a vacuum pump, a gauge to monitor the vacuum level and a control system to regulate it; a sample of molten aluminum solidifies under the chosen vacuum level. The reduced pressure in the vacuum chamber causes the dissolved hydrogen to come out of solution in the molten aluminum and form bubbles in the solidified sample.

After solidification, the sample is cut in half vertically and its cross section is compared with visual samples, similar to those shown in Fig. 7-53. As porosity number increases (number in the center), density (bottom number) decreases. Samples #1, 2 and 3 are considered as standards for subsequently high, good and commercial quality castings.

Despite the fact that this test is a semi-quantitative test (because it is not a true measure of hydrogen content), it allows for the correlation of metal density and actual hydrogen content. It is a quick, simple and low-cost technique, widely used in aluminum foundries.

Special equipment (Fig. 7-54) is used to provide information on the level of oxides and other inclusions in the melt at all stages of the aluminum castings process. A small sample of liquid aluminum representing the heat is poured into special unit. The computerized apparatus records the filtration rate curve during a standardized pressure filtration test and compares it with preprogrammed benchmarks for each alloy processed at this foundry, and after 3 min measures the molten aluminum cleanliness. The same sample may be used for microscopic evaluation to determine inclusions content and grain size as well as for SEM inclusions identification.

Fig. 7-51. Noncontact pyrometers measure molten metal temperature without contact in the range of 600–3000°C (1100–5500°F).

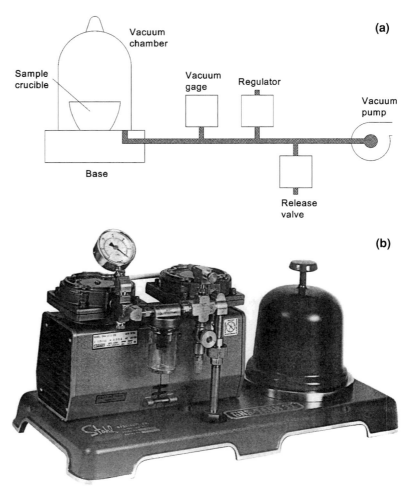

Fig. 7-52. Schematic representation of reduced pressure (vacuum) test (a) and testing unit for measuring hydrogen content in molten aluminum alloys (b). (Courtesy: Stahl Specialty Co)

STAHL
Aluminum Comparative Standards for Gas
Percent Surface Area Porosity
Densities for 356 Alloy
100mm Pressure

#6
5.3
2.38

#5
2.9
2.45

#4
1.3
2.52

#3
0.84
2.56

#2
0.18
2.59

#1
0.10
2.60

#0
0.00
2.68

#12
30.3

#11
24.5
2.16

#10
19.5
2.19

#9
15.4
2.22

#8
11.8
2.26

#7
8.3
2.30

Fig. 7-53. Example of aluminum A356 cross sections standards used for visual comparison and for hydrogen porosity control. (Courtesy: Stahl Specialty Co)

Fig. 7-54. Liquid inclusion sampler to measure the relative cleanliness of aluminum melts.

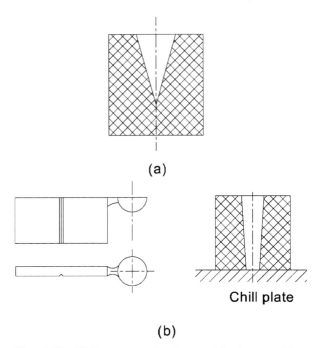

(a)

Chill plate

(b)

Fig. 7-55. Chill test methods used in iron melting practice: (a) triangular-shaped test specimen is poured in an open-top sand mold; (b) the tip of the test specimen is poured against chill plate.

7.5.4. Chill Control in Iron Melting

Solidification structure and properties of cast irons depend upon many variables such as chemical composition (carbon equivalent, alloying element content), casting wall thickness, pouring temperature, mold material, gating position, etc. To control solidification, the use of a special chill wedge-type specimen, poured in a sand mold, is common in cast iron practice. The ASTM A-367 standard recommends two types of chill testing methods (Fig. 7-55):

- For low carbon equivalent, high tensile strength gray irons, a triangular shaped test specimen is poured in an open top sand mold (Fig. 7-55a)

- For softer, higher carbon equivalent grades of gray iron, the tip of the test specimen is poured against a chill plate made of metal (iron, steel or copper) or graphite (Fig. 7-55b). Despite the necessity of maintenance of the chill plate, this method is more universal and adapted in high productivity iron foundries making a variety of cast irons grades.

Regardless of the method used, the chill wedge, after pouring, is removed from the mold as soon as it is completely solid, cooled in water, and then is fractured in the middle by striking with a hammer. The chilled area usually consists of two zones: clear and mottled. The portion nearest the apex, entirely free of graphite, is designated as clear chill, followed by the portion in which spots of white iron or cementite are visible, called the mottled zone. Chill is measured as a distance from the tip to the edge of the mottled zone, or as a width of chilled area in the fractured cross section of the wedge.

For more precise chill measurements, an image analysis system may be used, which also takes into account chilled areas on the corners of the chill wedge. Indirectly, chill tendency is evaluated utilizing principles and apparatus for thermal analysis of the iron solidification curve.

References

1. *Ductile Iron Molten Metal Processing*, American Foundrymen's Society, Inc., Des Plaines, Illinois USA (1986).

2. *Ductile Iron Handbook*, American Foundrymen's Society, Inc., pp 148-166 (1993).

3. "Mold Inoculation for Ductile and Gray Iron," *Metallurgy and Foundry Technology*, Tecpro Corporation, pp 6-8 (2005).

4. Lerner, Y.S., Riabov, M.V., "Iron Inoculation: An Overview of Methods," *Modern Casting*, pp 37-40 (June 1999).

5. Lerner, Y.S., Graig, D., Aubrey, L.S., Margaria, T., Siclari, R., "Development of In-mold/In-filter Inoculation for Thin-Wall Cast Irons," *AFS Transactions*, vol. 112, Paper No. 04-092 (05) pp 1-25 (2004).

6. Lerner Y.S., Tukhin I.E., "Ductile iron treatment using pure Magnesium in the modified pressure vessel and sandwich methods," World Symposium on Ductile Iron, South Carolina, Oct. 19-22, (1993).

7. Henych I., "The development trends in the ductile iron metallurgy," George Fischer Ltd., Switzerland (1997).

8. Alagarsamy, A., "Ductile Iron Treatment Using Pure Mg in a Modified Tundish Ladle," *AFS Transactions*, Vol.100, pp 235-238 (1992).

9. Lerner Y.S., Panteleev G.V., "Magnesium Treatments in Ductile Iron Production," Part 1, *Foundry Management & Technology*, volume 130,number 8, pp 25-31 (Dec. 2002); Part 2, *Foundry Management & Technology*, volume 131,number 2, pp 24-29 (Feb. 2003).

10. Lerner, Y.S., Laukhin N.Y., "Development Trends in Pouring Technology," *Foundry Trade Journal*, Nov. 2000, pp 16-21.

11. *Foundry Management & Technology*, May 2007 and Jan. 2008.

12. Huangu, E.P., Naranjo R.D. and Bentz K.M., "Combating Energy Bills," *Modern Casting*, Apr 2006, pp 20-22.

13. Lerner, Y.S., "Modern Casting of Ductile Iron", AFS (2006),178 p.

Review Questions

7.1 Describe the lining materials used in melting furnaces. Define slag basicity.

7.2 Describe the constructional features of a cupola furnace.

7.3 Discuss the major operations of a cupola furnace for melting cast iron.

7.4 List the charge mix content in a cupola furnace.

7.5 Explain the functions of flux in melting metals and alloys.

7.6 Explain why the chemical composition of the iron obtained from a cupola changes during melting.

7.7 Differentiate between cold and hot blast cupolas.

7.8 Explain the difference in construction and applications between a coreless induction furnace and a channel induction furnace.

7.9 Define batch and tap-and-charge melting operations.

7.10 Describe a duplex process.

7.11 Explain the refractory installation procedure in an induction furnace.

7.12 Define iron inoculation and its fading.

7.13 Discuss the different methods of inoculation used.

7.14 Explain the ladle inoculation methods.

7.15 Explain the benefits and problems of late inoculation.

7.16 Discuss the advantages of in-mold and in-filter inoculation.

7.17 Give a few recommendations for selecting the inoculation methods for thin-walled iron castings.

7.18 Explain the advantages of using pure magnesium treatment for ductile iron production.

7.19 Describe the plunging magnesium treatment method.

7.20 Explain the cored wire magnesium treatment method.

7.21 Explain the treatment converter used for ductile iron production.

7.22 Describe the treatment methods that use magnesium masteralloys for ductile iron production.

7.23 Explain the tundish process for treatment with magnesium masteralloy.

7.24 Give an example of the in-mold magnesium treatment process. Explain the necessity of the installation of a filter.

7.25 Describe the flow-through treatment process for ductile iron production.

7.26 Summarize how an electic arc furnace operates.

7.27 Differentiate between acid and basic steel melting practice.

7.28 Give examples of different crucible furnaces used for melting nonferrous alloys.

7.29 Explain the reverberatory furnace design features and applications.

7.30 Briefly describe major problems in aluminum melting and the methods used to solve them.

7.31 Discuss the necessity of degassing in aluminum melting. Give a description of rotary degassing.

7.32 Describe each of the ladles which can be used for pouring molten metal into the molds.

7.33 Explain the difference between automatically-operated ladles and ladleless pouring systems.

7.34 Describe the pouring system widely used in diecasting. Give a brief description of the system.

7.35 Describe control systems used in automatic pouring lines.

7.36 Discuss control methods used in foundries during melting.

7.37 Differentiate between optical emission spectrometry and thermal analysis system applications for chemistry control.

7.38 Describe the methods used for molten metal temperature measurements.

7.39 Explain one method used for hydrogen control in melting of aluminum alloys.

7.40 Explain chill control in iron melting practice.

Problems

7.1. The iron foundry is using a charge for the cupola consisting of 20% pig iron 1, 25% pig iron 2, and 55% scrap iron. Assuming a carbon pickup of 0.30%, sulfur pickup of 0.03%, 10% loss of silicon, 25% loss of manganese and no change in phosphorus, calculate the final melt composition.

Charge materials	Carbon, %	Silicon, %	Manganese, %	Sulfur, %
Pig iron 1	3.20	1.70	0.80	0.03
Pig iron 2	3.50	2.40	0.60	0.01
Scrap iron	3.25	2.30	0.65	0.08

7.2. Foundry needs to melt in a 3,000 kg (6,600 lb) capacity coreless induction furnace pearlitic ductile iron Grade 100-70-03. Required chemical composition: C = 3.6–3.8%, Si = 1.6–1.8% (before inoculation), Si = 2.4–2.6% (after inoculation), Mn = 0.5–0.7%, Cu = 0.6–0.8%, S ≤ 0.02%, P ≤ 0.03%. Calculate charge using the data given below.

Charge materials	Percentage	Carbon, % in material	Carbon, % in charge	Silicon, % in material	Silicon, % in charge	Manganese, % in material	Manganese, % in charge	Copper, % in material	Copper, % in charge	Phosphorus, % in material	Phosphorus, % in charge
Ductile iron returns	50.0	3.70		2.60		0.55				0.03	
Steel scrap	50.0	0.20		0.20		0.60				0.03	
Totals without melting loss	100.0	--									
Melting loss		10.00		10.00		10.00					
Total with melting loss											
Carbon raiser*		98.50									
Pure copper (scrap)								100.00			
FeSi75, (recovery 0.9)*				75							
Estimated composition											

* For chemistry adjustment use the same method as described in Examples 7-2 and 7-3.

SPECIAL CASTING METHODS

8

Objectives

A variety of special casting methods have been developed as an alternative to convensional sand casting to provide specific economical and technical advantages. After studying this chapter reader should be able to:

- Discuss the permanent mold casting process, including required equipment
- Define various types of diecasting methods and their applications
- Compare the centrifugal casting process and its variants
- Explain the investment casting process and its advantages
- Identify the ceramic molding process and its applications
- Explain the lost foam casting process and its advantages and limitations
- Describe the continuous casting process and its variations
- Define the countergravity casting process
- Discuss the semisolid casting process
- Discuss the vacuum molding process and its advantages and limitations

Keywords

Permanent Mold Casting, PMC, Gravity Permanent Mold Casting, Gravity Diecasting, Metal Molds, Mold Cavity, Mold Ejection System, Molten Metal, Casting Solidification, Casting Process, Mold Cooling System, Mold Coatings, Thermal Barrier Coating, Mold Design, Cooling Methods, Water-Cooled Permanent Mold, Air-Cooled Permanent Mold, Gray Iron, Ductile Iron, Mold Coating, Cooling Jacket, Die, Metal Die, Graphite Die, Pouring Machine, Vent, Mold Life, Mold Erosion, Insert, Heat Sink, Permanent Mold Machines, Stationary Permanent Mold Machine, Tilting Permanent Mold Machine, Multi-Station Turntable Permanent Mold Machine, Metal Core, Graphite Core, Sand Mold, Sand Core, Mold Distortion, Shrinkage, Diecasting, Pressure Diecasting, Rapid Solidification, Nonferrous Alloys, Copper Alloys, Cold Chamber Diecasting, Hot Chamber Diecasting, Die Ejection System, Flash, Die Operational Temperature, Infrared Noncontact Thermometer, Low-Pressure Diecasting, Centrifugal Casting, Semicentrifugal Casting, Centrifuging, Investment Casting, Lost Patterns, Ceramic Molding, Shaw Process, Unicast Process, Lost Foam Casting, Evaporative Pattern Casting, EPC, Expendable Polystyrene, EPS, Continuous Casting, Tundish, Dummy Bar, Horizontal Continuous Casting, Steel, Countergravity Casting, Hitchner Process, Countergravity Low-pressure Air-melt Casting, CLA, Loose-Sand Vacuum-Assisted Casting, LSVAC, Semisolid Casting, Rheocasting Process, Thixocasting, Vacuum Molding, V-process, Permanent Mold, Solid Model, Solidification Modeling, Solidification Behavior, Numerical Modeling, Meshing, Simulation, Aluminum Alloy, Hot Tear, Microporosity, Niyama Criterion, Density, Freezing Point, Casting Solidification, Finite Difference Method, Rapid Tooling, Heat Transfer, Gating System, Risering System, Chill, External Chill Insert, Water-Cooled Chill, Air-Cooled Chill, Copper Chill, Iron Chill, Cooling Fin.

In all previously studied casting processes, a separate sand mold needs to be prepared for each casting produced. For large-scale production, making a mold for every casting to be produced may be time-consuming and expensive. In addition, conventional sand casting is neither dimensionally accurate nor economical in many applications, whereas the special casting processes would be more appropriate. These processes include precision casting methods that are able to produce precision cast parts with an improved surface finish, while providing excellent details with a higher degree of dimensional accuracy.

Several special casting processes use high-precision sand molds; others, called permanent mold casting, utilize metal molds, in which molten metal is poured into reusable metal molds with the assistance of gravity, tilt, pressure, vacuum, or centrifugal forces.

Use of permanent molds or precision thin-wall sand molds is not only cost effective, but is also environmentally friendly because it eliminates or significantly reduces foundry sand consumption and associated emissions, waste generation and disposal.

This chapter discusses the special casting processes most often used by the foundry industry.

8.1. Permanent Mold Casting (PMC)

Process overview

In conventional permanent mold casting (PMC), molten alloy is poured into a reusable metal mold under gravity (static mold) or into a tilt mold. This process is also called gravity permanent mold casting or gravity diecasting, since the metal enters the mold under gravity. Rapid solidification permits almost immediate shakeout of castings, reducing production cycle and enhancing mechanical and service properties of the castings. Near net shape parts made by this method feature exceptonal dimensional accuracy and surface quality.

The traditional permanent mold casting process is predominantly a mass production method that becomes cost-effective only when used for properly selected parts. Matched with the proper casting design, there are definite advantages in cost, quality, energy reduction and environmental issues.

Metal molds can be used to produce a large number of castings, anywhere between 100 to 250, 000, depending on the alloy used and the complexity of the casting. Typical permanent mold design incorporates the mold cavity, cores (metallic or sand), gating system, mold cooling system and casting ejection system. (Figs. 8-1(a) and 8-1(b))

Mold material plays an important role in permanent mold casting, determining technical and economic effectiveness of the process. Commonly, the selection of the mold material is based on the type of casting alloy, its pouring temperature, size of the casting, and frequency of the casting cycle and cost. The thermal impact of molten metal flow in the mold is the major factor determining mold life, as well as the casting quality. The permanent mold process operates at a range of high temperatures, and the mold material is subjected to significant molten metal erosion and thermal stresses.

Typical permanent mold materials are iron, steel, copper or graphite. Cast iron is a recognized mold material that offers good thermal conductivity and heat resistance. It is used to make molds for iron and aluminum castings. Tool steel H-13 is also a common mold material for aluminum PMC, where mold life may reach up to 75,000 parts, while iron molds may produce up to 40,000 similar castings.

In iron and some nonferrous permanent mold practice, steel water-cooled molds are cast or machined of low-carbon steel 1015 or 1020, or of low-alloy Cr-Mo steel 4115 or 4120. After casting, steel mold blanks are normalized at approximately 900°C ±5°C (1650°F ±41°F) for about 2 or 3 hours and then stress relieved at 620–650°C (1150–1200°F) for 2 or 3 hours and cooled in the furnace. Copper molds are made of Cu-Be or Cu-Cr alloys supplied as continuously cast plates. Graphite, because of its high thermal conductivity, is another material that is used in PMC, mostly of steel, or for small volume production from aluminium and magnesium alloys. Graphite is also used to make cores and inserts, playing the role of heat sinks that set up the desirable solidification mode.

Mold Coatings. Permanent molds are coated with either refractory (insulating) or lubricating (releasing) material.

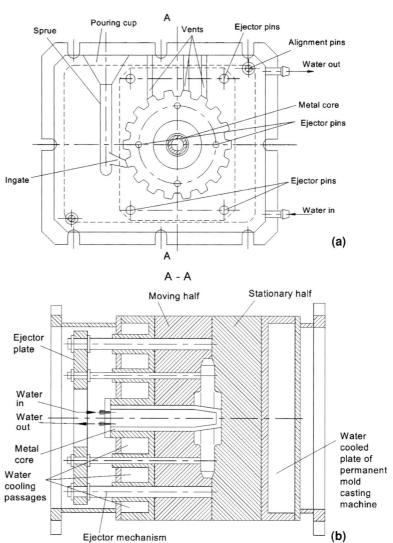

Fig. 8-1(a and b). Typical design of a water-cooled permanent mold gear casting, incorporating mold cavity, metal water-cooled core, gating system, mold cooling system and casting ejection system.

These coatings are used to increase the mold life by preventing the soldering of metal to the mold, minimizing the thermal shock to the mold material, and helping to control the rate and direction of the casting solidification. The coating also reduces friction and thermal losses that, in turn, prevent premature solidification of the metal in the mold. These coatings drastically extend the mold life.

Depending upon the alloy cast, the coating may consist of one or two layers. Lubricating (releasing) coatings are used in low-temperature alloy practice such as alumunum and magnesium. For the higher pouring temperature alloys, protective coatings or a combination of two layers are prefereable. The first layer is an insulating, thermal barrier coating, applied to the mold surface before the mold is placed into service. This is a semipermanent coating that must be reapplied periodically. The second coating is a lubricant, usually a carbon-containing material, which is deposited on the mold surface prior to each pour. It may be a water-based refractory coating sprayed on the previously preheated (up to 120–150°C (250–300°F)) mold surfaces, or a solid ceramic coatings applied by thermal spray or plasma spray techniques.

Cores for making any hollow portions are also used in permanent mold casting. Cores can be made out of metal or sand. When sand cores are used, the process is called semipermanent molding. The metallic core cannot be complex with undercuts and the like. Also, the metal core is to be withdrawn immediately after solidification, otherwise its extraction becomes difficult because of shrinkage. For complicated shapes, collapsible metal cores (multiple-piece cores) are some times used in permanent molds. Their use is not extensive because it is difficult to securely position the core as a single piece, and also due to the dimensional variations that are likely to occur.

In PMC, the cost of tooling is a significant fraction of the initial investment. Therefore, when considering this process, the foundry must always add mold life as a factor to the cost of the casting. Mold life is one of the major factors determined effectivness of the PMC. Within a wide variety of measures that extend mold life and, in turn, increase the recuperation of the initial investment, appropriate mold cooling and mold operational temperature control systems are all important.

Mold Design. Depending on the part complexity, molds are designed with a horizontal or vertical parting line, having from one to several identical cavities. The gating and risering systems used are very similar to that of the sand casting (see Chapters 4 and 5).

The mold cavity should normally be simple without any undesirable drafts or undercuts, which interfere with the ejection of the solidified casting. In designing the permanent molds, care should be taken to achieve directional solidification toward the riser. If the casting has heavy sections, which may solidify for a longer time and are likely to impede the directional solidification, the mold section around that area may be made heavier to extract more heat. Metallic inserts or chills supported by a heavy air blast may also be used to remove the excess heat. Alternatively, cooling channels may be provided at the necessary points to get proper temperature distribution.

Cooling Methods. A properly designed mold cooling system must regulate the heat flow and ensure desirable productivity of sound castings as well as extend the mold life. Figure 8-2 schematically illustrates the relationship between the permanent mold operating temperature and production cycle time for different cooling systems. It is obvious that when the temperature range a mold must withstand is kept within a narrow range, it will extend the life of the mold, but at the cost of increased cycle times. Careful consideration must be made to the priority of cycle times and mold life.

Air-cooling gives a very "soft" cooling rate and provides effective heat transfer from the mold when thin-walled castings are produced, but it is less effective than water-cooling in the production of thick-walled castings.

Mold temperature control is very important to the casting quality in terms of establishing the desirable thermal gradients in the mold and regulating the casting's solidification. Another factor that affects mold life is the control of hot or cold spots in the mold. Uniform cooling will eliminate localized areas that would be subjected to thermal shock or liquid metal erosion and, therefore, prolong the mold life.

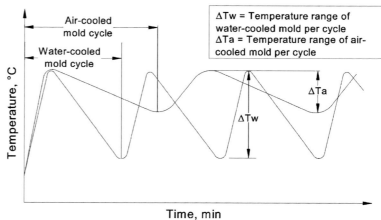

Fig. 8-2. Relationship between the permanent mold operating temperature and production cycle time for air-cooled and water-cooled molds.

Abrupt changes in the cooling rate within the mold cavity caused by cold or hot spots, are also detrimental to the casting's quality, causing shrinkage-related defects and hot tearing. Uneven solidification also produces a high level of residual stresses that result in casting distortion and dimensional instability during the process and service of the castings .

To regulate the temperature in permanent molds, there are a variety of cooling methods available. Each of these methods has advantages and disadvantages, which should be carefully analysed.

Air-Cooled Permanent Molds. Figure 8-2 represents one of the simplest methods of permanent mold cooling. These molds have limited cooling capabilities that may be enhanced by contouring the mold, adding cooling fins and using compressed air. Figure 8-3(a) illustrates typical design of an air-cooled permanent mold where the back of the mold shell is contoured to maintain uniform mold thickness around the mold cavity.

The contour of the mold back may be thickened or thinned out, as needed, to increase or decrease the cooling rate in localized areas. Cooling fins are placed across the back of the mold to aid heat transfer. The back of the mold could also be designed flat, as shown in Fig. 8-3(b), rather than contoured with the addition of cooling fins.

The cooling fins may have a circular or rectangular cross-section. Rectangular fins have an obvious advantage due to the increased surface area. The back of the mold could also be designed without the addition of cooling fins. The air-cooled mold will have a longer service life because of its gradual cooling, rather than the immediate cooling effects of water-cooled molds.

Water-Cooled Permanent Molds. Within diverse designs of water-cooled molds, the following are the most used in foundry practice.

Cooling Jacket Welded to Mold (Fig. 8-4). In this specific design of water-cooled systems, the water jacket is welded directly to the back of the steel mold.

Effective heat transfer in this mold design is achieved by circulating water through the jacket. This method allows the back of the mold to be contoured in an effort to maintain uniform cooling. This cooling system works

well to reduce or eliminate hot and cold spots on the mold. Actually, the cooling system works so well that the mold life is drastically increased due to elimination of the thermal shock experienced by the mold.

However, this cooling method is limited to molds made of steel, to allow the water jacket to be welded onto the back of mold. In addition, water-cooled permanent molds with wall thickness of 25–38 mm (1–1.5 in.) made of low-carbon cast steel exhibit longer life, because mold cracks and other deteriorated areas may be periodically repaired by welding.

Cooling Jacket Affixed to Casting Machine (Fig. 8-5). Compared to the water jacket welded directly to the back of the mold, this design provides more moderate cooling, because it cools the mold indirectly.

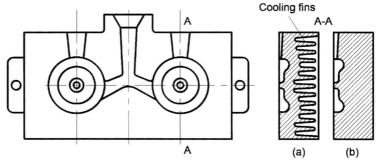

Fig. 8-3. Air-cooled iron permanent mold with contoured back (a) and flat back (b).

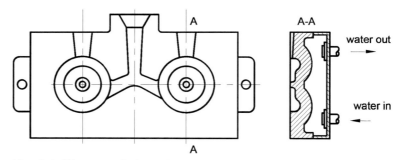

Fig. 8-4. Water-cooled steel permanent mold with a cooling jacket welded to the back of the mold.

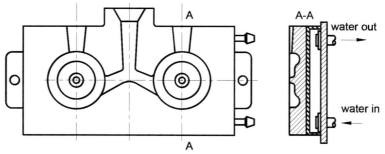

Fig. 8-5. Water-cooled permanent mold with a cooling jacket affixed to casting machine; mold can be made of iron or steel.

The advantage of this method is that the water jacket can be made from materials other than steel, for example cast iron, and it is suited for relatively small and thin-walled casting applications and for operations that include frequent changes of the mold.

The main drawback of this system is the air-gap often occuring between the mold and cooling jacket, due to the thermal related stresses and distortion occurring in the mold during operation. As a result, some areas the mold will have no contact with the water jacket and, therefore, experience less cooling than other areas of the mold.

Drilled Cooling Passages (Fig. 8-6) may be placed with relative precision in the mold and may be applied adjacent to certain casting sections within the mold cavity.

The major disadvantage of this design is the inability to set up uniform or differential cooling and to avoid hot or cold spots in other regions of the mold. Another restriction to this technique comes from the mechanical problems associated with the drilling of the passages. The fact that drilling of the passages cannot be curved means that paths of cooling that are perpendicular to each other will require elaborate drilling patterns. After drilling such paths, the excess openings must be closed with special manufactured threaded plugs. Once plugged, the mold needs to be pressure-tested to ensure no leaks are present. If this testing shows a leak formed by porosity in the mold material, the mold is worthless and must be scraped. This leak may not even be evident during testing. Some leaks are discovered during the use of the molds, when heating the mold increases a small defect in the material to a large (and dangerous) problem. Since the drilling and testing follows machining of the mold blank, the cost of machining would be lost as well. Plugging of the leaking molds has never been successful, because the plugs can often leak due to differences in thermal expansion. One solution to this problem would be the use of a prefabricated steel pipe that is cast into the iron permanent mold.

Prefabricated Steel Pipe Cast-in the Iron Permanent Mold (Fig. 8-7). In this method, steel pipe is prefabricated to the desired cooling pattern and then cast into the iron mold during production of the cast mold blank. This method allows water to pass directly across any areas that would need cooling without restriction to straight-line distances. Another advantage of this system, in comparison to the drilled passages, is the virtual elimination of problems related to

the mold leakage. Prefabricated water cooling passages may be designed with one circuit or two separate circuits.

The prefabricated water cooling passage method is limited to mostly simple shapes, flat castings without deep pockets. The disadvantage of this cooling method is that the mold is deteriorated more rapidly in the areas that are close to the cast-in pipe.

Spray or Vaporization Cooling of Permanent Molds (Fig. 8-8). In this design of cooling system, vertical passages in the mold are sprayed with water from the nozzles located in the top manifold. As water contacts the hot surface of the passages, it changes its physical state from liquid to steam. The necessary energy required for this change of state is captured from the mold heat. This, therefore, significantly reduces the temperature of the mold. The condensed water is then collected at the bottom, by the collector manifold.

The cooling passages can be cast into the mold blank or machined so that an elliptical cross-section can be achieved, rather than a circular. The elliptical shape allows greater surface area for a more effective heat transfer. The commonly used materials to make these types of molds are iron or copper alloys. While this process is one of the most effective methods of mold cooling, it is a less uniform method of cooling. The lack

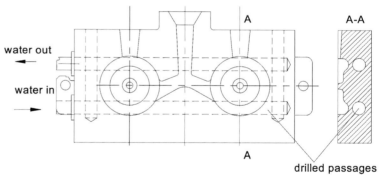

Fig. 8-6. Water-cooled iron permanent mold with drilled cooling passages.

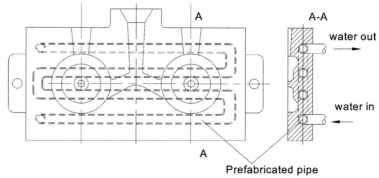

Fig. 8-7. Water-cooled iron permanent mold with cast-in prefabricated steel pipe cooling passages.

of uniformity causes more thermal shock to the mold and, therefore, reduces the mold life.

Any water-cooling system requires proper maintenance due to the fact that, during service, passages will become clogged with scale from minerals in the water. To prevent this, demineralized water can be used and the passages must be regularly cleaned. Common for all water-cooled molds is a constant flow rate. This can be disadvantageous, because the mold needs different water flow control throughout the solidification process. Figure 8-9 illustrates a computer-controlled water-cooling system that monitors the temperature at various locations throughout the mold and inputs temperature readings to the computer.

The computer, in turn, sends a signal to the water flow-control unit to vary the flow of water to the mold. This allows for supplying more coolant when the mold temperature is higher and less coolant when the temperature is lower.

Careful technical and economic analyses should be performed before choosing the suitable cooling system design. In selecting the most cost-effective mold cooling system, several technical factors must be taken into account, such as the weight, moduli and section thickness of the casting, production cycle times and quality, the total number of castings to be made, and expected mold life. Generally, the final decision should be made on the basis of the estimated cost of finished castings.

The effect of a cooling system is often best evaluated by the use of specialized simulation softwares that can analyze heat transfer through the mold and solidification behavior of the casting.

One very important thing should be kept in mind when considering the water-cooled systems: since the water passages are made as a permanent part of the mold, incorrect placement of the coolant lines or their relative distance from the mold cavity would be an expensive mistake.

Metallic inserts (chills) or heat sinks, made of a material with higher thermal conductivity than the mold material, is another way to control solidification and heat transfer in PMC.

This is particularly important when the gating and risering system is not capable to setup a desirable solidification mode; i.e., directional or progressive solidification due to the specifics of casting design, for example, in thick hub gears. In this case, an insert can be placed in thicker casting section areas to enhance the solidification process in that area.

Figure 8-10 illustrates the typical design of a thick hub gear and four possible locations of heat sinks/inserts to reduce shrinkage.

Figure 8-10 (A) shows a flat-ended insert on one side of the casting at the hub location. The insert will draw heat out of the hub so the hub and adjacent rims can solidify concurrently. Figure 8-10 (B) shows a projected-end insert to draw heat out of one side of the hub. The

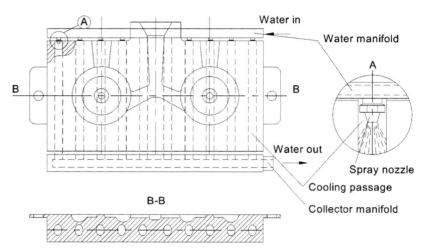

Fig. 8-8. Water-cooled permanent mold with spray nozzles for vaporization cooling; mold can be made of iron or copper alloys.

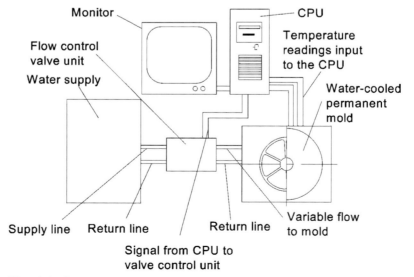

Fig. 8-9. Computer-controlled water-cooling system for permanent mold casting. Note: CPU is the abbreviation for central processing unit.

Special Casting Methods

advantage of this design compared to the flat-ended insert is that the projected end can reach further into the casting to draw the heat out more effectively.

If this setup is not sufficient, two inserts can be used as shown in Fig. 8-10 (C). This setup can obviously be used with the flat-ended insert design as well. If more rapid cooling is needed, a water-cooled insert could be used as shown in Fig. 8-10 (D). This setup is the same as a single projected-end insert design. However, the insert has water passages inside, which allows cool water to pass and, in turn, draw heat from the hub at a faster rate.

If using heat sinks/inserts or chills is not functionally possible, another alternative to accelerate the solidification process is to remove the cooling pins from the back of the air-cooled mold or use anti-chills. Basically, an anti-chill does the exact opposite of a chill.

After multiple cycles, metallic inserts can deteriorate and will need to be replaced. If an insert can be replaced quickly, it will minimize permanent mold downtime. Possible designs of inserts allowing for their easy replacement are shown in Fig. 8-11.

As can be seen, the insert, having a slot at the end (Fig. 8-11A), can be inserted through the face of the mold and locked into place with a wedge from the back of the mold. In this case, the insert could be easily replaced if deteriorated. Possible limitations to this design are that there might not be sufficient room for the wedge on the back of the mold, and the fact that there is a chance of the wedge coming loose. The latter may be solved by using a threaded insert and nut to fasten the insert into place more securely, as shown in Fig. 8-11B. If the space on the back of the mold is still limited, a threaded hole could be machined into the mold and the threaded insert could be tightened from the face of the mold as shown in Fig. 8-11C. This insert design would most likely be more practical, but more expensive, due to additional cost of machining.

For aluminum alloy permanent mold casting, see Section 8.12 at the end of this chapter, which is a case study of external chill selection.

Measuring Mold Operation Temperature. Under the regular casting cycle, the mold operation temperature depends on the pouring temperature, casting cycle frequency, casting weight, casting shape, casting wall thickness, wall thickness of the mold and the thickness of the mold coating. If the metal is poured into a cold mold, the first few castings are likely to have misruns until the mold reaches its operating temperature. To avoid this, the mold should be preheated to its operating temperature and it must be controlled.

There are two commonly used methods for measuring permanent mold operation temperature:

- Thermocouples are inserted into the mold cavity or into its proximity
- Noncontact infrared thermometer or system with laser sighting is used, which allows scanning temperature profile of the mold surface or to measure temperature at different mold points.

The hand-held infrared noncontact thermometer (Fig. 8-12) provides accurate mold temperature measurements from a distance, and is able to check and monitor mold

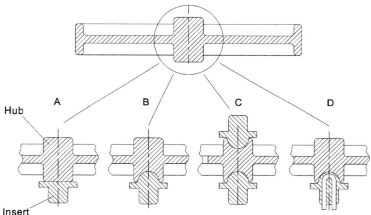

Fig. 8-10. Typical design of thick hub gear and possible locations of heat sinks/inserts: A–Flat-end design of insert to draw heat out of one side of the hub; B–Projected-end design of insert to draw heat out of one side of the hub; C–Two projected-end inserts to draw heat from two sides of the hub; D–Projected-end insert with water passages to draw heat out of one side of the hub.

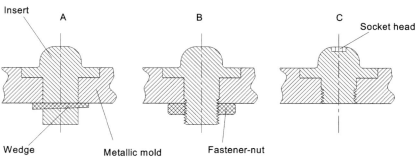

Fig. 8-11. Replaceable insert designs in permanent mold casting: A–Locked in the mold by internal slot and a wedge; B–Fastened from the back of the mold with a nut; C–Threaded insert fastened in the mold with a socked head.

temperature up to 1600°F (870°C) either on stationary or molds moving on a permanent mold machine. Laser sighting makes it easy to pinpoint the spot at a distance, even at a low light conditions. Data output on the infrared noncontact thermometer provides a direct interface to chart recorders or printers. The noncontact infrared line scanning system (Fig. 8-13) provides accurate temperature monitoring for a whole mold surface.

Zone temperatures are monitored and controlled via three analog outputs. Unlike point sensors that measure a single target point, the line scanning system measures multiple temperature points across a scan line. This is achieved by the rotating optics within 90 degrees. A motorized mirror scans at twenty lines per second, and the unique internal blackbody system standardizes the sensor on every scan. A high-speed microprocessor calculates the temperature of the individual measurement points. Temperatures are compared to process setpoints for each of three user-defined sectors. Each sector has an adjustable 0–20 mA current output through a serial communications line to a personal computer. The linescanner is complemented by software that generates real-time color profiles of the mold temperature distribution.

Mold Repair. Mold cracking or mold erosion is a very common problem in permanent mold casting. In a vertically, as well as horizontally parted permanent molds, the area that suffers the most deterioration is the sprue-well (Fig. 8-14). Due to the nature of design, the sprue-well receives the highest initial thermal shock as the molten metal is introduced into the mold. This high degree of shock is due to the impact of both the temperature of the molten metal and the energy of the falling stream, as it strikes the sprue-well. Liquid metal erosion may also hit some protrusions of the permanent mold or metallic core.

The resultant cracks and erosion destroy the molds and they must then be repaired. The following summarizes the practical applications of various means available for repair and extending the life of permanent molds.

Solution 1: Grind the sprue-well area and create a new sprue-well by enlarging the old one. This practice, though successful, is only a temporary cure and yields mixed results. Though the mold is repaired, the repaired areas will eventually deteriorate again. It is also important to note that the mold can only be ground to within a reasonable distance, usually from 68.75–75 mm (2.75–3 in.) from the mold edge, to prevent mold leakage. If this distance has been compromised, the mold must be scraped. Additionally, it should be kept in mind that if the choke is located in the sprue, it may also be burned, but grinding and enlarging will eliminate the predetermined ratio between the choke and other elements of the gating system.

Solution 2: Replaceable Inserts. Another possible solution may be to use replaceable inserts that can be put in the spruewell area (Fig. 8-15). The insert can be designed either in a circle or square shape.

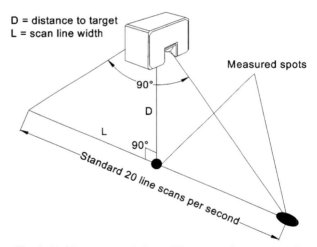

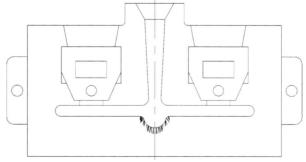

Fig. 8-13. Noncontact infrared linescanning system for monitoring permanent mold operational temperature.

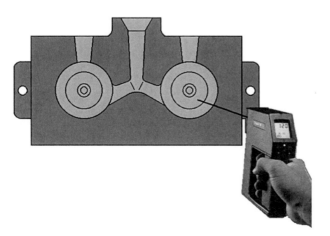

Fig. 8-12. Hand-held infrared noncontact thermometer with a laser sighting used for measuring permanent mold surface temperature.

Fig. 8-14. Schematic of a vertically parted permanent mold showing the most deteriorated sprue-well area.

Special Casting Methods

The circular design has an obvious advantage, as its shape can be more easily machined in the mold. The insert may be shaped on both sides, so it can be flipped if needed. The insert is bolted from the back of the mold, and precautions must be taken to insure that molten metal would not enter the thread holes from the inside of the mold. Certainly, the insert material must be the same as the base mold, having an equal coefficient of thermal expansion. When choosing the insert's method of production, as-cast surfaces should be given preference over machining.

There are some disadvantages to the insert solution. Flash occurring at the contact area between the mold and the insert may make the ejection of the casting difficult. This area may also be prone to the same form of deterioration. That is why the replaceable inserts may be considered only as a temporary measure to prolong the life of the mold.

Solution 3: Repair by welding. Permanent molds made of steel exhibit longer life, because deteriorated areas may be repaired by conventional welding using a special surfacing material and nickel-base alloy electrodes. The repaired mold areas do not require subsequent heat treatment if the hardness of the welded area is in the range of 171–185 HB and can be easy machined to desirable shape and size. A PMC iron foundry that currently employs this technique claims they can do this up to 15 times.

When cast iron is used as a mold material, repairing by conventional welding is not effective. Another method that may be employed to extend the life of the cast iron mold is the use of thermal spray welding technique. A special Fe-Ni-based alloy in the form of powder could be used to fill fissures and points of wear on the iron mold surface. Once again, it should be noted that the thermal expansion of the sprayed metal must be in common with that of the mold material.

Solution 4: Cast to the net-shape mold blanks. Another effective measure to extend the mold life is the use of cast to the net-shape mold blocks, utilizing the as-cast gating system and, in some cases, cast to the net-shape mold cavity. The as-cast surface advantage is the presence of burned-in sand on the surface. This "skin" features a good thermal resistant barrier, therefore, extending the life of the most deteriorated areas of the mold. To make as-cast mold blanks, precision tooling and casting methods, such as shell, ceramic or even PMC, are used.

Mold Cleaning with Dry Ice. The common way to remove coating buildup before reapplying a new one is to clean the hot metal mold manually with a wire brush or wire wheel, or blast the mold with silica sand, glass or another abrasive material at high pressure. The manual method is time-consuming and dangerous to employees because of their proximity to hot surfaces of the mold. Sand or glass blasting, due to the abrasive nature of the blast media, may cause excessive mold and ejection pin wear. In addition, abrasive particles can be trapped in the pin-bush alignment mechanism (guideway) resulting in castings dimensional instability, and eventually after repeated cleaning, to complete mold scrapping.

Recently developed dry ice blasting [Ref.11], in which small pellets of CO_2 are blown onto the mold to remove the coating. This is an alternative method, which will not cause mold surface or guideway erosion. This nonabrasive, wasteless process allows the PMC machine a longer production time, without interruption, due to more efficient and faster mold cleaning.

Permanent Mold Machines: Depending upon desirable productivity and casting design, stationary permanent mold machines (Fig. 8-16), operating in opening-closing cycle, or tilting permanent mold machines (Fig. 8-17) are used.

In a tilting permanent mold machine, molten metal is poured into a pouring basin while the mold is in a horizontal position and flows into the cavity as the mold is gradually tilted to a vertical position.

The major operations of the typical PMC are performed in the following sequence:

1. A metal mold is preheated to 120–150°C (250–300°F) and a refractory coating is applied to its surface

2. Sand or metal cores, if needed, are inserted to form internal cavities, and the mold is closed

3. Cast alloy is poured into the mold and metal fills the mold cavity under gravity, either statically or by tilting from a horizontal position to a vertival position

4. Rapid solidification rate allows quick removal of the casting from the mold, following core knockout, gate cutoff and casting finishing operations

5. A new casting cycle begins, in which all the above described operations are repeated

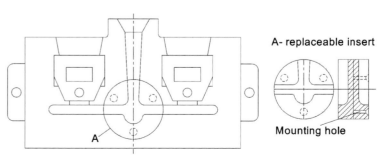

Fig. 8-15. Permanent mold with a replaceable insert in sprue-well area.

A- replaceable insert

Mounting hole

For high volume production, multistations (4, 6, 8 or 12 stations) of semi-automatically operated carousels-turntables that automate mold pouring, mold opening, casting knockout and mold recoating in a preset cycle (Fig. 8-18) are widely used. Carousels-turntables for thin-walled and low-weight castings rotate continuously in 2.5 to 3.5 min cycles; for indexing turntable-carousels the total revolution cycle time may vary from 5 to 10 min depending upon castings wall thickness and weights.

Figure 8-19 shows the typical layout of a permanent mold gray and ductile iron foundry utilizing a 12-station turntable permanent mold machine in high volume production of automotive brake cast parts.

As can be seen, there are two integral production lines: one (left side) for gray iron and a second one (right side) for ductile iron parts. Each line is furnished with induction melting furnaces and induction holders that continiously supply molten metal to PMC carousels. The carousel sequence of operation during the casting cycle is similar to single head machine and is as follows: in one of the positions, the mold is coated; in the second position, the sand core is set; in the third position, the mold is poured

Pouring Position

Ejection Position

Fig. 8-17. Tilting permanent mold casting machine used primarily for aluminum alloy castings. [Courtesy: C.M.H. Manufacturing]

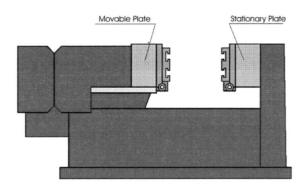

(a)

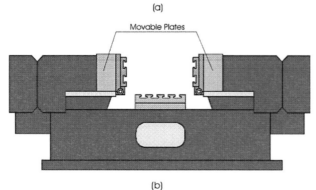

(b)

Fig. 8-16. Stationary, permanent mold machine used for the production of vertically parted ferrous and nonferrousalloy castings: (a) with single, movable head; (b) with double, movable head. [Courtesy: C.M.H. Manufacturing]

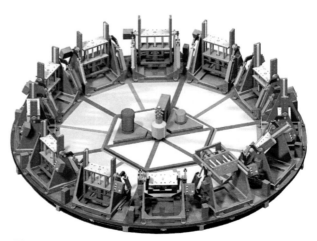

Fig. 8-18. Multi-station turntable permanent mold machines are used in high volume production. [Courtesy: C.M.H. Manufacturing]

Special Casting Methods

with molten metal; in the fourth, fifth and sixth positions the casting is held in the mold for the time needed for solidification; in the seventh position, the mold is opened to knockout; and in the next five positions, the mold is cooled to operational temperature, cleaned and prepared for a new casting cycle.

The following summarizes PMC advantages in comparison with convention sand mold casting.

Process Advantages of PMC

- Castings have fine-grained microstructure with improved mechanical properties, due to rapid solidification rate
- Closer dimensional tolerance control can be obtained
- Castings have superior surface finish and better appearance
- Small cored holes may be produced
- Inserts of different materials can be readily cast in place
- Cost of castings is reduced due to less labor involved in the mold preparation, mold shakeout, casting cleaning and sand reclamation
- Better environmental and working conditions

Process Limitations of PMC

- Complicated shapes cannot be produced with desirable cost effectivness
- The cost of the tooling is high and can only be justified for large-scale production
- The maximum weight of the casting that can be produced is limited because of the available equipment
- Not all materials are suited for permanent mold casting; for instance, steel, essentially because of the very short mold life

Applications of PMC

High-volume, small, simple shaped castings with uniform wall thickness without any intricate details cast in aluminium, copper-based alloys, magnesium and zinc alloys, gray and ductile irons. Some of the components that are cast in permanent molds are automobile pistons, parts for automotive brake systems, air conditioners and refrigerators, stators, gear blanks, connecting rods, aircraft fittings, cylinder blocks.

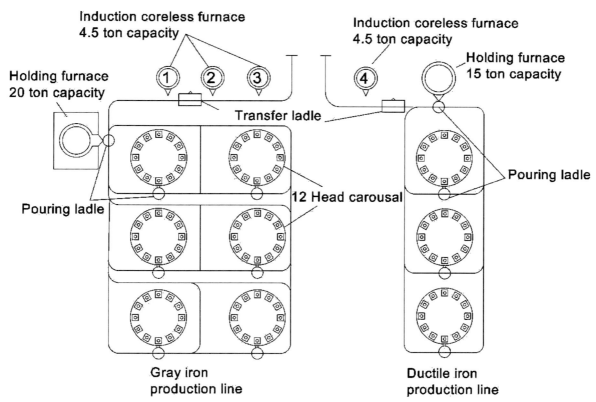

Fig. 8-19. Typical layout of a permanent mold gray and ductile iron foundry utilizing 12-station turntable permanent mold machines for high volume production of automotive brake parts.

8.2. Diecasting

Process Overview

In diecasting, also called pressure diecasting, parts are made by injecting molten metal at high pressures of 10–210 MPa (1450–30,500 psi) into a metal die. Diecasting is considered as a variation of permanent mold casting, because both processes employ reusable metal dies.

Compared to conventional gravity permanent molding, in diecasting the molten metal is forced into the die cavity under pressure, allowing the production of castings with very thin-walled sections, complex shapes, closer tolerances, and excellent surface finish and details.

Die Design and Material. The die for diecasting consists of two die halves: the stationary or cover die half which is fixed to the diecasting machine, and the moving or ejector die half, which moves out for the extraction of the casting.

The typical design of a diecasting die (Fig. 8-20) includes a casting cavity (single or multiple) with located air vents allowing for effective air removal, a sprue providing molten metal transition from the nozzle of the gooseneck (hot chamber process), or from the shot chamber, (cold chamber process shown here), runner and ingates, controlling metal flow and delivering metal to the casting cavity, and die cooling and casting ejection systems.

The casting cycle starts with the two halves of the die apart. A lubricant is sprayed on the die cavity, then the two die halves are closed and clamped. Guide pins are used to properly align the die halves. The required amount of metal is injected by the plunger into the die. After the casting has solidified under pressure, the die is opened and the casting is ejected.

An injector plate moves the ejector pins through the moving die half to free the casting. The number of ejector pins must be sufficient to remove the hot casting without any distortion. The placement of ejector pin positions should be so that the pin marks left on the casting surface will would not interfere with quality requirements.

The cores used are all metallic and are of two types: fixed and moving. The fixed cores are the ones that are secured to the die halves. These are parallel to the die movement. The others, called moving cores, are not parallel with the die movement and, hence, are to be removed before the casting is ejected from the die.

Sometimes, overflows are provided in the parting plane to accumulate the first metal, entering the die cavity, which is normally cold. Overflows are mostly used for small components to supply enough heat input to the die, so that no cold shuts occur. Also, the overflows can be utilized

for positioning the ejector pins so that no unacceptable ejector pin marks appear on the casting surface.

With the short cycle time, the dies would readily get heated, particularly in the sprue area or heavy sections of the casting. To maintain required operational temperature, water or oil is circulated through the cooling channels in identified hot regions of the die. Higher heat flow can be obtained by inserting heat sinks made of beryllium-copper or tungsten-based alloys.

Water spray or compressed air can also be used to remove the heat from the die surface. Die lubrication serves the same purpose, as it helps remove the heat from the die. The die works as a heat exchanger, being continuously heated and transfering the heat. Any interuptions of this cycle are detrimental for die life, which is one of the major concerns in diecasting. It is also important to preheat the die at the start of the shift and maintain die heat during production breaks. Typically, electric resistant heaters are used for this purpose, which prolongs die life and reduces scrap associated with improper die temperature.

Risers are not used in diecasting due to fact that shrinkage is compensated for by the increase of metal pressure at the end of the injection cycle. If necessary, pressure pins or squeeze cores may be applied to specific areas of a casting prone to shrinkage.

Hot working tool steels are normally used as material for the dies, die inserts and cores. For zinc alloys, the common die material is steel AISI P20 for low volume, and tool steel H13 for high volume. For aluminum and magnesium alloys, steels H13 and H11 are used. For copper alloys, tool steels H21, H20 and H22 are the usual die materials.

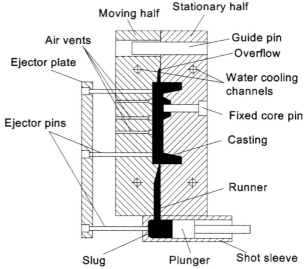

Fig. 8-20. Typical design of a die used in the cold chamber process.

Special Casting Methods

In diecasting, some excess metal may be forced into the parting plane and is termed as flash. Before using the castings, the flash, together with gates and overflows present in the casting, are to be removed. The trimming of the flash is done either manually or, more preferably, with hydraulic trim presses using trim dies, similar to sheet metal shearing dies.

Diecasting Processes. There are two types of diecasting processes used by the industry: hot chamber and cold chamber diecasting.

The main difference between these two processes is that in the hot chamber process, the holding furnace for the molten metal is integral with the diecasting machine and the injection mechanism is submerged into the furnace; whereas, in the cold chamber process, the alloy is melted in a separate furnace and then poured into the diecasting machine with a special small ladle for each casting cycle, called a shot.

The hot chamber process is used mostly for the low melting temperature alloys such as zinc, lead and tin. For the higher melting temperature alloys, such as aluminum, magnesium and copper-based alloys, due to their erosion attack on the gooseneck and injection mechanism materials, the cold chamber process is preferable. In the cold chamber process, the molten metal is poured with a ladle into the injection chamber for every casting cycle. This process reduces the contact time between the molten metal and the shot chamber. Accordingly, diecasting machines are classified as hot or cold chamber machines.

Hot Chamber Process. In a hot chamber diecasting process (Fig. 8-21), a special channel called gooseneck is used for pumping the molten metal into the die cavity. The gooseneck is submerged in the holding furnace containing the molten metal. The gooseneck is made of gray, alloy or ductile iron or of cast steel. A hydraulically operated plunger, made of alloy cast iron, moves up in the gooseneck to uncover the entry port to access the molten metal into the goose neck. The plunger can then develop the necessary pressure for forcing the metal into the die cavity. A nozzle at the end of the gooseneck is kept in close contact with the sprue located in the cover die.

The operating sequence of the hot chamber process is presented in Fig. 8-22. The cycle starts with spraying the die lubricant and closing the die. At that time, the plunger is in the highest position in the gooseneck, thus facilitating the filling of the gooseneck by the molten metal. The plunger then moves down forcing the metal in the gooseneck to be injected into the die cavity. The metal is then held at the same pressure until it is solidified. The die is opened, and any cores, if present, are also retracted. The plunger then moves back returning the unused molten metal to the gooseneck. The casting, which is in the ejector die, is now ejected, and at the same time the plunger uncovers the inlet or filling hole, allowing the molten metal from the furnace to enter the gooseneck.

Cold Chamber Process. The operation sequence of this process (Fig. 8-23) is similar to the hot chamber process. The operation starts with spraying the die lubricants throughout the die cavity and closing the die. Then, the molten metal is poured into the shot chamber of the machine, either manually by a hand ladle or by means of an automatic ladle. An automatic ladling device scoops molten metal from the holding furnace and pours it into the die at the exact instant required in the casting cycle. Then the plunger forces the molten metal into the die cavity and maintains the pressure until it solidifies. Next, the die opens and the casting is ejected. At the same time, the plunger returns to its original position completing the operation. The metal volume and pouring temperature can be precisely controlled with an automatic ladle and, hence, the desired casting quality can be obtained. A cold chamber diecasting machine is shown in Fig. 8-24.

The main disadvantage of the cold chamber process is the longer cycle time needed, compared to the hot chamber process. Also, since the metal is ladled into the machine from the furnace, it may lose the superheat, and sometimes may cause defects such as cold shuts.

One of the problems commonly seen in aluminum diecastings is air bubbles trapped in the solidified metal. These bubbles expand during heat treatment or welding,

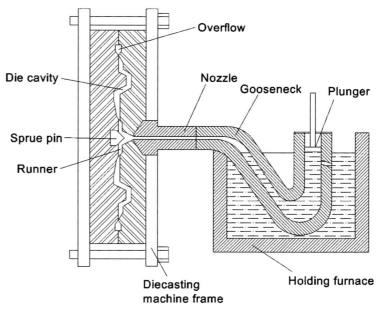

Fig. 8-21. Schematic of a hot chamber diecasting process.

causing blistering on the surface of the cast components. In the modification of the cold chamber diecasting process (Fig. 8-25), vacuum is applied to reduce air bubble formation in the solidified metal.

The process uses a two-step consecutively performed vacuum operation: in the first step, a vacuum circuit is connected with the die cavity via the shot sleeve; after this, the second vacuum circuit, connected with the die cavity via vent sleeve, is activated. As a result, nearly the entire volume of air can be removed from the die cavity within as little as 0.5 to 1.0 second.

During the casting operation, a special PC-based process control system monitors and documents the main vacuum process parameters, such as the ultimate pressure in the die cavity along with changes in leakage rate and other monitored parameters, and displays them for each shot.

Process Advantages of Diecasting

- Ability to cast high volume near-net-shape thin-walled castings with excellent surface finish

- Thin-walled parts can be easily filled because the molten metal is injected at high pressure: minimum wall thickness of 0.9 mm (0.035 in.) for aluminum and magnesium alloys; 0.6 mm (0.025 in.) zinc and tin alloys and 1.5 mm (0.06 in.) for copper alloys is typical for diecasting

- Closer dimensional tolerances on the order of ±0.08 mm (0.0032 in.) for small dimensions can be obtained

- Very high production rates can be achieved. Typically, about 200 castings per hour can be produced since the process is completely automated

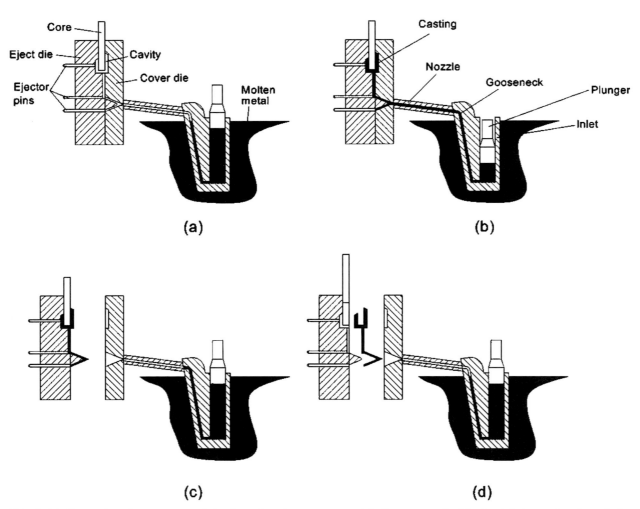

Fig. 8-22. Operational sequence of the hot chamber process: (a) die, sprayed with the lubricant, is closed, the plunger is in its highest position and gooseneck is filled with molten metal; (b) the plunger moves down and injects a portion of molten metal into the die; (c) die is opened, plunger moves up and unused metal returns to the gooseneck; (d) casting is ejected, the plunger is back in position, allowing the molten metal from the furnace to fill the gooseneck.

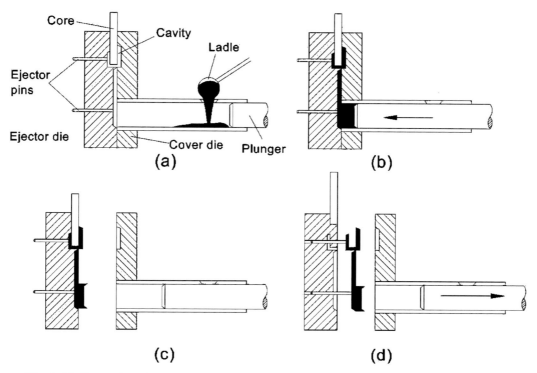

Fig. 8-23. Operational sequence of the cold chamber process: (a) die is closed and molten metal is poured into the shot chamber of the machine either manually by a hand ladle or by means of an automatic ladle; (b) the plunger injects molten metal into the die; (c) the die is opened; (d) the casting is ejected.

Fig. 8-24. Cold chamber diecasting machine. (Source: NADCA)

- The die has a long life, of approximately of 300,000 castings for zinc alloys and 150,000 for aluminum alloys
- Due to rapid solidification, diecasting gives better mechanical properties and fine-grained microstructure
- Inserts of other alloys can be readily cast in place
- Assembly of a variety of parts made by other manufacturing processes are replaced by diecastings at significant cost savings

Process Limitations of Diecasting

- Size and weight (up to 34 kg/75 lb) of the castings is restricted due to limitation of the machine capacity
- The process is not suitable for all cast alloys, for example steel, because of the limitations on the die materials. Normally nonferrousalloys such as zinc, aluminum, magnesium and copper alloys are diecast
- Gas porosity, due to the air in the die cavity being trapped inside the casting, is a potential problem with the diecastings
- The dies and the machines are very expensive and, therefore, are only economical when large quantities are produced

Applications for Diecasting

The typical parts made by diecasting are carburetors, crank cases, magnetos, handle bar housings, parts of scooters, motor cycles and mopeds, zip fasteners, head lamp bezels and other parts for automotive, electrical and general engineering applications.

8.3. Low Pressure Diecasting (Also known as Low Pressure Permanent Molding or LPPM)

Process overview

In this process, molten metal fills a metal die from a pressurized crucible located under the die. The process is illustrated in the example of an aluminum automotive wheel (Fig. 8-26). Here, a previously preheated and refractory coated die, having a horizontal parting line, is mounted on the top of a sealed holding furnace and is connected to the molten metal by a ceramic feed tube or stalk.

After the mold is closed, the furnace is pressurized by the introduction of air above the surface of the molten metal causing it to rise up in the feed tube or stalk and fill the mold. Typical air pressure is between 1406 and 3515 kg/m^2 (2 and 5 psi). The air from the mold cavity is removed through vents in the die, and when the cavity is filled, solidification begins. After the metal has solidified,

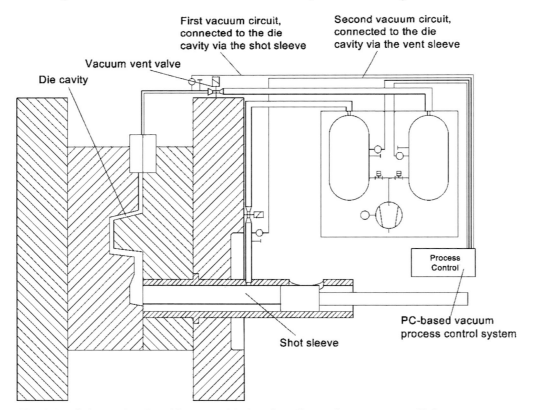

Fig. 8-25. Schematic of multi-step cold chamber diecasting process utilizing vacuum.

pressure is released in the furnace and the molten metal left in the stalk returns to the holding furnace. A further short cooling period is needed for complete casting solidification, then the mold is opened and the casting is ejected. The capacity of the furnace is usually sufficient to make around 8 to10 castings before refilling is necessary.

Correct die air and water-cooling system design combined with optimal process parameters ensures casting directional solidification and shrinkage-free castings. The die is made of tool steel H-13, and a water-cooled copper chill is installed to more rapidly cool the transition area between the spokes and the well of the wheel.

Besides die cooling, properly selected casting parameters such as alloy pouring temperature and mold operational temperature all are important. For example, for aluminum wheels, pouring temperature needs to be around 750°C (1382°F) and mold temperature in the range of 280–300°C (536–572°F).

One of the problems frequently seen in the process is limited service life of feed tube material, which is in constant contact with molten metal and subjected to thermal shock, wetting, and erosion. Currently used, fused silica feed tubes typically last about one week. Applying a zircon-based coating to the surface of fused silica tubes extends tube life from three to five weeks.

Process Advantages of LPPM

- By achieving directional solidification, need for risers are eliminated
- Because there is only one ingate and no risers, casting yield is exceptionally high, generally over 90%
- Controlled mold filling allows production of sound castings without defects related to metal turbulence and air entrapment in the gating system

Process Limitations of LPPM

- The process is limited to aluminum alloys although it can also be used for magnesium and other low melting point alloys

- Large castings, more than 100 kg (220 lb) can be made if cost of the metal die can be justified
- Both the machine and its dies are expensive, and for this reason, the process is economical only for high-volume production

Applications for LPPM

Typical applications include aluminum automotive wheels, cylinder heads, blocks, manifolds and critical aerospace castings.

8.4. Centrifugal Casting

Process Overview

In this process, the molten metal is poured into a mold that is rapidly rotated about its central axis. The spinning mold generates centrifugal force to throw molten metal against the wall of the mold and make the desirable shaped casting. Depending on the application, forces can range upward of over 100 times the force of gravity. Molds may be made of metal (cast iron or steel), sand or graphite.

The prime advantage of the centrifugal casting process is its increase in yield over static sand molding or gravity permanent mold casting. Most castings that can be made using the centrifugal process don't need gates and risers. This results in better material utilization or yield and also reduces cleaning time. Using permanent molds to

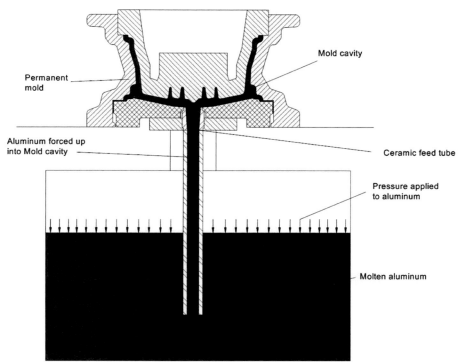

Fig. 8-26. Schematic of low-pressure diecasting of aluminum automotive wheels.

---

centrifugally cast a part considerably reduces molding time, core making and setting time.

Though all known cast alloys have been centrifugally cast and most castings could be made centrifugally, only certain castings are practical to be centrifugally cast. The process imposes limitations on shape of castings, and is normally restricted to the production of cylindrical geometric shapes (in the case of true centrifugal casting).

Practically, there are three basic centrifugal casting processes:

- True centrifugal casting
- Semicentrifugal casting
- Centrifuging

True Centrifugal Casting. This is normally used for the making of pipes, tubes, cylinders, bushings, sleeves, etc., which are axisymmetric with a concentric hole. Since the metal is always pushed outward because of the centrifugal force, no core needs to be used for making the concentric hole. The axis of rotation can be horizontal, vertical or any angle in between.

Very long pipes are normally cast with a horizontal axis, whereas short pieces are more conveniently cast with a vertical axis (Fig. 8-27). A typical horizontal centrifugal

casting machine used for making cast iron pipes in sand molds is shown in Fig. 8-28.

First, the molding flask is properly rammed with sand to confirm to the outer contour of the pipe to be made. Any end details, such as spigot ends, or flanged ends are obtained with the help of dry sand cores located in the ends. Then the flask is dynamically balanced so as to reduce the occurrence of undesirable vibrations during the casting process. The finished flask is mounted in between the rollers and the mold is slowly rotated. Now, the required amount of molten metal is poured into the mold through the movable pouring basin. The amount of metal poured determines the thickness of the pipe to be cast. After the pouring is complete, the mold is rotated at its operational speed until it solidifies, to form the required tubing. Then, a machine replaces the poured mold by a new mold, and the process continues.

Metal (iron or steel) molds can also be used in the true centrifugal casting process for large-quantity production. A water jacket is provided around the mold for its cooling or the mold may be cooled by water spraying onto its external surface. Before pouring, metal molds are preheated to approximately 150°C (300°F) and protective coating (mold wash) is applied to its surface.

In the case of metal mold usage, the movable pouring machine is furnished with a long spout extending to the other end of the pipe to be made. To start, the mold is rotated with the molten metal being delivered at the extreme end of the pipe. The pouring machine is slowly moved down the track allowing the metal to be deposited all along the length of the pipe. The machine is continuously rotated until the pipe is completely solidified. Afterward, the pipe is extracted from the mold and the cycle is repeated.

Iron and steel pipes, structures and tubes in any section size can be readily produced by horizontal centrifugal casting. This process (Fig. 8-29) is also successfully used to make bimetallic tubes, consisting of two materials: inner layer made of wear- or corrosion-resistant material (more expensive material) and less expensive backing material.

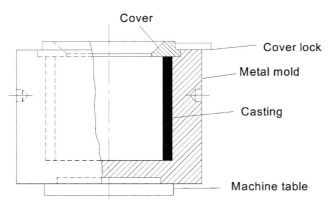

Fig. 8-27. Schematic of vertical true centrifugal casting.

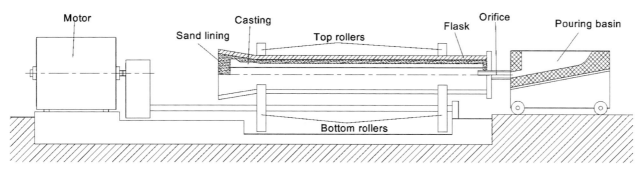

Fig. 8-28. Schematic of horizontal true centrifugal casting machine.

Special Casting Methods

Semicentrifugal Casting. Semicentrifugal casting is used for parts that are more complicated than those possible in true centrifugal casting, but are symmetrical about a centerline (axisymmetrical). Using this process, molds are usually spun about the vertical axis and molten metal enters the mold through the central pouring basin, as in Fig. 8-30.

Molds can either be made of steel or graphite (permanent) or sand-lined flasks. Depending on the part, cores may or may not be used. For larger production rates, the molds can be stacked one over the other, all feeding from the same central pouring basin. The rotating speeds used in this process are not as high as in the case of true centrifugal casting.

Centrifuging. In order to obtain higher metal pressures during solidification, when casting shapes are not axisymmetrical, the centrifuging process is used. This is suitable only for small parts of any shape. A number of such small part molds are joined together by means of radial runners, with a central sprue, on a revolving table, as in Fig. 8-31.

Process Advantages of Centrifugal Casting

- Quality of centrifugally cast parts are better compared to other processes, because the inclusions, such as slag and oxides, get segregated toward the center and can be easily removed by machining

- Due to pressure acting on the molten metal during solidification, combined with optimal casting parameters, it is possible to control solidification rate and produce shrinkage-free high-density castings

- No cores are required for making concentric holes in the case of true centrifugal casting

- There is no need for ingates and runners, which increases the casting yield to approximately 90–92 percent

Process Limitations of Centrifugal Casting

- Only certain shapes, which are axisymmetric, and have concentric holes are suitable for true centrifugal casting

- The equipment is expensive and, thus, is suitable only for large quantity production

Applications for Centrifugal Casting

Ferrous, nonferrous or bimetallic pipes, tubes, rollers, hydrauluc cylinders, bushings and sleeves, gear blanks, wheels, pulley sheaves, impellers and a wide variety of industrial components of similar shapes.

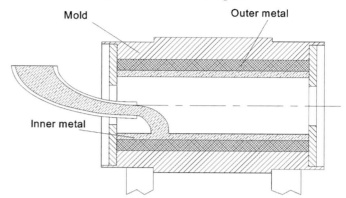

Fig. 8-29. Schematic of bimetallic centrifugal casting process.

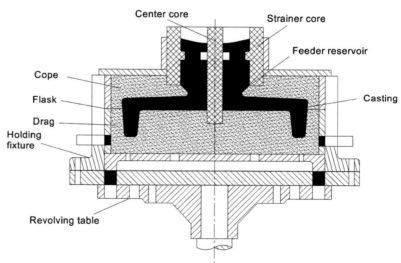

Fig. 8-30. Schematic of semicentrifugal casting process.

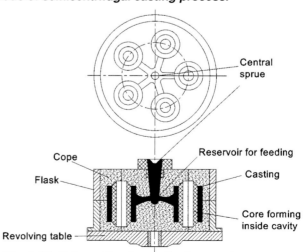

Fig. 8-31. Schematic of centrifuging casting process.

8.5. Investment Casting

Process Overview

This process utilizes ceramic shell molds made by the use of heat-disposable patterns. These patterns, called lost patterns, are typically made of wax or plastic or some other material that can be melted or burned away. The first step in this process (Fig. 8-32) includes the preparation of the pattern for every casting made. The patterns and gates are then attached to a central sprue.

The molds are uniformly placed on the table around the periphery so that their masses are properly balanced. The process is similar to semicentrifugal casting. Centrifuge casting is usually reserved for castings that are difficult or impossible to feed by static casting methods. This method in combination with investment molding is applied to make orthopedic implants, jewelry and dental appliances.

The pattern assembly, called a tree or cluster, is then coated (invested) with multiple layers of a refractory, made by suspending fine ceramic materials in a binder such as ethyl silicate or sodium silicate to build-up a thin ceramic shell around the pattern. Dry refractory grains such as fused silica or zircon are "stuccoed" on this liquid ceramic coating.

The shell is then dried and the process of dipping in the slurry and stuccoing and drying is repeated until a desirable shell thickness is achieved. The next step, aimed on removing the pattern from the mold, is done by heating the mold to melt/burn the pattern.

Before pouring, the molds are preheated (fired) to a temperature of 800–1000°C (1506–1840°F), depending on the size, complexity and type of metal to be cast. This produces a more rigid ceramic shell, reduces any traces of pattern material, and improves filling of all mold sections, which are too thin to be filled in a cold mold. The molten metal may be poured under gravity, vacuum, or by using centrifugal or countergravity methods, or under slight pressure, depending on the type of casting.

Process Advantages of Investment Casting

- Capability to cast parts of complex shapes, which are difficult to produce by any other method, since the pattern doesn't have a parting line and is removed by melting

- Very fine details and thin-section castings can be produced by this process, because the mold is preheated before pouring

- Castings are near-net-shape and feature very close tolerances and better surface finish, which are ready for use with little or no machining

- The process can be used for mass production

Process Limitations of Investment Casting

- The process is limited to the small sized, low

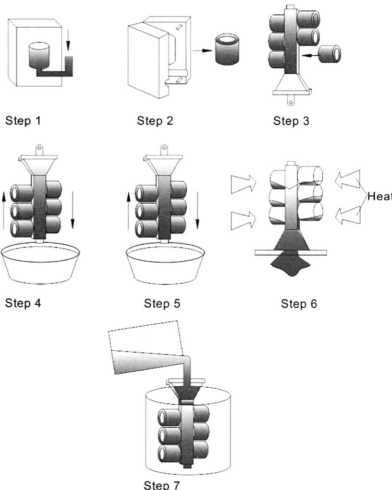

Step 1   Step 2   Step 3

Step 4   Step 5   Step 6

Heat

Step 7

Fig. 8-32. Schematic of investment casting: Step 1: Injection of pattern material; Step 2: Removal of pattern; Step 3: Cluster assembling; Step 4: Cluster dipping or investing; Step 5: Stuccoing; Step 6: Dewaxing and firing of shell mold; Step 7: Mold pouring.

weight parts, typically, up to 5 kg (12 lb)

- The process requires special equipment and tooling for patternmaking and mold preparation
- This is an expensive process because of the large amount of manual labor involved in the preparation and multiple handling of the patterns and the molds

Applications for Investment Casting

Highly precise, near-net-shape, small size and weight castings for aerospace and aircraft jet engines, vanes and blades for gas turbines, impellers for turbo chargers, surgical instruments and implants, dental appliances, jewelry, etc. Parts can be cast of a wide variety of nonferrous, ferrous and special alloy/superalloys. Figure 8-33 illustrates some examples of typical investment castings used for various applications.

8.6. Ceramic Mold Casting

Process Overview

This process, also known as Shaw process or Unicast process, employs conventional patterns (wood, metal or plastic) to make a highly refractory mold by pouring ceramic slurry around the pattern into the flask or jacket. The pattern can be made by any conventional method, from CNC machining to rapid prototyping. Because the molding process is done at ambient temperature, almost any material is suitable for pattern use. The process offers the simplicity of sand mold casting, combined with the quality of precision casting: close degree of tolerance and exceptional surface finish. Using the process, casting weight up to several tons with minimal wall thickness of 1.5 mm (0.06 in.) can be cast. Typical tolerance of ±0.08 mm/0.003 in. on dimension size up to 25 mm (1 in.) and on dimension over 375 mm (15 in.) tolerance is ±1.14 mm (0.045 in.). There are no alloy limitations and most of the standard ferrous or nonferrous foundry alloys can be readily cast. The process (Fig. 8-34) begins with preparing a ceramic slurry by mixing the refractory material (alumina or fused silica or zircon) with a binder (colloidal silica or ethyl silicate).

The slurry then is poured over the pattern kept in a flask or jacket and allowed to solidify. No ramming or vibration is required. The pattern then is removed and a gas torch is used to remove any moisture in the mold at relatively low temperatures.

After all moisture is removed, the mold is fired or sintered at approximately 982 to 1095°C (1800 to 2000°F). Depending upon alloy type and casting section size,

molds may be heated or not heated before pouring. Duration of heating depends upon size and section thickness of the mold. While this step is not always necessary, especially for lower melting metals, it is

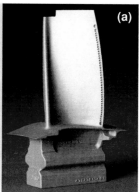
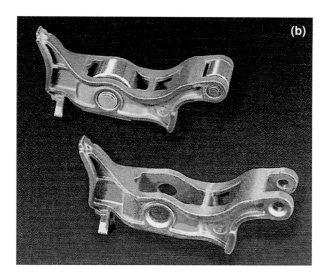
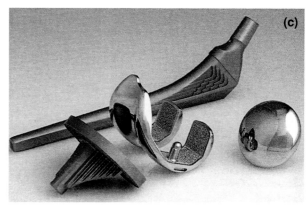

Fig. 8-33. Examples of investment castings used for various applications: (a) aerospace and gas turbines blades and vanes; (b) valve train for automotive gasoline engine cast of 30CrMoV9 alloy; (c) orthopedic implants for the hip, knee and shoulder, cast of supperalloy.

recommended, as this process fully converts the ceramic phase, thus increasing the already high refractory qualities of ceramic, improving mold strength and minimizing the possibilities of mold/metal reaction.

The process is also utilized in the production of precision molds for the casting of sculptures. Due to lower cost, the process is considered as an alternative to investment casting, but without limitation on size and weight.

Process Advantages of Ceramic Mold Casting

- Process may be used to make solid or faced molds
- No alloy limitations, most of the standard ferrous or nonferrous foundry alloys can be readily cast
- Offers precision castings identical to investment casting at lower cost, but without limitation on size and weight
- Short lead time
- Cast-to-size tooling eliminates the majority of machining that is ordinarily required in making

rubber, plastic and forging dies and permanent molds, cast core boxes and patterns. This cuts down delivery times and overall costs of production

Process Limitations of Ceramic Mold Casting

- High temperature and long heating is involved in moldmaking operations
- Process is limited to low-volume production rate

Applications for Ceramic Mold Casting

Rubber, plastic, glass, extrusion and forging dies, dies for diecasting, permanent molds, patterns and core boxes for foundry industry, precision cores and molds for pump impellers, diffusers and valves. Cast parts routinely made by this process include various applications for dies and tools and cores and molds for the pump and valve industry, where internal precision and surface finish are very important.

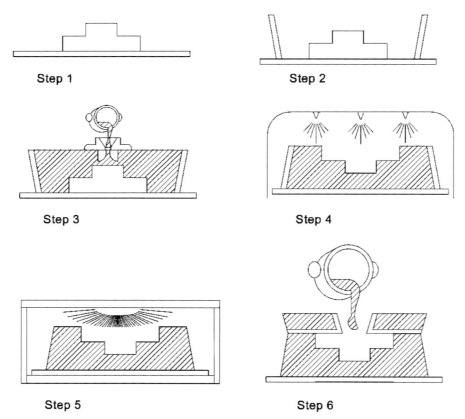

Step 1

Step 2

Step 3

Step 4

Step 5

Step 6

Fig. 8-34. Schematic illustration of major steps in ceramic molding: Step 1: Pattern of the cast part is prepared; Step 2: Pattern is placed in the mold box; Step 3: Ceramic slurry is poured over the pattern and allowed to solidify; Step 4: Pattern is removed and the mold is cured at a relatively low temperature; Step 5: Mold is then fired after removing all the moisture; Step 6: Molten metal is poured into the ceramic mold.

8.7. Lost Foam Casting

Process Overview

Lost foam casting, also known as evaporative pattern casting (EPC), is a unique and economical method for producing complex, close-tolerance castings using an expandable polystyrene pattern and unbonded sand as the molding media. Because molten metal burns the pattern, a pattern is required for each casting. In this process, the pattern is made of expendable polystyrene (EPS) beads. For high-production runs, the patterns can be made in a die by injecting EPS beads into a die and bonding them together using a heat source, usually steam. For shorter runs, sheets of EPS can be used in the pattern shop. Pattern shapes are cut out of the sheets using conventional woodworking equipment, and then assembled with glue. In either case, internal passageways in the casting, if needed, are not formed by conventional cores, but are part of the mold itself. Thus, no cores are required.

After the gating and risering system is attached to the pattern, the pattern assembly is coated with a refractory wash, which covers both the external and internal surfaces of the pattern, and is suspended in a one-piece flask. The flask is then placed onto a compaction or vibrating table. Additional sand is added while the flask is vibrated, until the pattern assembly is completely embedded in sand, creating a rigid mold. As the molten metal is poured into the mold, it replaces the EPC pattern, which vaporizes. Gases formed from the vaporized pattern permeate through the coating on the pattern and the sand, and finally through the flask vents. After solidification, the mold is moved to the shakeout area where the unbonded sand is dumped out of the flask, leaving the casting with an attached gating and risering system for further finishing operations.

Examples where the advantages of the lost foam process are fully utilized with significant reduction of machining operations and cost, include aluminum engine blocks, cylinder heads and other parts (Fig. 8-35).

Process Advantages of EPC

- Complete elimination of cores and associated cores defects
- Close dimensional tolerances and excellent surface finish
- Decreased or completely eliminated machining
- Capability to cast all cast alloys with no limitation on the size and shape
- Castings can be made to closer tolerances with walls as thin as 3 mm (0.120 in.)

- Because the process uses dry, unbonded sand, there are no moisture- or binder-related defects
- Flasks for containing the mold assembly are inexpensive, and shakeout is simplified due to the use of unbonded sand; no shakeout equipment is required
- Casting cleaning is minimized since there are no parting lines or core fins
- Easily recycled sand and extremely low external emissions and clean solid waste disposal
- Improved working environment: no noise, dust, fumes or heavy lifting
- The need for skilled labor is greatly reduced

Process Limitations of EPC

- A special die is needed to make the patterns
- A special, properly applied surface refractory coating must be used
- The pattern coating process is time-consuming; pattern handling requires great care; if glued, glue marks may be found on castings

(a)

(b)

Fig. 8-35. Typical castings made via lost foam process: (a) cylinder head, (b) aluminum engine block with as-cast fluid distribution lines.

Applications for EPC

Wide ranges of weights and overall dimensions, cast parts for automotive power train and marine engines, machine tool and military use.

8.8. Continuous Casting

Process Overview

Continuous casting process is employed for producing various shapes of cast bars in nonferrous (aluminum, copper alloys) and ferrous alloys (steel, gray, ductile and alloy irons). There two variations of continuous casting process: vertical and horizontal. Vertical continuous casting is used primarily at steelmaking facilities for production of steel forms that can be further directly rolled on mills, thus bypassing conventional ingot casting.

In this process (Fig. 8-36), molten steel is poured from the ladle into an intermediate reservoir, called a tundish ,with a stopper rod. From there, it is poured into an open-ended, vertical water-cooled copper die or mold. To initiate the casting, a starter bar or dummy bar is installed before the process begins. The first metal solidifies on and around the starter bar and a solid skin is formed at the surface of the die. As the molten metal rises in the mold to a desirable height, the starter bar is withdrawn at the rate equal to the steel pouring rate. The solidified shell supports the molten steel and, as it moves down by rollers, the bar passes through the secondary cooling zone, where complete solidification is achieved by spraying water on its surface. After complete solidification, the bar is cut to the desirable length by cutoff equipment. To prevent steel from sticking to the copper mold, the mold is oscillated during the casting process and lubricant is added to its surface.

Horizontal continuous casting offers ease of operation. It was first applied for casting aluminum and copper alloys, then used for gray and ductile irons and steel. In this process (Fig. 8-37), molten metal is tapped from the transfer ladle into the metal receiver.

The receiver may be furnished with a heating system, such as channel type inductor or gas torch. This will maintain a certain metal temperature range and compensate for temperature losses during the drawing process. For aluminum, copper alloy and iron castings, a graphite die, inserted into a water-cooled jacket, is attached to the side of the receiver. In horizontal continuous casting of steel, a copper water-cooled die is used. The die's life depends on die finish, part intricacy and process operation parameters. Figure 8-38 illustrates typical continuous casting die designs used in aluminum, copper and iron practice, consisting of a water-cooled jacket and inserted in a graphite die.

The internal die cavity is machined from solid blocks of graphite and must have the same profile design as a vertical cross section of the bar intended to be cast. Graphite is recognized as an excellent die material because of its high thermal conductivity, low coefficient of thermal expansion, high thermal resistance and good machinability. Another advantage of graphite die material is that it provides nonwetting properties and does not require lubricant. Graphite can be machined quite readily to provide excellent surface finish. Figure 8-39 illustrates a sequence of operations typical for horizontal continuous bar casting of nonferrous alloys and irons.

The process operates in semicontinuous mode: drawing is followed by the pause. The pause is necessary to create a solid skin bar in the die to support molten metal in the center. Figure 8-40 illustrates typical shapes

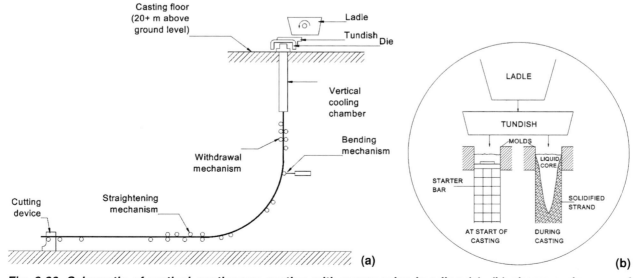

Fig. 8-36. Schematic of vertical continuous casting with progressive bending (a); (b) shows a close-up of pouring area.

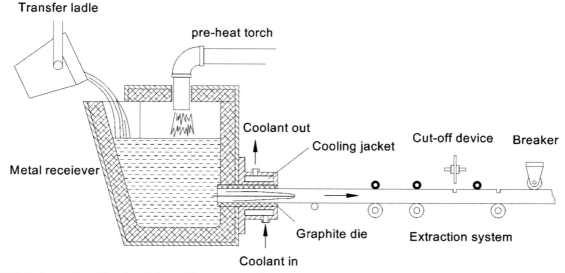

Fig. 8-37. Schematic of horizontal continuous casting.

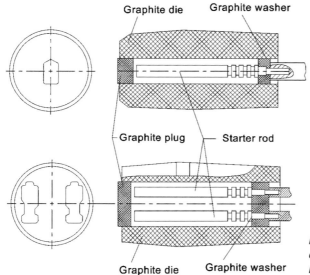

Fig. 8-38. Typical designs of graphite dies with one (above) and two cavities (below) to cast relatively simple shaped bars.

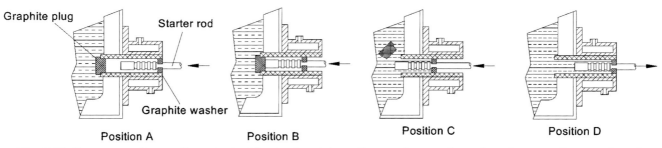

Position A   Position B   Position C   Position D

Fig. 8-39. Sequence of operations typical for horizontal continuous bar casting of nonferrous alloys and cast irons: A–the graphite plug is installed at the entry to the die assembly and the starter rod is inserted from the direction of withdrawing until a sufficient amount of molten metal is in the receiver; B–the starter rod is moved toward the graphite plug by reverse motion of the withdrawing mechanism; C–the graphite plug is pushed away from the entry to the die, allowing access of molten metal into the die. The metal fills the die and begins to solidify around the starter rod; D–The withdrawing of a solid bar begins and the bar is pulled out by the extraction system, which controls stroke length and frequency.

of horizontally cast continuous bars. Upon complete solidification, a special mechanism cuts and breaks the bars to required lengths.

Process Advantages of Continuous Casting

- High casting yield of 90–92%, since it eliminates traditional feeder needs due to the fact that molten metal in the receiver plays the role of a preheated riser. The riser continuously supplies liquid metal to feed the bar during solidification and compensate for shrinkage
- The absence of casting defects usually related to sand molding (such as sand inclusions), in combination with a dense, gas and shrink porosity-free macrostructure, makes this product ideal for hydraulic and pneumatic component applications
- Due to the same reason—a very uniform grain structure—continuously cast iron bars feature excellent machinability

Process Limitations of Continuous Casting

- Process is limited to relatively simple shapes without internal cavities, because no cores can be used, although hollow bars using graphite central cores are made in short runs
- Overall dimensions of bars produced by this method may vary from 12.5 to 560 mm (0.5 to 22 in.) in diameter, to rectangular up to 457 x 559 mm (18 x 22 in.)
- Each production run of certain bar shapes need a machined graphite die
- Wear of the graphite die, which, in turn, depends upon the length of operations, impair dimensional accuracy of bars

Applications for Continuous Casting

Housings, plungers, shafts, rotors and pistons for hydraulic apparatus and pumps; shafts, sheaves and gears for power transmission and machine tool; bushings and gears for automotive industry, etc.

8.9. Countergravity Casting
Process Overview

This is a relatively new casting process, utilizing vacuum to fill the mold. In conventional gravity casting, liquid metal falls down the sprue and enters the casting cavity at a high rate from the metallostatic pressure, causing stream turbulence. As a result, oxidation occurs, forming oxides and dross defects.

In the countergravity process, a permeable sand or vented metal mold is placed into a special container and submerged into the bath of molten metal. Vacuum is applied to the container, and the clean metal below the surface is transferred into the mold cavity, which is filled at a controlled, stationary rate. After mold filling, the applied vacuum is released and residual metal in the central

Fig. 8-40. Typical shapes of horizontally cast continuous bars.

sprue flows back to the furnace. High casting yield can be obtained since the ingates are not attached to the sprue.

One of the techniques using vacuum assisted filling is known as the "Hitchner process" or the countergravity low-pressure air-melt (CLA) casting. It was developed by Hitchner Manufacturing Company in the mid-1970s, and was initially applied to investment casting. The loose-sand vacuum-assisted casting (LSVAC) is one of the modifications of the countergravity casting process. Figure 8-41 illustrates the sequence of this process operation.

In this process, the shell or investment or nobake sand mold is placed in a vacuum chamber with the sprue facing down. The chamber is filled with loose dry sand, sealed, and lowered a precise distance into the bath of molten metal. The metal is siphoned into the mold cavity, ensuring complete filling of casting sections. After a brief hold time has elapsed, allowing the ingates and a portion of the parts to solidify, the vacuum chamber is lifted and the residual metal in the central sprue flows back into the melt.

Process Advantages of Countergravity Casting

- Ability to produce thin-walled castings that are free from oxides and other nonmetallic inclusions
- Due to controlled mold filling, overall casting quality is improved and is superior to castings produced by conventional methods
- Casting yield is increased compared with gravity casting, where much of the cast weight is in the sprue and gating system.

Process Limitations of Countergravity Casting

- The size of the sand mold and casting weight are limited by the size of the furnace and its capacity
- Special equipment is needed
- Process productivity is relatively low

Applications for Countergravity Casting

The process was sucsessfuly applied to cast a variety of thin-walled (1.5–2 mm/0.06–0.08 in.) castings such as stainless steel exhaust manifolds, track wheel centers, aircraft fuel pump impellers, missle wings, etc .

8.10. Semisolid Casting

Process Overview

The semisolid or Rheocasting process, often referred to as thixocasting, involves injection of a semisolid casting alloy into a metal die. The principal difference between the semisolid and conventional diecasting process is that metal is heated only to its mushy state between liquidus and solidus; in other words, the alloy is not fully melted. With approximately 50% solid base, the semisolid alloy is plunged into the die, requiring removal of less heat to solidify and thus, less time to cool. This results in less shrinkage and better quality of casting. Die design, die material and sequence of operations (die preheating, die lubrication and part ejection) are similar to diecasting.

In general, the process utilizes conventional diecasting machines. In some cases, such as for semisolid casting of magnesium alloys, the machine design is more complicated, as shown in Fig. 8-42. In this machine, the hopper is filled with cold chips or pellets of Mg-alloy, which are gradually heated in the barrel in the neutral atmosphere of argon gas. Continuous heating and dynamic agitation of the semisolid alloy produces a highly fluid, castable slurry. Upon accumulation of the required shot size, the screw accelerates forward, injecting the semisolid slurry through the nozzle into the die cavity. In this particular machine, used for Mg-based alloys, the barrel has a diameter of 70 mm (2.8 in.) and length of approximately 2 m (80 in.). The die is preheated to 200°C (392°F), slurry temperature is 580°C (1076°F) and the alloy is injected at a screw velocity of 0.6 m/s (24 in./s).

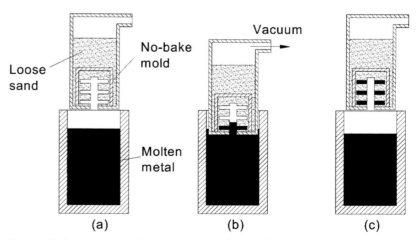

Fig. 8-41. Schematic of the countergravity casting process showing the sequence of operations: (a) nobake sand mold with the sprue facing down is inserted into the vacuum chamber. The chamber is filled with loose dry sand; (b) Vacuum chamber is lowered into the molten metal and vacuum is applied; (c) After mold filling is completed, the chamber is lifted up and rotated to shakeout position.

Current injection casting machine sizes range from 75 to 1600 metric tons (165,000 to 3,520,000 lb) clamp capacity, and machine cycles times range from 35 to 40 seconds up to two minutes, depending upon part size. Melt loss is about 2 percent.

One of the chief improvements in comparison with conventional diecasting is that parts made by the semisolid process have significantly less gas porosity (density 98% vs. 95%). This allows application of heat treatment for improving mechanical properties. Due to a closed environment and the presence of a protective atmosphere, oxidation of semisolid alloys is prevented, which is particularly important for Mg alloys having a high affinity to oxygen.

Attemps to apply this process for aluminum castings have revealed one of the major limitations of this technology: the size of billets (no more than 7.62 x 10.16 x 10.16 cm/3 x 4 x 4 in.) limits size of the castings. Any bigger billets collapse under their own weight. The later also limits the weight of the part—less than 6.8 kg/15 lb. An improved process [Ref. 12] uses rapid cooling and applied convection (steering) to create a nondendritic semisolid slurry, which is then injected into the die cavity. To create a semisolid alloy, molten metal is tapped out of the same type of furnace used in diecasting. It is poured into a special crucible or pouring ladle, where the metal cools up to a certain temperature and then is stirred by mechanical (with graphite rod) or electromagnetic means. This process produces a wide range of high-integrity, near-net-shape parts, from thin-walled propellers to 12.25 kg (27 lb) four-cylinder engine blocks and other parts for marine engines. They feature high strength and ductility compared to squeeze and permanent mold cast components (Table 8-1).

Process Advantages of Semisolid Casting

- Ability to cast extremely thin walls on the order of 0.5 mm (0.02 in.)
- Die is filled with semisolid slurry, having high and controllable viscosity that promotes nonturbulent filling of the die, thus increasing die life

Table 8-1. *Comparison of Mechanical Properties of Aluminum Alloy 356 after T6 Heat Treatment cast by Three Different Methods.*

Casting Method	Mechanical Properties		
	Tensile Strength, MPa (ksi)	Yield Strength, MPa (ksi)	Elongation, %
Semisolid diecasting	314 (45)	223(32)	9.0
Squeeze casting	300(43)	223(32)	9.0
Permanent mold casting	255(37)	150(22)	5.0

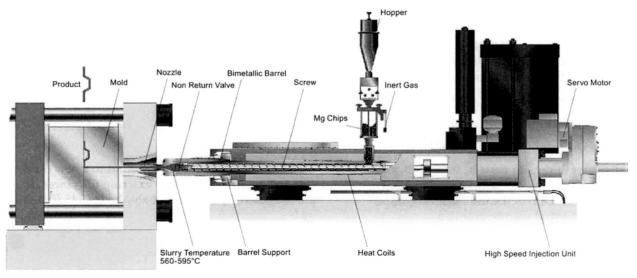

Fig. 8-42. *Illustration of the injection casting or thixomolding machine for a semisolid Mg alloy.*

- Parts have less gas defects, shrinkage, and reduced warpage after removal from the die
- Process completely eliminates or significantly reduces finishing as well as improves properties and overall part quality

Process Limitations of Semisolid Casting

- For some alloys, for instance, magnesium alloys, process requires specialized and costly equipment
- Although cast alloys that may be made by the process include most of the ferrous and nonferrous alloys, the present commercial interest is limited to aluminum and magnesium alloys

Applications for Semisolid Casting

Aluminum alloys: oil pump housings and other thin-walled (2.5–12 mm/0.1–0.47 in.) hydraulic pump parts, thin-walled propellers, swivel arm brackets, four-cylinder engine blocks and other parts for marine engines. Magnesium alloys: consumer electronics (laptop computer cases, keypads for cell phones and cases, digital cameras and camcorders), home hardware and structural automotive components (engine, body and interior cabin parts).

8.11. Vacuum Molding or V-Process Casting

Process Overview

In this process, molds are made of dry, unbonded sand, which is compacted through application of a vacuum or negative pressure. The process is carried out in eight subsequently performed steps, schematically illustrated in Fig. 8-43.

As in conventional sand molding, the process utilizes the cope and drag halves of the pattern, mounted on plates or boards. The difference is that each board and pattern is perforated with vent holes connected to a vacuum chamber.

First, the cope half is made. A preheated sheet of highly flexible plastic film with a typical thickness of from 0.050 to 0.125 mm (0.002 to 0.005 in.) is draped over the pattern and board. When the vacuum of 200 to 400

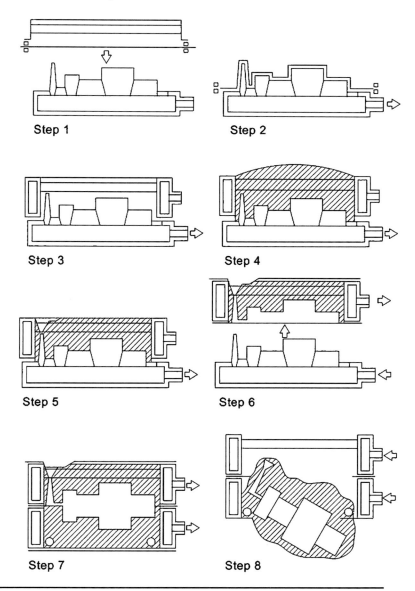

Fig. 8-43. Schematic of vacuum molding or V-process. (Courtesy: Roberts Sinto Corp.): Step 1. Pattern (with vent holes) is placed on hollow carrier plate. A special heater softens plastic film; Step 2. Softened film drapes over the pattern, with a vacuum acting through the pattern vents to draw it tightly around the pattern; Step 3. Double-walled flask is placed on the film-coated pattern; Step 4. Flask is filled with dry unbonded sand. Slight vibration compacts sand to maximum bulk density; Step 5. Sprue cup is formed and the mold surface leveled. The back of the mold is covered with unheated plastic film; Step 6. Vacuum is applied to the flask, atmospheric pressure then hardens the sand and, when the vacuum is released on the pattern carrier plate, the mold strips easily; Step 7. Cope and drag assembly forms a cavity, lined with a plastic. During pouring, molds are kept under vacuum; Step 8. After casting cooling, the vacuum is released and dry unbonded sand drops away to be reused, leaving a clean casting.

Step 1   Step 2   Step 3   Step 4   Step 5   Step 6   Step 7   Step 8

mm Hg is applied, the plastic film clings closely to the pattern contours. Then a flask is placed on the pattern and is filled with dry unbonded sand. Slight vibration compacts the sand to maximum bulk density. Then, the cope half of the mold is covered with a second sheet of plastic film, and vacuum is applied to the unbonded sand, which becomes hard and rigid. Releasing the vacuum on the pattern plate allows the pattern to be easily stripped from the mold.

The drag half of the mold is prepared in the same manner. The two halves of the mold are assembled and cores, if necessary, are set into the mold cavity before closing. Vacuum is applied during pouring, when the plastic material melts and is replaced by the molten metal. After casting solidification and cooling, the vacuum is released and the sand falls away for reuse.

Molding equipment is simple and usually consists of a vacuum system, film heater, vibrating table, pattern carrier and flasks, and can be automated for high volume production.

The process is suited for castings varying from a few ounces to approximately 10 tons and permits the use of cores for complex configurations. Figure 8-44 shows some typical castings made by the V-process.

The modified V-process, utilizing lost foam (EPC) patterns, has an advantage because vacuum is applied only during pouring, which significantly shortens the overall process time. The latter allows for better economics and expanding applications of the process to a wide variety of complex shaped cast components.

Process Advantages of V-Process Casting

- There is no need for mullers and mixers for molding sand preparation, and no need for costly sand reclamation and reconditioning equipment
- Pattern life is extended because there is no direct contact between the sand and the pattern, and the pattern is not subjected to the impact of any forces related to conventional molding methods, such as jolting, squeezing or ramming
- This process yields excellent finish and good dimensional accuracy of castings, and can reduce cleanup and rough machining operations
- Castings are free from gas defects and other defects related to conventional green sand and nobake molding
- Process features better environmental conditions, reduced noise, smoke and fume levels, than does conventional sand molding

Process Limitations of V-Process Casting

- The V-process requires special molding equipment, plated pattern equipment and double walled flasks for effective vacuum
- Sand grains must be carefully selected for optimal mold compaction
- Close synchronization of mold and metal readiness is essential in foundry practice

Applications for V-Process Casting

Using the V-process, castings of all sizes and shapes ranging from thin-sectioned curtain walls cast of aluminum to cast iron pressure pipe fittings, as well as stainless steel valve bodies in weights up to massive 8-ton ship anchors, are produced. Other components being routinely cast include bathtubs, railroad bolsters and side frames, machine tools, engine parts and agricultural castings. Any cast alloy (gray, ductile, malleable iron, various grades of steel, or aluminum and copper-based alloys) may be poured, with the possible exception of magnesium. Besides industrial applications, the process is used to make aluminum and bronze art castings, such as sculptures, statues and ornaments.

8.12. Case Study: External Chill Selection for Al Alloy PMC

Introduction

Two of the major problems commonly seen in permanent mold casting of aluminum-based alloys possessing medium to long freezing ranges are shrinkage porosity type defects and a high level of residual stresses, often resulting in hot tearing.

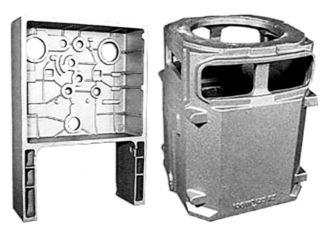

Fig. 8-44. Typical industrial castings made by the V-process. [Courtesy: Roberts Sinto Corp.]

A number of techniques have been developed to address these problems. In addition to the control of gas content and the diminution of oxide incorporation, a special key element in producing a quality, defect-free aluminum casting is the promotion of directional or sequential solidification. Typically, this can be accomplished through good casting design and correct placement of the feeding system.

However, in many cases, casting design adjustment does not permit directional solidification. For example, in the casting of wheels and pulleys with large hubs, directional solidification is difficult to accomplish without local cooling means, such as cooling fins and external heat sinks (chills).

Yet, there are few specific recommendations regarding the application of chills to PMC casting. With the increasing use of cast aluminum alloys for critical safety of cast parts in automotive and aerospace applications, these issues become very important. In the case of PMC cast parts design, the determination of the number and placements of heat sinks, based on trial and error, is clearly very expensive. Contemporary computer software permits simulation of mold filling, solidification behavior, internal stress formation and distortion appearing in castings. Thus, simulation of casting and solidification is able to reveal critical areas with a high propensity for defect formation.

This case study investigates the capability of external chill inserts in the prevention of hot tears and shrinkage formation, by accelerating the cooling rate in critical locations of aluminum PM castings. Because hot tearing and shrinkage are common problems in foundry practice, the development of methods, which permit avoidance of such defect formation at the design stage of cast production, will significantly reduce the production and service costs.

Experimental Procedures

Test Casting of PM with Chill Insert Design

An aluminum alloy A206 wheel was selected as the test casting for this study. The wheel comprises a massive central hub, eight cross-sectioned spokes, and rim. Figure 8-45 illustrates the vertical gating system design selected for a permanent mold containing two wheels. The solid model was built by using Pro-E software.

The particular wheel shape was chosen since this configuration indirectly involves two widely accepted tests for hot tearing susceptibility and is likely to be extremely prone to shrinkage-related defect formation. An example of a ring-test (similar to the wheel rim) was

described by Kurdjumov [Ref. 13], and a schematic design for a restrained bar casting (so-called "I-beam," similar to a spoke with junctions) has been described by Sigworth [Ref. 14].

The permanent mold was designed of cast iron in the shape of a rectangular block with external dimensions 790 × 125 × 470 mm (31 × 5 × 18.5 in.). The top of the mold is open, and the chill inserts enter the mold cavity from one side. The chills are inserted from the inner side of the permanent mold half and are fixed from the back of the mold by a nut within a mounting pocket (Fig. 8-46). Six different configurations of chill inserts were evaluated via solidification modeling experiments (Fig. 8-47).

Fig. 8-45. CAD model of casting with two attached wheels and the vertical gating system.

Fig. 8-46. Permanent mold designed to cast wheels (front half of the mold is not shown); chill is inserted into the left cavity of the mold.

- copper air-cooled chill with flat surface (F1)
- copper water-cooled chill with flat surface (F2)
- copper air-cooled chill with hemispherical surface (S1), forming an adequate recess/depression in the hub
- copper water-cooled chill with hemispherical surface (S2), forming an adequate recess/depression in the hub
- steel water-cooled chill with flat surface (F3)
- steel water-cooled chill with hemispherical surface (S3), forming an adequate recess/depression in the hub

Because a direct comparison between the effects of chills having flat or hemispherical contact surfaces would be inappropriate (since hemispherical chills lead to significant decreasing of the hub volume) special measures were taken. To make these chills comparable, two different reference casting designs were considered. The first one was the casting with a solid hub (N1), and the second one was the casting with a hemispherical recess in the hub (N2). Both designs have been used as reference castings during simulation. The recess possesses the same shape and dimensions as the contact surface used in the hemispherical chills. Thus, the chill effectiveness was measured relative to the original casting and to the casting with impressions in the hub area, accordingly, for both flat and hemispherical designs of chills, as shown in Fig. 8-48.

Computer Simulation Parameters

The simulation software SolidCast, based on the finite difference method that allows simulating filling and solidification behavior in a real 3-D model has been used in the study. The Niyama point was set at 65%, and the Critical Fraction Solid point was 60%. For all simulations, the mesh was generated with 1,500,000 nodes. Each simulation included 5 cycles of mold filling—casting shakeout with mold opening time equal to 30 sec. Running 5 cycles of the simulation assured stable temperature distribution through the mold.

For all chill configurations, a pseudo-thermocouple was embedded into each hub, allowing simulation of temperature changes during solidification. The conditions relating to thermal contact and to those of water cooling were those provided by the software.

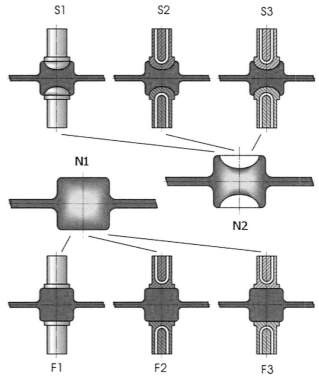

Fig. 8-47. Six different designs of external chills along with cross-sections of test castings with no chills. Flat (N1) and hemispherical (N2) chill efficiency evaluations are shown in Figs. 8-49 through 8-53.

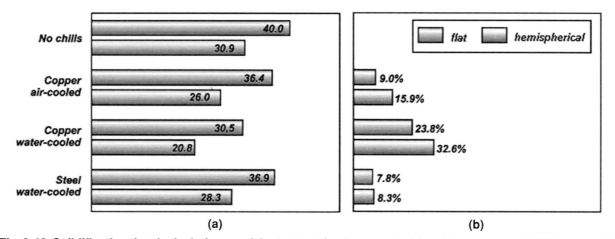

Fig. 8-48. Solidification time in the hub area of the test casting in seconds (a) and improvement of this parameter (%) achieved by applying different chills (b).

Establishing Baseline Data

Preliminary solidification modeling did confirm the major problems expected in the test casting:

High porosity in the hub caused by premature solidification of the spokes through which the hub is fed; Hot tears in junctions of the spokes and the hub, caused by an unacceptably steep temperature gradient. It was assumed that using external chills placed into the hub area could solve both of the problems.

Effectiveness of Chills

In order to evaluate chill effectiveness, a number of criteria such as solidification time in the center of the hub, minimal density in the hub area and maximal value of the Niyama criterion, were used. Each of these criteria was measured for the same reference casting, one poured without chills and one with the chills. Finally, an improvement factor was calculated as:

$$I_C = \frac{|C_{NCh} - C_{Ch}|}{C_{NCh}} \cdot 100\%,$$

Where

I_C = improvement of the criterion C;

C_{NCh} = value of the criterion C measured on the reference casting with no chills;

C_{Ch} = value of the criterion C measured after application of the chill

Results and Their Analysis

Solidification Time

It is widely recognized that minimizing solidification time leads to an improvement in microstructure (such as

fine and uniform grain structure) and a decrease in alloy segregation, etc. In the case considered, when metal in the area of the hub remains liquid after all spokes, acting initially as feeding channels are solidified, solidification time of the hub becomes important. Decreasing solidification time in the hub area reduces the difference between the solidification times of the spokes and the hub, which, in turn, will lead to a reduction of shrinkage related defects. Figure 8-48 shows solidification time in the hub area of the reference casting in seconds (a) and improvement of this parameter achieved by applying different chills (b).

As can be seen, not all chills are equally effective in reducing solidification time. Surprisingly, the effectiveness of the steel water-cooled chills was less than that of the copper air-cooled type. The application of the spherical, copper, water-cooled chill permitted the reduction of solidification time from 30.5 sec to 20.8 sec or up to 32.6 %, and clearly outperformed all other chills.

Shrinkage

Casting density distribution in the cross section of the hub area was used to qualitatively evaluate chill effectiveness, in terms of internal shrinkage porosity reduction. Figure 8-49 illustrates minimum material density in the hub area of the reference casting, and improvement of this factor was achieved by different chill applications. Figure 8-50 shows the impact of chill's design on the hub cross-section area where density is lower than 98 percent.

It is obvious that the copper, water-cooled, hemispherical chill achieves the best results. This chill improves minimal observed density by eliminating areas with density lower than 90%, and significantly reduces areas with density lower than 98%. Steel

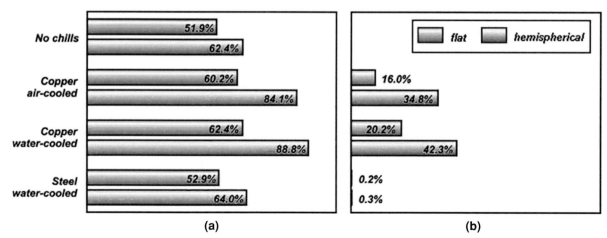

Fig. 8-49. Minimal density observed in the hub of the test casting (a) and improvement of this factor achieved by applying different chills (b).

chills, both flat and hemispherical, are not as effective as copper chills, only slightly reducing shrinkage porosity in defective areas. The difference between flat and hemispherical chills was more significant for coarse shrinkage defect elimination (areas with density less than 90%). Changing the shape of the chills from flat to hemispherical had a more noticeable effect on solidification behavior, than did the application of water-cooling as opposed to air-cooling.

Hot Tearing

The Niyama criterion, which numerically equals the temperature gradient during freezing in a given area, divided by the square root of the associated cooling rate, has been used as an indicator of both feeding efficiency and hot tearing tendency. The software application calculated the temperature gradient in each cell of the enmeshed model as well as its cooling rate. Analyses of the simulation results showed that the most critical part of the casting, in terms of hot tearing formation risk, was the junction between the bottom vertical spoke and the hub. Niyama values in this section were used for evaluation of different chill effectiveness in terms of hot tear prevention (Fig. 8-51).

As can be seen, all chill configurations showed somewhat similar results: 14–23% improvement for flat and 13–17% for hemispherical chills. However, the results need careful interpretation; for instance, the relative effectiveness of copper hemispherical chills is less than the flat variety. This is probably caused by the large difference between the two reference castings: those with and those without the hemispherical recess in the hub. More reliable data can be obtained by comparison of data for values of area cross section of the casting with the Niyama criterion higher than "1," as it is shown in Fig. 8-52.

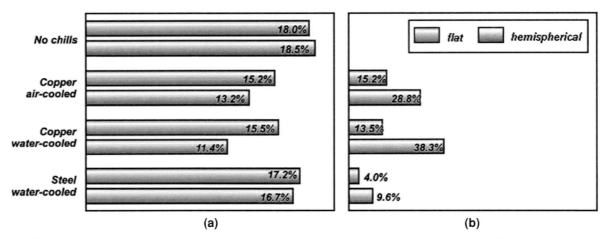

Fig. 8-50. Percentage of hub area of the test casting with density lower than 98% (a) and improvement of this factor achieved by applying different chills (b).

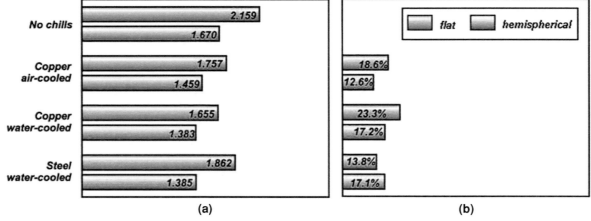

Fig. 8-51. Niyama criterion values in the junction between the bottom vertical spoke and the hub of the test casting (a) and improvement of this factor achieved by applying different chills (b).

Special Casting Methods

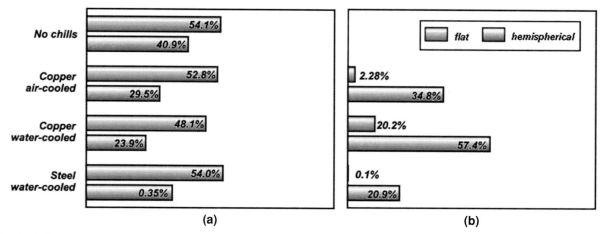

(a)   **(b)**

Fig. 8-52. Percentage of the hub area of the test casting with Niyama criterion higher than "1" (a) and improvement of this factor achieved by applying different chills (b).

Conclusions

1. Application of the various external chill/heat sink configurations studied suggest that different degrees of reduction of porosity in shrinkage-prone areas may be possible through the promotion of sequential solidification in the PM casting of aluminum A-206.

2. The most effective chills are those of the hemispherical, copper, water-cooled design. Changing the shape of the heat sinks from a flat to a hemispherical configuration has a more noticeable effect on solidification rates than does the application of water-cooling as opposed to air-cooling.

3. From a practical standpoint, the effectiveness of the various chill configurations studied can be arranged into the following order (from more effective to less effective): copper water-cooled; copper air-cooled; steel water-cooled. This order is valid for both chill designs: flat and hemispherical. In turn, hemispherical chills are seen to be more effective than the flat type in comparison with normalized parameters, where reduction of the hub volume is possible.

4. The relatively high efficiency of the hemispherical chills may be explained as a result of their larger contact surface area through which heat transfer occurs. In addition, the hemispherical chills have greater mass and, accordingly, heat capacity. An additional factor here, which will require further work, is the fact that castings will shrink into internal chill configurations, rather than forming an air gap, as is the case with flat (external) configurations, thus providing a more perfect degree of thermal contact.

5. Local modification of solidification behavior by applying external chill inserts is common in sand casting. However, control of metal solidification by this method in PMC is significantly more complicated than in sand casting. The thermal conductivity of the mold material in the case of PMC is considerably higher than in sand casting. Accordingly, differences between heat transfer from casting to mold, and from casting to chill, is much less than in sand casting. The latter explains why chill inserts for permanent mold casting are significantly more powerful in terms of heat transfer.

References

1. *ASM Metals Handbook, Vol. 15, "Casting"*, American Society of Metals, Metals Park, 2008.

2. Lerner, Y.S., "Status and New Developments in Gravity Diecasting of Iron," *Foundry Trade Journal*, England, May 1999, pp. 27-30.

3. Lerner, Y.S., "Mold Life Improvement In Permanent Casting" *Transactions from 5th International Conference on Permanent Mold Casting of Aluminum*, AFS, 2000, pp. 81-94.

4. Lerner, Y.S., T. Frush, "Counter-Gravity Casting of Thin-wall Ductile Iron," *Proceedings of The Ductile Iron Society's 1998 Keith D. Millis Symposium on Ductile Iron*, Hilton Head, SC, 1998, pp. 313-446.

5. Lerner, Y.S., "Microstructure and Properties of Continuous Cast Ductile Iron," *AFS Transactions*, pp. 349-354 (1993).

6. "Dura-Bar: Ductile Iron With A Difference," *Ductile Iron News*, DIS, No 2, p. 6, (1992).

7. Lerner Y., Griffin G; "Developments in

Continuous Casting of Gray and Ductile Iron," *Modern Casting*, Nov 1997, pp. 41-44.

8. Lerner, Y:, "Continuous Casting of Ductile Iron. Solidification, Microstructure, and Properties," *50th Electric Furnace Conference Proceedings, ISS*, Vol. 50, Atlanta, USA, Dec 13-15, 1992, pp. 331-340.

9. *Die Casting Engineer*, Nov. 2004, pp. 51-58.

10. Gzerwinski, P.,"Assessing Capabilities of Magnesium Alloys," *International Journal of Cast Metals Research*, Vol 16, 2003, pp. 389-396.

11. Wetzel, S.,"Protect Your Permanent Molds," *Modern Casting*, Feb 2009, pp. 47-49.

12. Kopper, A., R. Donahue, D. Olson, "Semi-Solid Casting Process Shows Muscle for Mercury Marine," *Modern Casting,* May 2005, pp. 35-37.

13. Kurdjumov, A.B., Editor, "Laboratory Works on Foundry Tech Production," *Engineering,*Moscow, Russia, 1990, p. 271.

14. Sigworth, G., "Hot Tearing of Metals," *AFS Transactions,*Vol. 104, 1996, pp. 1053-1062.

Review Questions

8.1 Explain the need for special casting processes.

8.2 Specify the reason for selecting a given mold material in the permanent mold casting process.

8.3 Describe the importance of mold coatings in permanent mold casting process.

8.4 Explain the need of cooling in permanent mold casting process.

8.5 Briefly compare at least two designs of water-cooled permanent molds.

8.6 Specify the purpose served by heat sinks in permanent mold casting process.

8.7 Explain the mold erosion problem as experienced in the permanent mold casting process and how it is solved.

8.8 Discuss the steps in a typical automatic permanent mold casting cycle.

8.9 Compare the advantages and limitations of permanent mold casting.

8.10 Describe applications of permanent mold casting.

8.11 Briefly explain the diecasting process.

8.12 Discuss materials typically used to make dies for the diecasting process.

8.13 Review types of cores used in diecasting.

8.14 Compare a cold chamber diecasting process with a hot chamber process.

8.15 Specify the reason for selecting cold chamber diecasting rather than hot chamber diecasting for aluminum.

8.16 Define the role of overflows in diecasting.

8.17 Discuss the advantages and limitations of diecasting.

8.18 Give examples of typical parts made by diecasting.

8.19 Discuss the justification for the following statement: Although sand casting is the most widely used process judging from the tonnage of castings produced, there are instances where one would choose diecasting in preference to the sand casting.

8.20 Compare advantages and limitations of low-pressure diecasting.

8.21 Describe the applications of low pressure diecastings.

8.22 Explain true centrifugal casting.

8.23 Explain how a sound hollow bar can be cast by true centrifugal casting. Give reasons in support of your answer.

8.24 Discuss advantages and limitations of centrifugal casting.

8.25 State the differences between centrifuging and true centrifugal casting.

8.26 Comment on the statement: Large parts cannot be manufactured by the centrifuging process.

8.27 Outline the investment casting process, giving typical applications of the castings made through this process.

8.28 Specify the advantages of the investment casting process over other casting processes and highlight its limitations.

8.29 Give examples of the typical products of the following processes: diecasting, true centrifugal casting, and permanent mold casting.

8.30 Describe the ceramic molding process.

8.31 Compare the advantages and limitations of ceramic mold casting.

8.32 Describe lost foam casting or EPC process and its major operations.

8.33 Discuss advantages of the lost foam casting process.

8.34 Briefly outline the vertical continuous casting process.

8.35 Specify the advantages and limitations of the

horizontal continuous casting process.

8.36 Summarize major features of the countergravity casting process.

8.37 Specify the advantages and limitations of the countergravity casting process.

8.38 Discuss the semisolid casting process.

8.39 Explain the advantages and limitations of the semisolid casting process.

8.40 Briefly outline the vacuum molding process and explain its advantages.

SHAKEOUT, CLEANING AND QUALITY TESTING

9

Objectives

After the casting is poured and solidified, it is necessary to remove it from the mold, clean and test it for any defects. After studying this chapter, the reader should be able to:

- Identify the optimal time for casting cooling and removal from the mold
- Describe the various shakeout equipment options
- Explain a variety of cleaning and finishing operations on the casting
- Discuss the need for testing the quality of the finished casting

Keywords

Shakeout, Cleaning, Cast Alloy, Cooling Rate, Sand Molding, Vibrating Conveyer, Rotary Separator, Casting Shakeout, Vibratory Knockout Machines, Liquid Nitrogen Jet, Degating, Core Removal, Casting Decoring, Chipping, Shotblasting, Shotblasting Machine, Tumbling, Robot, Quality Testing, Nondestructive Testing, NDT, Videoscope, Surface Defects, Warpage, Crack, Hot Tear, Shrinkage, Slag Porosity, Dye Penetrant Testing, Magnetic Particle Inspection, Microstructure Evaluation, Graphite Shape, Nodularity Tests In Ductile Iron, Radiographic Testing, Ultrasonic Technique, Ultrasonic Velocity, USV, Resonant Acoustic Method, RAM, Borescope.

The operations discussed in this chapter are final operations in the process of manufacturing castings. Although various steps of the metalcasting process have increased and are more automated, the process of cleaning castings, in most cases, remains labor intensive. It is estimated that approximately 25 to 35% of the manufacturing cost can be attributed to cleaning and or finishing operations.

9.1. Shakeout

In this operation, the casting, after being poured and solidified, is removed from either the sand or metal mold.

In the case of sand molds, they are taken to the shakeout area, where the mold is broken to extract the casting from the flask. In the case of metal mold (permanent and diecasting), castings, after being ejected from the mold, are transferred to the next cleaning operation. If a sand core is used, the casting is subjected to further core knockout.

Casting shakeout from the mold is to be done only when the casting has sufficiently cooled. Premature casting removal may lead to faster and uneven cooling (air quenching) that, in turn, cause warpage, cracks or induced thermal stresses. Early mold shakeout is also unsafe because of possible molten metal spill from incompletely solidified pouring basin, ingates and risers.

In sand molding, the castings remain in the mold for a certain time to ensure a desirable cooling rate. The molding sand provides a uniform cooling medium for the casting while producing the least amount of residual stresses. In the mechanized foundry equipped with a pouring conveyer, molds are cooled on the conveyer line, the length of which controls the cooling rate. In low-volume production, the molds remain on the foundry floor after pouring, from where they are transported to the shakeout area.

The cooling time depends upon the type of alloy cast, casting section thickness, total weight as well as the type of mold. Approximate values of cooling times for sand mold iron castings are given in Table 9-1.

Late mold shakeout causes a slower cooling rate, creating conditions where castings are mold annealed. The latter

Table 9-1. Approximate Cooling Times for Sand Mold Iron Castings Depending Upon the Type of Mold and the Weight of the Casting.

Sand mold type	Casting weight, kg (lb)	Cooling time, hours
Green sand mold: simple to moderate complexity	< 20 (44)	0.4–0.75
Green sand mold: moderate to high complexity	21–100 (46–220)	0.75–1.5
Dry sand mold: moderate to high complexity	< 20 (44)	0.6–1.0
Dry sand mold: moderate complexity	101–500 (221–1100) 501–1000 (1101–2200)	2–6 6–9
Dry sand mold: complex shapes	1001–3000 (2201–6615) 3001–5000 (6616–11,020)	8–18 18–30

has an adverse impact on certain alloy mechanical properties. For example, in the case of cast irons, it reduces hardness, impact and tensile strength.

Ideally, the sand mold castings should be shaken at a temperature where no phase transformation occurs. For example, the shakeout should be done at a temperature below 700°C (1292°F) for ferrous alloys. If the castings are thin and fragile, they should be removed at a temperature as low as 400°C (752°F), whereas for the heavier castings, a little higher temperature of 500°C (932°F) may be suitable.

Typically, mechanically or automatically operated equipment is utilized for casting shakeout. Shakeout machines are designed to separate molding sand from the casting through a perforated/grizzly deck, fixed to a vibrating frame (Fig. 9-1). These machines operate with vertical action at a high frequency to facilitate sand lump reduction. Used sand drains through the vibrating conveyer and goes to the sand reclamation system. Due to air contamination, the shakeout device should be enclosed and furnished with an effective dust and fume collection system.

In contemporary automatic molding lines, the shakeout station is a part of the whole line, where molds are transferred and castings removed from the mold, automatically.

A rotary separator or rotary drum is another type of shakeout equipment used in high-volume production foundries. Poured molds are delivered to the intake end of the rotary drum (Fig. 9-2). As the molds tumble through the drum, the molding sand is separated from the casting, reduced to grain size, and dissipated through openings in the lining to the outer chamber, where it is conveyed to the sand discharge point.

The cleaned castings travel to the casting discharge end of the drum, where they exit and move to the next stage of processing in the cleaning room. The tumbling

Fig. 9-1. Shakeout machine operates with more vertical action and at a higher frequency to facilitate sand lump reduction. [Source: Foundry Management & Technology]

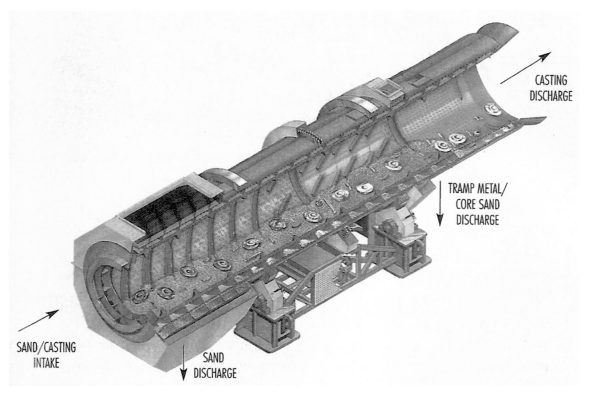

Fig. 9-2. Rotary drum is another type of equipment used to separate molding sand from the casting. Source: Foundry Management & Technology]

action in the separator crushes sand lumps, removes core butts, and empties sand pockets. The openings in the specially designed lining act as a rotary screen to prevent tramp metal, core butts, and other foreign material from entering the sand system. Moreover, the sand is homogenized and uniform in temperature, since the cooler sand from molds entering the unit is constantly mixed with hotter sand as it passes through the lining into the sand chamber. This allows for better sand control at the muller. Use of this equipment eliminates manual operations, improves working conditions by keeping sand in the system and reduces air contamination.

9.2. Cleaning and Finishing

The following operations are cleaning and finishing. The process involves the removal of the sand cores, gating and risering system elements, cleaning of the casting surface, chipping of fins along the parting line, core prints as well as veins and stickers and other unnecessary projections on surfaces.

9.2.1. Core Removal (Decoring)

The dry sand cores can be removed manually by simple knocking off with an iron bar, or mechanically by employing special vibratory knockout machines, or by means of a high-pressure water blast device called hydroblasting. The method used depends on the size, complexity and the core material as well as the production volume. The knockout machine is typically furnished with a clamping device to hold and rotate the casting during operation. These machines are enclosed to keep the working place safe and environmentally clean.

One of the latest developments in core removal technique is the utilization of a liquid nitrogen jet technology. After the flashing, riser and ingate removal, the casting is moved to a robotic device where the robot picks up the casting and moves it over a jet of liquid nitrogen for final sand core removal. The system compresses liquid nitrogen from 35 to 380 MPa (5000 to 55,000 psi) with temperature between −150°C and −95°C (−240 and −500°F) and creates an ultra-high velocity jet that has a density comparable to water. As the casting is positioned over the rotating nozzle, liquid nitrogen is propelled into the sand core. Within milliseconds after leaving the nozzle, the liquid nitrogen changes from a supercritical fluid to a gas. As this change occurs, the liquid nitrogen expands up to five times its volume, rupturing the core without damaging the casting. Additional cleaning is achieved when the displaced core material and the speed of

the liquid nitrogen stream are combined. According to the manufacturer, the developed technology offers several benefits:

- The process is totally dry, since the liquid nitrogen turns to a gas
- No heat is introduced into the casting
- The process is environmentally friendly because no secondary waste is created, thereby eliminating all environmental problems and cost associated with waste disposal

9.2.2. Ingate/Riser Removal (Degating)

The ingates and risers can be removed by various methods such as hammering, chipping, mechanical cutoff machines (band saw, abrasive wheel, friction sawing, shearing, water-jet cutting), flame or arc cutting. Removal of ingates and risers can be simplified by providing a reduced metal section or V-notch at the casting joint, as shown previously in Chapter 4 (Fig. 4-12) and Chapter 5 (Fig. 5-6), resulting in gating system break off during shakeout.

For brittle materials such as gray cast iron, hitting with a hammer can easily break the ingates. For steel and other similar materials, sawing with any metal cutting saw, like a hack saw or band saw, would be more convenient. For large-sized iron and steel ingates and risers, it may be necessary to use flame or arc cutting to remove them. In the arc-air cutting process, the electric arc melts the metal and air blows it away.

Similarly, abrasive cutoff may also be used for removal of ingates. Most of the abrasive cutoff can be carried out by portable grinding machines with an angled grinding head. Typical wheel speeds used are in the range of 45 to 80 m/s.

Plasma arc cutting or the plasma jet employs heat generated by applying electrical energy to a gas to remove ingates and risers from castings made of any electrically conductive cast alloy. The method is used mainly to cut risers of plate-shaped castings, whose wall thickness and shape allow full penetration of the plasma torch.

The shearing method is typically employed to cut off ingates as well as trim parting line flash, primarily in aluminium and zinc diecastings. The method uses a trimming die mounted on a press, and can trim horizontal and vertical planes, as well as cut ingates, in the same operation.

When the gating system is removed, it becomes part of the charge material or foundry returns and will be remelted in the melting furnace.

9.2.3. Fin and Excess Metal Removal

After removal of the ingates, the casting surface may still contain some fins and other projections on the surface near the parting line and core prints. Also remaining may be some rough surfaces left at the time of ingate removal or sand that is fused to the surface. These need to be cleaned thoroughly before the casting will be used. The fins and other small projections may easily be chipped off with the help of hand tools or pneumatic tools, mechanical cutoff or arc cutting units, or trim presses (mentioned earlier). For smoothing the rough-cut ingate edges, either a pedestal or swing-frame grinder is used, depending on the size of the casting.

Shotblasting and Tumbling. For cleaning the sand particles sticking to the casting surface, an abrasive impacting method or blasting method is the fastest approach. The abrasives used are sand, metal grit and/or metal (iron or steel) shot.

In the air blast method, the abrasive normally used is sand that is carried in a high velocity air stream directed at the casting surface. The casting is kept in a closed box and a jet of compressed air with a blast of sand grains or steel grit is directed against the casting surface, which thoroughly cleans the casting surface. In the airless-

blasting devices, the metallic particles (grits or shots) are thrown against the castings by centrifugal force from a rapidly spinning wheel (Fig. 9-3).

The typical shot speeds reached are in the order of 80 m/s (262 ft/s). The shots used are either chilled cast iron grit or steel grit. Chilled iron is less expensive but is likely to be lost quickly, by break-up.

A rotating-table shotblasting cabinet (Fig. 9-4) is one of the typical batch-type pieces of equipment suited for cleaning small- to medium-sized cast parts. In a similar machine intended for larger sized castings, a satellite table is positioned in front of the operator or loading robot for loading and unloading, while another satellite table is positioned within the shotblasting zone of the machine. Parts are uniformly covered with a wide jet of shot launched by centrifugation by one or more turbines, which cover from a minimum of 500 mm (20 in.) to a maximum of 2400 mm (96 in.). Based on the same principle, a three-table satellite machine, with tables of 1000 mm (40 in.) each, is used in large-scale casting production.

Because the parts being shotblasted are fixtured onto the shotblasting table, the parts are not banging and hitting into each other, lending this machine to the shotblasting of delicate parts as well. This shotblasting machine is also well suited for shotblasting of parts that have deep recesses that also require cleaning.

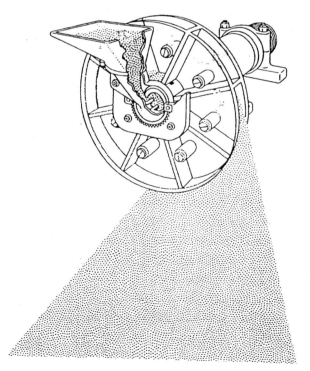

Fig. 9-3. Schematic of airless shot- or grit-blasting machine head, which employs centrifugal force from a rapidly spinning wheel.

Fig. 9-4. Rotating table shotblasting cabinet. [Source: Foundry Management & Technology]

For large and heavy-weight castings weighting up to 230 t (506,000 lb), special blast equipment, called a blast room, with a turntable of up to 4 m (12 ft) in diameter and multiple airless centrifugal wheels is utilized.

In continuous flow shotblasting cleaning equipment used in high production rate foundries, castings are moved through the cleaning chamber via a flat belt conveyor or monorail-type conveyor.

Due to great flexibility, these units can be easily integrated into existing casting production lines, creating continuous, entirely automatic casting flow from molding/pouring and cooling stations directly to blast cleaning without any manual operations. This minimizes air pollution and ensures better working conditions.

Shown in Fig. 9-5, is a typical example of a fully automated drum-type blast cleaning machine that has capacity up to 35 t/h (77,000 lb/h) of parts weighing up 150 kg (330 lb). After leaving the molding line, castings pass through the blast cleaning area, where the high-powered abrasive streams, aimed at the castings from above, effectively clean all surfaces, cavities and internal passages. The machine is equipped with a polygon-shaped trough, which rocks back and forth about its longitudinal axis for gentle rotation, exposing surfaces for more thorough cleaning of the castings. An oscillation conveyor moves blast-cleaned castings from the cleaning station for further processing.

Tumbling is another useful method for cleaning the casting surface. The tumbling machine is a large drum into which castings are placed along with jack stars. In this operation, the castings and stars tumble and scrape each other as the drum rotates. Here, the castings are kept in a barrel, which is completely closed and then slowly rotated on a horizontal axis at 30 to 40 rpm. The barrel is reasonably packed with enough room for castings to move so that the sand, unwanted fins and projections will be removed. However, one precaution to be taken for tumbling is that the castings should all be rigid with no frail or overhung segments, which may get knocked off during the tumbling operation.

Some shotblasting machines combine tumbling of parts with shotblasting. These rotary-tumble shotblasting machines, with centrifugal projection of shot, have very high efficiency and are suitable for cleaning medium-sized pieces of cast iron, steel, bronze, etc. Designed to allow high production levels of small and medium-sized castings, in intermittent loads, their characteristics include a continuous conveyor belt made of special anti-abrasive rubber or steel plates for the rotation of the pieces during blasting. Machine loading may be manual or automatic via a hydraulic tipping bucket whose capacity varies from 60 kg (150 lb) to over 2500 kg (5500 lb). Automatic discharge is accomplished by reversing the direction of the conveyor belt. These machines represent batch-type operations.

9.2.4. Robotic Cleaning Operation

In order to eliminate manual operations, achieve better productivity and improve working conditions in cleaning rooms, robots are often used in high volume casting production. Typically, the robotic system is designed as a cell, in which castings are degated, ground and moved within the operation by robots.

The robotic system similar to that shown in Fig. 9-6 features robotic part handling, automated grinding wheels to remove risers, burrs, and parting line fins. Main grinding wheels handle exterior operations; mini grinder attachments finish the inside of the casting. These grinders are fully programmable allowing operators to "teach" the grinding system to execute the same

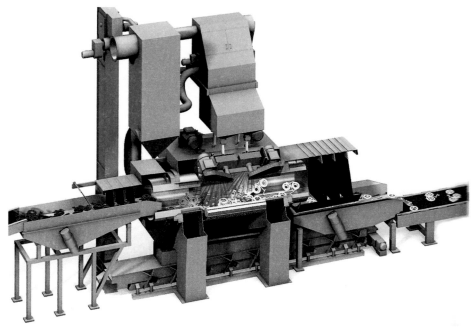

Fig. 9-5. Drum-type continuous blast cleaning station that has capacity up to 35 t/h (77,000 lb/h) of parts weighing up 150 kg (330 lb). [Courtesy: DISA Industries.]

operations that would be performed manually. Casting changeover can be performed in minutes by changing fixtures and uploading new programs.

Another robotic cleaning system is equipped with digitizing programs where the castings are scanned prior to running and the machine eliminates unneeded operations. Figure 9-7 illustrates some typical automotive castings processed by a robotic cleaning system. Some robotic systems are capable of performing other tasks while parts are cleaned, such as stamping, ultrasound and hardness tests, washing and painting.

Specialized automated cleaning systems, similar to that shown in Fig. 9-8, are built for automotive and tractor engine blocks, heads and crankshafts, and have a productivity rate of up to 600 castings per hour.

Implementation of the robotics not only drastically increases productivity of cleaning operations, but also results in dramatic improvements in safety, since manual operations are completely eliminated or significantly reduced. The environmental impact is also notable, since noise and dust are now contained within a soundproof safety enclosure.

9.3. Quality Testing

Before castings are shipped to customers, they are subject to final inspection and quality testing, to confirm that the castings are free from defects and satisfy requirements of the standards and specifications. These procedures are done in addition to conventional testing methods that begin when materials enter the

foundry and accompany each step of metalcasting process.

Typical inspection of castings includes dimensional and shape control using gauges or measurement instruments previously described in Chapter 2. To detect flaws or defects on the casting surface, castings are inspected visually or using nondestructive testing (NDT) methods. The NDT provides information on casting quality without any alteration of its shape or the structure.

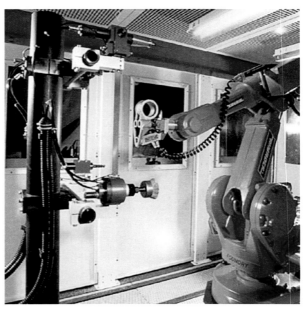

Fig. 9-6. Robotic grinding cell. [Courtesy: Rimrock Corp.]

Fig. 9-7. Typical automotive parts processed by fully automated finishing system. (Courtesy: MAUS Automation)

Shakeout, Cleaning and Quality Testing

Where nondestructive methods are used in foundries, there are three major problem areas: surface defects, internal defects and microstructural irregularities.

Surface Defects. Tests to detect surface defects such as hot tears, cracks, pores and other surface imperfections affecting quality that cannot be detected visually. Dye and fluorescent penetrant testing techniques as well as magnetic particle inspection are typically used for this purpose.

Dye and fluorescent penetrant testing uses a penetrating dye for detection of defects that are open to the surface only. In this test, a part, after being cleaned of oil and other contaminants, is dipped or sprayed with a visible or fluorescent penetrant. Visible dye, which is typically red in color, after applying special developer and viewed under a bright light, produces red lines or dots indicating surface flaws. If fluorescent dye is utilized, the defects are revealed as glowing yellow/green dots or lines under ultraviolet light.

Magnetic particle testing is applicable for surface inspection only of ferromagnetic materials. Aluminum, magnesium, copper alloys castings as well as titanium and austenitic stainless steel castings cannot be inspected by this method. The casting is magnetized, and then a magnetic powder is sprayed onto casting surface. The powder will be localized at the areas of cracks or other discontinuities, showing their location and shape. This method is more effective and sensitive than dye penetrant testing, because it allows the detection of defects located beneath the surface that may be closed during cleaning operation (such as shotblasting).

These two tests (fluorescent penetrant and magnetic particle) are relatively simple and less costly than other NDT inspection methods.

Internal Defects. Tests to detect internal defects, such as shrinkage, slag and gas porosity, may employ radiographic or ultrasonic methods.

Industrial radiographic (IR) testing techniques involve film x-ray radiography, as well as digital radiography, electromagnetic radiation and computerized axial tomography (CAT scanning). The latter provides 3-D images as well as cross-sectional views of the casting. These methods utilize various radiation sources for inspection of critical and high-temperature application cast components. For example, in aerospace, aircraft and turbines, detecting small defects and recognizing damage accumulation at earlier parts of the manufacturing stage (before being assembled and shipped for service) is important. These defects, such as shrinkage, gas porosity or slag (nonmetallic) inclusions, differ by density from the density of the casting alloy and will reveal themselves as dark or light areas on the film.

In comparison with conventional radiography, new real time radiography is filmless. It produces no film records, but an electronic image is displayed on an operator's monitor and may be recorded and saved. In addition, the speed of each examination is substantially reduced to make possible immediate, in-line inspection of high-volume parts such as automotive aluminium wheels, intake manifolds and cylinder heads. Based on these techniques, manual, semi-automatic or fully automatic systems are currently used in metalcasting facilities as a part of quality testing procedures for the detection of microporosity, cracks and hot tears.

Ultrasonic testing (UT) uses beams of high-frequency waves to detect surface and subsurface flaws or discontinuities in the production of safety-critical cast components such as automotive suspension and brake systems. In this method, sound waves generated by a transducer travel through the material with the loss of energy or velocity. The reflected beam, after being analyzed, shows location and size of the defects. This method is also used for measuring the thickness of the material and evaluating graphite shape in cast irons.

The drawback of UT technique is that testing cannot be performed on a rough or oxidized surface and requires the use of a liquid couplant or part immersion.

Fig. 9-8. Robotic cells in automated cleaning operations. (Source: Modern Casting and Foundry Solutions & Design [http://www.foundrysd.com/]

Another approach is using an electromagnetic acoustic transducer (EMAT) to generate the sound in the inspected part. This is found to be more flexible and capable of more accurate defect detection in complex castings of iron, aluminium alloys and other metals, without liquid couplants or tank immersion.

Microstructural Irregularities. For microstructure evaluation, such as the shape of graphite in cast irons (nodularity tests in ductile iron), the *ultrasonic velocity (USV) technique* is widely used.

In this method, nodularity is checked using an ultrasonic velocity (USV) measuring instrument, which measures velocity by sending and receiving sound waves as they travel through the section of a casting. With a known thickness of the object, USV is calculated and nodularity is determined, based on previously established relationships.

Currently, some automotive foundries are using the USV method for 100% nodularity testing in high-volume production of castings intended for safety-critical applications, such as brake systems and suspensions. For this purpose, contemporary PC-based USV stations are used in which the USV nodularity test is combined with ultrasonic tests for internal defects, such as shrinkage porosity.

The PC-based USV station (Fig. 9-9) consists of one or two immersion tanks coupled with part-holding fixtures designed for specific part configuration. These fixtures are furnished with the necessary quantity of transducers, testing first for casting flaws and then for nodularity. An additional channel can be used for precision dimension measurements. Parts loading into the fixture and sorting by quality may be done manually or automatically. The

USV test procedure takes a couple of seconds, and hourly productivity may vary from 600 to 800 parts.

One of the disadvantages of traditional USV is that it commonly analyzes nodularity in only one section of the casting; nodularity in other areas would not be detected. Another problem is that it needs a fluid coupling or immersion.

An alternative NDT technique, called *resonant acoustic method (RAM)*, utilizes a method in which the test casting is impacted by mechanical means and a highly sensitive microphone is used for listening and analyzing its acoustic spectrum. The controlled impact provides broadband input energy to excite the part, and the microphone allows for noncontact measurements of the resonant frequency, which is then correlated with nodularity. This method eliminates the need for fluid coupling or immersion and is suitable for high-volume automated inspection.

For visual inspection of heavy-duty industrial pump housings, valve bodies and other hydraulic application

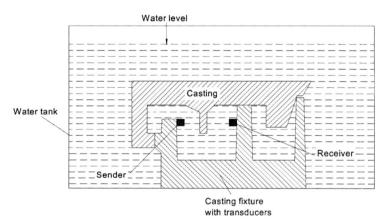

Fig. 9-9. Schematic of a PC-based USV station for simultaneous nodularity and internal defects testing in ductile iron castings.

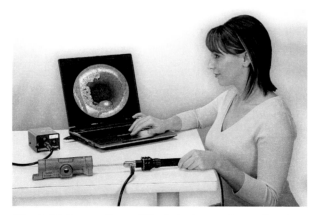

Fig. 9-10. Inspection of the interior surface of an iron casting using a Hawkeye Pro Hardy rigid borescope and video system. [Courtesy: Gradient Lens Corp.]

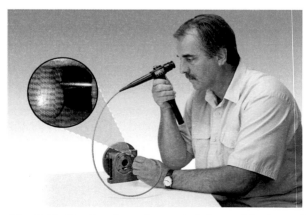

Fig. 9-11. Casting bore inspected for residual sand using a Hawkeye Pro Flexible borescope. [Courtesy: Gradient Lens Corp.]

castings with small-cored passages, a special visual diagnostic instrument, called a borescope, is used. Borescopes are available in both rigid optical (Fig. 9-10) and flexible fiberoptic (Fig. 9-11) versions. The borescopes can be used by eye or attached to a video camera system.

This instrument has been effective for spotting burned sand, excessive porosity and other hidden defects in cored hydraulic passages as small as 3 mm (0.125 in.) diameter.

Newer borescopes are equipped with either rigid or flexible attachments, along with a portable video camera, which allows the operator to view, capture and store the inspection images. These instruments are lightweight and more portable than conventional borescopes, allowing the inspector to bring the scope to the casting for easy inspection of heavy parts with complex internal passages, thus avoiding unnecessary transport of the casting.

Typical final metallurgical control includes chemistry, microstructure, hardness and mechanical properties testing. Coupled with this textbook, the Lab Manual describes, in detail, some of these testing procedures as well as safety precautions related to these tests.

Besides those mentioned, some special tests may be required, such as pressure testing to find leaks in hydraulic application castings, or residual stress checks in castings used in aircraft and aerospace equipment (see Chapter 2, Section 2.2.2.).

References

1. "Liquid Nitrogen Jet," (editorial), *Foundry Management &Technology*, May 2005, p.16.

2. *Safe Practices in Cleaning, Testing and Finishing*, American Foundrymen's Society, Des Plaines, 1970.

3. *Analysis of Casting Defects*, American Foundrymen's Society, Des Plaines, 1996.

4. Brown, J.R., ed.: *Foseco Foundryman's Handbook*, 10th Ed., Butterworth Heinemann, Oxford, 1994.

5. *ASM Handbook Vol. 15*, "Casting," ASM International, Metals Park, 2008.

Review Questions

9.1 Discuss the ideal conditions for extracting a casting from the mold.

9.2 Explain the term degating and list methods used for this purpose.

9.3 Differentiate the methods available for the removal of ingates and risers from the ferrous and nonferrous castings. Give examples.

9.4 Explain the term decoring; list methods used for this operation.

9.5 Describe the methods that can be used to clean the casting surface.

9.6 Specify the functions of robots in metalcasting cleaning operations.

9.7 Briefly highlight the advantages of robot applications in casting cleaning.

9.8 Define the objectives of final quality testing of castings.

9.9 Specify the methods typically used in the final quality inspection.

9.10 List three major NDT methods currently used in the foundries and their applications.

9.11 Briefly describe the dye penetrant test and its applications.

9.12 Explain advantages and limitations of magnetic particle inspection.

9.13 Explain the purpose of radiographic testing, and describe the steps of the process.

9.14 Explain the primary applications of ultrasonic inspection in casting production.

9.15 Explain how NDT USV nodularity testing is done and used by foundries.

9.16 Describe a videoscope (borescope) and its applications.

CASTING DEFECTS AND PREVENTION

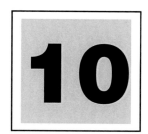

Objectives

Proper identification of castings defects and understanding their root causes is essential for production of defect-free castings with optimum performance. After studying this chapter reader should be able to:

- Classify casting defects depending on their appearance
- Describe different types of shrinkage defects
- Identify the various gas-related defects in casting and their proper corrective measures
- Recognize different types of mold-related defects in castings and their causes
- Discuss procedures to eliminate casting defects due to improper pouring practice
- Explain reasons for the occurrence of breakages in castings
- Be able to develop measures preventing defect reoccurrence

Keywords

Casting Defects, Shrinkage, Shrinkage Porosity, Hot Spot, Molten Metal, Metal Solidification, Flask, Corebox, Blowhole, Open Blows, Air Porosity, Molding Sand, Mold Venting, Core Venting, Sand, Gas Porosity, Pinhole, Blister, Body Scar, Cut, Wash, Metal Penetration, Metal Fusion, Gating System, Directional Solidification, Runout, Riser, Rattail, Buckle, Swell, Drop, Expansion Scab, Spall, Erosion Scab, Shakeout, Degating, Shift, Misrun, Cold Shut, Slag Inclusion, Nonmetallic Inclusion, Metal Filtration, Crack, Hot Tear

The main goal of every foundry operation is preventing casting defects and reducing the rate of rejected and scrapped castings. As in every manufacturing process, the foundry is dealing with quality issues on a daily basis, and it is very important to use the proper approach to this problem. In general, defects must be recorded and carefully analyzed for possible causes and corrective measures. Follow-up procedures have to be developed to prevent their reoccurrence in the future.

The following material describes the major categories of defects that are likely to occur in all castings, and suggests their causes and remedies. It needs to be highlighted that this division is very relative; each of the defects has multiple causes, which are interconnected and, in turn, may be the cause of other defects and may be attributed to the same foundry process operation.

10.1. Shrinkage-Related Defects

This type of defect occurs during the solidification of the casting and manifests itself as an internal concentrated shrinkage cavity or hole, or in the form of dispersed porosity or depressions on the surface. Figure 10-1 illustrates a typical shrinkage cavity in the thick section of the casting caused by a lack of feeding or improper gating and risering.

Figure 10-2 shows a shrinkage depression on the surface of a casting opposite from the existing riser. It is obvious that riser is not effective to ensure sufficient feeding.

Poor casting design involving abrupt changes of section thickness or isolated heavy sections, which cannot be fed, or the lack of adequate fillets produce this defect. Shrinkage also may occur due to incorrect pouring practice: pouring too cold or pouring too hot makes the riser system ineffective. Another shrinkage cause can be attributed to poor molding practice—sand mold wall movement under molten metal pressure.

Fig. 10-1. Typical shrinkage cavity in the thick section of the casting caused by lack of feeding or improper gating and risering.

Applying principles of directional solidification, usage of proper gating and risering, proper casting design, and appropriate molding and pouring practice can eliminate this defect. While Chapters 5 gives more details on casting risering and feeding aids practice, Chapter 11 contains some practical recommendations on casting design to eliminate the shrinkage related defects.

10.2. Gas-Related Defects

The defects in this category can be classified into blowholes and open blows, air and gas porosity. Pinholes, blisters and body scars as well as certain types of porosity are variations of gas holes. All these defects are caused to a great extent by low gas-passing tendency of the mold/core material, which may be due to poor venting, low permeability of the mold or core and/or improper design of the casting.

Low mold permeability is caused by finer grain size of the molding sand, higher clay content, higher moisture content, or by excessive ramming of the molds. Excessive or improper usage of some gas-producing additives in core and molding sands also can cause the occurrence of this defect. Improper gating can also cause some of the gas defects, as can improper melting practice that allows air and gas pickup.

Blowholes and open blows are the spherical, flattened or elongated cavities present inside the casting or on the surface or subsurface, as shown in Fig. 10-3. On the surface, they are called open blows and inside, they are called blowholes. Excess moisture in the mold and the core causes these types of defects. Due to the heat of the molten metal, the moisture is converted into steam, part of which when entrapped in the casting ends up as blow holes, or as open blows when they reach the surface. Apart from the presence of moisture, they can occur due to the insufficient mold/core venting and lower permeability of the mold.

Fig. 10-2. A shrinkage depression on the surface of the casting due to insufficient feeding (area surrounding bore to the right and opposite side from the riser).

Air and Gas Porosity (Fig.10-4). The atmospheric and other gases absorbed by the molten metal in the furnace, the ladle, and during the flow into the mold, may be trapped inside the casting and weaken it, if not allowed to escape. As the molten metal solidifies it loses temperature, which decreases the solubility of dissolved gases, allowing their evolution. While leaving the solidifying metal, very small-diameter pinholes may develop, showing the path of escape. These series of pinholes may cause the leakage of fluids under high operating pressures and lead to part failure.

The main reasons for this defect are: higher pouring temperatures, which increase the amount of gas absorbed; poor gating design such as straight sprue in nonpressurized gating, abrupt bends and other turbulence-causing practices in the gating, which increase the air aspiration; and finally, the low permeability of the mold itself. The remedies would be to choose the appropriate pouring temperature and improve gating practices by reducing the turbulence.

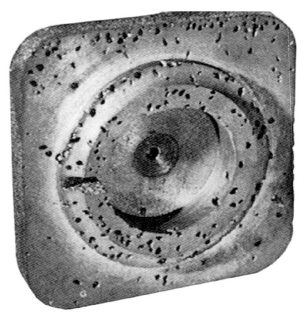

Fig. 10-3. Pinhole porosity on the surface of the casting due to excessive moisture in molding sand. [Source: Ref.1]

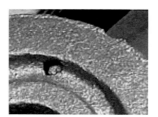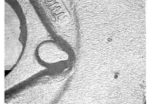

Fig. 10-4. Typical gas evolution cavities on the cope surface of castings.

10.3. Mold-Related Defects

These defects occur essentially because the molding materials are not of the required properties or are due to improper moldmaking methods. In addition, incorrect gating and risering, creating irregular metal flow or localized mold heating, contribute to these types of defects. These defects can be categorized as cuts and washes, metal penetration and fusion, runout, rattails and buckles, swell, and drops, etc.

Erosion, Cuts and Washes. Cuts and washes appear as rough spots and areas of excess metal. They are caused by the erosion of molding sand by the flowing molten metal. Inadequate mold strength or a high velocity of the molten metal may cause this. The former can be remedied by the proper choice of molding sand and using an appropriate molding method, and by altering the gating design to reduce the velocity of the molten metal, by increasing the size of ingates or by using multiple ingates.

An erosion scab is a defect usually occurring in the drag where the loosened sand has been eroded away by the motion of the molten metal, and has left a solid junction between the casting and the defect. If not deep, this defect sometimes can be removed by grinding usually leaving a solid surface. The erosion scab may also result in sand holes or sand inclusions.

There is a fine line of distinction between an erosion scab and a cut or wash. As far as molten metal flow alone is concerned, the two defects have the same cause. In the case of an erosion scab, there is not enough impingement to actually form a cut (in the absence of expansion), but is enough when expansion stresses exceed the strength of the sand.

Metal Penetration and Fusion. When the molten metal or metallic oxides enter the gaps between the sand grains, the result will be a rough casting surface. The main reason for this is that, either the grain size of the sand is too coarse, or no mold wash has been applied to the mold cavity, or soft ramming of the sand. Excessive sand permeability, high pouring temperature and improper gating and risering placement, which promote local overheating of the mold, can also cause this. Choosing an appropriate sand grain size, together with proper mold wash and gating ratio, should be able to eliminate this defect.

Fusion is another type of defect where metal or its oxides penetrate the mold, giving a brittle, glassy appearance on the casting surface. The main reason for this defect is that the clay in the molding sand is of lower refractoriness or that the pouring temperature is too high. The choice of an appropriate type and amount of bentonite would cure this defect.

Expansion defects represent a family of defects that include:

- *Rattails and buckles.* Rattails are irregular lines on the cast part surface. When the casting surface may have a number of V-shaped small crossing lines, they are called buckles. Buckles may occur by themselves or under an expansion scab.

- *Expansion scabs* are rough layers of metal connected to the main body of the casting by a vein of metal. Blackening scabs are a special form of a scab in which the defect is related to the mold or core coating rather than to the sand.

- *Spall or pull downs* are indentations in the cope surface of the casting. Depending on the time of formation, they may have the appearance of a buckle, rattail, shrink or blow.

The main cause for these expansion defects is poor expansion properties or low hot strength of the molding or core sand, or the metal pouring temperature is too high. Also, the foundry sand applied does not have enough carbonaceous material or cellulose to provide the necessary cushioning effect. The proper choice of foundry sand ingredients and the pouring temperature are the measures to reduce the rate of these defects. Nonuniform ramming, an improper type of wash or excessive wash, as well as casting design with abrupt section changes, are also responsible for this defect.

Swell is a local enlargement of a casting section due to mold wall movement under the influence of the metallostatic forces, created during molten metal pouring and solidification. As a result of mold wall movement, the casting dimensions may be off and the feeding requirements of the casting is increased, which should be taken care of by the proper choice of risering. Another cause of this may be faulty moldmaking procedures or plugged flask vents. Proper ramming and venting of the mold should correct this defect.

Drop. The dropping of loose molding sand or lumps, normally from the cope surface into the mold cavity, is responsible for this defect. This is essentially due to improper ramming of the cope flask (not uniformly rammed or soft rammed), or insufficient mold strength, or rough handling during mold assembly and transportation (Fig. 10-5).

Runout occurs during mold pouring when the molten metal leaks out of the mold resulting in an incomplete casting. This may be caused either due to improper mold making or because of faulty molding flask or pattern equipment, or insufficiently weighted and clamped molds.

Shift (Fig. 10-6) is a mismatch of the casting at the parting line. This is mostly due to misaligned or worn patterns (pins or locators) or coreboxes, or warped flask equipment. Corrective action must be directed to change worn, bent pins and bushings on flasks, and properly designing and maintaining patterns and coreboxes, and utilize chaplets in case of complex castings.

10.4. Pouring-Related Defects

The likely defects in this category are misruns, cold shuts and slag or other nonmetallic inclusions.

Misruns and Cold Shuts. A misrun occurs when the molten metal is unable to fill the mold cavity completely, thus leaving unfilled sections. A cold shut occurs when two metal streams meeting in the mold cavity do not fuse together properly, thus causing a discontinuity or weak spot in the casting (Fig. 10-7).

Sometimes, a condition leading to cold shuts can be observed when no sharp corners exist in a casting. These defects are caused, essentially, by the low fluidity of the molten metal, or that the section thickness of the casting is too small. The latter can be rectified by proper casting design. The remedy available is to increase the fluidity of the metal by changing the cast alloy composition or raising the pouring temperature. This defect can also be caused when the heat removal capacity is increased, such as in the case of green sand molds. The castings with a large surface area-to-volume ratio are more prone to these defects. This defect is also caused in molds that are not properly vented because of the backpressure of the gases. The remedies are basically affected by improving the mold design.

Slag and Other Nonmetallic Inclusions. During the melting process, flux is added to remove the undesirable oxides and impurities present in the metal. At the time of tapping, the slag should be properly removed from the ladle before the metal is poured into the mold. Otherwise, any slag entering the mold cavity will weaken the casting and also damage the surface of the casting. Another source of this defect is eroded molding or core sand or

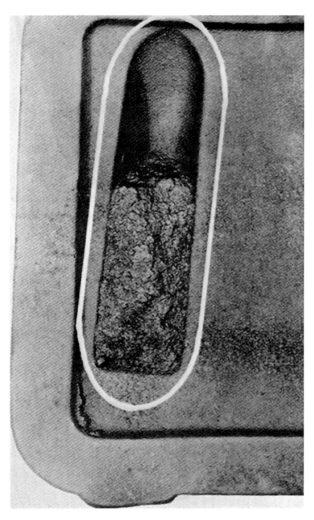

Fig. 10-5. Typical appearance of a drop on the casting surface. [Source: Ref.1]

Fig. 10-6. Shown is a cast iron pulley scrapped because of shift at the parting line resulting mostly from misaligned or worn patterns (pins or locators) or warped flask equipment.

Fig. 10-7. Cold shuts (laps) on the surfaces of these stainless steel elbows occurred because pouring temperature is too low.

Casting Defects and Prevention

mold/core coating. These inclusions, after cleaning, leave holes on the casting surface, as shown in Fig. 10-8.

This can be eliminated by proper melting, pouring and gating practice and utilization of some of the slag trapping methods discussed in Chapter 4, such as filters, runner extensions, etc.

10.5. Hot Tears and Broken or Cracked Castings

A hot tear is a crack in the casting, which occurs while it is still hot, or either solid or semisolid. Figure 10-9 illustrates a cracked casting caused by the core failing to collapse. In this case, internal core restrains metal contraction during solidification.

Primary causes are improper casting and pattern design, such as an abrupt change in section thickness and

design, which cause the mold or core to resist metal contraction, and the use of molding or core sand with poor collapsibility. Additional causes to this type of defect are gating and risering that prevent normal contraction, as well as interfering with flask bars, which also may restrain casting contraction. For more details on casting design optimization, see Chapter 11.

Broken or cracked castings refer to castings that have been broken or cracked as a result of mechanical impact during shakeout, degating and cleaning, or rough handling. This casting defect is mostly caused by an improper casting design that incorporates irregular sections or isolated heavy and light sections or combination of all the above, which require careful handling at shakeout, cleaning, finishing and heat-treating. Another possible cause is gating and risering design that doesn't provide proper break-off notches (Fig. 10-10), or a lack of adequate fillets.

Fig. 10-8. Typical slag/nonmetallic inclusions can be eliminated by proper melting, pouring and gating practice and filters installations.

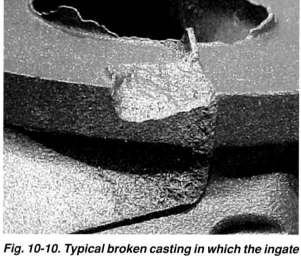

Fig. 10-10. Typical broken casting in which the ingate did not have proper break-off notches and lack of adequate fillets.

Fig. 10-9. Hot tear (cracked casting) caused by internal core failure to collapse. In this case, the core restrains metal contraction. [Source: Ref.1]

Fig. 10-11. Early shakeout of this gray iron casting broke the gate into the casting. Source: Ref.1.

Early, rough shakeout of these castings can also break the gates into the castings while they are hot and weak, as shown in Fig. 10-11.

Additionally, poor collapsibility of molding sand or core material due to excessive hot or dry compressive strength or a very hard-rammed mold may also produce this type of defect.

As seen, any irregularity in the foundry process that causes defects in castings may in many cases, be minimized or prevented with proper gating, molding or melting practice. More detailed information on casting defect analysis can be found in AFS publications on this topic [References 2-5].

References

1. Analysis of Casting Defects, American Foundry Society, Schaumburg, IL, 1974, reprinted 1999, 2007.

2. American Foundry Society, *Casting Defects Handbook: Iron & Steel,* George Goodrich, Technical Editor, American Foundry Society, Schaumburg, IL (2008)

3. American Foundry Society, *Casting Defects Handbook: Aluminum & Aluminum Alloys,* David Neff, Technical Editor, American Foundry Society, Schaumburg, IL (2011)

4. American Foundry Society, *Casting Defects Handbook: Copper & Copper Base Alloys,* David Neff, Technical Editor, American Foundry Society, Schaumburg, IL (2010)

5. International Committee of Foundry Technical Associations, *International Atlas of Casting Defects,* English Edition, translated and edited by Mervin T. Rowley, American Foundry Society, Schaumburg, IL, 1974, reprinted 1999, 2007.

Review Questions

10.1 Explain shrinkage-related casting defects.

10.2 Explain how shrinkage cavities or shrinkage impressions are formed in a casting and the measures undertaken to prevent their occurrence.

10.3 Describe the casting defects that may be caused by improper gating system design. Name at least three defects.

10.4 Discuss any three common green sand mold-related casting defects and give their causes and remedies.

10.5 Give reasons for the occurrence of the following mold-related casting defects: shift, runout, and drop.

10.6 Give reasons for the occurrence of each of the following casting defects: cold shut and misrun; blow hole and pinhole porosity.

10.7 Describe the various defects that are likely to be caused in sand castings because of higher pouring temperatures.

10.8 Give reasons for the occurrence and prevention of each of the following casting defects in sand casting: metal penetration and fusion; rattails, cuts and washes.

10.9 Discuss why hot tears appear in the casting and how to prevent them.

10.10 Explain possible causes of broken castings.

10.11 Explain how slag and nonmetallic inclusions can be prevented by proper melting practice, gating system design and liquid metal filtration.

DESIGN OPTIMIZATION FOR SAND MOLDING

Objectives

Optimizing the design of a part for its suitability for sand molding helps to reduce the cost of the casting as well as improve its quality. After studying this chapter, the reader should be able to:

- Design castings to improve the economics of sand molding
- Design castings to reduce possible defects
- Design handling provisions for castings to facilitate during production
- Discuss the use of Finite Element Analysis (FEA) methods to optimize the shape of the casting

Keywords

Sand Mold, Permanent Mold, Mold Cavity, Casting Geometry, Casting Design, Design Optimization, Sand Molding, Casting, Parting Line, Core, Pattern, Casting Defect, Boss, Shrinkage, Distortion, Cast Alloy, Tooling, Graphite Precipitation, Pinhole, Blowhole, Solidification, Cope, Drag, Flask, Hot Tear, Coreprint, Gray Iron, Ductile Iron, Steel, Chills, Fins, Restrained Contraction, Deformation, Warping, Hot Tear, Diecasting, Venting, Finite Element Analysis, FEA, Mesh, Meshing, Residual Stresses, Stress Analysis, Stress Contour, Dimensional Accuracy, Heat Flow, Fluid Flow Analysis.

In designing a casting, the responsibility of the designer includes much more than just ensuring proper functioning of the cast component. Optimal casting design must allow the production of sound, defect-free cast parts. Consideration for economy in molding procedures should also be incorporated in the development of the casting design. Furthermore, other foundry operations, such as finishing, or the elimination of finishing where possible, in whole or in part (i.e., assembly of one part with another part) and economical servicing during the life of the casting, must also be taken into account.

Accordingly, the casting design process should be considered under the following categories:

- Designing for economical molding
- Designing casting defect prevention
- Designing to aid handling of castings

The design rules applied to cast components are differentiated by the type of cast alloy used. For example, different rules are applied to iron versus steel, or even between gray iron versus ductile iron castings. The difference is laid out in the casting alloy's specific behavior during solidification. Steel is prone to shrinkage and hot tearing, while high-CE gray iron, due to extensive graphite precipitation during solidification, may not show any shrinkage at all.

While some of the castings' design basics are common for many casting methods, special consideration should also be given to their specifics, capabilities and limitations. For instance, a cast part intended to be made by permanent mold casting or diecasting, employing rigid metal mold/die, which restricts alloy contraction, may cause hot tearing or distortion. As a result, different rules need to be adopted than those for a sand casting design.

11.1 Designing for Economical Molding

11.1.1. Parting Line Determination

The parting line determines the position of the casting in the mold, and its location depends upon the shape of the casting. Selecting the best parting line should be based on several considerations such as: providing proper metal flow into the mold cavity; minimizing or eliminating cores, which would simplify molding; providing sufficient core support and venting, and preventing risk of casting defects.

The simplest parting line is one that runs through the centerline of the casting, as shown in Fig. 11-1. The optimal solution is to design a casting with a parting line that is straight, or as nearly straight as possible. Complex parting lines increase the cost of tooling and the cast component.

As an example, Fig. 11-2 shows the possible redesigning of a part in order to simplify the parting line. In the original design (Fig. 11-2(a)), the hub and arms are located in different planes. To make this casting, a complicated and costly tooling will be required. By modifying the casting design, as shown in Fig. 11-2(b), the parting line becomes straight and, thus, simplifies the molding procedure and, eventually, reduces the cost.

When an irregular parting line results in a deep mold pocket, it may be more economical to redesign the pattern equipment and change to a straight parting line involving the use of cores.

11.1.2. Core Positioning

Cores are placed in the mold to provide castings with contours, cavities and passages, which are not possible to obtain by normal molding. In case of any back drafts, cores are used so that the pattern can be withdrawn from the mold.

Frequently, a minor change in the casting design may economize the production cost by eliminating or optimizing cores. Figure 11-3(a) shows an original design, which required a dry sand core to form the interior of the casting. By redesigning the casting as shown in Fig. 11-3(b), a green sand core was substituted for the dry sand core, thus achieving the economy. Such a change in design may alter the parting line from straight to irregular, and the cope may contain either a cavity or a hanging sand pocket, but it is still cost-effective.

When the use of cores cannot be avoided, the designer should strive to make them as simple as possible (in the interest of economy) by using simple surfaces, which are easy to produce. An example of such a core is the massive coreprint presented in Fig. 11-4, which is optimized.

Also, the cores must be properly supported so that they do not become displaced during mold assembly and pouring. The arrangement shown in Fig. 11-5(a), for example, is not recommended because the left core has only one coreprint. This coreprint

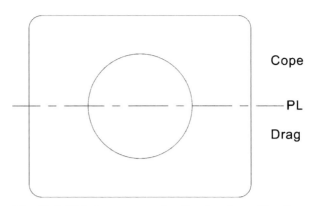

Fig. 11-1. This is an example of a simple parting line.

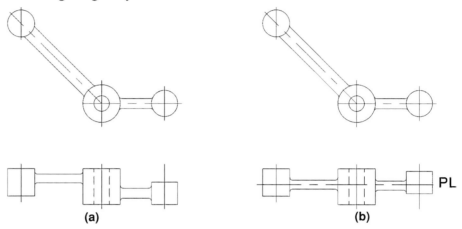

Fig. 11-2. Parting line modification: (a)-original design; (b)-casting design is modified and parting line is a straight line.

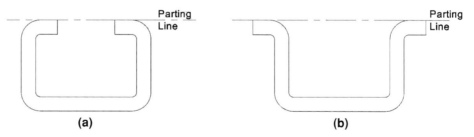

Fig. 11-3. Eliminating a dry sand core by modifying the draft angle: (a) original design, incorporating dry sand core; (b) design in which a green sand core was substituted for the dry sand core.

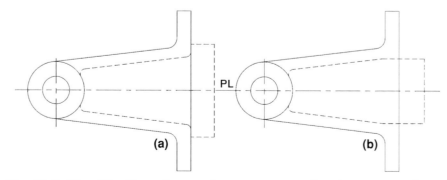

Fig. 11-4. Simplification of core shapes, representing two approaches: (a) expensive; (b) economical, in which coreprint is optimized.

cannot be extended due to space limitation, and chaplets are required. In this case, combining two cores must provide further support, eliminating the need for chaplets. The new core (Fig. 11-5(b)) has additional coreprints, which prevent core displacement during mold assembly and pouring.

If several cores are needed, they are best positioned on the same plane and have identical parting lines, as shown in Fig. 11-6.

In general, cores should be avoided or minimized to reduce the cost associated with their production and additional shakeout operation. Furthermore, placement of a core would diminish the dimensional accuracy of the assembled mold and, eventually, of the casting.

11.1.3. Boss Positioning

Bosses are frequently used to increase the sectional thickness of housings and the like, in order to provide longer bolt or tap holes, or to improve the strength of certain parts of the casting. This may be satisfactory if the axis of the cylindrical boss is parallel to the direction in which the pattern is drawn out of the mold, or if the centerline of the boss is in the parting plane. When this is not the case, the boss on the pattern must be loose, and the skilled technique of molding a loose pattern must be employed. The section, shown in Fig. 11-7(a), illustrates the positioning of a boss well below a flange whose upper surface is chosen as a parting line. To make this casting, a loose piece pattern or an external core is required to permit removal of the pattern from the mold. In both cases, the production of such a casting, as shown, will involve more labor and cost. In addition, accurate positioning of the core is difficult; any shifting of the core results in surface irregularities and weakens dimensional accuracy. This solution may be appropriate for low

volume production run. A somewhat less complicated and more economical design in Fig. 11-7(b) extends the boss to the flange, eliminating the possible undercut and the need for a loose piece pattern or external core. This makes this pattern design suitable for high volume machine molding.

11.1.4. Simple Economics

Generally, a two-part mold with one parting line is simpler and more economical, compared to a three-part mold, which has two parting lines and requires the

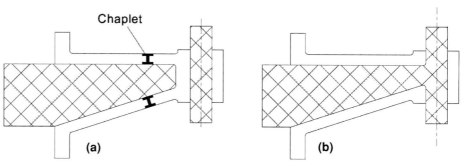

Fig. 11-5. Providing proper core support: (a) incorrect design, central core has only one coreprint, which cannot be extended due to space limitation, and chaplets are required; (b) correct design, by combining two cores, the new design has three coreprints, which prevent core displacement during mold assembly and pouring, eliminating need for chaplets.

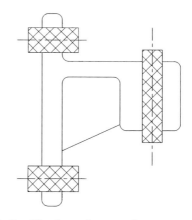

Fig. 11-6. Positioning of several cores on the same parting line.

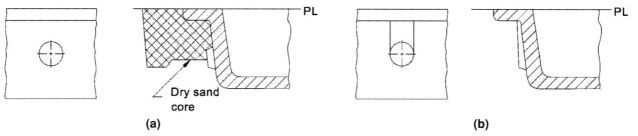

Fig. 11-7. Modification of bosses: (a) boss is located below the flange and a loose piece pattern or external core is required to remove the pattern from the mold; (b) boss is extended to the flange and no extra core is required to make the casting.

---

use of a cheek (intermediate flask). But when the part configuration, as shown in Fig. 11-8(a), is necessary, it may be desirable to modify the molding procedure by providing an external ring core (Fig. 11-8(b)) to avoid the intermediate flask. But this is also is an expensive alternative. The best choice would be to redesign the casting by eliminating the bottom flange, as shown in Fig. 11-8(c), which makes it unnecessary to use the external core and thus is more economical.

11.2. Designing for Casting Defect Prevention

11.2.1. Shrinkage

As discussed earlier, the main reason for shrinkage defects is volumetric contraction, both in the liquid and solid state. The solidification process progresses from thin to thick sections; when the casting is not properly fed during solidification, shrinkage usually appears in heavy sections or at junctions of walls (hot spot), as shown in Fig. 11-9.

The best way to avoid volumetric shrinkage is to design a casting that has no isolated hot spots that cannot be properly fed. With this purpose in mind, the designer should try to place and proportion members and their intersections in such a way as to establish a positive temperature gradient. The temperature gradient should be at its lowest point farthest away from the riser, but gradually increase toward it, ensuring directional solidification. The ideal directional solidification pattern is solidification that progresses from thin to thick sections and then to the riser. Tapered design is one of the simplest ways to enhance directional solidification and finally prevent shrinkage occurrence.

If the casting part design cannot prevent shrinkage-related defects, various foundry techniques such as the use of chills or fins, or feeding aids may be used.

The shrinkage problem is particularly severe in junctions, where a concentration of metal always occurs at the point where two walls of equal thickness come together. Such a concentration is reduced, however, if one of the walls is made thinner. That is why, in steel castings for example, ribs are always made thinner than the wall in the ratio:

$$\frac{\text{Rib thickness}}{\text{Wall thickness}} = 0.6 \text{ to } 0.8$$

A rib, which enters a wall at an angle, gives a larger concentration of metal than one that enters perpendicularly. This design should, therefore, be avoided where possible. Commonly, five types of junctions, which are represented

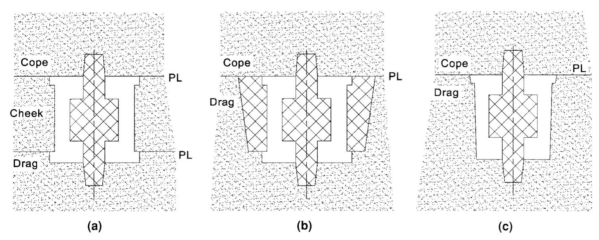

(a)   **(b)**   **(c)**

Fig. 11-8. Example of cast component redesign to simplify the molding process and avoid three-flask molding: (a) with a cheek (intermediate flask); (b) with the external core; (c) two-part molding, which makes use of the external core unnecessary and, thus, more economical.

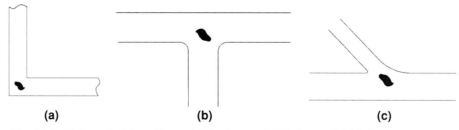

(a)   **(b)**   **(c)**

Fig. 11-9. Hot spot at junctions: (a) L-shape; (b) T-shape; (c) Y-shape.

by the letters L, T, V, X and Y, are used in any part design. In designing a casting, complex junctions like X, V, Y and X-T junctions should be simplified to T or L junctions if possible.

Examples of junction at L sections are shown in Fig. 11-10. It shows that using moderate radii at the corners eliminates defects. Note that a large radius may lead to a bigger hot spot.

Practical applications of these recommendations are illustrated in the examples of a steel flange casting, thick hub steel wheel and ductile iron cast compressor frame (housing), shown in Figs. 11-11, 11-12 and 11-13.

Figure 11-11 shows a typical junction of a cylindrical opening with a flange, where the original design in Fig. 11-11(a) is compared with recommended practice in Fig. 11-11c.

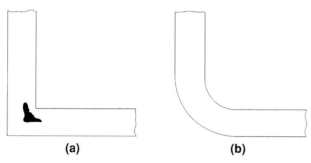

(a)   (b)

Fig. 11-10. Typical L-shape junction shows how the addition of radii on inside and outside corners eliminates shrinkage and stress concentration: (a) poor design, when shrinkage and hot tears may occur at the sharp corner; (b) recommended design.

The hubs of wheels are other places where the concentration of metal is likely to occur, as shown in Fig. 11-12a. An acceptable practice is to core the hub as in Fig. 11-12(b), which is better but still likely to cause shrinkage defects, if no feeding elements or local cooling is available. The best design would be as shown in Fig. 11-12(c) where the excess metal is completely removed by applying radii on the inside and outside corners.

Another example (Fig. 11-13) shows how the redesign of the massive elements in a ductile iron cast frame can eliminate defects. The modification shown in Fig. 11-13(b) is comparatively better, but venting of core gases may be a problem. This is completely taken care of in the design shown in Fig. 11-13(c). Rapid cooling by the use of chills should be provided in the sections where massive elements are inevitable.

11.2.2. Distortions

Internal stresses appear in the casting walls when shrinkage is restricted because of the resistance of the mold or core elements, or the action of the adjacent walls. Increased internal stresses make the casting warp and may lead to the development of cracks.

Shrinkage stresses develop during the cooling when the metal loses its plasticity within 500–600°C (930–1110°F) for cast iron, and 600–700°C (1110–1290°F) for steel. At higher temperatures, the change in dimensions is readily compensated for by the plastic flow of the metal and, thus, the shrinkage manifests itself only in the thinning of the walls.

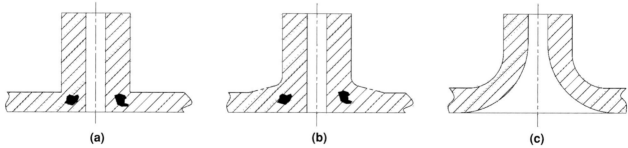

(a)   (b)   (c)

Fig. 11-11. Reducing metal concentration at the joints of a cast steel flange: (a) poor design; (b) improved, but not recommended; (c) recommended design.

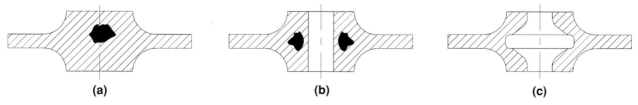

(a)   (b)   (c)

Fig. 11-12. Avoiding concentration of metal in the cast steel hubs of wheels: (a) original design; (b) redesigned with the use of core, but not recommended unless additional local cooling or feeding elements are available; (c) recommended design.

In the box-shaped casting (Fig. 11-14), the internal partition formed by cores cools at a slower rate than the horizontal walls, because of the core sand being heated from all sides. While cooling below the temperature at which metal passes from the plastic to the elastic state, the partition material hardens and contracts, and as a result, it undergoes tension. If the tension exceeds the strength of the vertical walls, they are likely to warp and introduce distortions in the casting.

Warping will increase in the casting with uneven section thickness and internal core resistance, as shown in Fig. 11-15. In this example, the thinner walls would have cooled down very quickly leaving the thicker wall still in the plastic state. When the thinner walls contract due to solid shrinkage, this contraction is resisted by the internal sand core, causing hot tearing at the joints with the thicker ribs.

11.2.3. Hot Tearing

Hot tears are formed in castings because of the differential cooling rates and the low strength of metal at higher temperatures. This, in fact, is an extension of warping.

In wheels or big gear wheels where the rims are connected to the hub through spokes, hot tears are likely to occur in the areas where the spokes join the rim, as shown in the design in Fig. 11-16(a). Making the spokes curved and having them occur in odd numbers, as shown in Fig. 11-16(b), ensures that the restraining force acts in only one direction, making the wheel less susceptible to hot tearing.

Based on this discussion, the following design rules, which would reduce the shrinkage-related stresses and the resulting distortions and hot tearing, may be laid down:

- Casting walls should preferably be of uniform thickness
- Internal walls of the casting, cooling under conditions of slow heat transfer, should have smaller cross sections to accelerate their solidification
- Transition between casting walls of different thicknesses should be smooth, with no abrupt changes
- Local metal accumulations and massive elements should be avoided, if possible

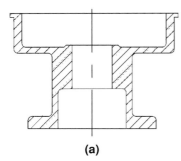 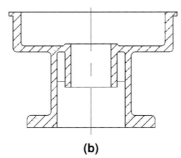 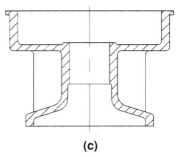

(a)   (b)   (c)

Fig. 11-13. Concentration of metal in a ductile iron cast frame (a); the first modification of design; (b) where complicated venting of core gases is a problem; and (c) final design, which has solved the problem.

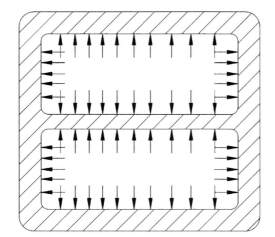

Fig. 11-14. Restrained contraction in the box-shaped casting resulted in a high level of residual stresses and distortion in sand castings.

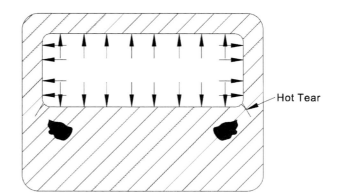

Fig. 11-15. Warping and hot tearing due to uneven section thickness in the sand casting resulted from contraction restrained by internal sand core.

- Sections where casting walls join massive elements should be gradually thickened towards the latter or reinforced with ribs

11.2.4. Gas (Blowholes and Pinholes)

The internal cavities of the castings, formed by cores, should be designed to permit the escape of gases evolving from the cores when the molten metal is poured. Internal cores, which are relatively thin and long, are also likely to pose difficulties in cleaning. Sand burned into core holes, and fins or veins, are very difficult to remove when they are hard to reach. Providing access holes or cleanout holes, allows the venting of core gases as well as permits the core sand to be removed.

For example, an unsatisfactory casting design is illustrated in Fig. 11-17(a). The gases accumulating in the upper side parts of the core do not have ways to be evacuated from the mold and may form blowholes and pinholes. This problem may be partially solved by making small vent holes (plugged afterwards, if necessary) for the escape of gases, as shown in Fig. 11-17(b). The redesigned vaulted shape of the upper portion of the casting, as in Fig. 11-17(c), would be the best way to ensure the escape of gases through the coreprints.

Another way of solving the problem is to change the position of the casting in regard to the parting plane. For example, in Fig. 11-18(a), where the casting is located in the cope, the core gases will be poorly vented. By locating the casting in the drag, as in Fig. 11-18(b), the core gases can be properly vented through the coreprint in the cope.

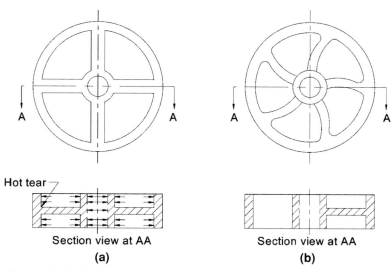

Fig. 11-16. Reducing residual stresses and hot tearing by making curved spokes in wheels: (a) original design with straight spokes—hot tears are likely at the areas where spokes join the rim; (b) modified design with curved spokes making the wheel less susceptible to hot tearing.

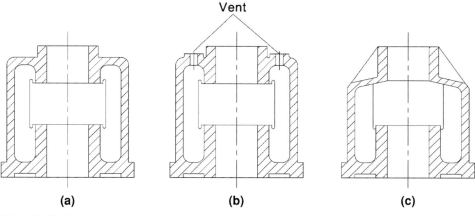

Fig. 11-17. Escape provision for core gases in a large gray iron housing: (a) with no passages for gas to escape from the side internal cavities of the core; (b) with small vent holes, requiring further plugging; (c) redesigned vaulted shape of the upper portion of the casting, allowing gas to escape freely through the coreprints.

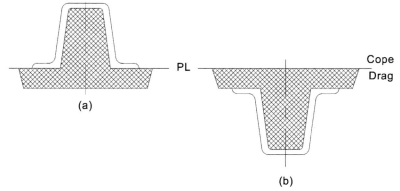

Fig. 11-18. Core gas venting by repositioning the casting regarding parting line: (a) casting is located in the cope; (b) casting is located in the drag.

Design Optimization for Sand Molding

11.3. Designing to Aid Handling

It is necessary to take into account the handling and transporting of castings, and to supply provisions for mounting a casting in the machine tool during the finishing process. Also, accidents may occur if large castings slip from the hitch because of improper hoisting surfaces.

When a casting is to be machined to a close tolerance, it is often desirable to do as much finishing as possible without removing the part from the machine tool. Figure 11-19 shows a chucking extension on a casting, which will permit the entire casting to be machined on a lathe in one setting, with the last operation being the cutoff of this extension.

Similarly, castings with tapered sides are difficult to chuck in a lathe and, if possible, should be provided with a holding surface such as pads or flats, as shown in Fig. 11-20. These flats also aid in safer hoist positioning during part transportation by crane or monorail, preventing possible slipping of the hoist.

11.4. Designing with Finite Element Analysis (FEA)

Today, casting design may be successfully optimized with a number of commercial finite element analysis (FEA) software programs. These programs allow thermal and structural stress analysis, minimization of draft angle, deflection and weight of the casting to be performed. Using FEA along with solidification modeling is one of the fastest and most reliable methods to simulate and predict defects in a solidified casting, at the design stage. Defects such as hot spots, cracks, pinholes, and areas with residual stress concentration (which can result in warpage) should be properly addressed before the first casting is made. By interacting with the foundry during the design stage, the designer can evaluate the potential problems and take remedial measures to reduce defect occurrence.

Finite element analysis (FEA) is a numerical analysis procedure that can be applied to a large class of engineering problems that otherwise would be very difficult to solve using classical analytical techniques. The FEA modeling process allows for discretizing (meshing) the intricate geometries into small fundamental volumes, called finite elements. It is then possible to write the governing equations and material properties for these elements. These equations are then assembled by taking proper care of the constraints and loading, which results in a set of equations. When solved, they give the results that describe the behavior of the original complex body being analyzed.

A typical example for using FEA is shown in Fig. 11-21. This is an aluminum piston for an automotive engine, which needs to be analyzed. The geometry of the piston is difficult to solve by the closed form solutions, and, hence, the need to adopt an approximate method. The finite element method (FEM) of discretizing (meshing) the part is shown in Fig. 11-22. When solved in the finite element solver, the resultant stress contours in the part are shown in Fig. 11-23. Different colors indicate the level of the stress with red representing the highest stress. Notice the high value of stress patterns that are close to the hole and in the part, due to the acting forces.

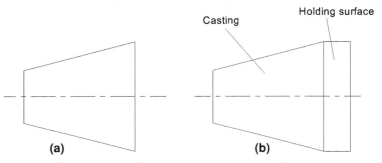

Fig. 11-20. Provision of holding surface for handling castings with tapered surfaces.

Fig. 11-21. An example of an aluminum piston from an automotive engine that requires the use of FEA software.

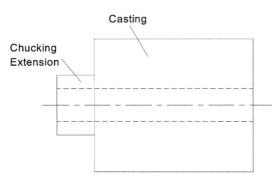

Fig. 11-19. Chucking extension permits the entire part to be machined in one setting.

Application of FEA is not limited to mechanical systems alone, but to a range of engineering problems such as:

- Stress analysis
- Dynamic analysis
- Deformation studies
- Fluid flow analysis
- Heat flow analysis
- Seepage analysis
- Magnetic flux studies
- Acoustic analysis

A large number of commercial, as well as free, software for the application of finite elements is available.

Fig. 11-22. The discretized (meshed) piston shown in Fig. 11-21.

Fig. 11-23. Stress contours in the casting shown in Fig. 11-22 due to the application of FEA software.

Generally, to solve a complex problem, a very powerful computer is needed. However, with the new developments in microprocessors, it is possible to carry out such analyses in most of the present-day desktop computers. With FEA software, it is possible to try a number of alternative designs before actually going for a prototype manufacture. For example, in the case of designing a cast part for diecasting, it is possible to perform stress, heat and fluid flow analyses, and, based on this knowledge, optimize casting geometry to prevent possible defects.

References

1. Marek, C.T.; *Fundamentals in the Production and Design of Castings*, John Wiley, New York, 1963.

2. Caine, J.B.; *Design of Ferrous Castings*, American Foundrymen's Society, Des Plaines, 1963.

3. *Metal Handbook, Vol. 15*, "Casting;" ASM International, Metals Park, 2008.

4. Johns, R.; *Casting Design;* American Foundrymen's Society, Des Plaines, 1987.

5. Doyle, L.E., *Manufacturing Processes and Materials for Engineers*, Prentice Hall, Englewood Cliffs, 1969.

6. Schleg, F.P.; *Technology of Metalcasting*, American Foundry Society, Des Plaines, 2003.

Review Questions

11.1 State any three considerations for choosing a proper parting line in sand mold castings.

11.2 In sand castings, apart from the stress concentration, is there any reason for rounding of the corners? Explain.

11.3 Are internal corners more prone to solidification shrinkage than the external corners? Explain.

11.4 Describe problems caused by bosses in sand castings. Explain the methods available to solve them.

11.5 Explain the formation of shrinkage cavities in castings. Discuss the design methods used for eliminating them based on the example of a flanged casting.

11.6 If possible, most of the casting should be in the drag instead of the cope. Is this statement correct? Explain your answer.

11.7 Define the considerations for choosing or avoiding cores in sand casting.

11.8 Discuss the measures a cast part designer takes to ensure proper gas evacuation from the core.

11.9 Discuss what provisions should be made to ease casting finishing and machining.

11.10 Explain the Finite Element Analysis (FEA) application in cast part design.

11.11 Examine the components shown in Fig. 11-24. Decide the optimal parting line, cope and drag position and core location in sand molding of these components. Discuss how these castings can be redesigned to improve the casting quality.

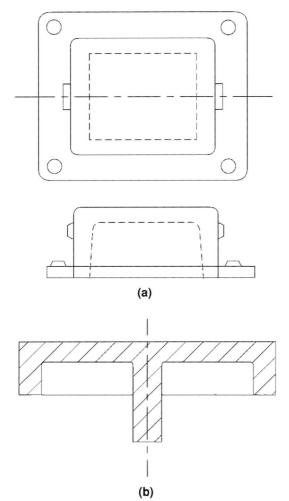

(a)

(b)

Fig. 11-24. Examples of castings referred to in Review Question 11.11: (a) gray iron housing with two bosses and hollow internal cavity; (b) ductile iron pump plunger.

11.12 Review the castings show in Fig. 11-25 and assume they are steel castings in sand molds. Discuss what types of defects are likely to occur. Suggest possible redesigns for these castings.

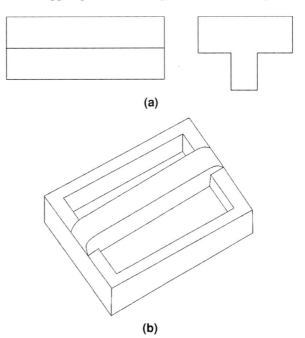

(a)

(b)

Fig. 11-25. Shown are examples of castings that are mentioned in Review Question 11.12.

11.13 Figure 11-26 shows some cases of hot tear formation in sand castings. Review and discuss how the hot tear formed and advise what measures can be applied to reduce the hot tear's occurrence.

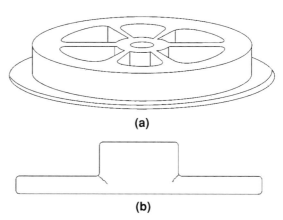

(a)

(b)

Fig. 11-26. Examples of castings that are prone to hot tear formation: (a) aluminum wheel; (b) cast steel blank for gear, as mentioned in Review Question 11.13.

RAPID PROTOTYPING AND RAPID MANUFACTURING IN METALCASTING

Objectives

Rapid prototyping (RP) has become an important area of metalcasting in the past decade, to decrease the product development time and reduce costs. After studying this chapter the reader should be able to:

- Identify the concept of rapid prototyping and its significance
- Describe the major steps involved in the layered manufacturing process
- Compare the range of processes available for rapid prototype development and their applications in metalcasting
- Determine the need for rapid tooling and methods to be employed for this purpose
- Explain rapid manufacturing and its capabilities

Keywords

Sand, Sand Casting, Investment Casting, Diecasting, Sand Mold, Permanent Mold Casting, Pressure Diecasting, Nonferrous Alloy, Nonferrous Alloy, Mold Life, Pattern, Corebox, Machining, Grinding, Rapid Prototyping, RP, Layered Manufacturing, LM, Computer-Aided Design, CAD, Standard Triangular Language, STL, Stereolithography, SL, Stereolithography Apparatus, SLA, Photo-Curable Resin, Laser, Ultraviolet Laser, Build Platform, Curing, UV Oven, Selective Laser Sintering, SLS, Powder, Electron Beam Melting, EBM, Laminated Object Manufacturing, LOM, Paper, Heated Roller, Fused Deposition Modeling, FDM, Plastic Filament, Extrusion Nozzle, Build Material, Support Material, Water-Soluble Support Structure, 3-D Printing, 3-DP,Inkjet Printer, Binder, Glue, Laser Engineering Net Shaping, LENS, Metal Powder, Direct Metal Deposition Tooling, Rapid Tooling, RT, Direct Tooling, Tool-Less Process, Pattern-Less Sand Molding, Lost Paper, NASA, Ceramic Shell, Heat Sink, Rapid Manufacturing, RM, Direct Metal Deposition, DMD, Computer Numerical Control, CNC, Rapid Solidification Process, RSP, Rapid Casting Technology, RCT.

12.1. Rapid Prototyping (RP)

Process Overview

Developing a prototype as a solid representation of the part, without all of the mechanical properties required for the actual product, has been used in the manufacturing industry with wood, wax or clay models. The term *rapid prototyping* (RP) is normally used in the current day to specify a series of processes utilizing specialized equipment, software and materials that are capable of using three-dimensional computer-aided design (3-D CAD) data (as well as 3-D scan data, such as from a coordinate measuring machine), to directly fabricate geometrically complex objects. Sometimes, these processes are also called additive processes since the material is added, compared to the conventional processes of material removal that are generally used for prototyping. The first commercial system was demonstrated at the 1987 AUTOFACT show in Detroit utilizing the stereolithography (SL) process. Though the initial demonstration had a number of limitations, a large number of processes and materials have been developed since then. As a result, this process has been widely adopted by a majority of manufacturing industries. The use of these processes drastically reduced the development process of a new product with significant, cost saving.

Rapid prototyping technologies are generally based upon a layered manufacturing (LM) concept. In this method (Fig. 12-1), a 3-D model of the object as a CAD file is transferred into the system and then sliced into equidistant layers with parallel horizontal planes. The system then generates trajectories for the material to be added in each layer by the RP machine. The sacrificial supporting layers are also simultaneously generated to keep the unconnected layers in proper position. The resultant separate cross-sectional layers of very small thickness, when assembled (glued) together, will form the final required object.

There are a number of ways the 3-D CAD data can be represented. However, the STL (standard triangular language or stereolithography language) format is

---

most common and is generally supported by all the RP equipment. Each physical layer from above is then deposited and fused to the previous layer, using one of the many available deposition and fusion technologies.

Traditional computer numerical control (CNC) machining can also be considered as rapid prototyping, though it requires custom fixtures and has inherent geometric limitations. In contrast to additive RP processes, it is subtractive prototyping and, still, can be effective in many RP applications. For instance, utilizing hard plastic instead of metal for making prototype patterns may reduce machining time up to 50%, because of superior machinability.

Advantages

- Product development time and cost will be greatly reduced compared to the conventional prototyping techniques used
- By reducing the prototype development time, the total product design cycle will be shorter, thereby getting products to the market sooner
- Communications between marketing, engineering, manufacturing and purchasing will be enhanced due to the availability of physical prototypes
- It will be possible to present the physical model at critical design reviews, thereby making the decision process more accurate
- In some cases, it will be possible to perform functional prototype testing before committing to the actual tooling
- By making available an accurate physical prototype, it will be possible to generate precise production tooling
- Utilizing RP technology in metalcasting for direct mold and coremaking from CAD files, without the need of tooling will drastically reduce the lead time and cost of the produced castings

Limitations

- The initial cost of the equipment is relatively high
- The build material choices for different processes are limited in terms of their properties
- In some cases only plastic materials can be used

Applications

Use of rapid prototyping will enable foundry personnel to:

- Check the feasibility of new design concepts
- Make functional models, with testing limited to the model material
- Conduct market tests/evaluation
- Create tooling for metalcasting (investment, permanent mold, die) injection molding, and some metal forming processes
- Build sand or metallic mold and core prototypes for sand, permanent mold and diecasting
- Fabricate a master pattern for silicone rubber and epoxy molds
- Manufacture many exact copies of models, simultaneously

The current trend of the industrial applications of RP is given in Fig. 12-2. As can be seen, tooling (almost 30%) is one of the major areas of RP applications, compared to the other applications. Also, the percentage of functional

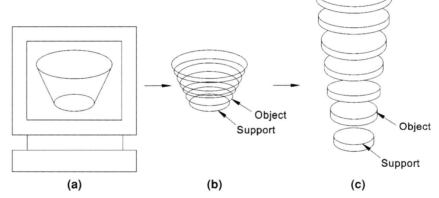

(a) **(b)** **(c)**

Fig. 12-1. Concept of layered manufacturing; (a) shape data as input in the CAD system; (b) CAD model is sliced into layers; (c) each layer is then deposited, starting from the bottom until the model is completed.

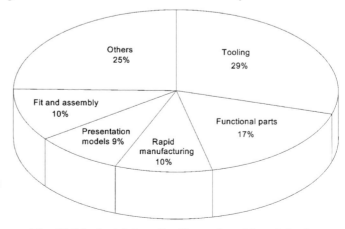

Fig. 12-2.Industrial applications of rapid prototyping.

parts is increasing over the years, with the development of the newer materials and processes.

12.2. Rapid Prototyping Technologies

The typical steps involved in all current RP techniques can be summarized as follows:

1. A CAD model is constructed and then converted to STL (standard triangular language) format to input into the software for creating the slice data.

2. The software processes the STL file by creating sliced layers of the model. The resolution of the built model depends upon the layer thickness.

3. The RP device creates the first layer of the physical model. The model is then lowered by the one layer thickness, and the process is repeated, layer by layer, until the model is completed.

4. The model and any supports are removed; the surface of the model is then finished and cleaned.

A large number of RP techniques have been developed in the past few years. However, the major technologies commercially in use in metalcasting are:

- Stereolithography (SLA)
- Laminated Object Manufacturing (LOM)
- Fused Deposition Modeling (FDM)
- Selective Laser Sintering (SLS)
- 3-D Printing (3-DP)
- Laser Engineering Net Shaping (LENS)
- Direct Metal Deposition (DMD)

A comparative evaluation of several RP processes is given in Table 12-1.

Table. 12-1. *Summary of Some Rapid Prototyping Technologies.*

System	Max. build size, mm (in.)	Overage Dimensional Accuracy ± mm (±in.)	Materials	Advantages	Disadvantages
Stereo lithography	1524×762×508 (60×30×20)	0.127(0.005)	Liquid photosensitive resins	High accuracy, medium range of materials, large build size, smooth surface finish	High cost process, support structures needed, post cure required
Selective Laser Sintering	550×550×750 (22×22×30)	0.254(0.01)	Nylon based materials, elastomer, metal-based powders, coated foundry sand, waxes and composites	Wide range of materials, fast build speed	High cost process, rough surface finish, limited build size
Fused Deposition Modeling	915×610×915 (36×24×36)	0.127(0.005)	ABS, elastomer and wax	Good accuracy, functional parts, medium range of materials	Rough surface finish, support structure needed
Laminated Object Modeling	815×560×508 (33×24×21)	0.1(0.004)	Paper foil, metal sheets	High accuracy, medium build size, fast build speed	Limited range of materials, support removal necessary, low part strength
3-D Printing	4000×2000×1000 (158×79×40)	0.1(0.004)	Powder of photopolymers, ceramics, composites and metals	Good accuracy, wide range of materials, unlimited part complexity, very large build size, low cost process, very fast build speed	Rough surface finish, low part strength
Direct Metal Desposition	1041×1981×610 (41×78×24)	0.08(0.003)	Powder of metals and alloys	High accuracy, capability of making large functional parts and restoration of worn/damaged components	Limited part complexity, low volume production runs, relatively slow and costly process

12.2.1. Stereolithography (SLA)

The most commonly used process for rapid prototyping is stereolithography or photolithography. These systems build shapes, using light to selectively solidify photo-curable resins. A stereolithography machine (Fig. 12-3) converts 3-D CAD data of physical objects into vertical stacks of slices. A low-power ultraviolet laser beam is then carefully traced across a vat of photo curable liquid polymer, producing a single layer of solidified resin—the first slice of the object under construction. The laser beam (UV helium-cadmium or argon) is guided across the surface (by servo-controlled galvanometer mirrors), drawing a cross-sectional pattern in the x-y plane to form a solid section.

The initial layer is then lowered, incrementally, by the height of the next slice. A re-coating blade passes over the surface to ensure that a consistent layer thickness is achieved. The re-coating blade was found to be necessary, without which air entrapment caused build problems. This procedure is repeated until the entire part is fabricated. On completion, the model is carefully removed and washed in a solvent to remove uncured resin, and placed in a UV oven to ensure all resin is cured.

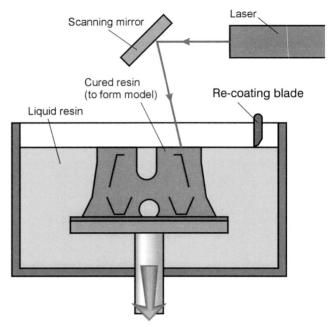

Fig. 12-3. Schematic of stereolithography (SLA) machine operation.

Though this was the first process commercialized, it is expensive and is limited to some of the photo-curable plastic materials only. However, a large variety of photo-curable materials have been developed, providing a large range of properties, as shown in Table 12-2. It is widely used for conceptual visualization, form and fit analysis, and pattern creation.

Accuracy available with these machines is much higher, compared to the other RP machines. As a result, it is widely used for a number of different applications. This further resulted in the development of a number of machines to make various part sizes ranging up to 1524×762×508 mm (60×30×20 in.).

12.2.2. Laminated Object Manufacturing (LOM)

A Laminated Object Manufacturing (LOM) machine (Fig. 12-4) works by actually cutting "slices" of the object out of a sheet of material (paper, foil or metal sheets) and then bonding them together. The foil comes off a material supply roll and the laser then cuts around the outline (perimeter) of the layer. The waste material around the slice is left in place to support the next layer of the model, but, to assist with subsequent removal, it is scored by the laser, to form blocks.

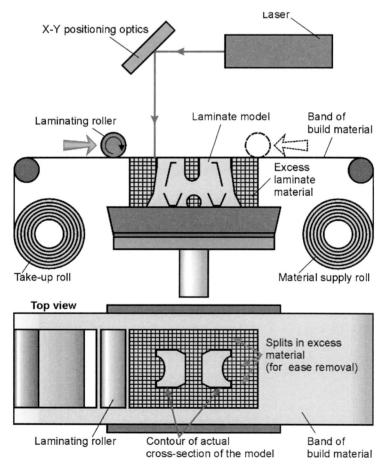

Fig. 12-4. Schematic of a laminated object manufacturing (LOM) device.

After the laser has cut out the top layer, a heated roller moves over the top of the foil to bond the layer to the rest of the object. A sensor is used to measure the thickness of the foil, as this can vary, and the machine will automatically adjust the dimensions of the layer being cut to account for any variation. During the manufacturing process, the heat of the build part needs to be maintained to ensure good adhesion. This can be achieved by altering the speed of the heated roller or the heat settings. The build part is removed from the metal plate and the excess

Table 12-2. Some Materials Available for Stereolithography (SLA) Machines.

Resin	Appearance	Viscosity cps @ 30°C	Flexural modulus, MPa	Elongation at break (%)	Notched Izod impact (J/cm)	Heat Deflection Temperature @0.46 MPa	General application
AccuGen Nd[a]	Clear amber	500	1930	4.6	0.171	--	Prototype parts, master patterns, RTV mold inserts, flow testing, etc.
AccuGen HC and Ar[a]	Clear amber	485	2494 to 2632	4.6 to 5.6	0.202 to 0.245	59°C	Prototype parts, master patterns, RTV mold inserts, flow testing, etc.
Accura 25[a]	White	250	1380 to 1660	13 to 20	0.19 to 0.24	58 to 63°C	Similar to polypropylene, functional components for mockups, master patterns, RTV and silicone molding, etc.
Accura SI 10[a]	Clear amber	485	2827 to 3102	3.1 to 5.0	0.187 to 0.277	56°C	Investment casting
Accura Amethyst SL[a]	Purple	350	3652 to 3721	0.56 to 1.04	0.009 to 0.012	77°C	High quality patterns for RTV molding, design evaluation models, patterns for direct casting
Watershed 11120[b]	Clear, colorless	260	2000 to 2400	11 to 20	0.2 to 0.3	46 to 54°C	Master patterns, investment casting
Somos White[b]	White, opaque	240	2200	8	0.24	53°C	Master patterns, functional parts
ProtoGen O-XT Clear 18120[b]	Clear, colorless	300	2600	6 to 10	0.15 to 0.17	68 to 74°C	High accuracy master patterns
ProtoCast AF[b]	Green, clear	250	2100	7	0.15 to 0.17	55°C	Very low ash, investment casting

a – ® 3D Systems
b – ® DSM Somos
RTV – Room Temperature Vulcanizing

material is broken away from the model, by hand. The part is then hand finished by rubbing down, creating a flat surface, free of the build material steps. The result is a part that looks like laminated wood.

This process can produce large parts economically with good accuracy. However, the choice of materials is limited and the properties of the build part are generally poor. Initially the LOM process was used for making large patterns for the casting process, but is now rarely used. Some examples are shown later in this chapter.

12.2.3 Fused Deposition Modeling (FDM)

In this process (Fig. 12-5) a plastic filament is unwound from a coil and supplies material to an extrusion nozzle. The nozzle is heated to melt the plastic and has a mechanism that allows the flow of the melted plastic to be turned on and off. The nozzle is mounted to a mechanical platform, which can be moved in both horizontal and vertical directions. As the nozzle is moved over the table in the required geometry, it deposits a thin bead of extruded plastic to form each layer. The plastic hardens immediately after being squirted from the nozzle and bonds to the layer below. Several materials are available for the process, including investment casting wax. Some FDM systems utilize two extrusion nozzles: one for deposition of a build material, and a second one for deposition of washable material to make a support environment. In one of these techniques, the temporary support structure is dissolved with water jets, rather than removing it by hand or with a chemical solvent.

A large range of FDM materials are available that include ABS (Acrylonitrile Butadiene Styrene), polycarbonate, polypropylene, PMMA (poly methyl methacrylate), and various polyesters. ABS is by far the largest used material in FDM. Some FDM materials and their properties are shown in Table 12-3.

One of the major problems with the FDM machines is the surface finish of the built part. Since the build material is melted and extruded through the nozzle, the minimum feature size that can be expected is about 0.4–0.6 mm (0.016–0.024 in.), while with SLA it is possible to get as small as 0.08–0.25 mm (0.0032–0.01 in.).

Another problem is the removal of the support structure material, particularly for parts with complicated interiors. Because of the availability of water-soluble support structure material, this problem is taken care of. Also, since these parts require very little cleaning and no post-processing, it is much preferred for functional parts. The materials provide better stability for the part dimensions with time and environmental exposure.

This process is widely used for concept models, form, fit and function models, along with patterns for the creation of molds and tooling. The size of the machines range from a low build envelope of 200×200×300 mm (8×8×12 in.) to a high of 915×610×915 mm (36×24×36 in.).

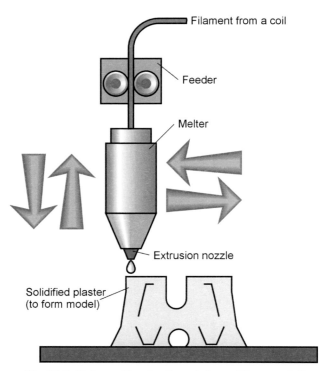

Fig.12-5. Schematic of a fused deposition modeling (FDM) device.

Table 12-3. Some Materials Available for FDM Machines.

Material	Appearance	Tensile strength, MPa	Flexural modulus, MPa	Specific gravity	Notched Izod impact (J/cm)	Heat Deflection Temperature @ 0.46 MPa
Polyphenylsulfone	Tan (silk)	55	2206	1.28	0.5873	189°C
ABS	Black, Blue, Green, Red, Yellow, Grey	22	1834	1.05	2.14	96°C
Polycarbonate	White	52	2137	1.2	0.5339	127°C

Rapid Prototyping and Rapid Manufacturing in Metalcasting

12.2.4. Selective Laser Sintering (SLS)

In the selective laser sintering (SLS) process, originally developed at the University of Texas at Austin, a modulated laser beam follows the shape of a slice of a CAD-generated object; it traces the object across a bin of special heat-fusible powders, heating the particles so that they can fuse or sinter together. In the SLS machine (Fig. 12-6), a layer of powdered material is spread out and leveled in the plane on which the layer is to be formed. A CO_2 laser then selectively traces the layer to fuse those areas defined by the geometry of the cross section along with fusing to the bottom layer. The powders can be joined by melting or surface bonding. The unfused material remains in place as the support structure. After the initial layer is formed, powder is reapplied, and the laser processes the next layer.

Some of the materials used are, plastics, waxes and low-melting-temperature metal alloys. Because of the use of metal powders, this process is greatly used in applications such as direct tooling for investment and diecasting.

A large variety of build materials are available for the SLS systems, as shown in Table 12-4. Plastic materials provide increased stiffness, heat resistance and mechanical integrity, which make them perfect for functioning prototypes. The materials will have properties similar to ABS and polypropylene, such that the parts made with them will have properties similar to injection molding. Some materials also have flexibility similar to rubber, so that parts requiring flexibility can also be made with these materials. Metallic materials have properties that are sufficient to use them for making direct metallic parts as well as tool making. They provide good surface finish and excellent machinability.

A wide range of machines is available with various build volumes. These provide a large build area, so that large

parts or tooling inserts can be easily produced. The RP process, called Electron Beam Melting (EBM) is similar to SLS and employs an electron beam for sintering, but uses only iron as a build material.

12.2.5. 3-D Printing (3-DP)

Originally developed at the Massachusetts Institute of Technology (MIT) in 1993, 3-D printing can be compared to SLS; the difference is that instead of a laser beam, liquid binder is applied to bond the powder particles.

A 3-D Printer is operated in the following sequence. The printer spreads a layer of powder from the feed box to cover the surface of the build platform and then prints binder solution onto the loose powder, forming the first

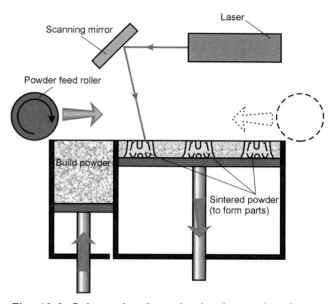

Fig. 12-6. Schematic of a selective laser sintering (SLS) device.

Table 12-4. Some Materials Available for SLS Machines.

Material	Melting point, °C	Tensile strength, MPa	Flexural modulus, MPa	Specific gravity	Notched Izod impact (J/cm)	General application
DuraForm PA®	184	44	1285	0.97	2.14	Prototype plastic parts, patterns for sand casting and silicone tooling
DuraForm GF®	185	38.1	3300	1.40	1.01	Prototype plastic parts, patterns for sand casting and silicone tooling
LaserForm A6 Steel®	--	470	138 000	7.8	--	Tooling inserts for injection molding and diecasting
LaserForm ST-200®	--	250	137 000	6.73	--	Direct metal parts, tooling inserts for injection molding and diecasting
CastForm PS®	<63°C	2.84	--	0.86	0<.11	Investment casting patterns

® 3D Systems Co

cross-section of the part (Fig. 12-7). Where the binder is printed, the powder's particles are glued together. The remaining powder is loose and supports the part as it is being printed. When the cross-section is complete, the build platform is lowered slightly, and a new layer of powder is spread over its surface. The process is repeated until the whole model is completed. The build platform is raised and the loose powder is removed, revealing the completed part.

The action of dispensing the glue is similar to that of an inkjet printer; it is possible to print in multicolor to make the build part have the requisite colors as an aid for better visualization. This is a low-cost process compared to the other processes considered so far. However, the mechanical strength of these parts depends upon the build powder used and is used for visualization purpose as well as prototype patterns and coreboxes.

Capability and applications of 3-D printing significantly widened with recently developed Direct Casting Metal Material, which is used to make sand molds for casting nonferrous alloys using the 3-D printing method. This material is a blend of foundry sand, plaster, and other additives that, when combined, produce strong molds with good surface finish. Direct casting metal material can withstand the heat required to cast nonferrous metals.

Users of this technology can create prototype castings without incurring the costs and lead-time delays of tooling. Currently, the largest 3-D printer is able to build large sand molds for industrial components 4000×2000×1000 mm (157.5 × 78.8 × 39.4 in.).

The world's first continuous 3-D printer represents a completely new generation of RP equipment allowing the building and unloading process steps run in parallel, without a need to interrupt the operations of the system.

While the printing process is active on one side of the system, unloading takes place simultaneously on the other side. It is possible with a horizontal belt conveyor that controls layer building. The layers are built at the entrance of the belt conveyor, while the unloading takes place at the exit. The new system makes unnecessary the build containers common in conventional additive processes.

The printing process, the core of this technology, is done on a level tilted to the horizontal. Printing is similar to conventional 3-D printing. First, the coater generates a layer of powder at an angle to the horizontal that is smaller than the repose angle of the powder. A high-definition, 600-dpi resolution print head then selectively bonds the layers. The conveyor system moves the entire fill toward the unloading area by one layer thickness. The finished component can simply be removed from the rear end of the system when it has gone through the entire material.

The build space of the first series machine measures 850 mm (335 in.) wide by 500 mm (198 in.) high. The length of the molds is virtually unlimited with this system, as there are no restrictions with respect to the length of the belt conveyor. The machine works with layer thicknesses ranging from 150 μm (0.006 in.) to 400 μm (0.016 in.). The usable build length is limited only by the manageability of the molds. The tilt of the print level enables the print head to take far less time for positioning movements, which improves the print speed.

The continuous printer does away with build containers and a separate unloading station, resulting in lower acquisition costs. The printer also scores points with the high re-use rate for unprinted particle material, which is returned straight to the build zone from the unloading area. Consequently, the machine requires smaller filling quantities and incurs lower set-up costs. In addition, operating costs are lower than conventional 3-D printing systems.

According to manufacturer, this advance technology raises the levels of speed, profitability, and flexibility for patternless small series production of metalcasting molds and prototypes.

12.2.6 Laser Engineering Net Shaping (LENS)

So far, LENS is the most advanced process in terms of the level of achieved mechanical properties of generated metallic parts among all commercialized processes, based on a layered manufacturing build principle.

The process uses a high-powered laser, focused onto a substrate, to create a molten puddle on the substrate

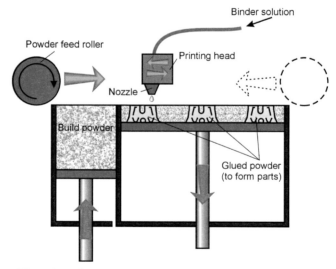

Fig. 12-7. Schematic of a three-dimensional (3-D) printing device.

surface (Fig. 12-8). Metal powder is then injected into the stream of an inert carrier gas, and into the melt pool to increase its volume. A powder ejection head moves back and forth according to the geometry of the first layer. After the first layer is completed, new layers are then built upon it, until the entire object represented in the 3-D CAD model is reproduced. Employment of a substrate makes this process different from others considered so far.

This method can utilize a wide range of metals and alloys (including superalloys) as build materials. The relatively high cost of operation and of produced parts on the one hand, and the very high mechanical properties of objects generated by this method on the other, do not allow consideration of this method as a plain RP technique or as a means of visualization. This technology became efficient only in the case of functional parts or tooling production.

12.2.7. Direct Metal Deposition (DMD)

DMD is an advanced additive technology, similar to the fused deposition method. It was originally developed at the University of Michigan and used for decades to repair and rebuild worn/damaged aerospace components that cannot be welded by normal processes [Ref. 11].

In this process (Fig.12-9a), a laser beam is focused onto a workpiece to produce a melt pool at the position where the laser is focused. Then a small amount of powdered metal is injected into the melt pool for building a thin layer on the part. The beam is continuously moved along the required path to deposit the material layer. The path of the beam is computed directly from the CAD geometry input and controlled, layer by layer, by a CNC unit. The laser head has 5-axes capability to cater to very complex part. It is provided with two optical feedback sensors (CCD cameras) that will help control the melt pool in real time to get a near-net-shape part. The powder is fed co-axially with the laser heating, thereby ensuring uniform deposition along the required path, with local shielding by inert gases (Fig.12-9b). Using DMD technology, it is possible to make large parts up to 1041×1981×610 mm (41×78×24 in.), with high dimensional accuracy.

Some of the main features of the DMD system are:

- **Co-axial** nozzle design gives full, five-axis deposition capability, along with local shielding by inert gases
- "Moving optics" capability allows processing of large, heavy parts
- Patented closed-loop optical feedback system monitors and controls the melt pool in real time, resulting in a near-net-shape part (Fig. 12-13(a))

- Multiple powder delivery system allows deposition of different materials—simultaneously or consecutively—at specified locations, enabling production of on-the-fly alloys/composites
- Deposits are fully dense and create a true metallurgical bond with the substrate/part

DMD has been used successfully on a broad range of materials, including, tool steels, stainless steels, high-speed steels, and alloys of nickel, cobalt, titanium, aluminum and copper.

12.3. Rapid Tooling in Metalcasting

The progress achieved in RP technologies, such as shortening of build time, increasing resolutions of building models, involving new materials for model creation, eventually led to wider RP applications. Models created by RP devices became functional and, in particular, resulted in the appearance of the Rapid Tooling (RT) concept. This concept utilizes the RP-generated objects (with or without special post-processing) as experimental or even regular tooling in industrial manufacturing (i.e., metalcasting, plastic parts production and metal forming).

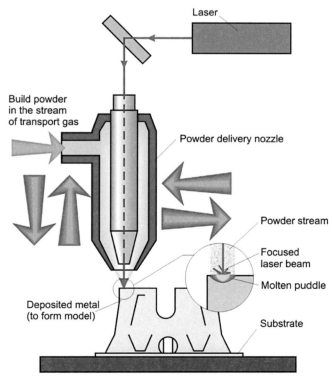

Fig. 12-8. Schematic of laser engineering net shaping (LENS) device.

Rapid tooling may utilize direct or indirect methods. Direct methods use the part fabricated by the RP machine, itself, as the tool, while indirect methods use the part fabricated by the RP machine as a pattern in a secondary process. The resulting part from the secondary process is then used as the tool. In some cases, the use of layered manufacturing simply eliminates the need for tooling, which leads to the concept of a tool-less process. In recent years, the term *rapid tooling* has been borrowed by practitioners of industry-standard methods, such as subtractive CNC, to refer to the ability to streamline these processes to compete with additive technologies.

12.3.1. Sand Casting

Major requirements for sand casting tooling are:

- Patterns, as well as coreboxes, must be made with sufficient dimensional accuracy
- Material for patterns and coreboxes must provide appropriate life in terms of wear resistance and dimensional stability

Direct tooling: Almost all RP techniques are capable of generating objects that can be used as patterns in sand molding (in cases of small- or medium-volume casting production) as a substitute for traditionally employed wood patterns. The steps taken are presented schematically in Fig. 12-10.

The major limitation is the size of the generated models, since the sand casting process is associated with the production of relatively large castings. Thus, the most widely used direct rapid tooling for sand casting was based on LOM technology (Fig. 12-11). The major weakness of paper made LOM patterns and coreboxes are their susceptibility to humidity, resulting in low dimensional accuracy. The latter can be fixed by applying special coatings or paintings, or using metal laminations.

Tool-less process or pattern-less sand molding: Current progress made in SLS technology allows sintering foundry sand coated with an ultraviolet curable resin. It provides the opportunity to generate sand molds and cores directly on an SLS machine. However, making sand cores or molds by laser sintering takes significantly

more time than does traditional methods utilizing patterns and coreboxes. Therefore, it is advantageous to use this method for pattern-less mold production in cases, when:

- it is necessary to make only one or a few castings, and making a reusable tooling set is expensive; and/or

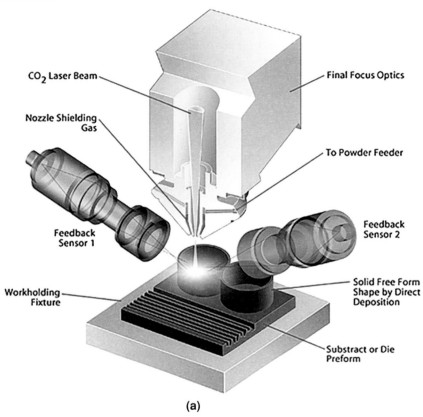

(a)

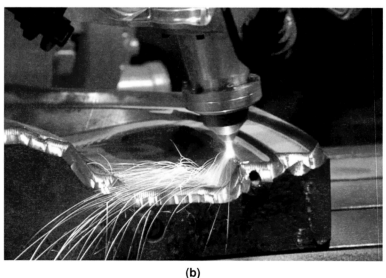

(b)

Fig. 12-9. The direct metal deposition (DMD) process: (a) schematic illustration; (b) industrial unit demonstrating actual process in action. (Courtesy: POM Group)

     Rapid Prototyping and Rapid Manufacturing in Metalcasting

- a casting is so complex that manufacturing the mold and core by traditional technology is extremely complicated or almost impossible (Fig. 12-12).

12.3.2. Investment Casting

The tooling in this process is a reusable die for lost pattern pouring. These dies are traditionally made from metal (usually aluminum) in the case of high-production runs, or from epoxy, or even rubber, in the case of medium- and low-run productions. RP-generated objects can be utilized indirectly in investment casting processes; i.e., as a master pattern for creating a silicone rubber mold, which can be used for small lots of wax pattern production (Fig. 12-13).

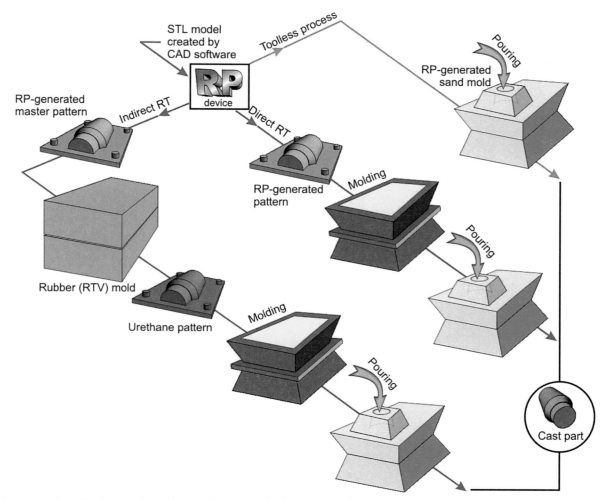

Fig. 12-10. Applications of rapid prototyping technique in sand casting for manufacturing tooling and molds.

Fig. 12-11. Gray iron casting and its LOM-generated prototype. [Courtesy: Foundry Management and Technology]

Fig. 12-12. Application example of complicated SLS sintered sand core and actual aluminum A356 casting. [Courtesy: Modern Casting]

Tool-less process: Major requirements for lost patterns made by direct RP technology are high dimensional accuracy and low cost. RP systems based on FDM principle are capable of dealing with traditional investment casting wax as a build material. Therefore, they have found the most applications in lost patternmaking systems. However, other RP technologies have also been utilized for direct lost pattern production. Polymer materials used in SLA are more difficult to burn out than are traditional materials used for lost pattern production. These materials also have a tendency to expand and crack the mold. To solve these problems, the SLA-generated pattern is built in hollow, thin sections, which tend to crumble during burn out, rather than expand (Fig. 12-14).

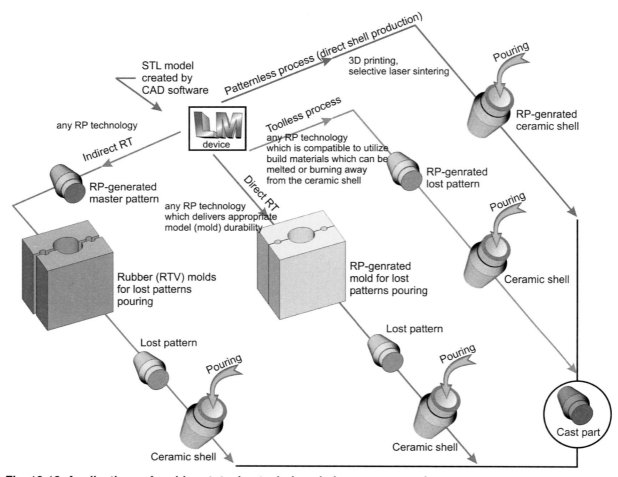

Fig. 12-13. Applications of rapid prototyping technique in investment casting.

Fig. 12-14. SLA-generated lost pattern and actual aluminum casting made via investment casting. [Courtesy: Foundry Management and Technology]

Modification of LOM technology, designed especially for lost pattern production, called "lost paper," generated objects that do not expand and do not crack the shell during the burn cycle. Similarly 3-D printing is also used to manufacture lost patterns.

NASA built a plenum gas-diverter component as a test case, to evaluate the various RP methods. The pattern built from the RP technique was then used to develop the cast part, using investment casting. The produced castings and the patterns were then evaluated for their critical dimensional accuracy and cost. Their results (Table 12-5) showed that high dimensional accuracy of a pattern was not really critical, but the accuracy of the final casting had a more important concern. Based on the cost effectiveness study of a variety of applicable methods, only 3-D printing was found to be most the effective in high-volume production of cast parts by investment casting technology.

Direct shell production: This technique can be considered as the next level in tool-less manufacturing, since even the need of a lost pattern is eliminated. The technology is based on the 3-D printing concept, utilizing ceramic build powder. The thin wall ceramic shell made by this method has an internal cavity, which defines the shape of the desired casting. This RT approach can be considered as a method of investment casting shell manufacturing with no lost patterns.

12.3.3 Permanent Mold Casting (PMC)

RP technologies can be utilized in the process of permanent moldmaking as *direct* or *indirect* tooling. Besides metallic cores, sand cores made by RP methods may also be used in permanent mold casting.

Direct tooling: Currently advanced SLS machines are capable of sintering metallic powders. It provides the ability to directly create permanent molds and cores for pouring low-melting temperature metals, such as aluminum, zinc and their alloys (Fig. 12-15).

At this time, two different options to sintering metallic powders exist. In the first option, parts are built by using a polymer-coated metal powder. The polymer is melted by a laser beam, and the metallic particles are bound together. To achieve the required mechanical properties, parts must go through a finishing process, in which the part is heated, the polymer burns away, and the metal

particles are sintered together. To eliminate porosity, the part must be infiltrated with another low melting point metal (typically copper-based alloy). The second option is to use a clean metal powder with no binder or coating. The laser partially melts the powder, and the particles are bonded together. For removing porosity, the part also must be infiltrated with another metal, like copper.

Parts sintered by laser are comparable in durability to cast or forged parts made from the same or similar material. Another possibility is to use the LENS process, which allows creating fully dense metallic molds without any sintering or infiltration. The major limitation of all these processes is the size of the created molds.

12.3.4. Pressure Diecasting

Because of similarities, methods used to make molds for permanent mold castings can also be employed to make dies for pressure diecasting. One of the recently developed rapid tooling methods, also called Rapid Solidification Process (RSP), combines rapid prototyping and metallization (spraying) technique to make dies for pressure diecasting. In one modification of this method, stereolithography or another RP device is employed to create a prototype in plastic.

Machined prototypes can also be used. From these shapes, the ceramic negatives (models) of molds are made, and then are sprayed with H13-steel or similar tool steel, to make the final tools. Virtually any tooling alloy can be used, though H13 results in a better die life than does any other material. Metal is atomized down to drops as small as 5 microns, which speeds its solidification, and then it is deposited onto the form.

The complexity of the tooling does not significantly influence the cost of produced tooling, making it particularly suitable for producing multicavity dies, i.e., for aluminum automotive parts. Currently, the process capability is limited by size (maximum size of 3225–4516 mm^2 (5–7 in.^{2}) for the finished part) and shape (it cannot produce core designs). Dies made by this process become cost-effective after yielding approximately 30 parts.

NADCA [Ref. 12] has compared the various RT methods suitable for diecasting applications, as shown in Table 12-6. As can be seen, all methods reduce the lead time compared to traditional manufacturing methods. While the majority of RT methods are limited to die sizes of

Table 12-5. Dimensional Comparison of RP Techniques for Investment Castings.

RP Methods	FDM	3DP	SLS	LOM	SLA
Pattern vs. CAD (mm/in)	0.356 /0.014	0.635/0.025	0.457/0.018	0.254/0.010	0.152/0.006
Casting vs. CAD (mm/in)	0.305/0.012	0.711/0.028	0.483/0.019	0.508/0.020	0.737/0.029

245 mm (10 in.), the Direct Metal Deposition method is capable of making larger dies. Even though tool life may reach up to 100, 000 production runs, dies produced by several methods may not be suitable for high-volume production where traditionally used heat-treated steel H13 provides longer life. But, some of these methods are cost-effective for pre-production models and limited production runs.

The Direct Metal Deposition method has also shown a lot of advantages as an RT technique for repair, restoration and hard facing of damaged large dies and cores. Another application this method has found is for making complex bi-metallic cores by producing copper cores with thick steel cladding on the outer surface. The copper serves as a heat sink, providing faster heat transfer and, hence, productivity, while the steel protects the core from dissolution by liquid metal.

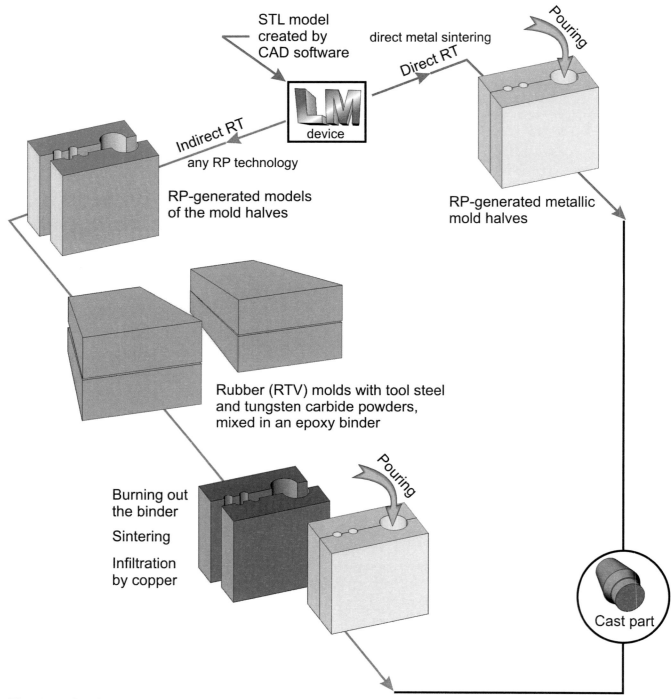

Fig. 12-15. Applications of rapid prototyping technique in permanent mold casting.

Utilizing rapid tooling techniques, which are based on printing technology, allows developing very complex designs of dies that would not be possible with other methods—even making dies with a cooling system placed precisely where it is needed. The latter sets up more effective cooling, drastically improving die life, and reducing the lead time and cost.

12.4. RP System Selection for Metalcasting

Figure 12-16 summarizes the capabilities of the various RP processes for metalcasting applications.

RP systems currently available differ not only in cost of the equipment and materials, but also in a wide range of capabilities. Most universal are systems based on SLA and SLS technologies, while most cost effective are systems based on FDM or 3-D printing technologies.

The following are major technical considerations for optimal system selection:

- Type (or types) of material of generated objects (plastic, wax, sand, metal, etc.)
- Maximum required size of prototypes
- Desired (required) accuracy of generated objects; resolution (layer thickness)
- Desired durability of generated objects (pattern or mold life)
- Maximum allowable cost per generated objects

The final selection of a system should begin with the exact definition of the necessary options and features of the system. A precise technical analysis will considerably reduce the list of allowable solutions that make the selection of a particular system easier. The final stage of a system selection will take into account the economic parameters, such as cost of build materials, cost of the equipment and its service.

Metal casting method	RP method	SLA	SLS				LOM		FDM		3DP		DMD
	build material / tooling	plastic	plastic	wax	sand	metal	paper	metal	plastic	wax	plastic	ceramic	metal
Sand casting	patterns/ core boxes	●	●	○	○	○	●	○	●	○	●	○	○
	sand molds/ cores	○	○	○	●	○	○	○	○	○	○	●	○
Permanent mold/ die casting	metallic molds/ cores	○	○	○	○	●	○	●	○	○	○	○	●
Investment casting	molds for lost patterns	●	●	○	○	○	●	○	●	○	●	○	○
	lost patterns	●	○	●	○	○	●	○	○	●	●	○	○

● Applicable ○ Not applicable

Fig. 12-16. Comparison of the RP methods for casting applications.

Table 12-6. Comparison of Rapid Tooling Methods Useful for Diecasting Dies. [Ref. 12].

Process	**Lead time**	**Tool life (shots)**	**Insert size (in)**	**Tolerances**	**Cost, $**
Direct Metal Deposition	1 week	1,000 – 10,000	41 × 78 × 24	0.003 in/39 in	2,500 – 60,000
Selective Laser Sintering	2 – 3 days	1 – 1,000	8 × 10 × 5	0.002 in	6,000 – 8,000
Direct Metal Laser Sintering	1 – 3 weeks	1,000 – 10,000	9.75 × 9.75 × 7.75	0.001 – 0.002 in/in	2,000 – 25,000
Rapid Solidification Process Tooling	2 weeks	1,000 – 10,000	7 × 7 × 4	0.003 in	1,500
Laser Engineered Net Shaping	2 – 4 weeks	10,000 and 1000,000	36 × 36 × 60	+/-0.005 in	250 per cubic inch
Electron Beam Melting	3 – 4 weeks	10,000 to 1000,000	8 × 8 × 7	0.013 in	2,500 – 4,500

12.5. Rapid Manufacturing (RM) Concept

Finally, the ability of some modern RP devices to build up plastic or metallic objects with the same or compatible mechanical properties to those achieved by conventional manufacturing processes, led to the emergence of the Rapid Manufacturing (RM) concept. Rapid manufacturing can be defined as the process of fabricating parts directly for end-use from a rapid prototyping machine. This is the manufacturing process that needs no tooling and no technological development.

It is predicted that in the near future, RM would be not able to replace conventional manufacturing for large or mass production. However, with decreasing cost of RP machines, this process may become efficient in low- or even medium-volume production. It is useful for some unique applications, such as the NASA experiments using RP machines to produce spacesuit gloves fitted to each astronaut's hands. RM is ideal for producing custom parts designed to the user's exact specifications.

The other major use of RM is for products that simply cannot be made by conventional processes, such as casting, machining, grinding, forging, etc. For example, objects with complex features, internal cavities, and layered structures cannot be made by conventional processes. An example is the versatility of the LENS process, which allows the use of separate sources of the build powder. Because of this option, it is possible to create parts with different materials at different layers, thereby providing the requisite properties at each of these layers. For example, a hard surface, and a soft core or heat-conducting core can be obtained by rapid manufacturing.

12.5.1. Rapid Manufacturing in Metalcasting

One example of an RM application in the foundry is the recently developed direct metalcasting process. This process involves the design of the mold and gating directly in a CAD system, and the use of an RP machine to produce the mold. The design of mold and gating follows the conventional procedures; however, because of the use of an RP machine (similar to 3-D printing), it is possible to use some unconventional practices, as well. The only caution is that the powder can be removed from the enclosed areas of the mold. The build materials used are an inexpensive starch-based powder or a high-definition plaster-based powder.

In the RP machine, a roller spreads a thin layer of powder (0.003–0.010 in.) on the printing platform. The print head then deposits the binder on top of the powder, and the process is then repeated for all layers until the mold

is completed. The loose powder acts as a supporting medium, allowing for any complex geometry to be made.

The mold is then dried in a convection oven at 200°C (390°F) for four hours or more, depending on the wall thickness. Once dry, the mold is treated with a mold wash, and poured. Because of low refractoriness, these molds are mostly used in nonferrous casting production.

Another variation of RP technology, called Rapid Casting Technology or RCT, uses a printing method to build sand molds and cores directly from CAD files, similarly to the techniques described previously. This pattern-less process can be used to produce prototype castings, economically, to validate mold design with various gating and risering systems (Fig. 12-17). It could also be used in certain applications to eliminate coreboxes or to produce especially intricate cores. The mold material is a mix of silica sand and furan resin binder. Machine capabilities include mold dimensions up to 1500×760×715 mm (59×30×28 in.) and cores up to 760×380×405 mm (30×15×16 in.). The molds or cores produced by this process can be used for producing castings in steel, cast irons, aluminum, copper and magnesium alloys in short runs.

12.6. Case Studies

Several practical applications of rapid prototyping in casting processes have been given here for the purpose of illustrating their versatility.

12.6.1. Industrial Applications Case Study No. 1 [Ref. 13]

The Rapid Prototyping and Fabrication Technologies Div. of the Naval Undersea Warfare Center Div. (NUWC), Keyport, Washington, has utilized a Prometal Rapid Casting Technology (RCT) S15 digital mold

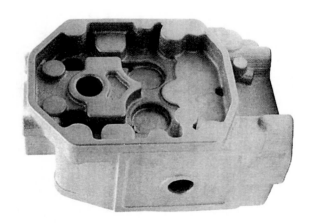

Fig. 12-17. Casting made by Rapid Casting Technology. [Courtesy: Foundry Management and Technology]

and coremaking printer with a working envelope of 57×28×26 in. (144.78×71.12×66.04 cm). The system creates sand casting molds with a furan-based binder directly from a CAD file, in two days or less. Whenever replacement parts are required, NUWC creates a CAD file of the part, using a laser scanner. The printer is capable of creating precise and complex molds with a layer thickness of 0.011 inch. The prepared sand mold is sent to a metalcasting facility for the requisite casting of the part. On average, NUWC cuts the costs for their low-quantity runs of parts by half. An example of molds from the RP machine and the castings produced from them are shown in Fig. 12-18.

Case Study No. 2 [Ref. 14]

A new concept for a US Air Force fighter plane component required long lead times and expensive prototypes. A stereolithography (SLA) pattern was used to reduce lead time and cost. The investment casting pattern for the aluminum electric motor housing shown in Fig. 12-19 was made hollow in CAD, and then the pattern was produced using the SLA process.

Case Study No. 3 [Ref. 14]

The US Army has used a sand printing prototyping machine to cast a new mortar base plate to replace an outdated heavy fabrication. The new base plate is to be stronger and also light weight. The Army decided to produce three different designs in aluminum and steel. Molds and cores required for the designs are produced using inkjet technology, with printer heads spreading a binder onto coated metalcasting sand. The mold is produced with all locators, core prints and gating system required for a production tool (Fig. 12-20).

12.6.2 Art Casting Applications Case Study No. 1 [Ref. 15]

Selective laser sintering (SLS) was used to produce the bronze statue of Father Basile Antoine-Marie Moreau for the basilica at Notre Dame Univ., South Bend, Indiana [Ref. 15]. The traditional process of producing this type of statue requires a very elaborate, time-consuming investment casting process. For this purpose, a smaller,

Fig. 12-19. Aluminum electric motor housing for U.S. Air Force fighter plane developed using SLA investment casting patterns [Ref. 14]. [Courtesy: Modern Casting]

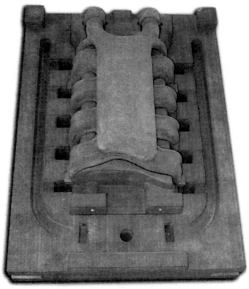

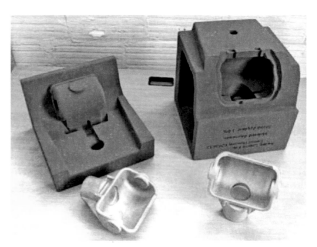

Fig. 12-18. Mold produced by RP machine at the NUWC facility with the castings shown [Ref. 13]. [Courtesy: Modern Casting]

Fig. 12-20. Pattern for a cast motor base plate produced using the direct sand casting process [Ref. 14]. [Courtesy: Modern Casting]

sculpted clay statue was used as a starting model. 3-D scanning of this model created a point cloud that was exported to a 3-D CAD file, where suitable scaling for the final size could be accomplished.

The CAD file was then hollowed out to facilitate the casting process, which required a 3.175 mm (0.125 in.) wall thickness. This hollowed CAD file was separated into manageable sections, suitable for the platform size 381×330×460 mm (15×13×18 in.) of the SLS machine. Each segment was scaled to account for differential shrinkage that occurred during the additive fabrication and casting processes. Flanges and bolt holes were designed into the file to facilitate casting and assembly.

It took a total of 11 days to completely build the 28 segments of the statue. Then, each piece was dipped into casting wax to produce the patterns used at the metalcasting facility to cast the statue in bronze. The finished statue can be seen in Fig. 12-21.

References

1. Hopkinson, N., "Rapid Manufacturing: what, why and how?"*Foundry Trade Journal,* Vol. 176, No. 3590, April 2002, pp. 12-15.

2. Lerner, Y., P. Nageswara Rao and V.Kuznetsov, "Rapid Tooling in Metal Casting,"*Foundry Management and Technology,* Vol. 130, No. 8, 2003, pp 47-55.

3. Rosochowski, A., and A. Matuszak, "Rapid tooling: the state of the art," *Journal of Materials Processing Technology,* Vol. 106, 2000, pp. 191-198.

4. "Rapid Manufacturing Technologies."*Advanced Materials and Processes,* May 2001, pp. 32-36.

5. Gustafson, R., "Rapid Prototyping: a tool for casting design and verification," *Modern Casting,* Vol. 89, No.3, March 1999, pp. 44-47.

6. Cooper, K., and G. Williams, "NASA on the Fast Track: A Case Study in Cost Savings with the Application of RP and Investment Casting," SME Technical papers, 2001, *RP01-335, Society of Manufacturing Engineers.*

7. Khaing, M.W., J.Y.H. Fuh and L. Lu, "Direct Metal Laser Sintering for Rapid Tooling: Processing and Characterisation of EOS Parts," *Journal of Materials Processing Technology,* Vol. 113, 2001, pp. 269-272.

8. Hanninen, J., "Direct Metal Laser Sintering," *Advanced Materials and Processes,* Vol. 160, No. 5, May 2002, pp. 33-36.

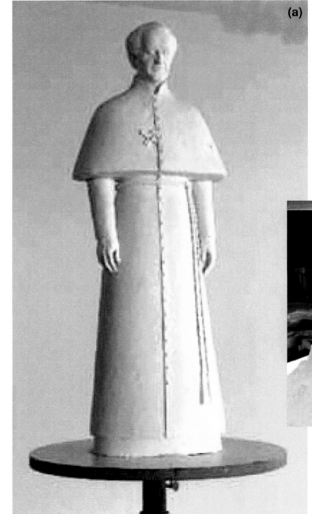

(a)

Fig. 12-21. Bronze statue (a) produced using SLS method; the patterns for hands (b) also made in SLS machine [Ref. 15]. [Courtesy: Modern Casting]

9. Clay, T.and Krauth,T"Direct Metal Casting," *Advanced Materials and Processes,* Vol. 161, No. 1, 2003, pp. 43-44.

10. *Foundry Management and Technology*, Oct. 2006, p.15.

11. Dutta, B., V. Singh, H. Natu, J. Choi and Mazumdar,J, "Direct Metal Deposition," *Advanced Materials & Processes*, March 2009, pp. 29-31.

12. NADCA, "Rapid Tooling Opens New Diecasting Doors," *Modern Casting*, Vol. 99, No. 10, Oct. 2009, pp. 30-33.

13. Anon, "Rapid Casting Delivers Parts to the Navy with Speed," *Modern Casting*, Vol. 96, No. 10, Oct. 2006, p. 44.

14. Gibbs, S. and Burrow G., "Be Proto-Type-Cast," *Modern Casting*, Vol. 98, No. 12, Dec. 2008, pp. 28-31.

15. Anon, "Rapid Prototyping Method Works for Industry, Art," *Modern Casting*, Vol. 99, No.2, Feb. 2009, pp.59-61.

Review Questions

12.1 Explain the term "rapid prototyping."

12.2 Outline the major steps involved in the layered manufacturing (LM) process.

12.3 Can computer numerical control (CNC) machining be considered as a rapid prototyping method? Explain why or why not.

12.4 Discuss the advantages of using rapid prototyping technologies (RP).

12.5 Describe the applications of RP.

12.6 Explain the principle of stereolithography (SLA).

12.7 Describe selective laser sintering (SLS).

12.8 Explain laminated object manufacturing (LOM).

12.9 Describe the principle of 3-D printing (3-DP).

12.10 Explain the concept of fused deposition modeling (FDM).

12.11 Describe laser engineering net shaping (LENS)?

12.12 Define rapid tooling (RT). What is meant by the terms direct tooling, indirect tooling and tool-less process?

12.13 Give examples of rapid prototyping technologies used in sand casting.

12.14 Specify the rapid prototyping technologies that can be used in permanent mold casting applications?

12.15 Explain the methods by which rapid prototyping technologies can be used in diecasting applications.

12.16 Give examples of rapid prototyping applications for investment casting.

12.17 Describe the major considerations for optimal RP system selection.

12.18 Define rapid manufacturing (RM) and its applications.

12.19 Explain the direct metalcasting process.

12.20 Give a brief description of rapid casting technology (RCT).

12.21 Describe the direct metal deposition (DMD) process and its main features.

INDEX

Bold pages indicate tables; *italics* indicate figures.

Copper molds, 176

Core blowing, corebox design features for, 121

Coreboxes, 50–54, **51, 52, 53,** *53, 54,* **59**
  features for core blowing design, 121

Cored wire method, 149–150, **150**

Coreless induction furnace, **135,** 135–136

Coremaking processes, 115–121, *117*

Core positioning, **230,** 230–231, **231**

Core prints, 50

Cores, 50–54, **51, 52, 53,** *53, 54,* **59**
  defined, 5
  dry (chemically-bonded) sand, 50
  green sand, 50
  removal of, 215
  strainer, 61, *61*

Core setting, 5

Corrosion resistance, 19

Countergravity casting, 200–201, **201**
  applications for, 201
  process advantages of, 201
  process limitations of, 201

Countergravity low-pressure air-melt (CLA) casting, 201

Cracked castings, **227,** 227–228

Croning, Johannes, 116

Crucible furnaces, 128, **158,** 158–159

Crushing machinery, casting in, 4

Cupolas, 128
  charge materials used in, 132–133
  cold and hot blast, 132, **132**
  construction of, *130,* 130–132, *131*
  melting of cast irons, **130,** 130–135, **131, 132,** *133, 134*

Cuts, 225

Cyaniding, 36

Cylindrical-shaped riser, 83

D

Dead riser, 83

Degassing, 158, 160

Dephosphorization, 129

Design optimization for sand molding, 229–237
  in aiding handling, 236

for casting defect prevention
  distortions, 233–234, **234**
  gas blowholes and pinholes, 235, **235**
  hot tearing, 234–235, **235**
  shrinkage, **232,** 232–233
for economical molding, 229–230, **230**
  boss positioning, 231, **231**
  core positioning, **230,** 230–231, **231**
  simple economics, 231–232, **232**
finite element analysis in, **236,** 236–237, **237**

Desulfurization, 129

Details, elimination of, 55, **55**

Diecasting, 4, 30, 186–190
  application for, 190
  cold chamber process, 187–188, **189**
  die design and material, **186,** 186–187
  hot chamber process, 187, **187, 188**
  process advantages of, 188, 190
  process limitations of, 190

Diffusion, 11

Dimensional accuracy, coordinate measuring machine (CMM) applications, 57

Dimensional stability, 17, **17, 18**

Dimension verification, 57

Direct metal deposition (DMD), 247, **248**

Distortion allowance, 49

Distortions, 233–234, **234**

Downsprue, 62

Draft allowance, 49–50, **50,** *50*

Drag, 5

Drilled cooling passages, 179, **179**

Drop, 225, **226**

Drop weight test, 15, **15**

Drum-shaped ladle, 163, **163**

Dry (chemically-bonded) sand cores, 50

Dry compression strength, 106

Dry reclamation (attribution) scrubbers, 123

Dry sand molds, 111–112

Dry sand reclamation, 123–124

Dry strength as sand property, 100

Dry tensile strength, 106

Patternmaker's shrinkage, 46

Pattern material
    plastics as, 42–43
    polystyrene foam as, 43
    wood as, 42

Patterns, 5
    cope and drag, 44, *44*
    dimensioning, 46–50
    follow board, 45–46, *47*
    loose, 43–44, *44*
    loose piece, 45, *45*
    match plate, 44, *45*
    metallic, 42, *42*
    single-piece, 43–44, *44*
    split, 44, *44*
    sweep, 46, *46*
    two-piece, 44, *44*

Pearlite, 13

Pearlitic malleable, microstructure of, 22

Permanent mold casting (PMC), 4, 30, 175, **176**, 176–185, 251, **251**
    air-cooled permanent molds, **177**, 178, **178**
    applications of, 185
    cooling methods, **177**, 177–178
    cores, 177
    measuring mold operation temperature, 181–182, **182**
    metallic inserts (chills) or heat sinks, 180–181, **181**
    mold cleaning with dry ice, 183
    mold coatings, 176–177
    mold design, 177
    mold material, 176
    mold repair, **182**, 182–183, **183**
    permanent mold machines, 183–185, **184, 185**
    process advantages of, 185
    process limitations of, 185

Permeability
    of green sand, **105**, 105–106
    as sand property, 101

Phase, 11

Phenolic urethane/amine process, **119**, 119–120

Phosphorus, 27, 129

Pig iron, 19

Plastic deformation, 13

Plasticity, 101

Plastics as pattern materials, 42–43

Plunging method, 148, **148**

Pneumatic scrubbers, 123

Polystyrene foam as pattern material, 43

Porous plugs, 169

Pouring basin, 60–62, *61*

Pouring cup, 60–62, *61*

Pouring ladles, 162–163, **163**

Pouring of cast alloys, *161,* 161–167, *162*
    automatic pouring control systems, 166–167, **167**
    ladleless pouring systems, **165**, 165–166, **166**
    ladles, 162–163, **163**
        automatically-operated, **164**, 164–165, **165**
        mechanically-operated, 163–164, **164**

Pouring-related defects, **226**, 226–227, **227**

Pouring sprue, 62, *62*

Pouring time, 67–69

Precipitation hardening process, 36–37, **37**

Prefabricated steel pipe cast-in iron permanent mold, 179, **179**

Premature casting removal, 213

Pressure diecasting, 251–253

Pressure ladle, **148**, 148–149

Pressurized, nonpressurized system versus, *69,* 69–70

Pressurized induction holding furnace, 143, **143**

Pressurized pouring furnaces, **165**, 165–166

Process control, 124

Pull downs, 225

Push-out furnace, 158

Q

Quality control and cleanliness testing in aluminum foundries, 170, **170, 171, 172**

Quality control in melting, 167–172
    chemical composition control, **167**, 167–168
    chill control in iron melting, 172, **172**
    gas and slag control, 169–170
        quality control and cleanliness testing in aluminum foundries, 170, **170**
        quality control (QC) and cleanliness testing in aluminum foundries, 170, **170**
    temperature measurement control, 168–169, **169, 170**

Quality testing, 218–221, **219, 220**

Quality verification, 57

Quenching, hardening by, 33

R

Radii, 54

Railroad industry, casting in, 4

Rapid casting technology, 254–255

Rapid manufacturing (RM), 254

Rapid prototyping (RP), 239–241, **240**, *241*, 241–247
  direct metal deposition, 247, **248**
  fused deposition modeling, 244, **244**, *244*
  laminated object manufacturing, **242**, 242–244
  laser engineering net shaping, 246–247
  selection for metalcasting, 253
  selective laser sintering, 245, **245**, *245*
  stereolithography, 242, **242**, *243*
  3-D printing, 245–246, **246**

Rapid Solidification Process, 251

Rapid tooling in metalcasting, 247–253
  investment casting, 249–251, **250**, *251*
  permanent mold casting (PMC), 251, **251**
  pressure diecasting, 251–253
  sand casting, 248–249, **249**

Rattails, 225

Real-time x-ray and neutron radiography, new
  development in, 6

Reciprocating wear tests, 18, **19**

Reduced pressure test (RPT), 170, **170**

Refractoriness, 109
  as sand property, 100

Refractory coatings or washes, 122

Refractory lining, 128–130, *129*
  installation of, 138–140, **139**

Refractory mold, 1

Residual stresses, 17

Resin/CO_2 process, 120

Resonant acoustic method (RAM), 220–221

Reverberatory furnaces, 128, **159**, 159–160

Risering and feeding, 81–98
  casting solidification and shrinkage, 81–83, **82**, *82*
  cooling aids, *87*, 87–88
  cooling aid selection for aluminum alloy sand mold
    casting, 92–98
  design of risers
    dimensioning, 83–85
      modulus method, 83–84, *84*

shape factor method, 84–85, *85*
  neck dimensioning, 86, *86*
  type and shape, 83
feeding aids, *88*, 88–89
feeding distances, 86, *87*
grouping castings, 89, *89*
solidification modeling, 89–91, *90, 91*

Risers, 5, 46, 82
  blind, 83, 88
  cold, 83
  cylindrical-shaped, 83
  dead, 83
  design of
    dimensioning, 83–85
      modulus method, 83–84, *84*
      shape factor method, 84–85, *85*
    neck dimensioning, 86, *86*
    type and shape, 83
  dimensioning, 83–85
    modulus method, 83–84, *84*
    shape factor method, 84–85, *85*
  function of, 82
  hot, 83
  live, 83
  open, 83
  spherical-shaped, 83

Riser sleeves, 88, *88*

Robotic cleaning operation, 217–218, **218, 219**

Rotary degassing system, **160**, 160–161, **161**

Rotary drum, 214, **214**

Rotating sliding test, 18, **18**

Rotating-table shotblasting cabinet, **216**, 216–217

Runners, 62–63, *63*
  defined, 5
  extension of, *60, 63, 68, 73*

Runout, 225

Russia, casting in, 2, *2*, 3, *3*

S

Sand
  chromite, 100
  fayalite, 100
  fosterite, 100
  olivine, 100
  silica, 99–100
  zircon, 100

Sand casting, 30, 248–249, **249**

Solution heat treatment, 37

Southern bentonite clay, 101

Space lattice structure in cast alloys, 10, **10**

Spall, 225

Spherical-shaped riser, 83

Split pattern, 44, *44*

Split tensile test, 106

Spray cooling of permanent molds, 179, **180**

Sprue, 6

Sprue base, 62, *62*

Sprue well, 62, *62*

Squeeze molding, 113, **113**

Stationary, bowl-type furnace, 158

Stationary tilting furnace, 158

Statistical process control (SPC), **56,** 57

Steel, 9
    hypereutectoid, 13
    hypoeutectoid, 13
    melting of, 156–158
        electric arc furnace, **156,** 156–157
        electric induction furnace, 157–158

Steel castings, 27

Step ingates, 64, *65*

Stereolithography (SLA), 242, **242,** *243,* 255

Straight lance technique, 160

Strain, 13

Strainer core, 61, *61*

Strength
    of cast alloys, 13–14, **14**
    of green sand, 106, **106**

Stress relieving, 32

Substitutional solid solutions, 11

Surface defects, tests to detect, 219

Sweep pattern, 46, *46*

Swell, 225

T

Tap-and-charge operation, 128

Teapot tundish ladles, 152, **152**

Tellurium, 168

Temperature measurement control, 168–169, **169, 170**

Tempered martensite, 34

Tempering, 102
    methods of, *34,* 34–35

Tensile stress, 108

Tensile test, 13

Thermal analysis system, **167,** 167–168

Thermal conductivity, 101

Thermal expansion, 101

Thermal sand reclamation, 124

Thermal shock resistance, 19

3-D printing (3-DP), 245–246, **246**

Time-Temperature-Transformation (TTT) diagrams,
    32, 32–34, *33,* **34,** *34*
    hardening methods and, *32,* 32–34, *33,* **34,** *34*

Tin, use in casting, 3, **3**

Titanium, 28

Titanium alloy, 9

Top ingate system, *63,* 63–64

Traveling pouring station, 164, **164**

True centrifugal casting, 192, **192**

Tsar Bell, 2, **2**

Tsar Cannon, **2,** 2–3

Tumbling, 216, 217

Tundish-converter, 153, **153**

Tundish ladle, 164–165

Tundish method, 151–153, **152, 153**

Tungsten, 27

Two-piece pattern, 44, *44*

U

Ultrasonic testing (UT), 219–220

Ultrasonic velocity (USV) technique, 220, **220**

Unicast process, 195

Unit cell, 10

United States, casting in, 3, **3**